THE MEANING OF AMERICA

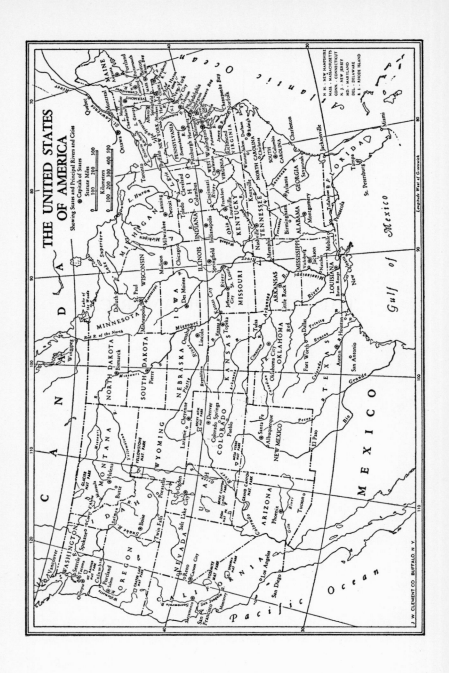

THE UNITED STATES
OF AMERICA

Showing States and Principal Rivers and Cities

⊙ Capitals of States

Statute Miles
100   200   100   100

Kilometers
100   200   100   400   500

J. W. CLEMENT CO. BUFFALO N.Y.

THE MEANING OF AMERICA

Essays Toward an Understanding of the American Spirit

by

LELAND DEWITT BALDWIN

UNIVERSITY OF PITTSBURGH PRESS

Library of Congress Catalog Card Number: 55-10721

973
B 181 m

55351

Copyright, 1955

UNIVERSITY OF PITTSBURGH PRESS

TABLE OF CONTENTS

MAPS

The maps in this book, except for the frontis-
piece, have appeared in other books by Leland
Baldwin.   They are used with the permission of
the American Book Company.   The one on page 5 is
reprinted from page 596, *Recent American History;*
the ones on pages 144, 153, 156 are reprinted from
pages 596, 195, 260, *Survey of American History.*

THE MEANING OF AMERICA

Most of us can live with our national history only because we know so little about it that we regard it all as good or because we know so much about it that we realize there was much good to offset the bad. Faultfinders usually are those who have read the scareheads of history and the front page summaries but have not followed the facts through the wearisome fine print of the back pages. Those who make a careful study of the histories of the democracies and would-be democracies will be struck by the many parallels among them—something worth remembering when one is about to preen himself upon the superiority of his particular history or way of life.

This book is an attempt to explain the United States by examining some aspects of its history and its historical psychology. Friends of my country will say that I could have told much more that was complimentary while its enemies will say that I could have added more that was derogatory. Both will be right. As a matter of fact I have made little attempt to rebut accusations, excuse mistakes, or convince the reader of the rightness of the "American way"; however I would not be human if I did not hope that improved understanding would bring some degree of tolerance and perhaps also the ability to draw something useful from American experience.

Much of the material that appears here was adapted from my *Stream of American History* and *Recent American History* with the kind consent of the publishers, the American Book Company and Richard R. Smith Publisher, Inc.

LELAND D. BALDWIN

I

One Out of Many

THERE is a story that Stalin, Truman, and Churchill came before St. Peter for adjudication. When they had passed the test the good saint offered to give each of them anything he wanted.

"I want the Americans to go home," said Stalin.

"And I want Russia destroyed," snapped Truman.

There was a twinkle in Churchill's eye and a sly smile on his cherubic face. "Is this on the level?" he asked. "Anything we want?"

"Yes, anything," answered St. Peter.

"Well, then," said Churchill, "I'll just have a cigar. But serve these other gentlemen first."

This story illustrates the changes which have occurred in the world during this century, and which only the most perceptive observers foresaw at its outset. The power and influence of the United States have mushroomed as those of no other nation in history, and yet few foreigners who have not resided there for a period of years have any adequate understanding of its character and ideals. Indeed foreign publicists take delight in presenting a picture of the United States which can only be described as a mixture of the fantasies of Hans Christian Andersen and the horrors of the Brothers Grimm.

The usual impression is that it is a country of rigid standardization and monolithic conformity. True, its gadgets are standardized where there is no particular reason to do otherwise, but it probably also produces as great a quantity of made-to-order goods as any country in the world. Far from being conformists, its people wrangle continually over cultural, social, economic, and political problems. Politically, the country is never swept by a single idea, and those elections which the foreigner sees as simple plebiscites on outstanding issues will upon examination be found to have hinged also upon a multiplicity of local problems and rivalries.

The national motto is *E pluribus unum*—one out of many—and denotes the deliberate acceptance of a sovereignty divided between states and nation and a consequent rivalry between the two forces. Indeed the struggle between localism and federalism offers the key to an understanding of American history because it has been the means of maintaining the balance of social conflict and cautious social advance which has formed modern America. The states have been artificial units, each with its separate constitutional and political history, though they have been significant as cradles of experiments in democracy, economics, and social welfare. The original theory of a constitutional division of sovereignty has survived even though the Civil War of 1861-65 made the decision that in case of vital conflict the nation was supreme. Nevertheless there is reason for holding that the real struggle in American history has been between rival sectional alliances of states which quarreled over the relative significance of nation and states. The realities have thus lain in the sections rather than the states.

Of late years the vitality of the states has been vitiated by vested political and economic interests. The Federal government has accordingly expanded to fill the vacuum left by the states, and national activities have increasingly focused public attention at the cost of interest in state activities. This may seem strange in the light of the fact that the citizen's daily life is far more affected by state than by federal actions. Nevertheless the seemingly smooth, uncreviced exterior which the United States presents to the world is really backed by an inextricable mass of rivalries which make it look as though the country is about to collapse. It may be this which has given to the totalitarian masters in the Kremlin the delusion that time will sweep aside the United States, the chief obstacle to Russian imperial rule. Actually what is going on in the United States is the normal democratic ferment. The old fights for life against the new, the individual against the many, the state against the region, the region against the nation, and each against the others on its own level. There is no disposition to regard frustrations as insurmountable or to adjust one's self to a program which announces that it is the historical dialectic and therefore inevitable; no acceptance of a perfect order of society.

*   *   *

It was said above that the struggle between localism and federalism has been the key to American history. This is still true. We shall presently have more to say about sectionalism as an historical phenomenon, but here we are seeking to lay the basis for an understanding of the diversities of the present-day United States. Sectionalism has carried with it such dire implications of civil and military strife and at times actual threats to the existence of the nation that recent commentators have preferred to use the weaker term *regionalism* for modern geographic sectionalism. Traditional American sectionalism looked toward cultural, social, and economic self-sufficiency and isolation, and finally political independence. Modern regionalism is to a very great extent created by problems common to the region; these may rise from conditions in a metropolitan area or a river valley or in a much wider geographical, social, or economic context. There are about one hundred metropolitan areas in the country and seventeen major river systems, so the basis for numerous subregions is well established.

But modern regionalism, whatever its present or future geographical boundaries, is quite different from the old sectionalism. It fosters certain cultural, social, and economic unities but it does not aspire to isolation or independence; it does not even aspire actively to administrative unity or autonomy, and sometimes there is not even a focal metropolitan center—or there may be two or three. It has a certain amount of geographic and climatic unity, but these must not be overstressed, for there is a great deal of internal variety. The nebulous nature of regional character is evidenced by the way in which writers on the subject differ from each other in the boundaries they draw between regions. The best guide, perhaps, is found in the local *feeling* of homogeneity, and this results from psychological and historical factors as well as from authentic cultural, economic, geographical, and climatic factors. But like factors may play entirely different roles in different regions—and all factors must be assessed with care. It must also be borne in mind that there are binding as well as separating factors. The effect of a common political and economic federalism is obvious. No less clear is the effect of the scores of privately-run national organizations which bring together businessmen, laborers, farmers, educators, churchmen, reformers, and veterans.

We thus see that it is impossible to make out regions with clearly defined boundaries or clearly defined common attitudes on all problems. The feeling of homogeneity may cover certain problems and interests and turn to bitter hostility on others. For this reason students of regionalism recognize (1) broad belts of uncertainty on the borders between regions where the people may turn first in one direction and then in the other, and (2) the existence of sub-regions in which the people may qualify or attempt to reject the regional attitude toward any given problem. The first exception is illustrated by the belt of states between North and South which attempted to remain neutral during the Civil

War and which has since then vacillated between the Republican and Democratic parties; the second by the mountainous area of East Tennessee which tried to stay with the Union during the Civil War, and has since then tended to vote Republican. There is a widespread belief that the people of the cities in all of the regions resemble each other more than do the people of the rural areas. Whether or not this is true there is an obvious interaction among cities which greatly modifies regional characteristics.

Having thus explained that it is impossible to bound regions exactly or to describe exactly the reasons why they are regions, we shall now proceed to name and analyze the regions of the United States. As a glance at the accompanying map will show there are three grand regions, North (or East), South, and West. These are not based solely upon geography.

(1) The North finds common expression in a balance between city and country, industry and agriculture, and in a rather general and conscious attempt to find progressive solutions for its problems.

(2) The South is still overwhelmingly rural and agrarian. It is united by a sense of historical injury, and by a long struggle to retain white supremacy and to attain economic equality with the North.

(3) The West is dominantly dependent upon agriculture, stock raising and the extractive industries and is united (at times divided!) by its desperate need for water and by a sense of current injury by the remainder of the nation.

The above are the grand regional divisions created by historical, cultural, economic, and geographic factors but each of them has regions within itself which have developed the *feeling* of homogeneity noted above as the chief criterion by which the existence of a region can be recognized. Thus the North is divided into the dominantly urban Northeast and the balanced Middle West. The South is the best integrated of all, more for historical than for natural or economic reasons. The West has its Missouri Valley with grain, cattle, and minerals; its Texas-Southwest with cotton, cattle, grain, petroleum, and chemicals; and its Far West with California, the Great Basin, and the valleys of the Colorado and Columbia rivers—each is jockeying for a larger voice in regional and national councils.

The connection between geography and national and regional character is close enough to make it worth devoting a few paragraphs to American geography. The continental United States occupies about one third of North America, is roughly 2,500 miles wide at the midriff

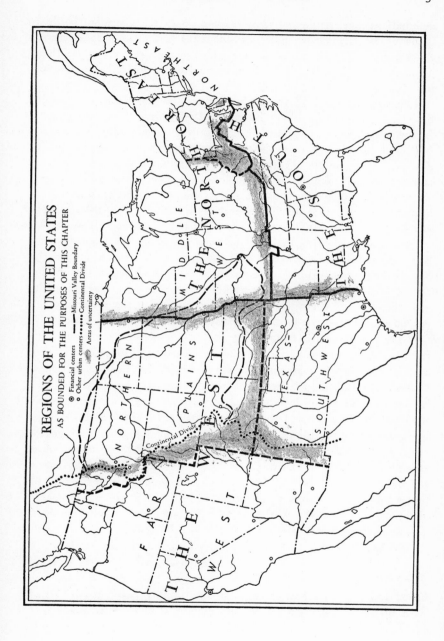

REGIONS OF THE UNITED STATES
AS BOUNDED FOR THE PURPOSES OF THIS CHAPTER

⊕ Financial centers —·— Missouri Valley Boundary
○ Other urban centers ·····Continental Divide
Areas of uncertainty

and half as much from the Gulf of Mexico to the Canadian border; it has 3,022,387 square miles and about 1,900,000,000 land acres; Alaska adds 586,400 square miles, which make the total more than 3,608,000. Canada, which lies immediately to the north, has 3,851,000 square miles.

The western third of the United States has the Rocky Mountain System, a scattered cordillera interspersed with deserts and farmlands. In the east there is a coastal plain backed by the old, eroded Applachian Mountain System. Between the two mountain systems lies a great plain, drained chiefly by the Mississippi and its tributaries which together afford thousands of miles of navigable waters. This great plain is open to the tropics on the south and to the Arctic on the north; so its super-heated southern winds bake the wheat fields of Canada in the summer, and its frigid winter winds make Texas blizzards famous. The Pacific coast is protected from extremes of temperature by the Cascades and Sierra Nevadas, and with the aid of the Japan Current it consequently has the most delightful climate on the continent. The winters in the rest of the country are seldom crippling except in the extreme north, and railroads and highways are usually open during the entire year.

One of the most remarkable climatic features of North America is that the eastern half (from about the 100th meridian) receives two thirds of the continent's rain and constitutes, next to Europe, the largest area of beneficently watered land anywhere in the Temperate Zones. Droughts and floods are both unknown (or would be if Nature had its way) except as local phenomena. American rainfall is more violent than that of Europe, and the result is that our soil is more likely to leach and erode than is the heavy soil of Europe under its more gentle rainfall. However, rainfall and fertile soil make this one of the most reliable crop lands in the world and consequently the world's largest and most consistent food producer. The grain production of the United States and Canada runs to about seven billions of bushels—probably about one third of the world's total—though the two countries hold only about seven per cent of the population of the globe.

The heavy rainfall and the long growing season in the southeastern states made the area suitable for plantation crops like cotton, and did much to give the region its separate identity. The area just below the Great Lakes—themselves gouged out by a series of glaciers—is blessed with glaciated soils rich in organic materials which have made it a farmers' paradise. The eastern half of the country was originally covered with forests. The vast deposits of coal and ores and its pools of oil once seemed inexhaustible and in fact are still considerable.

* * *

One of the most magnificent and yet least publicized wonders of the modern world can be seen on any clear night by the traveler on a plane flying between Boston and Washington. For a distance of four hundred air miles the observer is never out of sight of the myriad, multi-colored lights of a metropolitan center. The impression left on the mind is that of one solid urban conglomerate—an impression not far from right, as one will see if he tries to breast the highway traffic the next day. It is this urban conglomerate, centered on New York City, which has become the financial and to a considerable extent the commercial, industrial, cultural, and political heart of the world.

And yet less than four hundred years ago there was nothing in this region but forests and the cornfields of the sparsely scattered Indian nations. In an economic sense this is the fulfillment of Alexander Hamilton's dream of an industrial empire; over a century and a half a succession of ruthless practical dreamers fought against the opposing agrarian concepts in order to make Hamilton's dream come true. The result is that today New York and to a lesser extent Chicago wield for good or evil a financial and economic power never before matched. Today the Northeast and the Old Northwest or Middle West are in virtual alliance both economically and politically and may be lumped together as the North or the East. For the last two generations the North has been able to stack the cards in its favor. The tariffs were written largely to favor industry. Corporations have been the chief beneficiaries of tax rebates, and they have at times been able to dragoon Federal and state governments into settling taxes for a fraction of the sums assessed. With some exceptions the great corporations are effectively controlled in the North regardless of where their stockholders live. This is aptly illustrated not only by the great manufacturing corporations but by many railroads, by telephones, movie production and distribution, and by the chains which now control so many drug, variety, grocery, and department stores.

Though it seems clear that the North's throttlehold on finance and industry is made possible only because of the historic community of interest among the bankers of Wall Street (the Street was shorn of most of its power by the New Deal), yet it is not likely that they either "conspired" or consciously sought to impose "tyranny" as such.

Their motivations were probably no more sinister than a logical and rather short-sighted search for profits. In this search they used many weapons to neutralize established competitors and to prevent the rise of new competitors—meanwhile mouthing and perhaps believing the shibboleths of free enterprise, laissez faire, competition, and the law of supply and demand. Businessmen point out, and justly, that they are largely responsible for the American standard of living and that its existence depends upon concentration, efficiency, expensive experimentation, and the other factors that go to make mass production possible.

The North has furnished much of the capital and the technical skills for the development of the remainder of the country, and it has in the process added to its capital and frequently kept effective control. More than this it has sometimes managed to appropriate the results even where local capital and initiative have built a business. That such injustices have not been remedied is probably as much due to inertia as to a deliberate congressional design to maintain the center of economic power in the North. Actually Congress has drained away much of the North's profits by imposing upon it a tax burden far greater than upon the remainder of the country. The complaint is frequently heard that the Northern corporation simply passes on its taxes to the ultimate consumer, yet it is difficult to see how this could apply to the income tax and to the excess profits tax. At any rate the North has paid not only the lion's share of the taxes which have gone to defray such national ventures as wars, but it has contributed to the "pork-barrel" appropriations to other regions—that is, Federal expenditures to placate local interests—to the appropriations to the states called "dollar-matching" funds, and to farm subsidies. The economic and political power of the North makes it ascendant in the nation despite a check held upon it by other sections; it is no less apparent that for the same reasons it is and will for some time remain influential in the world despite the checks exercised upon the United States by other nations.

Of the parts into which the Northeast falls New England gives the impression of greatest antiquity—indeed it is often accused of being arid, meagre, and decadent, a civilization which has been completed and has nothing more to say. It is true that the New England capitalists, managers, and technologists who did so much to make America have passed on. Today Boston's "spendthrift" trusts sit on their millions while the gadgeteers of Connecticut and Rhode Island turn to New York for inspiration. Inundations of immigrants—Irish, Slav, French-Canadian, and Latin—have swept over the area and altered its face and its religion, but strangely enough have found an affinity for some aspects of its Puritanism. New England remains what it always was, a dualism at once pragmatic and transcendental.

There is reason as well as humor in the quip that the Pilgrim fathers fell first on their knees and then on the aborigines. New England still presents the seeming paradox of democracy and cliques, of mediocre conformists and eccentric "againsters." Its towns may be primly beautiful or awsomely ugly. At one extreme Boston offers a boiling of Irishmen, Jews, Italians, Middle Yankees, and "Brahmins." The latter exhibit facets of ritualism, provincialism, and public spirit along with ruthless flouting of political and economic ideals which would be called cynical in a less self-assured city. At the other extreme Vermont is rural, canny, neighborly, individualistic—and completely self-assured. An intensely democratic state which invariably goes Republican it is not strange that Vermont gave to America its leading Utopians, those zealous searchers for the City of God. There was significance in the decision of Vermont's first legislature "to adopt the laws of God . . . until there is time to frame better."

The New England states are strangely diverse and yet strangely unified. The contrasting ethnic groups, cultures, and mores now simmering within its borders offer a sound basis for a rich future broth. If the old New England stock has of late been "wanting in roundness" this roundness will presently be furnished by Irish ward heelers, French Canadian laborers, Connecticut gadgeteers, boys from the potato fields and lobster pots of Maine, and maverick Boston Brahmins. However that may be the historical influence of New England is beyond dispute. Its reformists laid an indelible stamp on education, literature, and social welfare; its inventors laid the basis for mass production and the American standard of living; its canny traders who knew how to take calculated risks contributed significantly to making New York City a paramount commercial entrepot; its financiers and managers did much to give the country its magnificent transportation system; and its statesmen contributed mightily to the idea of nationhood.

Moving from the sawtooth mountains of New England across gangling Lake Champlain to the colorful lake-gemmed Adirondacks one enters the so-called Middle Atlantic States. New York is as rich in history and natural wonders as any state in the Union, and as paradoxical as New England though in a different way. Its upper stretch, though highly industrialized, preserves many of the conservative traits of its New England settlers and has imposed upon New York City (which outnumbers it) a position of inferiority in the councils of the state. Nevertheless Upper New York was long unable to put through its cherished scheme of a St. Lawrence Waterway built in conjunction with Canada which would give it cheap power and would probably make Chicago (or Toledo) the world's greatest seaport. New York City, mindful of its position as the world's leading seaport, has with the aid of private power interests long managed to kill the project in Congress. Recent enabling legislation passed by Congress may help Upper New York to realize its dream.

That New York City is a giant needs no emphasis here. It may not be the world's largest incorporated city but it has with the aid of New Jersey and Connecticut the most populous metropolitan area (13,000,000). It leads in commerce, in finance, and in industrial production. Its budget is larger than that of most states and of most nations. It is the cultural capital of America (it would fain assert of the world) : at least it leads in publishing, art, music, opera, ballet, and the theater—Hollywood is merely a convenient "shooting" location a short hop from Forty-Second Street. It is the clearing house for news and opinion. It leads in styles, fads, and the argot of the underworld. As the Vanity Fair of the entertainment world, the nexus of luxurious hotels and restaurants, and the center of universities, libraries, museums, art galleries and laboratories it teems with playboys, gourmets, dilettantes, scholars, and scientists. It abounds with bridges, boulevards, skyscrapers, penthouses, slums, and bathing beaches, all on a commendably colossal scale.

Its population is polyglot: it has more Negroes, more Jews, than any other city in the world, more Irishmen than any city except Dublin, more Italians—fill it in to suit yourself—but not least of all it probably has more Americans born somewhere else than any other city except Los Angeles. For the city offers power enough to satisfy the most towering ambition, variety to satisfy the most curious and restless, values to stimulate those who would study life and eternity, and charm to lull the fevered senses.

And yet its people are surging, intense, callous, supercilious, provincial beneath a shell of sophistication, and obsessed with a craze for money and high living—a craze not confined to New Yorkers or to Americans. Religious, racial and ideological rivalries are always on tap, for New York City with its abortive Americanism combines the most raucous Europeanism. And yet there is a sort of tolerance as thin as the surface tension that floats a needle on a glass of water. Its people get along.

They have to. The rest of the country regards New York with an amusing mixture of awe, admiration, contempt, envy, and resentment—all well justified. The accusation is made that New York City is more parasite and dictator than reflector of American attitudes, so there is resentment that it should presume to act as spokesman for the country. William Allen White complained that New York would take God himself on its knee and tell him the facts of life.

Across the Hudson River lies New Jersey, a bedroom, coast resort, and vegetable patch for New York and Philadelphia and a manufacturing center in its own right. Philadelphia, oozing history from every pore, prosperous with its sprawling industries—a city which until quite recently seemed to have lost the civic consciousness of Franklin and Rush but preserved the snobbishness which once caused its social leaders to cross the street to avoid having to speak to that arch-radical, Vice-President Thomas Jefferson. To the north of it lie the anthracite coal fields; to the west the rich agricultural lands of the Pennsylvania Germans; beyond the Susquehanna are the forests which paradoxically are teeming with deer and bears. Among the mountains and west of them are coal and steel centered on Pittsburgh, a city of blackened spires and homes, vigorous, rough as its mill hands, with the spiritual rigidity of its Presbyterian founders, yet groping for ideals of civic, cultural, and spiritual consciousness.

In the old days Mason and Dixon's line was the southern boundary of the imperial North but industry has encroached upon the South. Delaware's sleepy fields are now the home of vast enterprises in munitions, chemicals, and nylons, spearheads of a mushrooming du Pont empire. The Free State of Maryland, once a planting colony cleft by Chesapeake, is now divided as sharply between industrial Baltimore and farmers and fishermen, while an enclave of Maryland soil has become the District of Columbia with its million government workers and their suppliers. Just as strange, West Virginia, which seized the opportunity of the Civil War to sever its ties with Virginia Tidewater, has made good with timber, coal, and steel.

The Old Northwest—the area between the Mississippi and Ohio rivers—became known as the Middle West after the rise of the trans-Mississippi West, and the name has stuck though it is no longer appropriate. There is no foolproof way of defining the Middle West, but one may cautiously affirm that it includes those states in the sphere of influence of Chicago in which there is a fair balance between industry and agriculture—the marriage of machine tools and Corn Belt. This would include not only the original five but Minnesota, Iowa, Missouri, and probably Kentucky. Their agricultural wealth has encouraged food processing (tobacco and whiskey in Kentucky) and other advantages have given them a leg up the ladder of other forms of industry. Southerners furnished the majority of settlers on both sides of the Ohio and in Missouri; Pennsylvanians and other Middle Staters moved westward just north of them; and New Englanders predominated across northern Ohio, Indiana, Illinois, and Iowa, and in Michigan, Wisconsin, and Minnesota. In later years Germans gave a distinct cast to Cincinnati, Louisville, and St. Louis, while Germans and Scandinavians settled in great numbers in Wisconsin and Minnesota.

The mechanical bent of the Middle West probably came not only from Yankee artisans but from these immigrant Germans and from the so-called Pennsylvania Dutch. No section, not even the Northeast, has enjoyed such good transportation, for there are not only the rivers and lakes but the terrain lends itself to railroad and highway building. Timber and minerals have been abundant and easily accessible, and the states favored entrepreneurs from the first. In no other section have public schools and state universities played such important roles, nor state and county fairs.

Few dispute that the Middle West is the heart of American physical and moral strength. It is, moreover, the epitome of the American mythus at its best and worst. There we see enlightened industrialists—and ruthless oppressors; militant and responsible labor leadership—and labor racketeers; tolerant and socially conscious churches—and cheap, emotional, anti-intellectual preachers of fear; courageous, responsible, and intelligent social and political leadership—and sowers of seeds of hatred. The area is often called the "Valley of Democracy" and indeed it does show democracy in successful action—but also the political machine at its most cynical. No other section of the country witnesses more desperate political battles nor ones in which the forces are better balanced. There is a saying in Kentucky: "We haven't made up our minds which side we're on, but when we do you can be sure we'll be damned bitter about it."

Nucleus of this vast region is Chicago, a metropolitan center of 5,500,000 people, blessed with an incomparable geographic position and cursed with extremes of weather—the temperature may fall forty degrees in an hour. Behind a magnificent lake front stretches a dead flat, humdrum waste of drab dwellings, factories, and tracks. Based on railways, steel, meatpacking, manufacture of agricultural machinery and countless other articles, and retailing (consider its amazing mail order houses) it holds an impregnable economic position and was at times boasted as one of the most corrupt city governments in the country with a minimum of reform interference.

Filled with foreign-born of all nations it is yet more typically American than New York. Folded in the heart of America it can see nothing else and has—at least until very recently—been dogmatically and profanely isolationist. Here is the citadel of the *Chicago Tribune,* operated in a totalitarian manner until his recent death by Col. Robert R. ("Bertie") McCormick, scion of the harvester family. The *Tribune* supported the war once we were in it but never ceased to picture it as an idiotic foray brought on by the ambition of "that man" in the White House. Col. McCormick was a warm favorite of German and Japanese press and radio; he was a long way from being a favorite of the Soviet Union. Probably McCormick was basically expressing Midwesterners' Anglophobia and distrust of a Europe from which their fathers had fled and which was the presumptive home of all evil. It may be significant that the isolationist senators of the Middle West toppled one by one during the 1940's and left behind less than a sergeant's guard of carefully cautious neo-isolationists such as Taft.

Chicago seems determined to match every quality with a paradox. Never has crime been more sordid than in Chicago; nor has any American ever made a more serious effort to sell philosophical absolutes ("the great books") than Robert M. Hutchins, recently president of the University of Chicago. Probably one of the more stimulating intellectual centers in America is the University of Chicago; yet most of the city's numerous promising poets and writers have drifted away. Wrote Sandburg:

> Hog-Butcher for the world
> Tool-Maker, Stacker of Wheat,
> Player with Railroads . . .
> City of the Big Shoulders.

In truth Chicago is a city of brawn, of clamor and strife, the living epitome of American giantism. Its winds are stronger, its crimes more Gargantuan, its politics more corrupt, its labor struggles bloodier. It is known for tight-fisted barons like Levi Leiter, Cyrus McCormick, and Marshall Field, organizers of crime like Al Capone, reactionaries like Bertie McCormick, and corrupt politicans like Big Bill Thompson who boasted that he would bust King George on the snoot. Yet out of it have risen Jane Addams of Hull House; Julius Rosenwald, who has helped to raise the Negro race; public spirited men like John Peter Altgeld, Carter Harrison, Harold Ickes, and Paul Douglas; thinkers like T. V. Smith; pioneer architects like Louis Sullivan and Frank Lloyd Wright; even poets like Vachel Lindsay, Carl Sandburg, and William Vaughn Moody.

The Middle West has been called the home of dead-level, democratic mediocrity, yet its states each show character. Ohio has long been a meeting ground of cultures—easternmost of the Western states, westernmost of the Eastern, and northernmost of the Southern. Here have met New England reformism, Western individualism, and Southern localism to create the most politically unpredictable state in the Union—hence the seven presidents born in or elected from Ohio who have given it the title Mother of Presidents. It may or may not be significant that all of them have been Republicans and none of them has been outstanding. Ohio's urbanism is pronounced and its cities are among the most civically and culturally conscious in the country. On the other hand its farmers are united and highly vocal and constitute the state's biggest pressure group.

Ohio was the first western state to reach maturity but Kentucky was the first admitted to the Union. Kentucky has historically been divided into rival sections, which has meant that few problems could be viewed on a statewide basis—hence its rural unprogressiveness. During the Civil War most Kentuckians stood by the Union, but during Reconstruction the state belatedly declared itself for the Confederacy. Ever since that Kentucky has been nostalgically Southern in its harking back to "the time that never was." Indiana has a balance between industry and agriculture, but is popularly regarded as rural—perhaps because of James Whitcomb Riley's ubiquitous "When the Frost Is on the Punkin." Local patriotism is high in Indiana and its citizens are perpetually bathed in a mellow sentimental glow. Nevertheless its mores are shrewd and conservative and its politics bitterly contested. As the abiding place of the American mythus (and a bastion of "Colonel McCosmic's Chicagoland") Indiana has been the harbor of nativist and anti-Catholic movements like the Ku Klux Klan—but also the home of liberals like Albert Beveridge, Wendell Willkie, and Paul Hoffman, and the "Irish" footballers of the Catholic University of Notre Dame. Its intelligentsia tend to migrate, but never lose their yearning for the moonlight on the Wabash. Downstate Illinois, despite its rich agriculture, cannot compete with Indiana for local consciousness, perhaps because of the pull of a Chicago which is plainly regional rather than local in its interests. An exception may be "Egypt" (with its towns of Cairo and Karnak), the extreme southern portion of Illinois, a delta-like region traversed by sluggish rivers and despite its coal mines still breathing the air of the antebellum South.

Missouri, "a Southern state with a Northern exposure," boasts of cotton fields, corn belt, hill billies, lead, zinc, coal, and two superbly corrupt and intellectually crass yet materially progressive cities, St. Louis and Kansas City. As locally conscious as Indiana its motto is popularly supposed to be *Show me!*—an attitude certainly not derived from the more easy-going side of the South. Iowa is the home of the corn-hog cycle and the farm state without a peer, though California surpasses it in total production because of fruit and vegetables. Prosperous, conservative, and penny-pinching—some of its farmers use airplanes because the roads are so bad—it yields allegiance to the American Farm Bureau Federation and its richly *American Physiocratic* philosophy, but is also busily engaged in food processing and light industry.

There remain the states which not only front upon the Great Lakes but which depend more vitally upon them as arteries of transport. They were in great part the creation of New Englanders, Germans, and Scandinavians. Minnesota relies on iron ore, timber, wheat, and dairy products. Less prosperous and conservative than Iowa it has experimented with one of the few successful third parties, the Farmer-Labor. Wisconsin, also long the home of a third party, the Progressive, boasts more industry. Michigan, with chemical industries, iron ore, copper, and timber slashings, now finds its mission chiefly in the automobile industry of the Detroit area. This industry, long notoriously anti-labor in its policies (perhaps partly because it was so sensitive to the national economic temperature), has attracted not only Negroes and immigrants—chiefly Poles—but great numbers of volatile and race conscious white Southerners. The result has been the mushrooming of a city which rivals Chicago in its vigorous and brutal materialism and surpasses it in explosive possibilities.

*   *   *

No section has been so persistently misrepresented as the South—and with such bland inconsistency—by the remainder of the American people. At one extreme there is the traditional "Dixeland" with its pillared mansions; dancing "darkies"; moonlight and honeysuckle; unexcelled cooking; and unlimited hospitality generously spiked with mint juleps or bourbon-and-branch-water. On the other extreme is the land of the frying pan cuisine; the country of merciless sun and rain, infested with cottonmouth moccasins; no less poisonous demagogues; moldy aristocrats; and shoeless sharecroppers whose only vitality comes with the kick of the white mule and the community summons to share in the regional sport of burning Negroes. There is a third mythus—the Southerner's impression of himself. Needless to say, all are some distance from the truth, yet there is some truth in all of them. Hence the Southern paradox which is in type also the American paradox.

One of the most remarkable aspects of American history is the continued vitality of the South. As early as 1750 its peculiar planter economy seemed doomed to disappear before the small farmer, but the Industrial Revolution gave cotton (and with it slavery) a stimulus which renewed the life of the planter economy. When once more it seemed about to fall, this time before the onslaught of its creator, the Industrial Revolution, Northern ineptitude, and the exacerbation of race antipathies gave it even in defeat a new psychological life which insured its immortality as a separate region even more certainly than had its planter economy in the old days. Under the leadership of its "Bourbon brigadiers" the defeated South drew together as a tight garrison devoted to the defense of its ideals. It yielded economic control to the North in the so-called "Treaty of 1877" in order to preserve the central values of aristo-agrarianism and white supremacy. Thereafter its internal politics were devoted to maintaining discipline in the Southern garrison, and its external politics to the search for a means of vetoing national policies which it regarded as inimical to its two cherished interests. The South blamed the Republican Party for the Civil War, so it gave its allegiance to the Democratic Party. Since that time the Solid South has been a significant factor in the threshing out of American policies, and thus far it has never been seriously breached except in two presidential elections; even then it remained stubbornly Democratic in local government.

The old rivalry of Massachusetts and Virginia for national ascendance has come down to us. Massachusetts has made this an industrial nation, has placed its stamp upon the newer regions to the west, and has even made deep inroads into the Texas-Southwest and into the South itself— but the South has built a psychological ark upon which the profane hands of Massachusetts are not likely to be laid in the predictable future.

Thus of all the regions of the United States the South is probably most homogeneous. This does not mean that its economic pattern is the same everywhere, beyond the fact that about three-quarters of its people are engaged in agriculture. Even its agriculture follows no definite pattern. Virginia, North Carolina, Tennessee, and Arkansas engage in general farming and tobacco growing, with the latter two growing some cotton. The cotton belt from South Carolina to Texas produces increasing amounts of other crops. Georgia has peach and pecan orchards, Florida citrus groves and truck gardens, and Louisiana has sugar and rice. Its manufactures are chiefly cotton textiles and products, steel and wood products, with some shipbuilding thrown in. One noticeable fact is that the South is still dependent upon the North for machine tools, so does not possess the ability to renew itself. The largest Southern metropolitan center is New Orleans (680,000) but it is not the capital except of a subregion. Birmingham, Memphis, Richmond, Norfolk, and Atlanta all have metropolitan districts with over 300,000. Of these cities Atlanta (665,000) has the best claim to be called regional capital, but even this claim remains to be proved. New York and Chicago are still the queen cities of the South.

The South is rich in material and human resources but lagging in capital wealth, in technology, and in the institutions which bring together the other factors to create a satisfactory society. The South therefore is a land where human and material resources are wasted, where imbalances reign in culture and economy, and where old fears and prejudices still are more powerful than scientific facts. The blame can fall upon the South only in part, for it has been the victim (as well as in some respects the beneficiary) of an expanding economy—the aphis to the industrial ant. The Bourbon brigadiers made their "Treaty of 1877" with the North on terms which seemed most likely to preserve the way of life which they and the South treasured; in other words, they sought to preserve the very status of agricultural and social imbalance which now is accused of being at the core of the modern South's difficulties.

The South is still rural and conservative in its outlook, even in the cities, and is tinctured everywhere with the paternalism which accompanied the old planter economy. Family ties are strong, and the traditional regard for religion is still potent. Labor is of a low order of skill but is improving. The white Southerner is not ordinarily given to analysis, least of all social analysis. He (even more than the Northerner) too often judges by sentiment and prejudice. Part and parcel of this attitude is the Southerner's supreme race-consciousness, what Odum calls the Southern Credo, the belief that the Negro "could not be expected ever to measure up to the white man's standard of character and achievement."

Southerners are inherently as intelligent and enterprising as any people in the world, but the typical diseases of the South are bred or encouraged by poverty, and they in turn discourage the victim from striving to emerge from poverty or to learn how to fight his ailments. Because of the low health and high mortality rates of the Negro, deaths from disease and childbirth as well as infant mortality are considerably higher in the South than in the North, and the region lags in its proportion of physicians, trained nurses, clinics, and hospitals. And yet the South's population gain outstrips that of any other region, while at the same time millions of its people have been moving into the North and West. These problems all throw an added strain upon the educational system. Actually the South devotes to education a larger proportion of its income than does the North, but the South is poorer and, moreover, it feels that it must maintain a double school system for whites and Negroes.

Opposition to change is not a Southern monopoly in the United States, but it is seen at its boldest in the South. The tendency is less to solve problems by finding and curing the causes than it is to impose social and legal controls. Prohibition won favor partly as a means of controlling the Negroes and partly from the Fundamentalist attitude that drunkenness is a venal sin. Few intended that it should deprive the white man of his liquor. The crusade against the theory of evolution was merely the spearhead of a group of movements to blot out the advances made by the modern heresies which were questioning the foundations of Southernism. The Ku Klux Klan of the 1920's, we are assured, was primarily intended to block the entry of Yankee ideas; its strength lay in its ability to lend its sheeted riders a sense of their dramatic unity with the heroes of the South in the defense of the Southern way against the world. Nevertheless reaction was bound to fail in the South: the region had too many men who were possessed of good sense and imbued by the old respect for learning. Moreover, there was shame at the ridicule of the world; and the leaven of modern ideas was working deep down, even in the masses.

On the other hand, the reactionism of the South cannot be completely sloughed off so long as it is bound up with vested interests in race, economics, and psychology. Hence the Southern demagogue. His mission is to strengthen reactionary economic interests by winning votes; this he does by favoring the voters' vested interests and prejudices, and it is notable that he is most effective with the illiterate, under-privileged, and yearning masses. Actually demagogues are in the minority among Southern politicians. The false impression of their number rises from the simple fact that it is news when a statesman in deference to his bare-footed constituents takes off his shoes before rising to address them. The majority of Southern politicians are conservative because the South itself is conservative, and the mechanics of Southern politics are designed to keep it that way. The one-party system lends itself handily to the creation of personal machines based often on court-house gangs and road contracts; and, since there is no other party to lead a popular revolt, they become entrenched and conservative, and then, new talent, especially if it is liberal, finds it difficult to rise. The poll tax (now rapidly vanishing) and primary systems contributed to one-party government.

Nevertheless, the South has had a long history of liberalism, and it is possible to show that it swings back and forth with the rest of the country. This tendency is concealed by the fact that it is always Democratic; when the country goes conservative Republican, the South merely supports conservative Democrats. Even on a "closed" subject like race relations the leaven of liberalism is working. Unsympathetic observers attribute changes to the threat of Federal legislation, to the slowly growing solidarity of white and Negro labor, and to the fear that the Negro will leave and deprive the region of a valuable cheap labor force. There may be something in these claims, but it would be unfair not to mention also the conscience of the South. Lastly, Southern conservatives do learn by experience—which is frequently more than can be said for Northern conservatives. Witness the reversal of South-ern conservative attitudes toward the TVA.

The general economic picture of the South has improved greatly during the last two decades, but it is still a colonial area, more so even than the other areas which have felt the heavy hand of the im-perial North. The Census of 1940 revealed that the Southeastern states enjoyed only about one-half the per-capita income of the rest of the nation. The agriculture of the South has suffered from a vicious circle not dissimilar to that which afflicts its people. Poverty forces the mining of the soil, with the result that production declines and poverty becomes deeper. Heavy rains quickly leach or erode the light soils of the South.

It is true that the rate of farm tenancy is no higher in the noncotton South than in some Midwestern and Missouri Valley states, but the income is certainly lower. The Cotton South, moreover, until recently at least, has labored under a peculiar system of sharecropping, which has notoriously discouraged both owner and tenant from making permanent improvements. Then there is the coming effect of the mechanization of cotton farming, which is sure to force hundreds of thousands of sharecroppers to leave the farm and to seek work in industries as yet unborn. For a generation swarms of migrant families, traveling in decrepit flivvers from harvest to harvest, have given witness of the economic maladjustments of the South.

The change and to a certain extent the maladjustments in the industrial scene are just as evident. The period of the 1920's was one of depression in Southern coal mines and textile mills, and this brought on a series of furious, almost revolutionary, strikes in the Upper South. The result was that the New Deal was greeted with greater enthusiasm in the South than in any other part of the country, even though its social ideals countered those of the South at almost every point. Reared in a Spartan school, which taught self-sacrifice in the cause of the garrison South, the Southern common man was bewildered by the New Deal's preachments that he should be a beneficiary rather than a martyr.

It was true that conservative Southern Congressmen supported the New Deal only on condition that the common man of the South should not be "spoiled" by equal benefits. Nevertheless the Southern industrial scene was radically changed, and that by other factors as well as the New Deal. Unions made entry against violent opposition, but they made entry. As one organizer put it: "They used to kill you for organizing a union; now they just knock all your teeth out." Mill owners increasingly lost control of their villages; this situation was not always clear gain for the workers, for while paternalistic duties passed, paternalistic privileges sometimes remained. A new middle class grew by leaps and exercised a moderating and progressive influence in politics and social legislation. The conditions of child labor (aided by Federal legislation) were mitigated.

One of the most potent factors in the rehabilitation of the South both in agriculture and in industry has been the Tennessee Valley Authority. There are certain cogent objections to the theory behind the TVA and to its processes, but here we are concerned with its effect upon the South. Flood control and aids to navigation have been among its important contributions. Not only has its cheap electrical power attracted new industries to the Southeastern states and expanded the old ones, but it has by its rural electrification program revolutionized the farm home and opened a new market for electrical equipment.

Of even more positive benefit has been TVA's battle against malaria, its program of agricultural education through demonstration, its reforestation and anti-erosion activities, and its restoration of the soil through proper plowing, crop rotation, and the provision of cheap phosphates and nitrates. In 1933 the Tennessee Valley (and adjacent areas in seven Southeastern states) was a poorhouse. In less than two decades it has become almost an agricultural paradise, while its significance as the home of important electro-metallurgical, chemical, aluminum, ceramic, woodworking, and atomic-energy industries is well known. TVA has consciously stimulated this advance not only by cheap power but by its research in new processes and equipment which are now handled by private enterprise. TVA is a strong reason for the clear fact that the South's wages, production, and general welfare are increasing at a rate greater than that of the nation as a whole.

*   *   *

No real American can think of the West without feeling a nostalgic pang for the days when men were ruggedly individualistic. Here is the explanation for the perennial popularity of the Western novel and moving picture, for the small boy's craze for cowboy togs. The West brings before our mind's eye a sweeping panorama: the mighty Columbia; hills clothed with giant redwoods and Douglas firs; vast pasture-lands; fertile secluded valleys; gold placers, and silver and copper mines; sunny haciendas, white beaches, the blue Pacific; and perhaps most poignant of all the Southwestern desert, which Bob Beverley calls "the land that seems to be grieving over something—a kind of sadness, loneliness in a deathly quiet." We are in love with solitude, with the ideal of the strong, silent, self-reliant man of Western legend.

Americans still think of the West as the land of promise. There the strong, silent man is still in style, but the landscape is big enough to include the pioneer with hands calloused from the plow and the mass production wheat farmer with 100,000 acres. Here one may find those vanishing races the cowboy, the desert rat, the champion liar, and the optimist—the last a quite different animal from the mere booster in search of a sucker.

"The West itself (says Ladd Haystead) is the place where you climb for water, dig for wood, look farther and see less, and the Powder

River runs uphill from Texas. It's a land of fable, myth, tradition and the lack of it, extremes of heat and cold, wetness and dryness, lowness and highness, of promise and bitter disappointment, of million-dollar schemes by the countless people who own no more than a jalopy or the down-payment on a radio. It's a land that has been exploited worse than almost any other part of the globe; and a land still incredibly rich in resources, in plans, hopes, and eagerness to find a 'pardner' who will grubstake a 'deal.' "*

Here we shall arbitrarily set the threshhold of the West at the western boundaries of the first tier of states west of the Mississippi, noting once more that there are broad belts of ambivalence along all regional borders and that Oklahoma and Texas are sometimes with reason assigned to the South. The states of the West have certain problems in common: (1) they are colonial areas subject to Northern financial and sales exploitation, and they claim that they suffer from unreasonable freight rates and other deliberate discouragements to industry; (2) great areas within the borders of most of the states are owned by the Federal government and are either withheld from use or carefully supervised in their use; (3) many of them depend upon Federal bounty to maintain essential public services; (4) they have a common Jeffersonian tradition with its deeply implanted suspicion of government; and (5) there is an all but general lack of easily available water.

Financial controls, inadequate and expensive transportation, and inability to get land cheaply and easily have been problems in every successive West from colonial times. But why, if the West has been so suspicious of government, did it vote repeatedly for the New Deal which certainly imposed government controls? Probably there were several reasons. For one thing the West was hit hard by the depression and its people desperately needed relief. Then New Deal policies were serious endeavors to carry out certain populist ideas long favored by the West and in addition to help the West to develop itself. One should be mindful also of certain welcome considerations, particularly in favor to silver and beet sugar interests. Last but not least, the West was able to perform the pragmatic operation of accepting the Federal aid that it wanted and denouncing as unconstitutional and oppressive that which it felt was not to its best interests.

---

* *If the Prospect Pleases* (1946), 7-8.

World War II gave the West thousands of new enterprises and doubled its industrial production. For a time it seemed that the change would be permanent, but government administrators of production and matériel were private managers on loan and they could not—or at least did not—divest themselves of their consciousness of the post-war competitive situation. They had the Eastern philosophy, that the West should produce only raw or unfinished materials which should be sent East for finishing. Moreover some of them had the state of mind of the "arrived"—that expansion and new methods must be examined cautiously, and avoided unless they are sure things. As a result of these complexes Southern California's great Fontana steel mill was located fifty miles inland instead of near a port, while the West Coast's giant airplane industry built no motors. There is as yet no certainty that the West, at least the Far West, can develop important fabricating industries. Even the booming Columbia Valley specializes in unfinished light metals. There is a real likelihood that such fabricating enterprises as survive will be held captive, for Eastern corporations have been moving in on them.

*   *   *

The western states of the Northern Plains Region, Montana, Wyoming, and Colorado, include the backbone of the Rockies and part of the western watershed; east of the Rockies the Great Plains slope gradually down to the Dakotas, Nebraska, and Kansas and at about the 98th meridian enter a belt blessed with generally adequate rainfall. Reading from left to right the region is notable for mining, cattle and sheep, and wheat and corn. One striking characteristic of the area is that despite its definite feeling of regionalism its capital is a city outside its borders, Chicago—for we may define the capital of a region as the place to which its entrepreneurs (not necessarily its bankers) go to borrow money. The western slopes of the Rockies are naturally attracted toward Salt Lake City and the Pacific Coast cities, especially San Francisco; if ever a readjustment of state boundaries is made those areas should certainly be joined to the Far West. The only city of the Northern Plains Region which has any right to call itself a metropolis is Denver, which with its 550,000 people holds 40 per cent of the population of Colorado.

The states of the Northern Plains have breadth, height, variety, and character. Their settlers came from all sections and included a large proportion of footloose Civil War veterans; the left wing of

Price's Confederate army, it was said, never surrendered but went to Montana. Later on the settlers were joined (least in Kansas) by Scandinavians, Germans, and Bohemians. Colorado is justly renowned for its scenery, its minerals, its beet sugar, wheat, and cattle. Mile-high Wyoming has a colorful history and a present economy based largely on cattle, sheep, and dudes. Montana, one-third mountain and two-thirds plain has poured billions of copper, lead, zinc, and silver into the world's markets and, until recently at least, was the puppet of the Anaconda interests. North Dakota has had a history flaming with economic revolt and has become quasi-socialist. South Dakota, strangely enough, has been more moderate. Nebraska, though it was the home of Bryan and Norris, has been almost conservative. Kansas "the most average of all American states" has veered among populism, conservatism, and Puritanism. Though it is fairly well diversified it still thinks in terms of agriculture. If there seems to be little consistency in the political and economic behavior of the people of the Northern Plains we may find the key in the fluctuating prices of wheat, beef, and wool, and in the number of inches of rainfall.

The Northern Plains have problems fully as serious as those that confront any part of the country. Water-power sites are legion in the Rockies, but either they are not used or the corporations which utilize them raise the price of electricity to unreasonable heights. As a result industry cannot enter, and apparently is not wanted. The amount of rural electrification is low, and not only do farmers lack conveniences but manufacturers are shut out of what should be a profitable market. The High Plains have been subject to flood and drought, and it was unwise to turn grazing areas into wheat lands. At any rate, overgrazing and dry farming have turned the subregion into recurrent Dust Bowls.

The result has been that the Northern Plains states have been the only ones in the nation to decrease in population. Federal and state governments have sought to teach soil-conservation methods, have controlled grazing, and have undertaken other measures to arrest erosion and restore fertility. But the states have not integrated their efforts, and the problem will probably not be solved until they do. The area close to the mountains has desired to increase hydroelectric and irrigation facilities, and it has found the old-established U. S. Bureau of Reclamation sympathetic to and useful in this endeavor. The areas farther downstream have been more concerned with using the rivers as cheap arteries of navigation to undercut the railroads, while the cities on the lower course of the Missouri have been concerned with both navigation and flood control; the lower river has found allies in the Corps of Engineers, which has had a long history of coping with navigation and flood control.

The difficulty (it is claimed) is that adequate irrigation on the High Plains will not leave enough water for a nine-foot channel down river; so the opposing subregions and government bureaus have been at each others' throats. Weary and disgusted observers in the region and in Congress have proposed a Missouri Valley Authority modeled somewhat upon the TVA, and they have demonstrated to their own satisfaction that only thus can the region be restored and developed. The threat of "socialism" brought the warring factions into a grudging alliance in support of a patched-up compromise called the Pick-Sloan Plan, drawn up by Army Engineers and Bureau of Reclamation men who were afraid of losing their jobs. The MVA project may or may not be dead. Much depends upon how effectively the Pick-Sloan Plan is revised and implemented.

*   *   *

The Southern Plains region offers a startling contrast to the Missouri Valley, not only in its superior resources but in the way in which it has developed. It is true that the area also has its problems of water, corporation domination, and Dust Bowl, and in addition acute minority problems in its Negro and Mexican populations. The difference may lie partly in the greater resources of the Southern Plains and partly in the frontier vigor of its people, but one suspects that it lies even more in the intense local patriotism which rose from Texas' consciousness of its mere *size* and of its unique history. If the Missouri Valley had developed as one state it is perfectly possible that it also would have exhibited many of the same characteristics. At any rate Texas has played such a major part in the development of what is often called the Southwest that we are warranted in calling it the Texas-Southwest to distinguish it from the Pacific Southwest. The gravitational attraction of Texas has not only pulled Oklahoma and New Mexico into its orbit but parts of Arizona, Colorado, Kansas, Arkansas, and Louisiana.

The region is divided from north to south a little east of its center— say along the 98th meridian—by geological, climatic, and social conditions. The eastern area, rather closely allied to the South, holds most of the cotton fields, the petroleum and gas wells, and the industries based largely upon sulphur and petroleum products. Eastern

Oklahoma, the old Indian Territory, holds about a third of the Indians of the United States but most of them are so nearly assimilated to white civilization that Oklahomans are not conscious of an Indian problem. Texas, however, has a heavy Negro population in its eastern portion and as heavy a proportion of citizens of Mexican extraction down its central axis and in its west. The lower wedge of Texas is largely given over to cattle except that irrigated land on the lower Rio Grande raises vegetables and citrus fruits, including the famous pink-meat Texas grapefruit.

The central part of the Texas-Southwest repeats the pattern of cotton and petroleum with the addition of wheat and cattle. The west, as any red-blooded American boy knows, is predominantly sheep and cattle country with some mining. New Mexico, of course, is the seat of an old and dignified Indian-Spanish-Catholic culture based on sheep, cattle, and irrigated land which grows respectable quantities of cotton. But overgrazing on the uplands has loosened the soil and is pouring mud into the valleys and dams along the Rio Grande, with the prospect that the entire irrigation system will soon be ruined. It is significant that El Paso is the queen of southern New Mexico and Amarillo of the northeast. Neither bustling Albuquerque nor the scenic capital city of Santa Fe can hope to compete with them.

What is the regional capital of the Texas-Southwest? Dallas (600,000) and Houston (800,000) each claim the honor, but neither has proved its claim. Houston, a curious mixture of progress and backwardness, has connected itself to the sea by a canal which has made it the country's fourth largest seaport. Dallas has lacked a seaport and some of the chemical resources of Houston, but has done well on oil, cotton, wheat, and cattle, and is apparently forging ahead in banking and insurance—which may yet make it the regional capital. This does not, however, gainsay the fact that, as one of its sons observed, "Texas is today the largest and most profitable colony in the world." Its railways, its petroleum corporations, and its new chemical industries are held in the fists of men in New York, Philadelphia, Wilmington, Pittsburgh, and Chicago, and these men are united not only by a community of interests but by an amazing system of interlocking directorates and stock controls. One result is that corporation taxes are held down and that Texas is unable to give proper attention to public works and social welfare. Texans, like the people of any area in which the rural tradition dominates, are inclined to be anti-labor— which is just what at least some of the corporations want. In order to preserve rural dominance the legislature for thirty years refused to redistrict the state in order to give the rising city population due weight, then passed an amendment which limited any county to a maximum of seven representatives. The trouble is that Texas cannot remain anti-labor and expect its war-born industries to flourish. In the light of the survival of pioneer individualism one should expect hell to pop when labor finally begins to march.

The remainder of the nation views the "beaming self-satisfaction" of Texans with attitudes that range from amused fondness to affectionate contempt. Texas, they quote, has "more cattle and less milk, more rivers and less water, more schools and less education, more miles of view and less to see—than any place on earth." Once at a banquet the Governor of Texas introduced the Governor of Oklahoma, "an outlying state of Texas." The guest rose to the occasion. "I want it understood here and now," he replied, "that *no* state outlies Texas!" However all this may be, the men who give names to books and movies insist that the word Texas in the title means money all over the nation. Texas is the epitome of the American manias for bigness and for self-advertisement. It has the most intense localism in the United States—Virginia, Indiana, Missouri, and California pale beside it, and even the narcissism of New York City is clouded.

As might be expected the Texans' own view of themselves is much like the movie version of their history; it saves a few stray facts but carefully builds a mythus which prunes off anything uncomplimentary and wrests history so far out of shape that Clio must weep into her nectar. There is real danger in this, for the Texas mythus is so self-complimentary that the Texan resents the implication that he can have a flaw (a sign of fundamental uncertainty) and of course this wars with any proposal to change the status quo. Un-Texan is a more powerful argument against a man or a policy than un-American, for though the Texan regards himself as an American he regards Texanism as the cream of Americanism. Texans regard themselves as a race apart, and the highest cachet a man can bear is to be a native-born Texan. There is a becoming note of modesty (Texas size) in the saying: "Never ask a man where he comes from. If he's a Texan, he'll tell you; if he's not, don't embarrass him."

No one can gainsay the significance of Texas. It leads in the number of farms and acreage of crops, and in the production of beef, cotton, wool, and mohair. It produces more petroleum and natural gas than any other state, and pipes the gas as far as New England.

This is enough to prove the point though any Texan can reel off a number of other *firsts* and *biggests*. Unfortunately these are countered by the state's rank far down the list in such things as disease controls, infant survival, social services, and education. There has been a tendency to drive out or cripple its intellectuals—but this was typical of the entire South until recently. For example the state university of Texas, one of the most promising in the nation, was deliberately shackled by political action to prevent it from teaching things as they are. The unheeding and at time unimaginative materialism of Texas is shown by the rather boresome exhibitionism of its millionaires and by their contempt for brain workers. "If you're so damn smart, why aren't you rich?" they seem to be saying. This is of course in the tradition of the Great Enterpreneurs and it may be expected to pass in good time.

At present Texas is engaged in a struggle to attain regional responsibility. It accepted industrialization as a modern manifestation of the traditional giantism of Davy Crockett, Sam Houston, and Pecos Bill. One of the most potent arguments against labor unions is that they will keep industry from getting bigger; even the populist farmer gives his support to giant corporations if they will only get things done in a big way. Strangely enough Texas, the home of giants and heroes, has no one outstanding figure either in business or politics. Nor does it have any journalistic leadership either liberal or conservative—and all of its big papers are conservative. Nevertheless it is slowly becoming accustomed to the idea that material changes will be destructive unless they bring social and psychological improvements, and young men are accepting the challenge.

In a sense Texas is still in the Jacksonian Era—which was a welter of anti-intellectuals, Bible shouters, populists, political lickspittles, and worshippers of social mediocrity and material accomplishment. And yet it must not be forgotten that the Jacksonian Era held the seeds of all that has made the United States a great material and spiritual power. Under the scum of dirty politics, of race prejudice, of crass materialism, and of a deplorable mythus, a new Hercules is struggling to emerge. And who knows what serpents he may strangle while he is still in the cradle?

*   *   *

When we look at the Far West we find that it falls into five principal subregions with jagged boundaries: (1) California, west of the

Sierra Nevada; (2) Southern California, the area south of the Tehachapi Mountains; (3) the Colorado Valley; (4) the Great Basin, the area between the Sierras and the Colorado Valley; and (5) the Columbia Valley. In a sense the Far West is a congeries of subregions rather than a region. There is relatively little communication among many of its parts. For example, though almost all the mountain ranges run north and south, the roads and railroads usually run east and west. State lines were drawn up to suit political exigencies or without much understanding of the climatic and other natural factors involved.

The states of the Far West have in common their colonial subjection to the East and the fact that their water resources are not distributed by Nature to the points where they are most needed. Of course, there is not enough water to irrigate the entire Far West even if that were topographically possible, but there is plenty of water for urban and farm use for a population possibly as great as that of the United States today. However this may be, we can be sure that vast areas of the Far West will always remain the refuge of solitude. The problem, then, is not so much in the scarcity of water as in its seasonal and geographical distribution, and not less in the baffling technical problems which follow on any attempt to use it. There is, moreover, grave doubt that wholesale irrigation is desirable in a time of agricultural surpluses, especially when there are vast tracts of rain-fed land in North and South which can be reclaimed with less trouble and expense. The usual argument in favor of Western irrigation is that the land will grow specialized crops. The trouble is that the lands are in fact often devoted to raising cotton, wheat, and other crops which might better be grown on unirrigated land.

Just as troublesome are the problems of politics and vested interest which are involved and which frequently doom any integrated effort to develop or preserve resources for the future. "What," demand some Westerners, "has posterity done for us?" They resent Eastern exploitation, but frequently the attitude rises less from a desire to preserve and use wisely their heritage than from a desire to share the gravy. Eastern interests never have any difficulty in finding allies in any Western state. For a price there are Western lawyers and publicists who will apologize for discrimination in freight rates and for high mortgage rates on real estate, and who will find reason for opening the national forests (and even the national parks) to unlimited grazing, timber cutting, and power exploitation.

A third and sometimes no less potent welding factor in the Far West is its common fear and distrust of California. Not only is California the oldest and most mature, but its population and developed wealth are greater than all the rest of the Far West combined. Separated from the remainder of the nation by a vast, sparsely inhabited area, endowed with statehood within two years after the gold strike, and guided by a group of articulate writers and politicians and self-sufficient financiers, California came to look upon itself as a nation, and like a nation developed its own regional and economic clashes for power and its own imperial tentacles. An urban state almost from the first, it was harassed by labor and agrarian discontent and dominated by mining, railroad, power, and food-growing and processing corporations.

San Francisco became a branch office of Wall Street, entrusted with the administration of the Far West. It was willing to accept disadvantages vis-à-vis the East in return for superior advantages in intraregional competition. As a result the Far West came to regard California as an exploiter and in many ways a double-dealer. This attitude was shown by Far Western alarm when California began to talk of developing out-of-state power sites for her own use and of bringing water from the Columbia River. California has managed to divert to its own use water which should go to Nevada, and despite an interstate compact it has managed to get the lion's share of Colorado River water and power—to the detriment of the Great Basin and Colorado Valley states. The development of the Central Valley has been left to the Federal government.

The capital of the Far West is still San Francisco despite the phenomenal rise of its rivals. It has had a turbulent economic and political history, but it early began to develop in the usual American urban pattern. But more than this, as the undisputed capital of the Far West during the last hundred years it took on a sophistication and cosmopolitanism found elsewhere only in New York. It is not without significance that the San Francisco area boasts the most varied and colorful residents, the best restaurants, the most vocal labor movement, and the oldest and most respected institution of higher learning on the Pacific Coast. But it also has its skeletons in the closet—civic corruption, corporate domination, race violence, and of course earthquakes. The calamity of 1906 when an earthquake shook down the city and fed it to the flames is still referred to by loyal 'Ciscans as "The Fire." San Francisco, be it recorded, was the place where a city father issued the famous call to civic betterment: "Let us grab the bull by the tail and look the facts squarely in the face."

The Central Valley of California, the heart of the state, is a bowl about 500 miles long and 100 miles wide. The northern part, drained by the Sacramento River, enjoys a greater rainfall than the south, and its mountains furnish more water than it can use. The extreme south is an area of seasonal rivers flowing into "dry lakes." Farther north, however, the San Joaquin (Wa-keen') River, fed by Sierra snows, flows through a fertile but arid valley to join the Sacramento and finally to discharge its waters into San Francisco Bay. The San Joaquin Valley is a natural hot house for the production of fruits and vegetables which needs only water for development. Irrigation has since 1871 been an essential interest of the Valley's inhabitants, and the New Deal finally stepped in to finance, at a cost of two billion dollars (2000 million) a plan which diverted the flow of the San Joaquin to irrigation canals and filled its lower channel with water pumped from the Sacramento.

Southern California occupies about a quarter of the state, but by far the most of it is uninhabitable. A strip about 250 miles long from Santa Barbara southward and never more than about sixty miles wide holds approximately half of California's population and wealth. The metropolitan area of Los Angeles (officially pronounced loss an'-juh-less) has about 4,500,000 while San Diego, known to the nation chiefly as a Marine Corps and naval base, is a flourishing district of 550,000. In the eyes of most people Southern California *is* California. It is known for its oranges, its movies, its forests of oil derricks, and its religious, dietary, economic, and political fads and cults. Probably there is too much leisure and boredom—too much loosening of life-long inhibitions among these "refugees from America." Aldous Huxley satirized Los Angeles as the City of Dreadful Joy—then decided to stay on. Southern California is a huge paradox. Its people are disinclined to go to much trouble—yet they have a mania for getting things done. There is intense materialism and a suspicion of abstract thought—yet the region is host to swarms of artists and intellectuals who are profoundly affecting American culture. Labor is taking over and reading the riot act to industry in an area where a generation ago a man was arrested for attempting to read the Declaration of Independence in public. It is a land of many moods, hospitable to reaction and to change, to sound ideas and to silly panaceas, to eccentricity and to the humdrum virtues.

The city of Los Angeles has grown by explosion. It is unique in the spotty way in which it has swallowed up hunks and patches of territory and has even reached a long tentacle southward to engulf the port of San Pedro twenty miles from city hall. New suburbs rise, literally in a season, thousands of homes complete with schools, churches, theaters, shopping centers, and bus lines. But with all its explosive efficiency Los Angeles has done little to solve the problem of public transportation, so it has become the city par excellence of the automobile and the boulevard. Los Angeles is a network of suburbs, each of them inhabited by people with similar interests, tasks, or economic standards. But economically Los Angeles and its parts and suburbs cannot be considered apart; next to the *rentier* who depends on investments the lifeblood of the whole complex lies in oil wells, movies, airplane factories, and numerous small fabricating plants—usually branches of eastern corporations. Moreover Los Angeles can boast more Mexicans than any single place outside of Mexico City and more Negroes than any other city in the West. Here then are the makings of racial strife, and thus far Los Angeles has tended to lean toward Southern interpretation of race relations.

The Colorado River Valley states have benefited greatly by Hoover Dam, but they have not had the money to construct the elaborate public works which they envisioned and which presumably would have made the desert blossom like the rose. Arizona has about 750,000 people, and these are mostly congregated about the mining towns and the irrigated areas of which Phoenix and Tucson are the centers. Despite the bitter feud between Arizona and California the two states are tied together, for California needs many of Arizona's products and Arizona needs the other's manufactures.

The Great Basin includes most of Nevada and parts of Utah, Idaho, Oregon and California. Unlike other parts of the United States it has no considerable rivers and those which it does have vanish into salt lakes or into the sand. Nevada, with 160,000 people, lives upon sheep, cattle, mining, gambling percentage, and the board-money attracted by a divorce mill. Dependent for water and power upon California's Sierras, and with its financial capital in San Francisco it has had no choice but to play second fiddle to its great neighbor. Utah is better off with 700,000 people, a majority of whom are vigorous, thrifty, hard-working Mormons. The economic power of Utah also is largely in the hands of the Mormon Church, one of the most successful cooperative enterprises in history. The population of Utah is centered largely in the agricultural north along the Logan-Ogden-Salt Lake City-Provo axis but continues diagonally southwest in a narrow strip along the old "Mormon Corridor." Utah's problem includes overgrazing, irrigation difficulties, corporate exploitation, and a perennial political rivalry between Mormons and "Gentiles." The Great Basin States—and the Colorado Valley—have never been thoroughly explored for their resources, but they give promise of supplying vast quantities not only of coal, oil shale, iron, copper, and aluminum, but also of the rarer metals. But the water problem will always be acute.

The Columbia Valley includes Washington, Oregon, Idaho, and parts of the neighboring states and Canada; the Puget Sound and Rogue River areas are inseparable sharers of its riches and its problems. West of the Cascade Mountains this subregion differs from the remainder of the Far West in that the Japan Current brings it plentiful rain and make it green and temperate. Here are the great urban districts of Seattle (725,000) on Puget Sound, and Portland (700,000) at the mouth of the Willamette ("the Willamette, God damn it!"), some manufacturing and a great deal of lumbering, fishing, and general farming. Seattle's significance rises not only from its rich hinterland and its advantage as the terminal of three transcontinental railways, but from the fact that it is the entrepot for Alaska's gold, fish, and timber. East of the Cascades the summers are hot and dry and the winters severe and snowy. Mining, lumbering, wheat growing, and cattle and sheep grazing are the pattern in the east, together with some irrigation which produces such products as the famous Idaho potatoes. The only considerable city in the east is Spokane (220,000) and it claims the mastery of the upper valley. Idaho is one of the least logically composed of the states. Its three settled areas owe allegiance to Spokane, Salt Lake City, and Oregon, while between them lies an area as large as Connecticut which is scarcely removed from primitive solitude.

The great fact about the Columbia River Valley is that in all the Far West it has the most favorable conditions for conquering the perennial problems of water and power and for developing a self-sufficient agricultural and industrial economy. Here the New Deal began to develop the second largest river on the continent. The Army Engineers built Bonneville Dam (1939) above Portland, and the Bureau of Reclamation built enormous Grand Coulee Dam (1942). Irrigation is in prospect in the near future. World War II put the newly available power to work in dozens of new enterprises, most notable of them the atomic energy plant at Hanford. Swarms of people moved in, chiefly from the Missouri Valley, and stayed when the war was over. The Columbia Valley has not been able to afford work for all, but it has hopes based on sound prospects. Already it is the country's chief center of light metals production.

The situation cries for an integrated plan of administration and utilization of resources—a Columbia Valley Authority—yet the usual conservative forces have managed to stave it off. The fact is that northwesterners are suspicious of too many changes of any kind. The Columbia Valley has bred a strong labor movement and its U'Ren was the father of the initiative, referendum, and recall, but it has never been notable for deep thought—or for that matter sweeping emotionalism. Living costs are high, but so are wages; there is too much rain in the west, but the country is green; the cities lack many of the cultural features enjoyed in other places, but they are manageable in size and it is possible to escape for a weekend without being crushed in traffic. There is a sense of relaxation and of plenty of time to spend, a feeling of permanence and assurance. The simple fact is that the citizens of the Columbia Valley live in one of the pleasantest regions in the world and they know it and want it to remain that way.

II

The American Quest

THE twentieth century revolution is far more than a demand by the peoples of the world for self government. It is also a demand that cultural and material resources shall no longer be the exclusive property of a few but shall become of service to all. Not only did the United States father this concept but its history has been the history of the quest to fit the evolution of the idea to the moral values of human dignity and freedom which it shares with the democratic wing of Western Civilization and which it believes are eternal.

The enemies of freedom tell the world that it is confronted by a dilemma. It must reject the cultural, religious, and moral values of the past if it wishes to accept mechanization's promise of a high standard of living, or it must reject mechanization if it wishes to preserve the old values. The pragmatic American refuses so simple a choice, for he knows that either alternative will result in the destruction of liberty. Rather he seeks to make mechanization serve morals. Out of the errors and struggles of the past he has begun to rebuild the unity which was destroyed by the entry of the modern age, to reconcile the spiritual and the material, and to conquer the material problems which have hampered the development of the good life.

For the first time in history democracy has the means to conquer its problems—the leisure and the implements for universal education, the relative economic equality which warranted the citizen in denying the power of a master, and the civil liberties to use in molding society to his needs and to the changing times. For the first time in history democracy has a fighting chance to win in the age old battle with authoritarianism. Mass production has the means of reconciling private enterprise and social welfare because it gives to both enterprise and society what they want—maximum profits by maximum production at minimum cost. More than this, mass production confirms democracy because it will fail without the free cooperation of both labor and society. We now have the prospect of replacing the old economy of scarcity by an economy of plenty and of carrying cultural and spiritual pursuits to undreamed of heights. The vista which opens before us is the most expansive in human history. Machines will be the servants which make it possible for us to place social aims first. Puritanism's compulsions can be moderated and economics once more subordinated to morals. Esthetics can at last find a secure base. The faith of the future can be affirmative, based upon human brotherhood and unity.

* * *

Historical action arises from influences as complex as the mind of man, his society, and the natural world in which he lives. If there is any permanent factor in history, it must be sought in human psychology and studied in connection with the way in which man reacts in his physical and social environment. Each man has an urge to get his own way, but he knows that to survive he must live in society and that society cannot exist unless individuals give up some of their independence. The amount of independence that must be surrendered immediately becomes a subject of conflict. Each person sets up a standard of justice (or good, or perfection) that coincides with the amount of independence he is willing to surrender. This personal standard of justice is controlled and changed from time to time by the struggle between his naked desires and his conscience, his conscience being his understanding of what God or society would have him do.

Out of this struggle for justice arises morality; man is by nature a moralist because he is always choosing between selfishness and society. When he has chosen, he seeks to convince his conscience that his standard of justice is right; he builds into his moral structure any course he favors, even if it only concerns taking the biggest piece of pie from a plate. And he is, in addition, consciously or unconsciously striving to force his standard on others—on society. His basic reaction to an idea is to ask about its morality; is it right or wrong, just or unjust to his concept of what the social order should be? This struggle between the individual and society is paralleled by a similar struggle between each nation and the community of nations.

It is obvious that without some influence to control and guide this interaction between the individual and his fellows, no society could be stabilized. It is law that provides the stabilizing influence. Law arises when one segment of society triumphs or when the various segments can agree on a compromise. Basically these are the only two ways in which society can be organized: by a triumph of part of the wills, or by a compromise of wills. Thus, any existing society is an expression of justice (or good) as understood by the nation or by the social caste in control.

The first method, of force, is characteristic of societies governed by an élite class, as the nobles of Europe in the past and the bureaucracy of Soviet Russia today. The aim of this method is to set up a "perfect" structure of state and society and jam humanity into it. The second method, of compromise, has been and is practiced chiefly by the peoples of the democratic nations. They insist that any attempt to force a rigid system on society will cause the triumph not of good but of evil. Their reason is simple: times change. The good law of today becomes the strait jacket of tomorrow. Compromise, they hold, is a gradual approach to good by realistic steps. Therefore they do not set up a structure; instead, they develop a process—democracy—that will enable society gradually to adapt itself to changing times. Democracy sets up a goal which it quite frankly admits it can approach but never reach: it is self-realization of the individual in a society which protects him by giving him a share in its day-to-day evolution. In English-speaking countries we believe that the first duty of men is to get along together by persuasion and compromise; we tend to define civilization as the substitution of persuasion for force.

Democracy has three readily recognizable standards: (1) it is government by law, not by the whims of rulers; (2) it is based on progressive compromises which affect anything except the basic integrity of civil liberties; and (3) it is a process, not a set structure, so can never lay claim to perfection. The test of democracy does not lie in the form of the constitution or the executive but in whether the people can and do put out the executive and the law makers and put in others more nearly to their liking.

Democracy, then, is a positive political process for putting the evolving will of the people into effect in order to advance toward liberty, equality, and fraternity. It bears in itself the means of improvement, but it is a process and not a structure, and therefore can never lay claim to perfection without destroying its essential nature. Democracy seeks to preserve and reconcile the rival sovereignties and moral values of the individual and of society and to use them as positive aids in developing a higher social and moral order. It means the federation of individuals to form society, not their complete surrender to society. In the long run democracy's controls lie in the individual's self-restraint and courage. Self-restraint is the monitor that tells us when to forego our own desires and opinions and yield to the general will: it is the basis of social order. Courage is the quality that enables us on occasion to stand up against the general will for what we believe is necessary because it is just: it is the means by which society advances.

Government in a practical sense must operate through popular pressures which effect a changing balance of social conflict—that is, a never-ending regrouping of social forces in temporary alliances to promote their own interests. Democracy—and only democracy—frankly seeks guidance in this interplay of social interests and is willing to change its program as the political, social, and economic balances shift. The method may be slow, but nothing in American history is so evident as that in the long run the people get what they want regardless of its wisdom. The political battle is fought between a "force" in office and a "counterforce" which is in opposition. They must adopt a satisfactory compromise on any mooted subject or else the "counterforce" may muster the support to displace its rival and assume office as the "force"; the ousted party then becomes the "counterforce" and in turn watches for an opportunity to unhorse its opponent. The conflict is carried on according to certain accepted rules (a "formalized conflict"), and the function of the party out of power to check on the other is so well recognized that in the British Parliament it is called "His Majesty's loyal opposition."

Democracy's method is political, but American democracy has demonstrated in every generation a consciousness that it cannot survive in the face of an ungoverned concentration of economic power. The crux of the democratic battle has not been against property as property, but rather against abuse or potential abuse of the power which the possession of property gives. Throughout American history there has been a determined effort to set up and preserve relative economic equality, and this was what Jefferson sought by trying to make the United States a nation of free farmers. By the time of the Civil War, however, it had become evident that relative economic equality was impossible in an industrial society. Democracy had to find a new economic base. The danger rises not only from concentration of property in private hands but from concentration of economic controls in pressure groups and in the government itself.

Throughout history the fates of democracy and science have been inextricably interwoven. The reason is plain: to remain in the position of power, an élite class must command the unquestioning faith and obedience of the masses. But science probes into current beliefs and attitudes and raises questions and doubts as to their validity and worth. Sooner or later it must begin to undermine the "perfect" structure. To save itself the élite class must crush science. Science, then, finds its only protection in the open minds of a democratic society, which actually encourages change. On the other hand, democracy depends for its existence upon popular enlightenment; and in a complex society this is possible only by the technical processes that give us paper, printing, easy transmission of news, and the time that the machine frees to us for education in childhood days and adult evenings.

Popular enlightenment has a never-ending task, for it must frequently try to alter or combat established ideas—the mythus. The mythus is the body of beliefs (true or false) which by its emotional appeal produces a spirit of loyalty to the leader or the ideal. It is the encrustation of wishful thinking and self-complimentary explanations that forms about human actions and institutions to explain their origin, nature, and development, and to "mobilize men for action."

Usually the mythus is interlaced with facts and so has a convincing air of authenticity. It may be a subtle or misleading explanation of destructive doctrines, as Nazism or Sovietism. Or it may furnish a positive urge to social and spiritual betterment; this is the way in which most people interpret the body of Christian doctrine and practice. Between the extremes lies the democratic mythus: democracy's aspirations are high, but the mythus makes such optimistic interpretations of democratic practices that it is possible to ignore the numerous exceptions that breed injustice. It would be far better to acknowledge the sordid facts of social ills and try to cure them.

*   *   *

Five hundred years ago, though Western Civilization was different in some ways from the civilizations of China and India, the latter two doubtless had the advantages. The Orient had known for thousands of years heights of art and luxury whose satisfactions perhaps we do not know yet—in spite of our gadgets. Moreover, it had reached a fairly satisfactory state of balance with Nature, which perhaps could have continued indefinitely. This balance was maintained at vast expense of human misery at the bottom of the social scale, but even the peasant knew how to live and die graciously and could find in religion and contemplation the consolations which society refused him. Still, the fact remains that the Orient failed to conquer Nature and provide its people with an abundant life. As Hu Shih, the Chinese statesman and philosopher, has pointed out, the Orient has a truly materialistic civilization because it is limited by matter and is incapable of transcending it. Its contentment with little and its fatalistic resignation are more materialistic than its actual hovels and images of the gods. Only the civilization which uses its full ingenuity to overcome and utilize the material in service to mankind is—or can be—highly idealistic and spiritual. That is, if it can utilize the material without worshiping it.

Western Civilization might have run the same course as the Orient had it not been that down through the ages there had been added special ingredients that were to set it on the track of a more successful conquest of Nature than had ever before been seen. Freedom, democracy, and science made several starts in the Mediterranean cultures, but in each culture the rise of a privileged ruling class defeated them. Science languished or was crushed; slavery brought contempt for manual labor, so that men were ashamed to perform practical experiments. Nevertheless, we have inherited much from all these societies. Greece passed on her great discovery that our desire to know the truth can never be satisfied until we are willing to submit our findings to the test of reason. Rome's most enduring bequest was a code of laws that today holds sway in most of the Western nations except those that speak English, and it has vitally influenced them also. The Roman Empire tried to seek the truce with Nature that China and India had sought. But the Empire was so complex and far-flung it could not solve the problems it had to solve to create a static society. It really fell of its own weight.

Christianity owed much to Hebrew monotheism and divine revelation; also it had elements of fatalism. But Greek philosophy and barbarian vigor refused to let Christianity lie quiescent. The Middle Ages wrought a mighty change. The Mediterranean world was inhabited by debased slaves, starveling peasants, commoners on the dole, and northern barbarians whom the lordly Romans regarded as incapable of becoming civilized. The Church took over the civilizing mission of Rome, fastened the yoke of discipline on the hot-blooded barbarians, and taught the dignity and necessity of labor to a society that had despised the laborer. Discipline and labor are two of the most important ingredients in an industrial society; they are two of the many gifts of the Church to the modern world. The Church also emphasized that Christian salvation was an individual matter, that each man was responsible for his own fate. This was the bridge between ancient statism and modern individualism. The idea that the individual exists for the benefit of the state began to yield to the democratic idea that the state exists for the individual *and* society.

The Renascence and Reformation split European society between the "Catholic Esthetic" and the "Protestant Ethic" and brought in changes which seemed to promote materialism. Let us see what actually came of it, how God has made the wrath of man to praise Him. Medieval man belonged to a unitary order of nature. The Church taught that there was a great deal of good in man, that he belonged to a great brotherhood, and that he was free to choose or reject salvation. Though his lot was cast with a class from which he had little chance of escaping, he enjoyed considerable emotional and practical individual freedom. Competition existed, but on the whole the economic was subordinated to the moral, and the troubles incident to human living received convenient theological explanations. Medieval man was imbued with faith, reverence, and love of beauty. Moreover he had a sense of responsibility, both to those above him and below him. On the whole the medieval order was such as to subject its members to a minimum of self-destructive compulsions. Men had a sense of belonging which is sadly lacking in the modern world.

The Renascence and the rise of capitalism destroyed this sense of unity by tearing up the social and economic roots and projecting the individual into a lonesome universe. It is true that there was a new sense of freedom among burghers and nobles, but it introduced fierce competition among them and brought the need to crush the new aspirations of the commoners. There was a new greed for power, pelf, and fame, for with the sense of social unity gone the individual was no longer satisfied with anonymity but craved immortality. The moral was now subordinated to the economic. By 1500 an upper crust of wealth and nobility had become firmly established, and just under it was a class of petty manufacturers and merchants who felt that they were estopped from rising. They could not assault the social order, for their welfare depended on order, so their hostility went out against both those who kept them from rising and those who menaced them from below. To satisfy his new ambitions the individual had to scrimp and save, take business risks, exploit those beneath him and cater to those above. It was the birth of snobbery.

It was the mission of the so-called reformers to rationalize and channelize these hostilities. Luther did it for Germany and Calvin did it for Western Europe and in the long run for the United States.

Calvin, following certain leads given by St. Augustine and St. Thomas Aquinas, taught that man was naturally depraved and unable to do good or even to desire to do good without the grace of God. For reasons best known to himself God had predestined some men to salvation and others to damnation. Men were therefore unequal; the damned must therefore submit to the "elect," and the latter must exercise a responsibility for the spiritual and temporal welfare of those beneath them.

How could one know that he was one of the elected? If he was sober in life and conversation, industrious, thrifty, and above all prosperous, he could be pretty sure of his status. Doubt was stifled by an inner compulsion to activity. Mere busyness displaced the old joy of creation; one must be busy in order to be good. Duty became an obsession, not merely a stimulus. Conscience from being a guide became a slave driver. These were accompanied by a distrust of freedom for others. As one of the elect it was the Calvinist's duty to see that others were saved from themselves by being forced to practice virtue, especially the virtue of industry. The belief that men must be forced to work for their own good has permeated the modern world and has become the core of the mythus both of capitalism and communism. The Calvinist's belief that his fellows were ruled by their natural depravity finds its parallel in the rather general belief that foreigners are ruled by their natural depravity.

Of course there were many gradations of opinions among both Catholics and Protestants: many Protestants did not adopt the harshness of Calvinism; on the other hand, there were many Catholics who practiced the precepts of Calvin's Puritans even though they rejected the theology. On the whole, however, Catholicism preserved the gentler virtues of reverence, faith, love for beauty, and the struggle for perfection.

There has been a great deal of praise for supposed Calvinistic virtues which actually did not exist. It was no part of Calvinism's plan to approve of religious liberty, democracy, or laissez faire; on the contrary it sought regimentation, and each of the three had to fight to break through the restrictive shell. However, after making due allowance for the evils of Calvinistic compulsives it is clear that they were powerful forces in Western Civilization's conquest of nature. Hard work, thrift, sobriety, self-reliance, a (limited) sense of responsibility for one's fellows, and the willingness to take calculated risks—these were among the economic foundation stones of the modern world.

We may now be in a position to reduce the compulsiveness which lay behind them, but there is no reason to suppose that society can continue to exist without these virtues.

American Puritanism, even in its early stages, was not completely Calvinistic. Rather it accepted the ideals of Pierre La Ramée, who distrusted Aristotelian logic and glorified common sense. This was, of course, only a restatement of the English tradition. The Puritan founders taught that though God was sovereign and absolute He had voluntarily limited himself in His relations to man; in other words God was a constitutional monarch. Man was caught in the toils of sin but he could still understand reason. The Puritan was thus realistic, tough-minded, self-confident, never completely disillusioned or fatalistic, but imbued with zeal and gusto.

Since God was a constitutional monarch, the Puritan knew how to approach him. Man might not be able to save himself, but at least he could approach God with the confidence of one who had *sought* to earn his passage and who knew that God helped those who helped themselves. This search was active; virtue required a world, a task, a field of operation—not a monastery. Since prosperity was the evidence of God's favor it may be that Puritans sometimes sought the prosperity rather than the favor. Closely allied to this was their belief in their responsibility for social welfare, and since they had to answer to God for results they could not afford to be too choosy of their methods. Breaking the moral law to uphold the moral law was sometimes necessary—indeed the very stuff of which morality was made. Call it hypocritical if you will, but do not make the mistake of calling it cynical. The view of the moral standard remained clear and the Puritan got back to it as soon as conditions permitted. It is a common complaint that conservatives and industrialists have frequently resorted to these tactics—a double standard of morality—but it has also been the resort of laborers, farmers, and political and social reformers. Each side is open to the accusation of moral double talk, for each has damned only the sins in which it does not care to indulge.

Puritan attitudes (not necessarily its theology) entered into the marrow of American life, into the Southern masses as well as those of the North. The Puritan lived in a state of constant warfare. He accepted privations, sacrificed many normal pursuits and desires, and took his turn at watch on the ramparts. Constantly he was reading bulletins from the front and being urged to give of his substance, to avoid complacency as evil, and never to acknowledge defeat. All this may have originated in the belief that his own and others' salvation was of first importance, yet the state of mind was obviously useful in conquering a continent. Such an activity demanded strict attention to business and unswerving allegiance to the sterner virtues. The Puritan was clearly giving an ethical meaning to material pursuits. He did not, like the European idealist, consign ethics to the realm of pure spirit.

Puritanism accepted human inequality as God's order. How then could democracy arise from it? Actually the seeds of democracy had already sprouted in the English soil and had taken such firm root that Englishmen would insist that even the Calvinistic virtues must conform to the Rights of Englishmen. As it was, Calvinism lent itself to the democratic mythus. It taught Natural Rights, the compact theory, and the right of revolution. Democracy found all of them useful. The Puritan belief that each man should strive to become prosperous and thus bear a share in social responsibility could be adjusted to the democratic belief that the benefit of one is the benefit of all and that all are responsible.

The Puritan's courage in standing up for what he believed and for the program he favored was part and parcel of democracy. The Puritan minister's authority stemmed from God and his congregation; that of the democratic leader from God and the people. The Puritan was self-reliant, but he had to respect his fellow Puritan who could quote scripture back at him or even put him in the pillory; give and take was also a part of democracy. The Puritan saw his material and social activities as the means to an end which lay beyond society; democracy also sees itself as a positive process for approaching a more perfect moral order.

Puritanism was a very human attempt to gird for a necessary conflict, and underneath its surface rigidity there was enough elasticity to make it adjustable to either liberty or authority. America forced it to adjust to liberty; Russia is adjusting a somewhat similar belief in determinism and human depravity to authority. American democracy, hewn from English oak, from frontier environment, and from Puritanism, has come to insist upon the dignity and ultimate worth of the individual; upon freedom of expression and action so long as they do not injure others; and the right and responsibility to share in community effort, benefits, and fun.

Calvinist ethics have been most deeply rooted in the middle class, which in America has historically included most of us. Its ethics fought against the mediocrity inherent in the practice of democracy and sought to develop leaders and to implant a respect for leadership. It has not always succeeded. It has frequently been observed that here and in Europe the top and bottom classes have been characterized by a greater measure of moral slickness and sexual looseness than the middle classes, though without so much hypocrisy. The New Deal violated the Puritan conviction that the poor and unfortunate were in those conditions because they did not deserve divine favor and should suffer until they mended their ways—that is, went to work. Nevertheless, in another sense the New Deal was fighting a rear guard action for Puritanism. The weakening of the middle class had weakened the humdrum Puritan virtues, especially respect for property. An upper working class civilization was rising which the New Deal fought to endow with at least that one virtue. It remains to be seen how well it succeeded. Certainly the undermining of the Puritan virtues had begun long before the New Deal.

The elements of the modern age were worked out in Western Europe. To Italy we owe the bases of that capitalism which in the restricted form of mercantilism was to rule early modern times and in the form of laissez faire was to become ascendant in the nineteenth century. To the French we owe the idea of progress and the impetus which their Revolution gave to nationalism, whether for good or evil. To England we owe the preservation and development of the democratic ideal and its twin, the scientific method. From these sprang the Industrial Revolution which, left to itself, would have broken down economic barriers and united the world into one great producing and marketing area. Perhaps in the end this would have led to a voluntary political integration. As it turned out, the continental monarchs, under the pretense of promoting unity and efficiency in the struggle for national survival, subtly and successfully prevented the rise of all but the mere forms of liberty. Particularly in the great states of Germany, Austria-Hungary, and Russia the tremendous power of the Industrial Revolution was chained to the chariot wheels of the national states and utilized less to raise the standard of living than to increase military power. In this deliberate frustration of the genius of the Industrial Revolution we can find the basic reasons for the wars and the economic decay of our own time.

Still, ever since the fall of Rome, the idea of unification has appealed to Europe, but her nations will accept only a unification that will preserve their precious diversities. Thus far Europe's political capacities have proved unequal to the task, though repeated attempts have been made to turn her states into a system of satellites revolving around a central sun. These attempts centered in the Holy Roman Empire of Charles V, the Spain of Philip II, the France of Louis XIV and Napoleon, and the Germany of Wilhelm II and Hitler. Though these attempts invariably involved complex economic rivalries, their significance to the future lay in the struggle between absolutism and democracy. The fate of both hung upon a rivalry between land and sea. Over a period of four centuries the sea conquered as the people of Great Britain constituted the core of resistance to the unification of Europe by force. From 1815 to 1914 there reigned the *Pax Britannica,* the longest era of comparative peace since the rupture of the *Pax Romana.*

* * *

The battle between Nature and Western man has had no more vivid illustration than in North America. The opening of the continent began just at the moment when European techniques had reached the stage where they could wage successful warfare against Nature and had already raped Europe's superficial resources in the preliminary skirmishes of the battle for the world. The demand for furs and timber was urgent, and it was not long until there was an even greater cry from an expanding population for food, minerals, and tropical luxuries.

Europeans, reared in an economy of scarcity, were dazed by the natural riches of the New World. Even the most unimaginative travelers became lyrical over the enormous expanse of the new continent, and there was a pardonable element of exaggeration in the tales they told. The fish off Newfoundland gathered in such shoals that ships could hardly make way through them; wild strawberries reddened the fields in early summer; clouds of pigeons darkened the sun and when they lighted bore down the stoutest trees; buffaloes covered the plains as far as the eye could reach; and trees were so tall that it took two men and a boy to see to the top. Here the men of straitened little Europe could find the elbowroom they craved, the freedom from feudal restraint, and the natural resources to give them a life so abundant that the like existed only in fairy tales. The "barbaric yawp" of Walt Whitman was only a faint and cultured echo of the exuberant whoops with which the pioneers fell upon the New World paradise.

It is customary to attribute American wealth to the stimuli of ingenuity and private enterprise. This is a sound view, as we shall see, but American ingenuity and private enterprise would never have exceeded those of a number of backward nations had it not been for two advantages which it is too often the custom to ignore. These were: (1) the existence of a rich continent with cream that could be readily skimmed off by the techniques of the time; and (2) the inheritance of English institutions, which meant that Federal and state governments were purposely designed to be relatively weak; along with this was the absence of certain restrictive European institutions, such as mercantilism and the guild system, which strait-jacketed European commerce and manufactures. In other words, the relative lack of privileged classes (either of politics, capital, or labor) in the new continent and the superabundance of natural resources operated together to build up a social and political system which not only promoted the skimming of the cream but measured it out for a large proportion of the people.

The natural riches of the North American continent have vitally influenced American psychology. The first and most obvious effect was the growth of what Stuart Chase calls the concept of infinity. Until the verge of our own century Americans were literally incapable of grasping the idea that there was any limit to their natural resources. They saw no more reason to save timber or minerals than would a gardener beside a waterfall see reason to be sparing of water. A man as cautious and observant as Jefferson thought that it would take the population sweep six centuries to reach the Pacific. Mineral and timber wealth was regarded as literally inexhaustible. The challenge to Europe's prodigal sons was irresistible. They were possessed of a furious yearning to conquer and strip Nature, to reduce it to order and usefulness.

The conquest was not easy. This generation, as it drives through the smooth green fields (say of Ohio), has no idea of the incredible toil that was necessary to fell the forest, log or burn off the trees, and to battle for decades with stumps, second growth, roots, stones, and briars. We see the drama of the cotton kingdom which in a single generation swept from the sea islands of Georgia to the plains of Texas, or of the lumber jacks who began life in Maine and died among the Douglas firs of Puget Sound. The drama conceals the fact that failures were more numerous than successes, that fortunes gained from cotton disappeared with the leaching of the soil and the dislocations of civil war, and that fortunes skimmed off the land by lumbering disappeared into the land in fake gold mines or wildcat oil wells. These are words of warning lest we paint too rosy a picture of the conquest of the continent; yet the fact remains that fortunes were made, and they were long-lived enough to give to the generalty of Americans the hope that they could found economic dynasties, however little they had in hand at the beginning. The medieval European dreamer retired to a monastery to nurse his frustrations; he was touted by future generations as a great idealist. The American dreamer became a builder, because it was possible for him to build; his reward has been to be called a crass materialist.

One of the most curious of American phenomena is the contradiction between the ideal of thrift and the practice of waste. Actually nothing could be more natural. The ideal of thrift is hereditary, not only because Europeans lived in an economy of scarcity and had to save, but because it entered into the religious teachings of Christianity, particularly Calvinism. Even more important, perhaps, is the fact that developing capitalism found savings essential for the purchase of machinery, raw materials, and transportation equipment, and so glorified thrift as the road to wealth and the respect of the community. In America, however, the concept of thrift and the concept of infinite resources have been at war. Those who favored thrift found themselves undersold by those in haste to be rich. The lumberman who threw away the waste and cut down more trees underbid the lumberman who thriftily utilized the less profitable waste. The miner who skimmed off the high-grade ore undersold the one who sought to utilize the lower grades. The oil man who wished to pump slowly found that rivals sank wells near his boundaries and drained off his oil. Regulation of such wasteful methods would have seemed wise, but Federal and state governments had been deliberately molded to prevent them from interfering with private business. The concept of infinity won. Thrift was found only in activities where cash had to be paid out for materials, and even there its hold was tenuous. Its safest retreat was found in children's copybooks.

Americans think of themselves as liberal and forward-looking. This concept is ordinarily true in the material aspects of their life, but it does not contradict the fundamental conservatism of their society. They change their machines and style of dress more easily than their mental and moral and social outlook. It is significant that no liberal political party has ever been able to assume power and remain liberal; basic political rivalries have not been between conservatives and true liberals, but between conservatives and ultra-conservatives. Americans sensibly asked themselves why they should plump for great changes when moderate changes in the distribution of natural wealth would solve their problems. They preferred to use the word liberal in a nonpolitical sense as denoting tolerance, generosity, public spirit, and most of all unbounded faith in the future of America and a willingness to gamble largely on that faith. Such liberalism was justified.

Conservatism had other legitimate origins. The Calvinist point of view dominated the colonists, whatever their theology. With a continent begging to be raped they could scarcely avoid regarding themselves as chosen of God, and they desired only to be let alone to exercise the individual responsibility which Calvin had made the basis of his system. Calvinist standards of success could apply only to a limited few in the bitter European economic struggle, but America's riches made possible their attainment by more people. John Calvin, and not Adam Smith, deserves to be canonized as the patron saint of American chambers of commerce and businessmen's clubs. He it was who saw a divine order in private enterprise and individual responsibility; and if he gave the state more power than we wish, it was only in order to enforce the ascendance of those who had proved themselves worthy. The eminent Episcopal jurist John Marshall had similar ideas—and so did Quaker Herbert Hoover and Catholic Al Smith.

Conservatism was strengthened in yet another way by natural conditions. The isolation and insecurity of the first settlers bred within them a fierce desire to hold on to the habits and beliefs of the homeland, altered only by the particular theologies or ambitions which had brought them to America. They clung to the moral and emotional content of their heritage long after material conditions had outmoded them, by setting up a tight little society, based upon state churches and a landed and merchant aristocracy, which attempted to enforce religious dogmas and social distinctions. They were Englishmen, and, like the proverbial Englishman on safari who dresses for dinner, they were determined to preserve the old ways. It is amazing how well they succeeded, in spirit if not in detail. Since their leaders were not noblemen but merchants and gentry, it was natural that their aristocracy was made up of merchants and gentry, but that was as far as they went willingly. The battle was joined from the beginning over the degree of change that was necessary and advisable. The defeated in any generation found it possible to move on west to new scenes where perhaps they in turn could become the successful and relatively privileged ultraconservatives.

This desperate clinging for comfort to the old ways in the midst of new conditions has accentuated the natural tendency to hold to a body of theory which is obviously contradicted by practice. On the frontier, where life was so radically different that it dissolved the social pattern into new and more democratic forms, people desperately sought an anchor in the religious dogmas and emotions and the antiscientific prejudices which they had brought with them. The split between ideas and realities led to astounding illogicalities, directly traceable to wishful thinking. When morality loses vital connection with facts, there is a tendency to offer legality as a substitute. Legality becomes a matter of technical adherence to laws, while at the same time it often shrewdly defies their spirit. Injustice can then be rationalized on the ground that no law is being violated.

Americans have too often been the apostles of waste and superficiality because these have at times actually been practical, workable national programs. The consequent drain on natural resources is viewed with alarm by an increasing number of observers. Of course, it is easy to point to denuded and eroding hills, lowered water tables, streams and coasts filthy with sewage and industrial waste, resources skimmed off by reckless competition or blown up in warfare, and to the fact that about one third of the population gets along on less than what is usually assumed to be a decent living standard.

But what is the significance of all this? Paradoxically, it means that for the first time in history democracy has a fighting chance to win in the age-old battle with totalitarianism. The riches of North America bred a society in which abundance took the place of scarcity; for the first time privilege could not snatch all the economic power for itself and tread down the common man. Democracy came into its own, and with it came the atmosphere of freedom which science and technology need in order to grow. Not only was this true in the United States, but the riches of America operated to extend much of the same atmosphere of freedom to the remainder of Western Civilization and gave to England, the champion of democracy, the strength to survive. Out of the blood and oppression of the Anglo-American sweep to the Pacific and out of the waste of this splendid continent has come the opportunity that we hold in our hands today. One can only stand in awe before the mysterious processes of history.

In this century the United States and the Soviet Union are the heirs of the two great conflicting forces of history: democracy and totalitarianism. For almost five thousand years totalitarianism or its kindred doctrines of aristocracy and special privilege ruled the Mediterranean world, except for a brief time in Greece. Today the machine makes it possible not only to do away with human drudgery but also to cast aside the psychological heritage of a slave-based society: contempt for manual labor, dictation over men's lives, and calling a segment of society inferior in race or ability as an excuse for exploiting it. For the first time we have the technical resources which make democracy possible in a complex society: the paper, the printing presses, the communication facilities, and the leisure for education. Democracy and science are working together, and if they win they must win as a team. On that union depends the issue of whether the common man shall walk in freedom and individual dignity or bow his neck to the yoke of slavery.

III

The Institutional Bases

THE colonies of England were planted later than those of most of the other nations, but they were the first to reach economic and political maturity. The reasons lay primarily in the nature of the English people and in their laws and institutions. Most important was the fact that mercantilism was never practiced more than half-heartedly by England; so it was possible for the colonies to attract swarms of immigrants, to build up their manufactures and commerce, and to exercise all but complete self-government. The colonists were self-governing because they were Englishmen and as such expected to manage their own affairs. Distance promoted self-reliance, troubles in England itself promoted a salutary neglect of the colonies, but the royal charters were liberal from the first and generally remained so. Immigrants were usually workers; few nobles came over and fewer remained. Liberal land policies promoted widespread prosperity, forced town employers to raise the wages of their workmen in order to keep them, and ensured a society that was relatively classless because there was an approximately equal opportunity for all.

It seems likely that the popular imagination has overrated the role of religious freedom as a reason for planting the colonies; on the other hand, it certainly had some share in attracting immigrants. British sea power protected the colonies from foreign conquest in one direction, while toward the land the rugged diplomacy of fur traders and royal governors weakened the Indians, the French, and the Spanish. Finally, though it was not generally recognized in that day, the Thirteen Colonies were highly favored by geographical position, climate, and soil. Their location between the Caribbean and Europe gave them a strategic commercial position; their climate was an invigorating aid to enterprise; and their agricultural staples and forest products afforded a firmer basis for economic strength and the growth of a transplanted European population than did the sugar, the cacao, and the silver mines of the tropics.

The colonies were settled largely by Englishmen and it was not until the close of the seventeenth century that other nationalities began to enter in large numbers. Even New York during the Dutch days had a large proportion of English settlers, and Dutchmen, French Hugenots, and Swedes were readily assimilated. The people of the United States, therefore, not only speak a form of the English language but they are basically English in blood, institutions, and mannerisms. The fact that most of the original settlers were Englishmen does not mean that most American blood today is English, but it is probably fair to say that there is still more English blood than any other. However that may be, the long historical interchange between England and America has made Americans, whatever their descent, more at home in England than anywhere else.

Americans have inherited or acquired the Englishman's love of action, distrust of logic, use of compromise, tolerance for minor differences, and reverence for the old and well-tried. Like Englishmen they are dualistic and so are always seeking to reconcile the practical and the moral and in the effort have found hypocrisy a way station on the road from vice to virtue. Their laws sprang from the English common law, and like the latter have grown organically by judicial decision in order to remain suited to the times. Though their liberties were concretely enumerated and specifically safeguarded, they also accepted John Locke's interpretation of Natural Rights, and from the latter deduced the doctrine that the protection of property was the central business of government. Finally they placed political authority in the hands of the elected representatives of the people and kept open the road to change.

German immigrants appeared in most of the colonies toward 1700 but most of them came to Pennsylvania—Quakers' Valley to them. By 1760 there was a broad belt with around a hundred thousand "Pennsylvania Dutch" between Philadelphia and the Susquehanna River. They gave a permanent color to the region, and some of their descendants still speak a German patois, especially in the communities founded by pietist sects like Dunkards and Mennonites. The Lutherans were readier to mix with their British and Irish neighbors.

Germans contributed one of the most valuable elements in the American heritage. They sought no short cut to affluence but relied on thrift, patience, industry, and big families. They were the only immigrants who we can say with certainty possessed the peasant's mystical love for the soil. German farmers were renowned for their thoroughness and intelligent application of scientific methods. Their manual dexterity and mechanical inventiveness, together with their agricultural methods, made the Pennsylvania-German counties the most prosperous and progressive region in the English colonies. Germans not only engaged in type founding, paper making, and glass making but were the finest wood and iron workers in the colonies; their Conestoga wagons and "Kentucky" rifles led the westward movement. Their folk arts have survived not only in museums but as a part of the American tradition. Music was greatly loved among them, and their town of Bethlehem was a center for the greatest of European music at a time when most Americans were still singing psalms and ballads through their noses.

The German flood was still running strong when, about 1718, Ulster Irishmen began to enter in large numbers through Philadelphia, Baltimore, and Charleston. These, often known as the Scotch-Irish, were descended from Lowland Scots and English who had been settled in Ulster by James I in an abortive attempt to drive out or exterminate the Irish and repeople the island with Protestants. The Scotch-Irish were rugged people, Presbyterian in religion, who settled in every colony, but most of them went first to Pennsylvania or the Carolinas. Ulster had been a frontier between Protestantism and Catholicism, subject like the new home to massacre and counter-massacre; so the Scotch-Irish had developed frontier characteristics before they emigrated. Contentious, boisterous, individualistic, restless, mentally rigid, impatient of restraint—and courageous and hardy—they were ideal pioneers. Essentially unimaginative and unaesthetic, yet always dreaming of better land farther on, they only scratched the soil, then moved on to the next valley and left to a German plodder the patient reclamation of the soil. In them the democracy inherent in one side of Calvinism found complete expression; the Presbyterian kirk was as important a school for self-government as the provincial assemblies. It was a rough-and-ready school for men who believed in self-reliance and direct action. It is no wonder that the Revolution was sometimes known as the Presbyterian Rebellion.

There was no readily distinguishable movement of Celtic Irish as there was of Germans and Scotch-Irish, yet there can be no doubt that they began to arrive even earlier and in even greater numbers. Scattered through every colony as redemptioners, many of them apparently lost their Catholicism and merged with their neighbors. On the frontier they formed an important element in the amalgam that was forming, and probably they did much to alter the English temperament. The Celtic Irishman has contributed a romantic dash and color to American political and military life. His companionableness and blarney, his large warm heart, his human sympathies, and his willingness to give kindly personal services at the expense of what he considers irrelevant rules · have given him a niche as a straw boss and politician. His lovableness has been transmuted into American friendliness, and his hyperbole has reappeared as giantism in American story and American ideals. Not English patter but the crackle of Irish humor has been adapted by the American; though along with it has also come Scots dryness and the English sense of incongruity. On the other side, Celtic slickness—reinforced by Yankee opportunism—has helped give us the too common idea that any action is justifiable if one can get away with it. Lastly, the Celt has heightened a certain volatility which has made us too often subject to national surges of hysteria and to the slogans and nostrums of quack statesmen.

The Scots came to America as families or small congregations and settled in every colony. The greatest single recorded migration was chiefly to North Carolina after the Young Pretender's defeat at Culloden in 1746. The poverty of Scotland had long been a barrier against the snares of luxury and political absolutism. The knightly tradition with its earmarks of lavishness and gentility never put down roots. Poverty made the Scot closefisted in spending for useless show, but in business matters he exhibited a persistence, carefulness, and cautious daring that made him the world's outstanding merchant. The Scots are the true shopkeepers, not the English. Nowhere is there more reverence for the things of the mind than there is in Scotland; this has led to a certain mental rigidity and disputatiousness which exalts logic. The Scots in America were prominent as merchants, ministers, lawyers, and schoolmasters. Their influence on the formation of American character was profound, in that it helped to alter the English tradition by giving the American a certain respect for logic and universal education—indeed, the Scottish universities were more the Meccas of American colonial youth than were Oxford and Cambridge—and the lawyers that Scotland sent to America were the logicians of the Revolution. The peculiar homespun brand of American democracy is as much the child of Scotland as of the frontier. Robert Burns examined fine clothes and fare, noble blood and high degree, and announced: "The rank is but the guinea's stamp; the man's the gold for a' that." This is the inherited belief of the average American.

Among the many immigrant elements the Negro deserves special
mention. The races of Africa are as diverse as those of Europe with
just as profound differences in physique, culture, and psychology.
However, it is impossible to assess their separate influences in the
American scene. The original claim that Negroes had to be imported
because white men could not stand the hard labor in the sun has
long since been exploded. Slavery was introduced because it furnished
quickly and with comparative cheapness a large and relatively docile
labor force which had no concept of civil rights, did not look forward
to freedom, and did not expect even the low standard of living of
European village life. The contribution of the Negro in the form of
labor to the economic enrichment of America is seldom realized by
whites and has never (even since emancipation) been rewarded by
more than a bare subsistence. Negroes absorbed rapidly the superficial aspects of American culture both because the race is readily
adaptable and because members of the various Negro tribes were
separated and had to learn English in order to communicate with
each other.

Christianity was readily adopted (and sometimes mixed with heathen
practices) because it is a religion of comfort for the lowly and oppressed,
a fact that is often forgotten today. A few Negroes learned to read,
and a few attained some distinction as writers, notably the poetess
Phyllis Wheatley. In their native Africa and in the plantation days
Negroes were apt and skillful artisans; and there seems no reason but
lack of background and opportunity why they should not be again.
Some of the Negro cultures were relatively high, but the only important vestiges that remain in the United States are found in folklore
and music. These, however, have become part and parcel of American
life and give it a mood, color, and dramatic value quite foreign to the
Western European.

*   *   *

All of the Thirteen Colonies were founded as a result of private
enterprise. Indeed, the British Empire has been chiefly the creation
of individuals and trading companies, and only with the greatest
reluctance has the government stepped in to remedy neglect and
exploitation—usually in response to an aroused public opinion. The
gradual change-over from proprietary and corporate (sometimes called
company or charter) colonies to royal colonies was therefore in keeping with imperial evolution and was hastened in many cases by the

colonists' hope that royal governors would be more lenient (they said impartial) than the governors sent out by proprietors or companies. The British government also desired the change because it could then act directly through its governors rather than through elected or proprietary governors. In 1775 Pennsylvania, Delaware, and Maryland were the only surviving proprietorships. Connecticut and Rhode Island were the only charter colonies, though in both the charters were held by the people and not by a British company.

The official point of view of the English government from first to last was mercantilist; that is, the colonies existed for the benefit of the mother country. It was the purpose of a long series of Navigation Acts to integrate the Thirteen Colonies (and all other English possessions) into a planned economy contained within a self-sufficient empire. It was the belief of that day that trade was a sort of warfare, and that the victor in a transaction was the party that came away with the most gold or silver.

The restrictions imposed by the Navigation Acts sound worse than they actually were. Of course, English merchants had promoted the Navigation Acts, and they expected to profit by them, but there was no intention to shut the colonies out. It was expected that colonial trade, also, would boom as a result—and it did. By and large the colonies were no exceptions to the economic thinking of the day. They were highly mercantilistic in their attitudes toward foreign countries, toward each other, and toward the mother country in so far as their own trading and manufacturing interests were involved. However, the advantages offered by imperial bounties and monopolies were so great that most colonists were highly in favor of the Navigation Acts until they were used as a means of taxation and imperial interference in local affairs. It is interesting to note that the limitations on enumerated products fell hardest on the West Indian colonies, which remained loyal; the greatest share of bounty payments went to the mainland colonies, which revolted.

Whatever else may be said about them, it is evident that the Thirteen Colonies were expanding enormously. From about two hundred thousand in 1688 their population grew to around two and three quarter million in 1775; at the latter date the British Isles had only about ten million people. The economic expansion was even more remarkable, as can be seen in the rising standard of living and the growth of commerce. On the other hand, colonial debts drained so much specie from the country that internal business was handicapped for lack of the

currency so necessary in an expanding economy. Attempts were made
to fill the need by issuing paper money, but the Crown disallowed the
practice. Such vetoes were generally favored by the creditor merchants
of the seaboard, but there was a swelling chorus of protest from the
debtor classes, who wished to pay their mortgages and quitrents with
cheap paper money. The result was the growth of hard feeling between
creditor and debtor sections, usually the coast and the interior respectively, and the planting of enmities which were to bear bitter fruit
in later years.

Colonial expansion, truly amazing for that century, was possible
because no serious attempt was made to enforce mercantilism until
1764. England, busy with internal strife and foreign wars or checked
by unconventional statesmen who distrusted mercantilism, let the colonies
go pretty much their own way. It is probable that during the eighteenth
century British mercantilism failed to crash because of the Americans'
free trade with the French and Spanish West Indies. As a result of
the wars of that century England added Canada and some additional
sugar islands, but Canada's temperate-zone products were more than
the Empire could absorb and only disturbed the economic balance
further. It is obvious that the British Empire was drifting toward
a crisis and that the more strictly mercantilism was enforced, the
sooner the crisis would come.

*   *   *

The possession of land had for thousands of years been the European's
Open Sesame to independence, wealth, power, and prestige. It is true
that the power of land was beginning to bow before that of commerce,
but the average man sensed that fact only dimly if at all and found
America's chief attraction in its cheap land. Here were millions of
acres of fat land waiting to be exploited either by the plow or by the
speculator. A history of the United States could easily be written in
terms of the history of real estate, and it would illuminate nearly
every problem that has confronted the country. The proprietors were,
of course, land speculators on a grand scale. Their concern was to
attract settlers who would buy land, and they were even willing to
give away fifty acres as a "head right" to redemptioners in order to
people the country and raise the value of the remaining land. Land
thus became the basis of American enterprise; and, because there was
land enough for all, it was natural that private enterprise should enter
into the warp and woof of the economic cloth the settlers were weav-

ing. Moreover, because most of the families in the typical farming community (not in the cities or in the tidewater-plantation areas) were about equal economically, there was a powerful impetus toward social and political equality.

Religious toleration was more a necessity than a conscious virtue, for there were too many sects to be combated successfully; and, moreover, real-estate speculators would not drive away a prospective sucker just because he believed in baptism by immersion rather than by sprinkling. Consequently, though state churches were established in nine of the colonies, there were only occasional flurries of persecution in the seventeenth century, and they died out in the eighteenth.

The result was a curious divergence in religious approaches. None of them wholeheartedly accepted Calvinist theology, but each of them retained some of its psychology. All, however, were American adaptations of current European trends. The first was "intellectual" in its sympathies; it followed the new scientific view of the universe as proclaimed by Copernicus and Newton and rejected the stern and high-handed deity of Calvin. Belief in predestination was weakened, and faith in freedom of the will strengthened. This was, of course, the American phase of the so-called Enlightenment. Men now, like the Greeks, sought truth in the things about them rather than in revelation and found no proof of the existence of sin and immortality. The universe was looked upon as the creation of an impersonal deity who set up laws to govern it, then took no more interest in it. This new view of God was known as deism, and after the middle of the eighteenth century it found expression in American periodicals and acceptance among great numbers of the educated class, including many of the men who were to become Founding Fathers of the new nation. The part of the Enlightenment which sank deepest into the masses was the belief in progress. This was not a philosophical acceptance but a practical one, drawn from the fact that the wilderness was giving way to civilization.

On the other extreme were the "enthusiasts." They laid emphasis upon emotional religion and found a ready response among the uneducated masses (especially on the frontiers) who could not appreciate the new importance of science and intellect. This movement was parallel to the evangelical movement on the European continent and to the Wesleyan revival in England. Evangelicals preached a vengeful God bent on sending sinful men to eternal torment, whose wrath could be escaped only by individual repentance and conversion. These were emotional and individual terms which the masses could understand, and the result was the Great Awakening, which during the generation after 1734 swept southward from Massachusetts and surged on to the frontier.

The upper classes regarded the moral precepts and the terrors of religion as necessary to keep the masses in order. Even a natural optimist and deist like Benjamin Franklin could say that "talking against religion is unchaining a tiger; the beast let loose may worry his liberator." As a result the gentry in general clung to the old forms, fought for the right of the established church to associate itself in political control, and even upheld much of the old theology even though they might not believe it themselves. The decaying theocracy of New England sought to preserve its control by replacing the loose congregational system of church organization with a more tightly knit presbyterianism. They failed to arrest the decline of their control, though they probably slowed it down, especially in Massachusetts and Connecticut.

Out of this religious ferment there arose factors of immense significance to the future of the United States. Minor religious differences led to a multiplication of sects and made control by state churches more hopeless than ever. Toleration was made necessary by diversity and was also promoted by the growing power of secularism. The decline of social uniformity forced relaxation of the so-called Blue Laws which regulated manners and morals. The revivalists' emphasis on individual responsibility for repentance and conversion was in line with growing democratic feeling, and so was the break-up of control by the state churches. The stimulation of religious activity also stimulated the interest of the denominations in higher education. The feeling of Christian brotherhood awakened by the revivals was a powerful humanitarian influence. There were also curiously contradictory psychological results of the religious ferment. Emotionalism (almost to the extent of a neurosis) entered into American life and was doubtless strengthened by Celtic influence. On the other hand, there were planted the seeds of respect for intellect and education. Individualism and social pressures grew side by side and later made possible the simultaneous flowering of "rugged individualism" and prohibition of alcohol.

These contradictions came in part from the contradictions of Calvinism but perhaps even more from the contradictions of human nature in a land where human nature attained unprecedented expression. Even while political democracy was maturing, its great enemy, concentrated and privileged economic power, was also maturing. Calvinism had followed historical precedent by setting up control of society by church and state, that is, ministry and gentry. When Calvinism and ministry decayed, the gentry retained the concept of leadership and responsibility (regardless of their church affiliation) and now came to exercise control through economic power. The shift in approach was significant, for it foreshadowed one of the most powerful conservative influences in later American development.

* * *

The political history of the colonial period can be compared to the struggle among three wrestlers in one ring; there can be nothing but mutual exhaustion unless two of them unite to toss the third out of the ring, and then go on to settle the issue between them. Just so the king, the coast, and the interior wrestled with each other at an increasing tempo for a century until, in the Revolution, coast and interior united to toss the king out of the country. Since then the American political story has been chiefly concerned with the struggle between the two victors or their heirs and assignees. The story of the colonial struggle is long and involved and well worth more attention than the bare reference we can present here. There were many alarums and excursions, and curious alliances were formed and broken. In general, coast and interior allied to oppose the royal power, and coast and king united against the interior. Somehow king and interior only occasionally found anything in common.

A century-long battle was carried on between governors and assemblies as the latter fought step by step for the same liberties that Parliament had wrung from the reluctant Stuarts. Out of the colonial political melée several facts and trends became clear. Two rival ideas of the structure of the Empire were growing up. The British regarded the Empire as an aggregation of states under the Parliament of the United Kingdom, with power flowing outward but none inward, except that Parliament was elected by the United Kingdom. The colonies were legally analogous to cities which, like the colonies, had been chartered by the king but were now subject to Parliament.

The American interpretation was that the Empire was made up of equal states, each under its own parliament, with the king as the coordinator and the Parliament of the United Kingdom legislating for him in matters that were distinctly of common imperial interest.

Basically, Americans rejected the idea that Parliament's laws, even if passed on through the king, could bind them: they would be accepted only by enlightened common consent. This was exactly the basis of the British Commonwealth of Nations in the first part of the present century. The tragedy is that in the eighteenth century British statesmen could not conceive of sentiment as being a tie that binds tighter than laws.

The assertion sometimes made that democracy did not exist in the Thirteen Colonies results from a failure to understand that democracy is a process, not a completed structure of popular government. As a process democracy was very much alive during the entire colonial period, both as (1) a movement among the common people to widen their political and economic rights, and as (2) an effort by the colonies to make good their rights within the Empire. The "compact" as an agreement among the people as the basis of government was well understood, and it found expression in the Mayflower Compact, the Fundamental Orders of Connecticut, and the Watauga Association, to mention only a few which preceded the great example of the Constitution of 1787. The people felt that the compact should be expressed in writing as their colonial constitutions (charters) were, in order to minimize uncertainty. It was this compact as concretely expressed in the charters and in the rights of Englishmen that was the goal of the colonial political struggle. Without the strength and experience gained in this struggle the colonists could never have succeeded in the War for Independence and the formation of the Union.

It is notable that though the democratic process was perfected in England, the Thirteen Colonies soon passed the mother country in the application. The reason sprang primarily from the wide spread of land ownership and the early adoption of land ownership as the chief qualification for the franchise. This was in line with the practice in England, but there the possession of land was limited to the few and only extremists like the Levellers dreamed of manhood suffrage. In America, however, the feudal tenure and transfer of land were unnecessary and, indeed, impossible. The common man suddenly found himself in the possession of political power and with sufficient land to make him all but economically independent. The attempts of the Tidewater gentry to concentrate wealth and power in their own hands he naturally and rightly regarded as an attempt to thrust him back into the pit from whence he had been digged, and so he fought with all his energies to preserve and extend his political and economic rights.

The battle of the coastal aristocracy against the governors was an essential step in the evolution of democracy. They represented themselves as promoting the welfare of the whole community (to get the votes of the lesser fry) and based their arguments on Natural Rights. Commoners thus came to accept and defend political equality, and even the unfranchised classes showed their vocal and muscular power in public affairs and gave the party they favored a radical tinge. The aristocrats had thus undermined their own control even while they were winning it from the governors. Once the common man's awe of them passed, the democratic movement would begin its irresistible march. "The mob," wrote Gouverneur Morris in 1774, "begins to think and reason. Poor reptiles! It is with them a vernal morning; they are struggling to cast off their winter's slough, they bask in the sunshine, and ere noon they will bite."

The American people emerged from the colonial period with the tenets of democracy burned into their hearts far more deeply than they were burned into English hearts at that time.

(1) They understood the reality of the democratic process and the method of advance by persistent struggle and temporary compromise. The changing balance of social forces as expressed in the political war of maneuver was accepted as the natural and inevitable means of progress.

(2) They understood the necessity of basic civil liberties, of popular control of legislative power, and the usefulness of the legislature's check upon executive and judiciary. It was generations before they lost their fear of a strong executive and an independent judiciary.

(3) They had a deeply ingrained fear of the union of Church and state. Though the union existed in nine of the Thirteen Colonies, it had been shorn of aggressive power and was to be wiped out by 1838.

(4) They understood the economic basis of democracy and realized that democracy could not exist in the face of ungoverned economic concentration. This was the crux of the democratic battle during the colonial period, and it has remained the crux down to our own day. The main battle has never yet been against property as property, but against the abuse or potential abuse of the power which property gives.

*　　*　　*

The American Revolution was caused by the British decision to enforce mercantilism. Like all oversimplifications, the statement requires explanation. For one thing the mother country needed aid in carrying the enormous financial burden incurred during the French wars. In the second place British manufacturers (not primarily the merchants) viewed with alarm the rising fabricating industries of America and pointed out that English prosperity would decline as America gained; they were wrong, of course, but their argument was consistent with mercantilism. Third, the West Indian sugar planters' lobby was determined to put an end to the mainland's trade with the French and Spanish sugar islands. Fourth was the resolve of George III to devote his life to the building up of his "prerogative," by which he meant the right of the king to dictate how Parliament should handle legislative and executive matters. In order to gain his ends it was necessary to build up the remnants of the old Tory Party in Parliament into a powerful party of the "kings's friends," strong enough to overthrow the great Whig families who had dominated British government since 1688. This the king proceeded to do by dispensing bribes in the form of sinecure jobs and lucrative contracts and by sedulous use of royal social favors.

George III was a shrewd operator, and he worked so quietly that it was not generally known that he was acting as puppeteer, and in fact the Thirteen Colonies supposed that the revival of mercantilism was the work of Parliament—which of course it was, in great part. Nevertheless, George III was striving consciously to fulfill his ideal of the "patriot king" and to bind the Empire into an efficient, well-articulated, and centrally controlled unit.

Each analyst of the causes of the American Revolution has his own way of handling the colonial reaction to the challenge of British policies, and doubtless one way is as good as another. Here we shall take them up in three categories: economic, political, and psychological. The British action in reviving mercantilism was a direct threat to American prosperity. The Seven Years' War had been fought to free the way for expansion, by which Americans meant commercial expansion into the Caribbean and expansion of trade and settlements into the Mississippi Valley. Indeed, the American debt structure was such that it could be handled only by such economic expansion as would provide the profits with which to pay British merchants and investors. During the decade after the Peace of Paris (1763) it became apparent that Great Britain envisioned the role of economic expansion as chiefly reserved to its own investors, merchants, and manufacturers, and the colonists found their expansion blocked on several fronts.

The rising manufacture of iron products, textiles, and other goods was limited or forbidden. The restrictions on trade with foreign nations and colonies were enforced, and smuggling was repressed. Tobacco planters, whose lands were worn out and who were mortgaged lock, stock, and barrel to British merchants, were relentlessly blocked when they sought to turn to food products and home manufactures. Westward expansion was discouraged lest it carry settlers away from easily controlled areas, and such land sales as were permitted were to be under the aegis of new colonies which would be strictly subservient to royal authority. The western fur trade was placed under the supervision of the governor of Quebec, who naturally desired to maintain the transmontane area as a great game preserve in which the Indian nations might trap for the benefit of British investors.

Hard money was drawn off in servicing debts owed to British merchants, and it was made more difficult to trade with the French and Spanish sugar islands, the old sources of gold and silver. The importation of British coins was prohibited, and so was the coining of Spanish bullion. The only substitute that could be used in carrying on business was paper money; and the British government ordered the retirement of old issues and forbade the printing of new issues. Last, a British army was quartered in the colonies, ostensibly for defense against the Indians—in Boston and New York City! There was a presumption that it was intended to enforce the legal and economic decrees of the British Parliament. At any rate, a part of the expense of its maintenance and a great deal of the bother of providing for it were saddled upon the colonies.

These measures affected not only merchants, planters, and land speculators. Farmers received low prices for their produce and paid high prices for merchandise; when they fell behind financially their mortgages were foreclosed, and they found it difficult to get new land farther west. True, it was not just to blame Great Britain alone for this, but they saw that the colonial magnates who were their economic and political oppressors were backed by British policies; so it was natural to blame the British. These economic measures, of course, could have been obeyed, but obedience would not only have resulted in a cessation of growth economically and territorially but would doubtless have brought widespread bankruptcy and a drastic cut in the standard of living. It was against human nature to obey.

The British action in reviving mercantilism was a direct threat to evolving American democracy. It would be a mistake to interpret the general American view of the Revolution as carried on in support of abstract principles of liberty and justice. On the contrary, Americans sincerely regarded the rights of Englishmen as constituting a concrete basis for a way of life and as having been in actual practice in the colonies. Now this way of life was in danger of being lost through Parliamentary action. They had a clear concept of civil liberties and of the English process, far clearer than did the English masses, and believed that they were menaced by the royal use of general warrants and by the trial of cases in admiralty courts, which sat without juries. They resented the English doctrine of "virtual representation" and insisted that representatives must be residents of the communities they represented; anything else was taxation without representation. They regarded the Empire as a body of equal and self-governing states under a common figurehead monarch and accused Parliament of changing its nature when it attempted to assert legislative (and in effect executive) authority over provinces which had their own legislatures.

It is true that Americans differed in details over the tenets by which they wished to be governed and agreed only that they wished self-government. Only a few aristocrats and job holders took exception to that, and the ideal was supported even by most of those who later became Tories. It is human nature to seek to support a desired course of action by a hog-tight, bull-proof, and horse-high legal fence. The first resort was to the colonial charters, but this ground had to be abandoned, for many of the charters gave the king the power of veto over colonial legislation and subjected the colonies to trade regulation. The second resort was to English precedents, the so-called "rights" of Englishmen. They soon discovered to their dismay that American evolution was moving toward somewhat different forms and goals. English representatives did not necessarily reside in the districts they represented; general warrants were legal; the English legal analogy to the colonial charters was the city corporation charters, which gave no power independent of Parliament. From the time of Cromwell, Parliament had actually legislated for the colonies. In other words, in these and other instances the American contentions were not indisputably sound *legally,* however *just* they may have been.

The Americans never abandoned their contention that Parliament's interpretation of the constitution was a menace to liberty, but they did seek a third trench which would be more widely understood and accepted. They found it in John Locke's doctrine of Natural Rights, which had come to be the basis of the French Enlightenment and which was thoroughly approved by most of the European intelligentsia. It will be remembered that Locke saw the Natural Right to hold property as the main balance wheel of society. Presto! Parliament was endeavoring to confiscate American property, so by analogy to Locke's own defense of the Revolution of 1688 the Americans had a right to insist that their government must obey the will of the governed (American property holders) and if it did not they had a right to change it. Of course there were problems: back-country men like Jefferson questioned the holding of property as a Natural Right, especially when it was held in great quantities; then there was the embarrassing fact that many of the Tories were great property holders. In the end the Revolutionists interpreted Natural Rights each in his own manner and left practical definitions for a later time. The beauty of Natural Rights as a defense was that nearly everyone acknowledged them even though they were incapable of legal and historical proof. It is both sound and popular to champion right and attack evil.

A significant phase of the democratic protest was the opposition to any attempt to strengthen the Church of England in the colonies. American democrats rabidly opposed the establishment of a colonial bishopric, and (perhaps consciously) exaggerated its dangers. New England's Congregational clergy had never seen much difference between Anglicans and Roman Catholics and now professed to see in growing English tolerance the prospect of a return of the Church of England to the Roman fold. The middle colonies and the backlands of the southern colonies were a welter of sects, all bitterly opposed to the Church of England, which they saw as the instrument of a political and social aristocracy.

As a matter of fact, there was little danger of the appointment of a bishop. Even southern Anglicans opposed it because it would have destroyed the parish vestry's control of the clergy. The British government opposed it because it would have raised America to an equality in ecclesiastical matters and would have set back the program of centralizing control of the Empire in London. Doubtless, intelligent Americans knew all this, but the issue had such an emotional appeal to the masses that it was a valuable anti-British weapon. The revolutionary movement was therefore given a decided (though specious) religious coloration.

In assessing the reasons for American revolt it is well to avoid over-emphasis on economics or politics or religion. It has been held that revolutions do not arise out of the desperation of misery but out of a vision of something better. British economic pressure was unwise and oppressive, but the Thirteen Colonies were even at the worst treated far more liberally than were the colonies of any other power in that century. Had George III realized his wildest dreams of imperial centralization, the Thirteen Colonies would still have been the freest on earth. No, the American Revolution did not arise from the desperation of misery, whatever the protests made by our shrewd and highly articulate ancestors. It arose from the belief that conditions could and should be better and that self-government was the only guarantee of this betterment. "The Revolution," says Van Tyne, "was one of the glories of British history. . . . The colonies of no other nation in that age had progressed so far in the attainment and enjoyment of political liberty as to have 'snuffed' the taint of tyranny in those acts of the British Government which precipitated the struggle." Well did he conclude with the words: "The freest of peoples were the first to rebel."

Possibly, and here opinions will clash, the Revolution was bred more in the psychology of the people than in their economic and political condition. There was considerable basis to the British plaints that the Americans were selfish, ungrateful, and obstreperous; on the other hand, the British laid themselves open to some of the same charges. There was American resentment at British sneers and patronization, at the opinion that an American was inferior simply because he was a colonial. There was resentment that the best governmental positions in the colonies went to English placemen. There was resentment that holders of the king's commission outranked colonial officers and at the open contempt with which British officers regarded American officers and soldiers. There was continually growing resentment that British investors, merchants, and manufacturers expected to pluck the American economy at will, demanding perquisites and privileges that were not so much impossible as insulting. Americans were relatively classless and very proud and self-reliant. They saw no reason for continuing to give down milk at the British behest, especially since they could put a stop to it. They were big enough to rebel, and they did.

On the morning of the Battle of Lexington, Levi Preston ran sixteen miles to get into the fight. Seventy years later he was asked his opinion of the oppressions that had led to the war.

"Oppressions?" exclaimed the old man. "What were they? I didn't feel any. The Stamp Act? I never saw one of the stamps. The tea tax? I never drank the stuff."

"Well," said the interlocutor, "I suppose you had been reading Sidney or Locke about the eternal principles of liberty?"

"Never heard of them. We read only the Bible, the catechism, Watts' hymns, and the almanac."

"Then what did you mean by going into that fight?"

"Young man," was his answer, "what we meant in going for those redcoats was this—we always had governed ourselves, and we always meant to. They didn't mean we should!"

* * *

The end of the Revolution found a congeries of thirteen sovereign states linked by the Articles of Confederation into "a firm league of friendship." The more democratic wing of the new nation—if it can be called a nation—wished the states to retain effective controls and opposed the granting of more powers to the central government. Conservatives, however, were determined to have a central government strong enough to ensure order and to protect business enterprise inside and outside the country. Though the 1780's were on the whole prosperous, conservatives managed to spread the conviction that economic hardship and political collapse loomed just over the horizon. They were aided by inflation, quarrels among the states, British trade aggression, discontent in the West, and finally by the revolt of dissatisfied farmers in western Massachusetts.

The convention which met at Philadelphia in May 1787 frankly launched into drawing up a new constitution to replace the faulty Articles of Confederation. To do that successfully it had to solve three problems which had often confronted constitution-makers but to none of which history had as yet offered any satisfactory answers. First was the necessity of reconciling the interests and jealousies of the large and small states; second, the problem of reconciling the sovereignties of states and nation; and third, the desirability of protecting holders of large property without hampering or antagonizing the holders of small property. These were the basic issues before the convention, and each one of them before it was settled was in danger of breaking down the deliberations.

The situation meant that the Federal system must be invented. It meant that each state must preserve enough self-government and receive a large enough share in the central government for its prestige and dignity to be preserved and for it to fear neither the central government nor its powerful neighbors. At the same time the central government must be strong enough to carry out its duites of protecting and promoting the general welfare. The Confederation and other historic confederations had depended on the goodwill of its parts, the states, and in fact the states had reserved to themselves the function of administering the general laws; the inevitable result was that local interests were in a position to block confederate policies and seldom hesitated to do so.

The Constitution was not an original creation. It was simply the next step in political evolution. Considerable reference was made to Greek confederacies and to the Bible, to Blackstone, and to Montesquieu; but on the whole the Constitution owed its nature to the examples offered by the Articles of Confederation and the constitutions of the states and, most of all, to the Anglo-Saxon genius for compromise. By the so-called Great Compromise there was to be a Senate composed of two members from each state, and a House of Representatives with membership proportionate to population and elected by popular vote. The question of an effective national government was settled, and in settling it the core of modern Federal government had been invented.

The new invention consisted of two parts: (1) the representation of both states and population in the central government, and (2) the right of the central government to operate directly upon the individual citizen without asking the permission of the state. The states could shape Federal law but they could no longer block it because they did not administer it. Though the states were the geographical units of Federal administration and of Congressional representation they were not to vote in Congress as units, but each Senator and Representative was to vote as he chose. The way was thus open for the formation of alliances that not only cut across state lines but also represented minority interests within the states. At the same time a step had been taken toward compromising the economic struggle, for the House, elected by the people, would represent little property, and the Senate, elected by the state legislatures, would represent the interests of big property. Compromise between them would be essential, for each would have a veto on the other.

Another feature of the Great Compromise was that five slaves were to be counted as three free persons in reckoning the population of the states for apportioning members of the House and for laying direct taxes. Following this feature of the Compromise was the problem of how to keep the North from dominating the South commercially, for it was feared that its more numerous population, greater number of states, and commercial facilities would enable it to treat the South as Great Britain had treated the Thirteen Colonies. The Three-fifths Ratio was a part of the answer, and the South, which was primarily an exporting section, was further protected by forbidding Congress to lay export taxes and by requiring all Federal taxes to be "uniform throughout the United States." At first the South insisted that "navigation" acts must be laid only by a two-thirds vote of Congress but finally accepted majority rule with the proviso that slaves could be freely imported for twenty years. This provision was to answer the demand of Georgia and the Carolinas. The South was further protected by the rule that treaties to be approved must receive the vote of two-thirds of the Senate.

It was recognized that in order to be strong the Federal government must receive the powers which concerned the welfare of all. As a result certain enumerated powers were assigned to the Federal government, and all of them (except a few with the consent of Congress) were forbidden to the states. Within its powers the state was sovereign and answerable to no one, and this sovereignty is essentially true today in spite of Federal aggrandizement. Certainly the individual citizen finds his life touched more by the state and its creature, the municipality, than by the Federal government.

The members of the convention seem to have differed in the interpretation of the language assigning powers to the Federal government, and it was inevitable that these differences later should become the subject of long political battles. Americans, like the other English-speaking peoples, search for legal excuses—and usually find them. The so-called "sweeping clauses" supplied the arguments that loose constructionists wanted. One of them, in the preamble, declares it the purpose of the Constitution to "promote the general welfare"; a second, in Article I, gives Congress the power to "provide for the common defense and general welfare." The so-called elastic clause has in particular been used to excuse the growth of Federal authority, because after the enumeration of Federal powers it provides that the government shall have the power "to make all laws which shall be necessary and proper for carrying into execution the foregoing powers." From this (as well as from the two welfare clauses) Congress has deduced that its taxing and borrowing power gives it the right to create national banks, emit legal-tender paper money, and erect a system of protective tariffs. The war power has been interpreted to authorize the annexation and government of territory and to make the President a virtual dictator with the consent of Congress. The power to regulate foreign and interstate commerce has been stretched to justify the control of immigration, the building of public works to aid and promote commerce, and the regulation of public carriers and local manufactures by controlling the terms of interstate commerce.

It will be noted that the Constitution provides not only for the division of powers between Federal and state governments but also for the separation within the Federal government of powers among executive, legislature, and judiciary. The state constitutions soon began to follow the same principles both in apportioning state and local powers and within the state government itself. In order to maintain this balance constitutions and customs have provided checks. In the Federal government the President appoints officials and makes treaties with the consent of the Senate, and he may veto legislation. The legislature initiates bills, restrains executive and judiciary by the power of impeachment, and overrides vetoes by a two-thirds vote. The judiciary may restrain executive officials from illegal acts, and it may declare legislation unconstitutional. Though there has from the first been considerable objection to this last power, and in fact it was only slowly and grudgingly accepted, there is now no doubt but that it was specifically envisioned by the framers of the Constitution as a judicial function.

Another aspect of the balance of powers is found in the way in which the framers sought to balance social forces. Most of the members of the Convention of 1787 had a profound distrust of the people and wished to place their own social class in control. This is not to deny that they loved their country or the sincerity of their belief that they were saving it from chaos when they sought to limit democracy. They could not go to an extreme, however, for it was evident that their document must meet the test of popular approval. They therefore sought to remove the people as far as possible from direct influence on policy: the President was given almost monarchic powers, but he was elected by an electoral college; the Senators were elected by the state legislatures; and the Senate was given the power of approval of treaties and presidential appointments. The popular demand for paper money was spiked by prohibiting the states from issuing it, and it was purposely left out of the powers given to the Federal government; later on it was interpreted back into the Constitution. The deliberate intention was to restrain the people from radical orgies by giving the President and the Senate large powers. Indeed, the only direct control given to the people was in the election of the House of Representatives. English and colonial custom led to the incorporation of the right of the popular branch to initiate money appropriations, but the Senate sometimes manages to get around it. Though in that day the House was regarded as the "arcanum" of the popular will and the Senate as the creature of conservatism, the present tendency is for the two houses to reverse the role.

Even though the Constitution was not democratic in our modern sense and was not intended to be, it is important to note that like the democratic process it kept the way open for change. This fact is evident in the provisions for amendment and for local control of qualifications for voting. More important than these was the use or inclusion of three basic American contributions to the democratic process. First, the Constitutional Convention implemented the compact theory in a practical way, and the method has found worldwide acceptance. Second, the Federal system found the practical compromise between the age-old rivals, nationalism and localism, and has been one of the important factors in making possible the growth of the modern state. Third, the old concept of empire as composed of a metropolis and permanently subject colonies or possessions was done away with; the constitution-makers deliberately provided for the admission of dependent areas to the same status as the old.

One curious intention of the framers in setting up their system of checks and balances was to prevent the growth of parties—"factions," they called them, though they seem to have used the word also to denote the pressure groups which today compose a party. Actually the system has promoted the opposite result, for the balancing parts of government co-operate well only when they are united by party discipline in support of common policies. The requirement of the consent of three-fourths of the states to pass an amendment would seem not only to have been to win the goodwill of the jealous states which feared the tyranny of their neighbors but also to hamper change, and indeed the method was so cumbersome that it succeeded until the rash of speedy amendments in our own day.

On the whole, technical amendments have made but few important changes. The vital changes have come about through interpretations; the growth of a body of political and technical customs and usages; and the arbitrament of arms, as the Civil War's decision of the problem of state rights. One bitterly contested provision in the convention was the right of Congress to admit new states on an equal basis with the old; the objection, of course, was based upon the perennial quarrel between the coast and the interior. Nevertheless, the right was essential to gain the cooperation of the West, which would never have consented to an inferior rank in the Union.

In looking over the Constitution one is impressed by the fears of the framers and the people as expressed by the Bill of Rights, the many compromises, and the elaborate checks and balances. These cumbrous mechanisms were so patently intended to prevent the interference of government in individual affairs and to prevent hasty action that it is almost fair to say that the document was as much intended to prevent government as to implement it. This was inevitable in an unformed nation which had just emerged from a war against tyranny and which was torn by rivalries among localities and between social classes and economic interests. These fears still are with us, but they do not control us as they did our fathers. It has been the mission of our century to carry out the positive functions of the Constitution, for most Americans now agree that they are there.

In casting up the balance sheets of the American Revolution, it is apparent that out of the war came both a tragedy and a blessing. The seed was sown of a long rivalry between the two nations. American development, unchecked either by experienced administrators or by a deeply rooted native aristocracy, entered upon a course of headlong democracy which was often as oppressive as liberating. Perhaps if the Americans had remained part of the British Empire and eventually become part of the British Commonwealth of Nations, the *Pax Britannica* might still dominate the world and encourage orderly growth. There might have been no world wars, no Russia and Germany resurgent in the same senses as in our time, because it would obviously have been foolish to combat so great a combination devoted to the cause of peace and law.

On the other hand, as things turned out, we have seen that democracy can appear in various forms. The United States has been a moderating influence in modern imperialism, both because of its example and because its existence has forced rulers to moderation—as Britain in Canada. It is conceivable that without independence America might have had a saner growth, but it would never have attained the tremendous power which has enabled it to cast a deciding sword into the scale against predatory doctrines.

IV

Hamilton and Jefferson

THE historian who looks back upon the formative days of the
nation can scarcely avoid the realization that it would have
been tragic for either of the two great wings of American
opinion to have won a clear-cut and sweeping victory. As it was,
the two great opponents, Hamilton and Jefferson, each had to consider the will of the other in carrying out his program, with the
result that something like an unhappy medium was struck between
them. Hamilton's Federalists got their way initially. They assumed
the state debts, thus centering the good wishes of the creditor class
on the Federal government, set up a bank, laid a light protective tariff
to encourage manufactures, and laid an excise on whiskey largely
to bring home to the frontier the fact that a strong central government was now in existence.

Alexander Hamilton came into the office of Secretary of the Treasury
at the age of thirty-two with his political philosophy already developed
and with an economic program for putting it into effect. It is wrong
to say that he dominated President Washington, yet Washington was
old and tired and so disposed to accept Hamilton's ideas, especially
since on the whole they agreed with his own. The touchstone of
Hamilton's life and policy was his fear and loathing of the people;
it is difficult to escape the conclusion that he was frantically striving
to differentiate himself from them and was haunted by the fear that
his foot might slip on the ladder and he would be precipitated back
to his obscure origins. *In vino veritas*: one evening when flushed with
wine he disclosed a little of his fear in the famous words, "The people—
your people, sir, is a great beast." He acknowledged that his social
ideal was met in Japan: "a mass of intelligent humanity, reckless of
their lives, yet filled with the joy of life, eager for distinction, hungry
for success, alert, practical, and merry; but at the same time subordinate,
humbly and piously subordinate, to a pure abstraction."

Hamilton favored monarchy and supported aristocracy because they
had nothing to gain by a change; he seems never to have understood

the value of the democratic process, though like all democratic conservatives (how he would have loathed the tag!) he yielded to the
rising counterforce. The British form of government as practiced
by George III he swallowed whole. Even its corruption was necessary,
he pointed out, because in order to ensure stability the rich must be
bound to the cause of government by self-interest. While he would
not have made serfs of the people or excluded them completely from
political rights, he proposed to thwart their disruptive demands by
seeing to it that the rich were cared for and thus, having a property
interest in the government, would support it against the storms of
democracy. He envisioned the United States as another England,
with great industrial cities, with workers crowding in from Europe,
and ruled over by an aristocracy which because it had everything
it wanted could not be subject to temptation. Hamilton knew nothing
of the aspirations and capacities of the poor at his own doorstep, and
nowhere do we find any suggestion from him that they could be
educated into good citizens.

Hamilton's program was in its essentials what the country needed
if it was ever to become a nation. Perhaps it was in the long view
fortunate that the counterforce was not in the beginning well enough
organized to block the force. Though the counterforce was represented
from the first by such leaders as James Madison of Virginia, it failed
to get much backing either in Congress or among the people until
the actual results of Hamilton's program demonstrated beyond the
shadow of a doubt that a new Tory party had developed and was
devoted to promoting the political, social, and economic ascendancy
of an aristocracy of wealth and position. Jefferson was the political
genius chiefly responsible for giving the inchoate opposition the semblance
of party discipline and a party program.

Thomas Jefferson came out of the Virginia Piedmont at a time
when it was more authentically western in spirit than California is
today. Though he is rightly called a philosopher, and like philosophers
dreamed of "the good society," it is notable that he expressed his
ideas and his program in concrete, practical terms. Aristocracy in
itself was certainly not an object of his hatred, for he sought to
spread its gospel of taste, refinement, education, and competent leadership—but not its abuses. Property was not the enemy, for he sought
to spread and increase it, though he did assert that its possession was not
one of the Natural Rights. Religion was not the enemy except as
it was used to uphold special privileges. Though he was probably a

deist, he did not evangelize. On the contrary, he reverenced the
teachings of Christ and read His words every evening. He was
an Episcopalian and, what is more, attended services more faithfully
and contributed more largely than many of his critics. And yet he
was hated by Episcopal and Congregational clergymen for his advocacy
of the separation of church and state, and they sought diligently in
his scientific writings for proofs of his atheism.

Jefferson was not (at least after the Revolution) a radical bent
upon overthrowing established institutions or uprooting the social
tree. He believed in working calmly and slowly by education, and
that if the people received light they would find their own way. And
yet he recognized the danger that popular "whims" might institute
a tyranny of the majority. The minority also had rights; the majority
to be right must be reasonable. He fought against any attempt to rivet
the ideological chains of one generation upon the next. Amendment
of the Constitution instead of being thwarted should be deliberately
undertaken every twenty years or so. Moreover, freedom was not
necessarily synonymous with peace. "The Tree of Liberty," he said,
"must be refreshed from time to time with the blood of patriots
and tyrants."

Basically Jefferson taught that government is the natural enemy
of man, hence his insistence that as many functions as possible must
be localized so that the people might be able to control them directly.
Government must not be permitted to do anything for the people
that they could do themselves, hence "that government is best which
governs least"; by protraction it followed that the cheapest government was the best, an idea which still has exponents. Jefferson opposed
the interference of the government to strengthen or enrich a class,
especially to give it the subtle and intangible forms of wealth (stocks
and bonds) which he believed arose from the exploitation of others.

He opposed this kind of interference because he feared that wealth
would sooner or later breed power, and power for the few is a menace
to the liberties of the many. Now since power and property are
inseparable, he desired that property be scattered as widely and as
evenly as possible; in other words, he favored the multiplication
of yeoman farmers. Great cities to him were great sores, and he never
trusted the proletariat because they were dependent upon the goodwill of employers. For this reason he was willing to break his tenets
and use the government to distribute land cheaply and protect the
farmer in its ownership. The good society was one of farmers; let

the United States remain content in agrarian freedom and import from other countries such products of wage slavery as it must have— and in British ships. He took direct issue with Hamilton's objectives and taught (1) government by the people; (2) the dominance of agriculture; and (3) the literal and strict interpretation of the Constitution.

In his political methods, Jefferson was too practical and too much the opportunist to be a saint. His political machinations were filled with the cunning which Hamilton tried to equal but never could. Though he was a voluminous letter writer, he possessed that elusiveness so valuable to a politician which hindered his enemies from pinning him down. If he did not encourage scurrility, he at least permitted it. He was accused, apparently with justice, of vindictiveness, and certainly he was persistent in seeking to break his political enemies. Nevertheless, he judged his enemies clearly and often admiringly without underestimating them or wasting his nervous energy in useless raving. But the secret of his political success did not lie in the use of such commonplace though deplorable weapons. He did not make Hamilton's mistake of organizing an army of generals. He sought to arouse the common people to an awareness of the value of the vote, he sought to break down excessive property qualifications for the suffrage, and he preached party discipline incessantly. He knew intuitively what the people at the grass roots were thinking and was able to build upon it. Even more important, he had that faith in the people which was necessary to inspire them in following him toward the bright goal of human rights which they may have glimpsed but dimly yet accepted because of their faith in him.

The democratic party which Jefferson now seriously undertook to mold was known as the Democratic-Republican Party but was soon to be shortened to Republican. The elements from which it was formed had existed in each colony from the earliest days, though they had never acted together until the Revolution. It was they who had settled Rhode Island and the Connecticut River towns, engaged in Bacon's Rebellion, fought the Stuart governors in 1689, comprised the Carolina Regulators, formed the Country Party of agrarian frontiersmen, composed the Lee-Adams Junto in the Revolution, and finally as Antifederalists had opposed ratification of the Constitution. The Jeffersonian Republican Party, therefore, was not in any sense a new creation or a foreign "ism" (as the Federalists pretended) but a legitimate growth of the seed of English liberties brought to this continent by the earliest settlers, planted in the American soil, and nourished and shaped in its growth by the peculiar conditions of the new environment.

Jefferson was little given to joining schools of thought, but until after 1800 he not only agreed with the Physiocrats that wealth came only from the land, but he (or at least his followers) regarded merchants, capitalists, and manufacturers as parasites. He had little comprehension of the part that capital and labor play in the creation of national wealth and did not learn until later. Physiocratic doctrines titilated the planter because they were designed to dignify and protect great landowners, and the small farmer because they made him the creator of national wealth. Since both planter and farmer were in debt, they naturally agreed that their creditors were parasites who did not deserve to be paid—that bankers and merchants not only drained away wealth without performing any true service in return, but they also flouted the natural law of free enterprise by using the government to carry out their schemes.

Just how much Americans owed to French thinkers is uncertain, for a predominantly agrarian society is sure to develop ideas of the importance of agriculture regardless of what economists may be doing. These ideas have been basic in American history, but there is no term adequate to express them. The word *agrarian* has come to carry little more meaning than *rural;* on the other hand, French Physiocracy was far more subtle and rigid than was the thinking of American agrarians. For lack of a better term we can use *American Physiocracy* to indicate the American form of agrarian laissez faire with its emphasis upon natural law and upon the fundamental importance of agriculture and its consequent right to dominate economics and politics.

A glance at the attitudes of Hamilton and Jefferson toward the powers of government is instructive. The Constitution was designed to provide a government that could not act too decisively, that in effect could not interfere with the current concept that the law of Nature was that business should regulate itself. True, there were "strong" government men in the Convention, but they had had experience with royal governors and courts and agreed to the checks held by the three branches of government on each other. It is significant that Hamilton was one of the few exceptions who did not fear a strong government. We usually oppose a strong government unless it operates in favor of our particular interest, so it is almost always true that the party in power tends to favor strong government and the one out of power desires weak government. Hamilton and Jefferson were no exceptions.

After two terms in the presidency Washington had been succeeded by John Adams. The war then in progress between Britain and France had deepened the split between Federalists and Republicans, the former taking the side of Britain and the latter of France. The Federalists indeed used their power to engage in a quasi-war against France and but for Adams's courage would have made it an all-out war. At the same time they sought to cripple the Republicans by the Alien and Sedition Acts which in effect identified opposition to Federalist policy with treason. Partly as a result of Federalist extremism the Republicans carried the election of 1800—though a tie in the electoral college put Jefferson in debt to Hamilton for his election to the presidency by the House of Representatives.

On 4 March 1801 in the little Senate chamber in the unfinished capitol building in Washington, Jefferson took the oath of office. His inaugural address was a model of moderation. "We are all Republicans," he said, "we are all Federalists. If there be any among us who would wish to dissolve this Union or to change its republican form, let them stand undisturbed as monuments of the safety with which error of opinion may be tolerated where reason is left free to combat it. I know, indeed, that some honest men fear that a republican government cannot be strong enough. . . . I believe this, on the contrary, the strongest Government on earth. I believe it the only one where every man, at the call of the law, would fly to the standard of the law, and would meet invasions of the public order as his own personal concern. Sometimes it is said that man can not be trusted with the government of himself. Can he, then, be trusted with the government of others? Or have we found angels in the form of kings to govern him? Let history answer this question."

What are the essential principles of our government, which consequently ought to shape its administration? "Equal and exact justice to all men, of whatever state or persuasion, religious or political; peace, commerce, and honest friendship with all nations, entangling alliances with none; the support of the State governments in their rights . . . the preservation of the General Government in its whole constitutional vigor, as the sheet anchor of our peace at home and safety abroad; a jealous care of the right of election by the people . . . absolute acquiescence in the decisions of the majority . . . a well-disciplined militia . . . the supremacy of the civil over the military authority;

economy in the public expense, that labor may be lightly burdened . . .
the honest payment of our debts . . . encouragement of agriculture, and
of commerce as its handmaid; the diffusion of information and arraignment of all abuses at the bar of public reason; freedom of religion;
freedom of the press, and freedom of person." These principles "should
be the creed of our political faith, the text of civic instruction, the
touchstone by which we try the services of those we trust."

Jefferson had honestly intended his accession to mark the beginning
of the decline of Federal power. It did not, and for three reasons:
(1) The Federalists had set the customs and precedents in the general
direction of their desires, had swollen the public debt, and had taken
over the judiciary, wherein judges sat for life; (2) international
problems complicated the situation and scuttled many of Jefferson's
dearest plans; and (3) Jefferson himself, as Hamilton knew, was
not a man to thwart a practical solution by sticking to a theory
(Hamilton said "principle"). Perhaps Jefferson learned by experience; perhaps, as John Taylor of Caroline asserted, he was a traitor
to his principles; perhaps he was like many of us who fight a power
when exercised by others but feel safe in assuming it ourselves because, of course, we will not abuse it. There is no proof that Jefferson
ever changed his basic thinking, but we see in his actual policies a
forecast of the characteristic modifications which inevitably come to
victorious liberal movements.

Jefferson, as he left the presidency, was a disillusioned man. He
had failed even as Washington to imbue public affairs with a spirit
of sweet reasonableness. His method of democratic compromise had
resulted in pouring out the baby with the bath. Most of the Republican
principles of 1801 were now so full of holes as to be unrecognizable.
Instead of strict economy, national expenditures were greater than ever;
instead of a navy at the docks, it had been busier than ever; instead
of peace, Jefferson had fought one war (in Tripoli) and barely
escaped another; instead of strict construction and preservation of
state rights, the way had been opened for Federal supremacy. Even
the hated Sedition Act had been aped by a no less tyrannical Embargo
Enforcement Act when Jefferson sought to free American commerce
from the interference of the warring powers by laying an embargo
on their exports to the United States. Secretary of the Treasury Galla-
tin, the enemy of the Bank of the United States, had become a convert
to its convenience and efficiency, and Jefferson had protested mildly,
then assented. From an *American Physiocratic* distrust of manufactures,

he had come to view them with pride and even counted them as a good result of the Embargo.

He but reflected the change in his party. Every election strengthened the Republican Party in the North, but the recruits were all but indistinguishable from the Federalists in economic principles and rejected only the Federalists' secessionism, merchant enterprise, and decadent aristocracy. Federalist principles were making way even in South Carolina as the cotton gin gave a new class of planters visions of busy textile mills. There were definite signs that even the Republicanism of Virginia was weakening; it was that which led the brilliant and erratic John Randolph and his Quids to part with Jefferson and fight a battle of invective for the strict construction of the Constitution. Yet another decade and the Old Dominion leadership even in the South would bow in everything but mere name to that of the Cotton States.

If Jefferson needed any proof of his basic failure, it was found in the long caravans of common farmers who in despair of relief from Republican policy were abandoning their sour and eroded acres and wending across the mountains to the fertile bottom lands of the West. If he needed any proof that his agrarian policies were not those of the developing future, he needed only to look at his followers in North and South who were furtively turning the pages of Hamilton's *Report on Manufactures* and dreaming not of a bucolic paradise but of bustling cities and whirring machinery. It was they who had pulled down the pillars of his Embargo when it was on the verge of success and brought down in ruin his hope of finding a substitute for war.

* * *

Most significant in the modification of Jeffersonian doctrines was the role of John Marshall, whom President John Adams had made Chief Justice of the Supreme Court and given a mandate to fight a rear-guard action for the defeated Hamiltonian forces. With the rise of Neo-Hamiltonianism Marshall found that his rear guard had become the vanguard of the new nationalism. No matter what fire-eating Republicans the Virginia dynasty might set on the bench, Marshall's clarity of reasoning and charm of manner steadily converted them to his opinions. The two principles steadfastly validated by his decisions were (1) the supremacy of the Federal government and (2) the role of the Supreme Court as the arbiter between states and nation and of the Constitutionality of legislative and executive actions. He did not, of course, draw these Constitutional principles out of the air (though the Old Republicans accused him of it) but "found" them implied in the Constitution itself.

Though Marshall was inclined to set his own common-law precedents, other judges saw that the bumptious American sense of legalism would demand legislative action unless long-accepted common-law standards were observed. The acceptance of Natural Rights in England, especially in the role of property as the automatic regulator of social order, had resulted in the freezing of the common law, except as needed to protect property. American patriots, anxious to be independent in all matters, proposed the formation of a more democratic code of laws, but the movement was stopped cold by two great jurists. They were Joseph Story of Massachusetts, associate of John Marshall on the Supreme Court bench, and James Kent, Chancellor of the State of New York. Their method was to show that English common law was based on natural law (moral law to the more pious) and must therefore of course be accepted. Their lives were devoted to fitting the common law of England to the facts, at least the supposed facts, of American conditions.

Now where law is supreme, there is a tendency for the lawyer to become supreme because the law is a "mystery" known only to the initiated. That the law was chiefly concerned with the protection of individual rights, principally those relating to property, does not mean that the Supreme Court was consciously promoting control by big property, for its decisions were aimed at giving little business a break as well—and this was then a nation of little business. The Federal government was defended against the assaults of the states because they were presumably more open to control by wild and subversive interests which would attack property. On the other hand, since the law is the lawyer's life, he finds it to his interest to preserve it from heedless executive and legislative encroachments; he watches over it with a jealous care which the average citizen, even in a democracy, would never have the knowledge or patience to imitate. On the whole the method works amazingly well.

To the lawyer, then, principally in the persons of the jurists of the Supreme Court, goes the credit for making the slightly considered third branch of the Federal government a decisive instrument for preserving balance within that government and between it and the states. It paved the legal road for the creation of a nation in place of the congeries of sovereign states which existed at the outset of the nineteenth century, and whose rivalries among themselves and with the Federal government might have torn the Union apart. Marshall, Story, and Kent also laid the necessary foundations for the growth of industrial capitalism.

* * *

When Jefferson retired from the presidency he placed his own bust and that of Hamilton facing each other in the great hall of his home at Monticello, and there they still stand, opposite each other in death as in life. This position is fitting, for they personify the two great forces of democratic evolution. Each was, and is, necessary to the other, just as without protagonist and antagonist there can be no drama. As Jefferson himself said: "The terms Whig and Tory belong to natural as well as to civil history. They denote the temper and constitution of mind of different individuals." In another place he was even more explicit: "In every free and deliberating society, there must, from the nature of man be opposite parties, and violent dissensions and discords; and one of these, for the most part, must prevail over the other for a longer or shorter time. Perhaps this party division is necessary to induce each other to watch and to relate to the people at large the proceedings of the other."

It was during the early years of the Republic that the nation set the direction of its development (democratic capitalism) and the method of its development (the democratic process). Hamilton stood for a strong central government, the dominance of commerce and manufactures, and rule by the rich, the well-born, and the able; Jefferson stood for a weak central government, the dominance of agriculture, and rule by the people as a whole. The lesson of the first twenty years is that we find either the two leaders or their followers deliberately contradicting in word or deed every item of their trilogy of principles. It is already evident that these "principles" were merely weapons for political combat and that a party out of power often held different standards from those it held when it was in power. This fact will become increasingly evident in later generations, so evident that only confusion can result if we try to distinguish the two sides by these superficial tags.

The true principles of Hamilton and Jefferson lie much deeper. They can perhaps be best expressed respectively in the two catchwords "order" and "liberty." Hamilton did not reject liberty, of course; he simply believed that it must give precedence to order.

Jefferson did not reject order; he simply believed that order without liberty is of no value, and that to preserve or extend liberty its tree must sometimes be refreshed by the blood of tyrants and of patriots. Hamilton was the realist, the practical man of affairs who thought in terms of dollars and cents and saw that they could not be amassed and protected without a high degree of public order. Jefferson was the idealist, the man of faith and optimism who believed that happiness is the end of human existence and the only defensible purpose of government—and how could a man be happy without liberty?

Both believed that where a man's treasure is, there will his heart be also. Hamilton looked upon order and property as treasures which are responsibly guarded only if they are entrusted to the select few. Property, as the rock of good order, must be preserved from direct injury or from limitations which prevent it from multiplying itself freely. The individual who sought either of these ends was not only trying to upset society but was also attacking the rights of a human being, the owner of the property. Jefferson sought to entrust the treasures of liberty and happiness to the many in the sublime faith that men who are trusted will prove themselves trustworthy. Therein lie the strength and the weakness of democracy. Obviously the Jeffersonians did not reject the holding of property; they simply believed that property should not become an instrument for limiting the rights, snatching the livelihood, or besmirching the dignity of the individual.

It is a curious fact that the philosophies of both Hamilton and Jefferson stemmed from *American Physiocracy,* though from different aspects; that if the individual were left free by the government to farm, manufacture, and trade, he would find an equilibrium with his fellows. Adam Smith adapted the general idea to trade and manufacture. He sought to smash the barriers of tariffs and governmental regulations and allow individuals freedom of enterprise both at home and in dealing with businessmen of other nations. To find the equilibrium, Smith insisted that neither nation nor individual must seek an artificial monopoly but must honestly obey the law of supply and demand. Hamilton sought to apply Smith's doctrines domestically, but internationally he sought to go back to some phases of mercantilism and have the government manipulate the tariff to protect and promote manufacture and trade. The fact that Hamilton did not live to see his ideas put into effect should not shear him of the honor of paternity.

The Jeffersonian relation to *American Physiocracy* was even more direct. The Republicans (at first) insisted that all wealth springs from the land and that manufacture and trade are parasites. Even before Jefferson's death the movement had split into two wings. For the sake of clarity it is well to define those wings here. Jefferson had sought both the welfare of society as a whole and the protection and expression of individual rights. One wing desired the government to promote public welfare even if it had to limit individual rights; to this now belong the plebeians and such of the farmers, laborers, and intelligentsia who are verging on socialism as they urge the people to add economic to political power. Probably Jefferson never realized that his theories could lead to such a result. The individualist wing has insisted that the government must stand aside and let the individual run his own affairs. In this wing there have been two elements. The rugged individualist, whether farmer or businessman, who has identified democracy with private enterprise, has often insisted that economic power carries the right to political power, and has often preferred Jefferson's weak government to Hamilton's strong government. The other individualist element, fostered by Taylor, Randolph, Calhoun, and the Tidewater aristocrats, was the die-hard, aristo-agrarian state-rights school which opposed business and insisted upon complete laissez faire; it was agrarian and *American Physiocratic,* and set up the Athenian ideal of a society of citizens erected on an economic basis of slavery.

Jefferson thought of the small farmers as the bulwark of democracy, because in their independence and economic equality he saw the only feasible way of reconciling liberty and equality. If there is complete liberty (individualism), the danger is that those with luck, initiative, or shrewdness will gain an undue share of economic power—and with it will come inequality, because they will have the power to oppress their fellows. If there is inequality to begin with, that is, an undue share of privileges in certain hands, it will be a serious obstacle to the preservation or the attainment of liberty; the alternative of setting up a government to preserve equality immediately shears the individual of part of his liberty to do as he pleases. There has always existed among some Americans an opinion that we are free so long as the government is not politically or economically tyrannical; many of us fail utterly to see that tyranny can come just as easily from the overwhelming economic power of individuals or corporations, or from social or religious restrictions.

Jefferson agreed with the ordinary American's distrust of government; it is notable that even in the century of the welfare state there is little tendency to agree with socialists that government is dependably "moral." However, Jefferson saw what many of us still fail to grasp: that to preserve liberty there must be throughout the nation a considerable degree of relative (*not* absolute) economic equality. It was to promote this end Jefferson fought and conquered primogeniture and entail in Virginia. This was why he violated his Constitutional principles: he made the Louisiana Purchase in order to obtain more land for the common man; he fought the Federalist judges because they were concerned chiefly with protecting property rather than liberty; he warded off war by the Louisiana Purchase and by harsh enforcement of the Embargo because he knew that war ordinarily makes the rich richer and endangers the economic equality necessary to democracy.

During his whole life Jefferson was concerned with finding the balance between liberty and equality, for he was not so foolish as to think that a wide distribution of property would be an automatic stabilizer. He proposed a solution that was quite in keeping with his faith in human nature. Let men be educated to their responsibilities, let them restrain themselves from deliberately overturning the balance between liberty and equality, and let them have the courage to fight any such attempts. The form of government was important, but secondary. What counted was the willingness of democrats to live virtuously and deal justly with their fellow men.

The problem of economic equality became acute after the Civil War with the growth of teeming industrial populations who could not live on their own land but were dependent upon the fortunes and the goodwill of others. Jefferson in his presidency had forecast the future when he sought to preserve economic equality by breaking his own partisan tenets. Since democracy tries to preserve balance between liberty and equality, it must create economic equality where it does not exist or has been lost. Thus MacArthur broke up the great corporations and the great landed estates of Japan. For the same reason both Democratic and Republican progressives have sought to enforce competition in manufactures by breaking up monopolistic corporations, and where "natural" monopolies exist they have imposed regulations (as on street railways) or taken them under government ownership (as the post office).

The people of the United States have found in capitalism the promise of popular welfare, and usually its delivery. The abundance of resources have given to our reform movements a color quite unlike that of older countries. Since nearly everyone here has been able to win some property if he is willing to work and save, the historic combat has not been a straight issue between property and human rights. It would be clearer and usually more accurate to speak of the struggle as between big property and little property.

While it is true that political revolts are always in progress somewhere in the country, the Jeffersonian side of the conflict nevertheless becomes clear in the national scene only about once in a generation (1800, 1828, 1860, 1896, 1912, 1932). The Democratic Party is the one with the *tendency* toward liberalism, but the opposition is never without its liberal wing, and Jeffersonian reforms may be implemented by either party. Lincoln once pungently illustrated this condition with a story: "I remember being once much amused at seeing two partially intoxicated men engaged in a fight with great-coats on, which fight, after a long and rather harmless contest, ended in each having fought himself out of his own coat and into that of the other." Lincoln himself, though a member of the party of Hamilton, has become a legendary hero of Jeffersonianism.

American political reform movements have never been root-and-branch crusades. They have pared, and altered, and regulated, but in the end the old tree is still alive. The aim has been not to kill our basic institutions but to revitalize them. Little property has sought to limit the overwhelming menace of big property to democratic equality. Liberal political movements usually have come on the heels of notable increases in the size or privileges of big property. It is also noteworthy that in a number of cases the rebels have been bought off by a handout of public land. Jefferson had to make recourse to this evasion when he lowered the price and terms of payment of public land. Hamiltonians and Jeffersonians have historically followed pretty much the same methods. Both have desired minimum government interference, though neither has scrupled to call for government aid in a pinch—little property against big property, and big property against labor agitators or foreign competitors. The tendency in this century, however, is for the Jeffersonians to demand regulation of big property or enforced competition.

It was Hamilton who first saw that the United States was poorly balanced economically and that manufacture and commerce needed to be fostered in order to promote prosperity and national security; it was only after years of buffeting that Jefferson got the point, and even then his consent was grudging. Certainly in this respect Hamilton deserves to be called progressive; by the same token Jefferson, with his desire to preserve a nation of small farmers, was a conservative. It is confusing, unless we interpret liberalism and conservatism as political attitudes, not necessarily economic or administrative tags.

Hamilton sought to maintain the political *status quo;* it was Jefferson who forced on him the pattern of democratic evolution through political conflict. Hamilton's legacy was intensely practical, mundane, and a little selfish; he lighted the furnaces of our iron mills, hoisted the sails of our trading ships, and posted the ledgers in banks and counting houses; his was the inspiration that brought us science and technology and that bred mass production and the American standard of living.

Jefferson's legacy was that of faith in humanity; he touched the moral consciousness of men with the spark of inspiration and sounded the trumpet call to battle for human rights.

Hamilton was the head, Jefferson the heart. Hamilton was science, Jefferson was democracy; and though they may clash, neither can live long without the other. Hamilton was might, Jefferson was right. Might gives to right the power to survive, and right gives to might the moral reason to fight for survival. Thus in eternal conflict, eternal compromise, and eternal interdependence Hamilton and Jefferson have lived since there were men on this earth and will live as long as men remain.

V

The Rampageous West

AMERICAN historians of the nineteenth century were overwhelmingly Easterners, or at least were trained in the East or in Europe. More than this, those of the first rank were for the most part New Englanders; even the exceptions usually lived no farther away than New York. The natural result was that formal United States history had an incorrigibly northeastern bias, and textbooks emphasized Plymouth Rock at the expense of Jamestown. Boston, often jokingly called the Hub of the Universe, was seriously presented as the center of most that was worth while in American political, economic, and cultural history. The point of view had a superficial plausibility simply because no one had yet tied into the national pattern the tremendous forces of the South and the West.

The role of the South in American history was thrust upon public attention by the Civil War. The West came into its own with dramatic suddenness in 1893 at the World's Columbian Exposition in Chicago when Frederick Jackson Turner, born in Wisconsin and trained at Johns Hopkins, read to a small group of historians a paper on "The Significance of the Frontier in American History." The famous Frontier Hypothesis, thus launched, held that the abundant free lands at the edge of the settlements not only caused the rapid advancement of the frontier to the Pacific but were instrumental in developing (from eastern and European seeds) American democracy and nationalism and in giving us a host of characteristics, such as individualism, inventiveness, freedom of opportunity, energy, equalitarianism, and exuberance. Hundreds of students sat under Turner's spell at the University of Wisconsin and at Harvard, and before long the effects of his hypothesis began to be felt not only in the historical field but in the other social studies and even in literature.

For a generation it was orthodox to present the West as the paramount molder of American institutions—indeed, Turner's followers were more dogmatic and sweeping in their claims than he ever was. Then the reaction set in. The political, social, economic, and cultural influences of Northeast and South upon the West began to be stressed. More than this, the heritage of the English democratic process was emphasized, and the bitter struggle of the honest mechanics of eastern cities for their democratic rights was shown to have been little influenced by the West. Probably the pendulum has gone too far to the opposite extreme, and the truth will eventually be found to lie somewhere between. At any rate, the present-day historian approaches the analysis of the West and its influence with reservations; certainly as yet he does not expect to find the answer to all his questions.

Turner seems to have used the words *frontier* and *West* as synonyms; there is something to be said for this, for certainly the two blend into each other so gradually that it is not always easy to tell where one leaves off and the other begins. Nevertheless it is well to preserve the distinction between the frontier as the area of contact and conflict (trading and crudely agricultural) between civilization and wilderness, and the West as the sparsely inhabited area of agricultural settlement; at times the West has also included mining and cattle raising. Turner also used the two words to denote a state of mind prevalent in those areas, either at the time of their existence or as passed on to later generations. The usage is well justified, for the *frontier* and the *West* had tremendous effects upon national psychology, but one must be careful in general reading to note the context in connection with each word. Eventually the term West was gradually shifted to the Great Plains states and to the Pacific Coast (or Far West), and these areas because of their special and irreconcilable interests are now closest to the West in its old meaning as an economic and cultural area and as a state of mind.

The settlement of new lands in the area east of the Great Plains usually followed a rather well-defined pattern. The frontier stage of penetration was by the fur trade, ordinarily engaged in by rough characters who had much in common with the Indian way of life; in fact, in later days they often were part Indian in blood. Their mission was to learn about the country and its possibilities, and they introduced alcohol and diseases of civilization which made white conquest easier. The second stage—which, however, did not always appear in the North—was the cattleman's frontier. Well before 1700 the Virginia back country had been overrun with great herds of wild cattle and horses which fed on the luxuriant pea vines native to that region. "Cowboys" found it profitable to organize hunts and to drive the animals into "cowpens," where they could be branded.

The third stage was that of the agricultural settler. It usually began before the traders or cattlemen passed on, for the first agriculturist was a squatter who mixed his activities. He lived in a rough cabin, girdled trees to kill them and let in the light on his corn patch, and then when neighbors pressed in sold his "improvements" and moved on where the hunting or forage was better. The permanent settler followed close upon the heels of the squatter. Last came the growth of industries which endeavored to meet the local need for manufactured products. When the industrial interests were powerful enough to control labor and join the speculators in boosting the price of land, the area had joined the East. The last phase was represented in the South by the rise of plantations, for they, like industry, represented the ascendance of capital.

* * *

The Piedmont area between the Fall Line and the mountains and the nearer valleys among the mountains are known as the Old West. From Pennsylvania southward the Old West was even in colonial days more of a unit than the coast. The Great Valley ran almost unbroken from the Hudson River to Georgia and furnished a highway along which the pioneers moved at will, and from which the waters of the valley flowed eastward to the Piedmont or westward to the Mississippi. As early as 1732 Germans moved southward along the valley from Pennsylvania, and very soon Scotch-Irishmen entered from both Pennsylvania and the Carolinas. The Appalachians and the hostility of the Indians delayed the westward movement for a generation, but the result was only to make the sweep more irresistible when it began. New England back country was a part of the Old West because there were a striking social and economic likeness and political fellow feeling from one end to another of the westward belt.

There can be no doubt that the Old West was the preparation ground for many of the economic and social techniques and for much of the psychological state of mind which the pioneers took with them as they burst the mountain barrier and began their sweep to the Pacific. The Old West was the meeting place of the nations, and its mountain valleys were the mixing bowls of the new nation. The Scotch-Irish took to the new environment with an aptness that made them its most prominent (at least its noisiest) element, thus giving posterity the idea that they monopolized the West. Such was far from the case. The restless, the adventurous, and the needy

of every race were there helping to mold the characteristics of the
West. The traveler in the hinterland saw what he chose to see.
The aristocrat called it a "lubberland," and even the best-disposed
admitted that dirt and laziness existed among the froth of outcasts
who were thrust continually ahead of the settlements or who were
left like islands in pockets of poor soil. But, as one observer recorded,
the European who went West felt a "sort of resurrection . . . he
now feels himself a man, because he is treated as such."

The Western European, long since removed from ancestral forests
and lapped in the security of town and castle, was now breeding the
pioneer once more. This was a free society and, like all free societies,
was democratic. The pioneers, like their surroundings, were in-
sensitive, uncouth, and at times semibarbarous, but taste and refinement were not proper weapons to conquer savage and wilderness.
The man of the Old West gloried in his freedom from restraint and
bitterly fought any attempt to subject himself to regulations. He
was subject to sudden gusts of passion, like his distant ancestor in
the German forests, and his religion was compounded of simple and
primitive emotions. The pioneer had no regrets for the civilization
of Europe or even of the Tidewater except as he hoped to make
his chosen region prosper; he was no longer English, Scotch-Irish,
or German, nor even Pennsylvanian or Virginian, but that new
man, an American. He lived in a log house, he ate of plentiful
but plain fare, he bred large families, he went to church or not as he
pleased, and he considered a man worthy or unworthy for his own
sake and not for his father's title or wealth. Education was all
right, especially for the ministry, but common sense and a knack
with rifle and ax were more useful.

He looked about him at the vast wilderness owned by Indians
and proprietors and held that "it was against the laws of God and
Nature that so much land should lie idle while so many Christians
wanted to work on it and to raise their bread." This was simply an
eighteenth-century way of saying, "The earth belongs to him that
gives it value"—to the cultivator, not the hunter, the speculator, or
even the cattleman. He therefore hated the Indians because they
in their dependence on game sought to stop the whites from leveling
the forests and killing off or driving out the game. He hated the
speculator (even though he might be a fellow Westerner) who got
hold of vast tracts of land and held them unoccupied for a rise in
value, or who sought to make the land a source of permanent income

in the form of quitrents. This attitude toward "engrossers" of land was fundamental and permanent and was used by the pioneers to justify all sorts of violence.

The man of the Old West was not a sensitive creature, and he found it perfectly possible to keep a clear conscience while he defied proprietors and quitrents, squatted wherever he found a fertile valley, and massacred the Indians who protested at his high handedness. His Calvinism lay broad and deep and made him look upon God as a business partner and a tribal deity who regarded with favor self-reliance and direct action. There is a story of a Western preacher —a Scotch-Irishman—who during the Revolution opened a recruiting meeting with this remarkable prayer: "Lord God, if Thou art unwilling by divine grace to assist us, *do stand aside and let us fight it out!"*

* * *

The West has always been recognizable by its problems. The most obvious problem was the Indians; even when the Indians were not on the warpath, the people of the West were concerned to get them pushed farther on in order to make more land available. Second was the problem of how to get control of land quickly, cheaply, legally, and in generous quantities. Third was the problem of transportation, for the pioneer's grain, meat, and lumber were too heavy to be carried far by primitive methods; even with the coming of the steamboat and the railroad, rates were so high that transportation remained a live problem. Fourth was the fact that the West was always a debtor area, for its products never brought enough to develop its resources and public utilities and leave enough for the people to live on in the style to which they wished to become accustomed.

As a result eastern capital was invested, but since the risk was great it charged all the traffic would bear and took much of its earnings out of the area; the effect was to reduce the circulation of cash, just as had happened in the Thirteen Colonies. There were many other western problems, but it will be sufficient here to name cultural sterility. This arose from several causes: the bitter struggle against Nature left little leisure for self-improvement; poverty in the pioneer era made it difficult to support colleges, churches, libraries, welfare agencies, and even common schools; and distances made social and institutional contacts difficult. The West inevitably in its second generation stepped a notch down the cultural scale below the men who had founded it.

Insatiability is the word which most readily comes to mind in connecting the Westerner with the land. Land was involved in the causes of all the colonial, early national, and Indian wars. Speculations in land, oversettlement, and sometimes overproduction were directly related to economic booms and busts. From colonial times insatiability for land exercised a powerful political pressure, and the satisfaction of this demand has vitally affected the growth of the democratic process, population shifts, foreign immigration, race relations, cultural indigestibility, growth of corporations and technology, American psychology and philosophy, and the present political pattern. The land was obviously not the only factor in American development, but if it did not affect all other factors the exception is not readily apparent. During and after the Revolution the states turned their claims to western lands over to the central government, thus endowing the nation with a magnificent public domain into which settlers could move and from which new states could be carved.

Land was the capital stake which the government offered to the settler, the speculator, the miner, the lumberman, and the cattleman. The settlers themselves were young people or foreign immigrants seeking a stake and farmers who had lost or worn out their land. Naturally settlers preferred fertile soil, so they left much unappropriated land between their holdings and added their political pressure to that of the speculators to force the government to buy more land from the Indians.

There was, from the first, agitation for free land—"vote yourself a farm"—but the policy was so clearly politically impractical that settlers had to content themselves by seeking more and better land at lower prices; on the other hand, speculators were hoping to make a killing by holding land for a rise. Though at one time or another most men with initiative or gullibility took a flyer in land speculation, the large-scale holder of "unseated" lands was all but universally hated, especially if he was successful and an absentee. Both the settler and the speculator wanted land, but under different conditions, and it may be said here that on the whole Congress was more responsive to the needs of the actual settler. However, since the first business of a politician is to get elected, Congressmen sought diligently to apportion the public domain to all interests as a capital stake for their ventures. Government gifts to private interests are not the creation of our own day but have been a historic American policy.

*   *   *

The West had a wealth of positive qualities. The first one that struck the traveler was the well-nigh universal optimism. The Englishman on the steamboat who listened to the native describe the great and beautiful city around the next bend was disappointed to find a collection of hovels with a few fever-racked inhabitants. The American probably had not been lying; the vision of the future had so filled his mind that he quite failed to see the reality, and what he described was merely what he saw in his mind's eye. The American of the pre-Jeffersonian era, it has been quite generally held, was indolent and indifferent. If that was true, something must have stirred him up by the time the War of 1812 was over—perhaps the hopes and visions offered by a continent full of opportunities. Except in certain backward and malarial regions he now became a live wire. He attacked his problems with intelligence, energy, initiative, and without undue scruples; he took calculated risks, and if he lost he picked himself up and tried again. He was materialistic, as was natural, for it was a material problem which he had set out to conquer. The whole country, it may as well be acknowledged, evidenced optimism and materialism, but these qualities were focused most sharply in the West.

The West was an economic opportunity rather than a stamping ground of freedom. Its citizens often worked hard to raise its religious, educational, medical, and cultural standards, but the standards they had in mind were imported from the East or from Europe. The Westerner quite sensibly looked at his problems primarily in economic terms, for economic disputes can be compromised; when they are transmuted into moral principles, they never can be. Lincoln was best illustrative of this attitude in his steadfast refusal to accept slavery as an inescapably moral issue. The Westerner refused to make sweeping reforms. He was democratic, but he did not give the vote to women, Negroes, or Indians; he agreed reluctantly to emancipation but preferred to leave the details to the South. He belonged, of course, to churches, missionary societies, temperance societies, abolition societies, and prison-reform societies, but these movements started in the East and for a long time were struggling and imitative in the West. The Westerner was not out to build a new Jerusalem but to duplicate settled areas on a somewhat better scale. Considering the obstacles, that gave him quite enough to do.

It has been the habit of the extreme proponents of the Frontier Hypothesis to claim everything in sight for the West. Not only were the breezes that blew from the West fresher and more invigorating than those from the East, but they bore on their wings all good gifts of politics, economics, and society. Unfortunately for the reliability of these interpreters, the West in its pioneer stage was all but sterile of new ideas in all three. The West was politically democratic, largely because at first its people were pretty much on an economic level, but it was equalitarian rather than socially conscious. The West itself was ostensibly convinced of its own superiority, but the heat of its protestations rose from a basic inferiority complex. It was jealous of eastern and British advantages and showed it by ridiculing and at times smashing manifestations of culture, luxury, and good manners.

Contrary to popular opinion the various Wests have not always been areas of progressive revolt; basically they have always upheld capitalism: their intention was simply to extend its blessings to themselves by pruning off the privileges which enabled eastern capital to drain away their surplus. Economic radicalism, indeed, is nearly always characteristic of agricultural areas, but it usually takes the form of panaceas (such as inflation by free silver) and is preached with the emotional zeal of crusades. Again, the Wests have contributed but few mechanical inventions, though they eagerly accepted and sometimes improved agricultural machinery; unfortunately, either because of circumstances or innate conservativeness, this tolerance was not for some time extended to scientific farming methods. The Westerner was an expansionist, but only in North America and certainly no farther than the Caribbean; he was an isolationist, but with a touchy sense of national honor; and a nationalist, but sometimes with his fingers crossed on policies (such as the tariff) which the East thought essential to national welfare.

Though the West may not have played quite the dominant role that its admirers would insist, it nevertheless had tremendous significance. Its drama has pervaded American literature, song, and story. Its psychological characteristics have strengthened certain trends in the pattern of national thought and action which would otherwise have been less pervasive. The West turned national attention inward and bred an illusion of isolation and self-sufficiency; at the same time the cotton and grain of the West slowed down the growth of industry, which might have given the United States an enlightened interest in world trade and consequently in world affairs. As it was, the tremendous domestic market afforded by the West (and the South) delayed an interest in world affairs even after industry had grown to almost unprecedented size.

The West drew surplus eastern farmers and thus by lowering the pool of prospective native industrial laborers raised wages and stimulated the flow of European labor; this in turn bequeathed to the country the problem of the melting pot and delayed the integration of American culture and the solidification of social and economic classes.

Lastly, this vast agricultural empire (cotton, corn, and wheat) has had decisive political influence. Even though population in industrial states has outgrown that of agricultural states, the number of the latter under the Constitutional system has given them a preponderance in the Senate. This has enabled them from time to time to check the arbitrary rule of industry, to enhance the growth of individual political rights, and finally to join in enhancing the growth of the individual's social rights.

The West sought to limit predatory individualism by demanding adherence to a concept of strict equality. This had as much to do with the development of modern American psychology as the land and the resources of the West have had to do with the growth of American power. A story is told that some officials, trying to get through a crowd to the speaker's platform, shouted self-importantly:

"Make way for the representatives of the people!"

"Make way yourself!" answered a voice from the crowd. "We *are* the people."

The spirit of equality found practical application in opposition to aristocracy, and it became so marked a characteristic of the West that it was transmitted without much dilution to later generations. Actually the aristocracy which was so distrusted was a plutocracy of slave-holding planters, land speculators, or industrial and investment magnates. In tracing the division of political parties one must recognize the fact that at least until about 1840 they were drawn more nearly on social and economic lines than they have ever been since. The alignment of sections in the Civil War was vitally affected by the antiaristocratic movement: in the Northwest the farmers were influenced by antipathy to the southern "slavocracy"; in the Southwest the poor white was influenced not simply by the social menace of abolitionism but by the old Jacksonian antipathy for northern capitalists. Politicians have known for generations how to win votes by invoking the little red schoolhouse and birth in a log cabin. Even in our own day red galluses and hill-billy bands are standard equipment of some Southern politicians, and Northern politicians have to shout down banks and corporations and extol the old American virtues, which they represent as having survived chiefly in the breasts of wage earners.

The turbulent individual's demand for personal dominance was in the end quelled by social pressure. The West's demand for conformity to a pattern of equality was so strict that mediocrity was glorified. To be socially acceptable, a man could not afford to rise above his neighbors; to show the marks of education and culture, to dress well, or to build a mansion was in many communities known as "putting on airs." The dead weight of public opinion favored the stodgy humdrum virtues, mediocrity, and complete predictability (what the English call "character"), and it made headway against the more self-assertive and lawless elements. The phenomenon is still familiar in small towns. It is no wonder that professional men, bored and frustrated by the sterile life about them, often drank themselves to death. The standard of success was property, not education, culture, travel, or work for building a better community in any except a strictly material sense. Everyone was perfectly free—to do the socially acceptable thing. As Jefferson put it: "The inquisition of public opinion overwhelms in practice the freedom asserted by the laws in theory."

All this shows nothing if not an innate conservatism in the West. Progress was a fetish, but it was strictly material progress; any other kind of change had to fight its way against general suspicion. The result was that the individualist threw himself into making money and amassing property and in the end brought about the very inequality which Jefferson had dreaded, and which now in fact menaced liberty. Western equality had failed to obtain a dead level of economic conditions and was in danger of being overturned. The successful were out to benefit themselves and were perfectly willing to let the devil take the hindmost.

VI

Democracy and Transcendentalism

THE War of 1812 against Great Britain occupies in Europe no more than a paragraph in the history of the Napoleonic Wars but it was big with significance in the history of the United States. As a matter of fact it was less a struggle for "free trade and sailor's rights" than a push on the part of the West and South to seize Canada and Florida. The war ended in an inglorious draw, partly because of the ineffectiveness of its promoters, President James Madison and the so-called War Hawks, partly because of the opposition of Federalist and pro-British New England.

Why, then, has it become a cardinal principle of the American creed that "we licked the British twice, and can do it again?" It reminds one of the fabled cock that contended his crowing brought up the sun. The explanation lies in the well-known psychological facts that we forget pain and remember pleasure and that we interpret events to our own credit. The War of 1812, from an obbligato of national dishonor, changed to a causal march of triumph to the tune of which our arms had carried one national objective after another. Occurrences in 1814 and later lent themselves very handily to wishful thinking by the heedless or the shallow. Let us examine them.

(1) The news of Jackson's resounding victory at New Orleans, won *after* the signing of the peace treaty, was followed immediately by news of peace. It was fatally easy to connect them as cause and effect.

(2) The handful of very creditable naval duels was somehow remembered with a pride which had no realistic connection with their significance. The fact that our navy was soon driven off the seas was quietly ignored in American song and story.

(3) Impressment and trade discrimination ceased. Here again completely separate occurrences were connected as cause and effect. The end of the European war in 1814 meant that England cut its navy in two and no longer had reason to impress sailors; at the same time the destruction of commerce by both Britain and France ended.

(4) There were no more significant Indian troubles in the Old Northwest. Yet the Indians could count only about 4,000 warriors, and many of these were disaffected. In contrast there were 200,000 white men of military age in the Ohio Valley alone!

(5) We were now relieved of foreign pressures and were able to turn with easy minds to the conquest of the North American continent. Here again the popular mind pitched upon the War of 1812 as the cause; actually the cause lay in the end of a generation of European wars.

(6) The War of 1812 promoted manufactures and thus gave us our industrial independence. This fact is true (with certain qualifications), but desire for industrial independence was not a cause of war, and industry was accelerated from dire necessity rather than choice. Curiously enough, the movement was most successful in New England, the section most opposed to the war. Still, it was the most valid gain that resulted from the war.

The decade after the War of 1812 was a period of reorientation. The War Hawks, though ready to take advantage of the public's belief that the United States had won the war, were keenly aware of the debacle which they had helped to promote and sought for means to prevent its recurrence. National strength and national welfare, it was apparent, could be assured only by nationalist political and economic policies. The party of Jefferson, which had laid Hamilton in his political grave, now exhumed his bones and adoringly enshrined them in the halls of Congress—and this with the approval of the aged Jefferson. The Federalists, still maundering into their stocks about the inevitable catastrophe that would follow in the wake of democracy, found their sons refusing to accept the roles of catastrophists and traitors. Young Federalists swarmed into the Republican fold and joined with the reconstructed Jeffersonians to pull the party ship out of its Madisonian doldrums and speed it before the winds of nationalism. The Federalist Party, which in twenty years had run the gamut from rabid nationalism to New England sectionalism, accepted the defeat of Rufus King in 1816 as its death knell and quietly folded up as a national organization.

The election of James Monroe in 1816 ushered in the last of the Virginia dynasty and a period of one-party government somewhat inaccurately known as the Era of Good Feeling. There was, however, a great deal of sparring for position among ambitious leaders. Though the young nationalists were distinctly ascendant, it became increasingly evident that there were two wings to the party: the Old Jeffersonian, or Antique Republican, and the Neo-Hamiltonian. Prominent in the Neo-Hamiltonian ranks were such men as Daniel Webster, John Quincy Adams, Henry Clay, and John C. Calhoun. Clay gained considerable attention by his American System, which proposed to lay a tariff to protect manufactures and use the money for internal improvements. Nevertheless it was Adams who reached the presidency in 1825, after a narrow contest in the House of Representatives.

Adams sought diligently to promote internal improvements, manufactures, and the march of science. He wished to make the public lands a source of regular income (particularly for the financing of internal improvements) instead of recklessly throwing them to squatters and speculators; such a policy naturally outraged the West. He even sought to decelerate the waste of natural resources, and the public gasped in wrath or amusement. Adams was indeed far ahead of his time, for he envisioned something very like the modern service state. He wished the government to promote and protect the public welfare and to tax away speculative profits and the unearned increment of land because they were the creation of society, not of the individual.

The political situation in the 1820's and 1830's was complicated by two trends that were, in that generation at least, quite irreconcilable. One was a movement for the enlargement of democracy; the other was the growth of sectional divergencies. This statement is perhaps an oversimplification. Actually the purpose of the democratic movement was to enhance local controls, and to do so it seized the Federal government in order to shear away its powers. The effect (as it had been under Jefferson) was to make the central government stronger, at least in certain ways, and to promote nationalism. Presently there emerged two wings of the democratic movement. One wing insisted that only by exalting the states could democracy survive; its weapons became state rights and sectionalism and, finally, southern nationalism. The other wing asserted that the strength necessary for democracy's survival in a hostile world could be furnished only by stressing the Union more than the states. In the struggle between the two the democratic movement faltered, then yielded precedence to the great issue of whether or not the nation should live.

*　　*　　*

The partial triumph of Neo-Hamiltonianism galled the remaining Old Jeffersonians, and they promoted the resurgence of democracy as a remedy for the hard times that followed on the War of 1812. The people, looking about for a scapegoat, were ready to find simple causes and to be sold on simple cures. What could be more simple than to assert that the people had lost control of their government since 1800, and what more simple cure could be found than to get it back? Politicians scurried to take advantage of popular resentments—undoubtedly they often shared them—and they filled the air with outcries and the newspapers with denunciations. The nationalist program had been for the benefit of business, so democratic fury focused upon upsetting it.

It has often been the custom to picture this democratic resurgence, called the Jacksonian Movement, as sweeping out of the West like a great wave. Actually it came from all parts of the Union. Look at the numerous local causes of complaint. The West was convinced that New England was blocking cheap land and internal improvements; the South blamed the Northeast for raising the prices of manufactured goods by the tariff; the Northeast blamed the rest of the country for bringing on the crash by its razzle-dazzle state bank currency. Pretty nearly everyone in trouble blamed the Bank of the United States, called B. U. S. for short, for its attempt to gain a monopoly of currency and attacked the Supreme Court for promoting national power. Eastern laborers complained that their wages were oppressively low and that employers could cheat them with impunity, for of course a poor man could not afford expensive legal redress. Moreover, membership in unions was punished by loss of the job, and courts went out of their way to prevent and to punish strikes.

In the East and South state constitutions preserved many earmarks of the conservative reaction of the 1780's, and suffrage was still based on property. State churches survived in New England. Presidential electors as late as 1824 had been chosen by the legislatures in six states. It was inevitable that a movement with so many springs should be amorphous. It was by no means confined to the common people and their political leaders. The ironmasters of Pennsylvania saw a chance to trade votes for a tariff on iron. State bankers saw a rich opportunity to overthrow their enemy, the B. U. S. The landed aristocracy, still charmed by *American Physiocratic* doctrines, joined in the attacks on their old enemies, the merchants and manufacturers. Even the leader of the movement was a poor boy (Jackson) who had fought his way up into the aristocracy and had become its leader in Tennessee.

The democratic wave began in the states and then invaded national politics, though it continued to swell in some of the states even after it had subsided on the national scene. In the states it was led by a remarkable galaxy of men, some of them horny-handed tribunes of the people, others ambitious young fellows from the élite—one of them the son of Alexander Hamilton!—who rode to fame on the tide. Like the Jeffersonian movement before it and every effective political reform movement since, the leaders were realists who carried daggers up their sleeves and got what they went after, whether it meant trading with the enemy or embracing a political friend and stabbing him in the back. Corruption was as much a weapon of the democrats as of the conservatives; and, indeed, it was the democratic leaders who invented the modern machine, fed it on the spoils of office, and manipulated it to seize control of political conventions from the old-line conservatives.

The nation was so well divided between sectional favorite sons that only by political maneuvering could a reasonably clear-cut decision be made in 1828. The followers of Andrew Jackson proceeded to groom the victor of New Orleans as the only person around whom the nation could rally. Their master stroke was their annexation of the democratic revolt. The democrats had the issues which appealed to the voters, they possessed the political machines, and they were able to get out the vote; the Jackson men had the nation's only outstanding hero. Together the two were unbeatable.

Jackson was first of all a man of will, contentiousness, and intolerance of those who differed from him, but these qualities were scarcely handicaps in a region where men stood up for themselves. In the light of his clearly aristocratic tendencies, it seems strange that he was destined to become the idol of American democracy even in the East. The answer may be found in these facts: he was a natural-born leader, and that was the only sort who could arouse the Westerner's enthusiasm; he sympathized with a strong policy against Indians and Spaniards and became its instrument; he represented a new phase of local self-determination as opposed to Federal dominance; and, not least, he expressed in his policies the growing leveling tendencies which declared every man a king in theory and a mediocrity in practice. If these factors seem incompatible with the nature of the man, it should be remembered that he was also a politician and knew as well as the next man how to convince the public that the deuce of clubs was the ace of spades.

But even more important than these was the national state of mind when he first sprang into public attention. The secret of his ascendancy over the national imagination can best be understood by contrasting his remarkable feats of will with the depression of national morale in 1814. After two and a half years of war the Madison administration was paralyzed, Congress shot through with treason, finances in chaos, military defense all but dissolved, and gloating New England stood poised to fasten her shackles on the nation or give it the alternative of being split asunder.

In the midst of military collapse and threatened disunion, only the will of Andrew Jackson stood between the nation and the bitter cup of national dishonor. The fact that his greatest victory was won after the peace treaty did not destroy the psychological salvation which he offered. Thereafter the common people gave Jackson an almost mystical acclaim. Whatever we may think of his later political course, that fact must not be forgotten. He was the realization of the common American's dream of himself; the man of will, the builder, the champion of democratic liberties, and the preserver of national honor and safety against the powers of foreign evil.

Jackson's presidency saw the high water mark of democratic reform in many of the states. Jackson himself, by his Maysville Veto, stopped the builders of turnpikes from tapping the national till and forestalled the same procedure by the builders of railroads. He prevented the renewal of the charter of the Second Bank of the United States on the ground that it was throttling free enterprise. He liberalized land policies and moved the Indians from the South to Oklahoma. Finally he blocked the effectiveness of South Carolina's movement to nullify the tariff. It was during his time that the Democratic-Republican Party split into the Democrats and the Whigs. The former were the heirs of Jefferson, the latter the heirs of Hamilton. Jackson left office grateful for the "happy result" of his reign and regretting only that he could not have shot Henry Clay and hanged John Calhoun. There is no indication that he ever thoroughly understood the full implications of his presidency. Indeed, he had significantly altered Jeffersonian concepts and placed marks upon American history which have never been erased, even though they were submerged for a while by the slavery crisis. Let us summarize six of his outstanding achievements.

(1) He turned the presidency into an aggressive force in contrast to Jefferson's belief that the President was the associate rather than the master of Congress. Some of his doctrines have disappeared: for example, Presidents no longer insist on their co-equal right with the Supreme Court to decide on the Constitutionality of policies. By no means are all Presidents strong and aggressive; but when the strong personality enters office or the crisis arises, the precedent is there.

(2) Jackson made the party a definite, disciplined instrument of policy, in contrast to the old idea that the mission of the party was to rally the unanimous support of the nation. Jefferson utilized the two-party system, possibly without thoroughly understanding its nature, and Jackson, who would gladly have hanged the leaders of the opposition and forcibly baptized their followers, was probably the unconscious agent of political evolution. The spoils system, of course, was an essential part of the President's control of his party.

(3) Jackson glorified mediocrity by his rule that one intelligent man could hold an office as well as another; Jefferson had believed in the election and appointment to office of men of experience, ability, and culture. Jackson was with the trend of the times. More than that, Americans have ever since preferred mediocrity, as is seen by comparing the brilliant pre-election records of every single President through and including Jackson with the mediocrity of *most* presidential candidates since then, regardless of their performance after the election.

(4) The Whig campaign of 1840 was proof of the success of the Jacksonian revolution. The Whigs wished to abbreviate John Adams' "rule by the rich, the well-born, and the able" to a short and sharp "rule by the rich," but this was not politically realistic. The Whigs now beat the drum for democracy louder and longer than the legions of Jackson ever did. It was a fateful switch in campaign methods, but the only way to keep a conservative party alive. Indeed, the basis of the vote had been so broadened that the privileged caste and its hangers-on could no longer win unaided. Since that time no party has been able coolly to deny democracy and still get elected. Nor is this change of conservative base necessarily cynical even though there always are some cynics among the leaders of any party, and probably many Whig orators talked so often and so eloquently about the beauties of democracy that they convinced themselves.

Much more important was the popular pressure for democracy, a pressure carried into the Whig movement by the Anti-Masons and by young men who had grown up in the time of the Jacksonian Movement. It is certainly significant that when we look for the perfect example of the democrat we always think of that rising young Whig politician, Abraham Lincoln. Originally American parties had a perceptible ideological basis; now in their efforts to woo the voters they tended to play down ideology and view the party as an administrative instrument. Despite the split which brought on the Civil War this has on the whole tended to be true ever since.

(5) Jefferson believed that the vote of a man who could not stand on his own feet economically—as the land-owning farmer could—would be controlled by whoever controlled his daily bread. Jefferson therefore (until late in his career) distrusted the working classes and feared their acquisition of the vote as a menace to democracy. Jackson swept away these fears. He divided society into producers and nonproducers and accepted farmers and industrial laborers into the first classification. He, or rather his eastern followers, basically rejected *American Physiocratic* doctrines and accepted Adam Smith's atomism; he fought monopoly, promoted competition, and tried to keep "fictitious" property (stocks and bonds) from eating up "real" property. He hoped thus to prevent wealth from controlling the worker's vote.

We noted above that Jackson probably failed to understand that the democratic party system seeks a changing balance of interests, not the complete and final victory of one interest. It has been claimed that the Jacksonian movement saw the beginning of the American class struggle. We do not as yet know enough of the facts to demonstrate such a thesis. In any case, right down to our own day, consciousness of class among wage earners has never been strong, and they along with probably ninety per cent of the total population regard themelves as "middle class." Class-consciousness, indeed has never been marked except among the propertied—as must be admitted by those who understand the tenets of Federalists, right-wing *American Physiocrats* like Calhoun, and the leaders of the modern urban rich. Such class-consciousness as existed among the unpropertied was probably pretty much confined to the city "Workies" of the East. They were keenly conscious of the fact that the franchise must quickly be protected by economic measures, or they would be smothered by the mere weight of the capitalists.

(6) Jackson was called upon to choose between the horns of the eternal dilemma, and he did choose whether or not he recognized the fact. He believed in Jefferson's dictum, "That government is best which governs least." He saw himself as called "to heal the wounds of the Constitution and preserve it from further violation," to peel away the excrescences on the body politic which had been created by misgovernment and undue corporate privileges. Once more the Anglo-Saxon pattern was repeated: the desire to return to the purity of the past. But Jackson was caught on the horns of the dilemma: weak government cannot protect individual liberty from other individuals with greater economic power, but a strong government can as easily become the weapon of tyranny as the instrument of public good.

Jefferson had faced the same dilemma and had yielded reluctantly to the pressure for the Hamiltonian method of strong government but never ceased to assert that each exception was merely temporary and that government was still the natural enemy of liberty. He realized thoroughly that every power which he added to government in order to protect the public welfare could also be used by conservatives against the public welfare when they came back into office. Calhoun, who saw the dilemma more clearly than Jackson, chose nullification under the illusion that he was protecting liberty by keeping the national government weakly submissive to the states.

Jackson never admitted to an abandonment of Jeffersonian suspicions, and he expected the Federal government, once it had "saved" the day, to retreat to its narrow sphere; it did momentarily, but thereby left more room for the regrowth of monopoly. Nevertheless, Jackson's use of the Federal government to promote the public welfare foreshadowed its enormous expansion during the Civil War and indicated the field in which private business and social reformers would fight after the Civil War. Jackson and Calhoun shared the hope that an order could be set up in which the government would not need to interfere; that hope seems to have gone the way of many other utopian dreams.

The trend of the future was forecast in Chief Justice Taney's decision in the *Charles River Bridge Case* in 1837. Massachusetts had granted a franchise for a second toll bridge over the Charles River which was to become free in six years. The proprietors of the first bridge contended that the second franchise was unconstitutional because it impaired the contract the state had made with the company. After long delays the case was considered by a Supreme Court transformed by Jackson's appointments. The second franchise was upheld. "The object and end of all government," said Taney, "is to promote the happiness and prosperity of the community by which it is established; and it can never be assumed, that the government intended to diminish its power of accomplishing the end for which it was created." This decision, of course, illustrated the Jacksonian opposition to monopoly, but even more significantly it showed that in a crisis the Jacksonians would with Hamilton and John Marshall grasp the strong-government horn of the dilemma.

It is not likely that Jackson ever understood the dilemma or understood that he had failed to reach his goal of governing least. He was not a thinker but a doer; he reached instinctively for the instrument that would do what had to be done. The confusion of historians over the Jacksonian Movement and the loss of some of its lessons has probably resulted from (1) the fact that there was no political philosopher to systematize its discoveries as Hamilton and Jefferson did theirs, and (2) that the sectional controversy followed so close upon its heels. And yet it would be wrong to belittle Jackson's sincerity. A man who for decades was touted as a great democrat, the personification of the will of the people, would be less than human if he had not himself come to believe it. The remarkable thing is that he was right. The old frontiersman had the spiritual dynamism which was necessary to weld inchoate popular discontents into a mighty crusade. He had found a real affinity with the democratic movement, and from it he drew his political sustenance. He was the instrument of democracy in hewing out the shape of the future.

The Jacksonian Movement was not intended as an attack on property but upon the abuse of power by the owners of property. It was basically the triumph of Little Property over Big Property. The problem then (and the problem now) lay in the definition of abuse. Jackson's answers were too often naive and prompted by anger at his political enemies. The result was that less progress was made toward solving the problem than serious thinkers had hoped. Western farmers saw the problem chiefly as one of spreading the gravy more evenly. They were not so much concerned with forbidding the means by which some men had waxed rich as they were in obtaining land and other aids to enable them to catch up. The Democrats, therefore, did not have to work out a permanent solution of the problem of monopoly's special privileges; they were able to evade the issue by writing a check for the farmers out of our abundant natural resources.

Eastern city workers, especially those who were unable to depend in part on subsistence farming, took more interest in shearing away the power of the Bank, reducing the expenses of government, stopping capital's abuses of labor, and clearing the way for their right to organize for their own protection. They were fighting for Human Rights versus Property Rights—the first time the issue had been boldly flung into the political arena. Even Jefferson had thought in terms of Little Property versus Big Property when it came to the practical political battle. Actually the industrial workers were neither united nor articulate; so, though they obtained a few of their desires, their principal gain was the franchise—a powerful weapon for future conflicts.

*　　*　　*

The ideal and practical streams in American history may be called by the names transcendental and pragmatic. American reform sentiment has thus been divided into two wings: the transcendentalists, who proposed to make a clear sweep, and the compromisers, who proposed to find a middle ground between the practical "evil" and the ideal "good"—to keep the advantages of the old while they tried out the new. In the main, Americans have sought ideals, but their method of getting there has been by the compromiser's gradual and practical approach. Thus, when an issue reaches the political realm the problem becomes one of "how" and "how much?" This is where the politician comes in. He is a man who has made a life-long study of methods of reconciling differences. That is why a politician as President is usually preferable to an engineer or a soldier. We pay politicians in the coin of prestige and power; but, if they make compromises which we regard as ill-judged or crooked, we pile on abuse even before we know the facts of the case.

The typical politician is as jittery as a man going into battle. The politician must straddle issues judiciously to win enough votes to get himself elected. Cynical observers say that the politician is trying to deceive the people; an even better case can be made that he is trying to guess what the people want. At any rate, politicians prove their usefulness by finding the ground on which the ideal and the practical can meet. Actually what politicians do is to refuse to recognize either as a moral ideal, for of course a principle cannot be compromised. If one side or both in an issue insist that it is upholding a moral ideal, there can be no practical political compromise, and war is likely to follow as it did in 1861.

The United States of 1830 was shot through with romanticism and sentimentalism. Even the Jacksonian Movement was sentimental in its self-deception as to the ease with which the democratic millenium could be whistled into the parlor and house-broken to live in civilized society. There were, however, many Americans who proposed to hew reality to their ideals. During the 1820's certain of the more liberal Unitarians were strongly affected by a number of influences too numerous and complicated to be analyzed here in detail. Classical philosophers, medieval mystics, and Oriental thought were all explored. The belief of the French Revolutionists in human perfectibility was appropriated. The idealism of Kant and his German followers was dissected and selections made. The English Lake poets were laid under tribute. All this at a time when we would have it that Americans were living to themselves in splendid isolation! Most significant, of course, were the twin streams of the American heritage; on one side the idealism and the Calvinist conscience which were related to these European borrowings; and on the other the self-reliance, common sense, optimism, and restless experimentation which were finding expression in the Jacksonian Movement.

Transcendentalism was not the creation of any certain group at any certain time, but it found its most famous focus in the meetings of the Transcendentalist Club which began in 1836 in Boston. Its members at one time or another included Ralph Waldo Emerson, William Ellery Channing, Theodore Parker, Henry Thoreau, Margaret Fuller, Orestes Brownson, George Bancroft, and Bronson Alcott. Among such a galaxy of individualists it was inevitable that there should be great differences of opinion, and these were freely expressed in a little magazine called the *Dial*. Nevertheless, there were fundamental agreements. They believed that knowledge of truth transcends experience and reason, and is implanted by God in the human heart. Knowledge of the ultimate truth (the Absolute) is thus possible to the individual who will listen to the voice within him. Since they were Americans, the transcendentalists felt the obligation of action, the necessity to preach and experiment and to put their God-given ideals into practice. Though they thus accepted the idea of progress, the relationship to Calvinism's self-righteousness is readily apparent. It is just as apparent that the expression of unalterable moral principles would cause trouble when they reached the political arena with its demand for compromise.

Nevertheless, transcendentalism had a relationship to democracy. Its emphasis upon courage and restraint, its glorification of self-reliance and social consciousness, and its belief that man is naturally good and that his divinely implanted instincts afford reliable guides to judgment and action—all these were inherent in Jefferson's democratic philosophy. With Jefferson transcendentalism distrusted too much government and denounced industrialism as materialistic and destructive of man's independence. Theodore Parker, appalled by industry's effect on the working class, led the attack and sought a social solution.

Henry David Thoreau, too much the complete individualist to be a loyal transcendentalist, pointed with alarm at the state, nationalism, and the machine. He wanted to stop them cold, not mold them into stepping stones to a better life; and he went to live in the woods at Walden Pond near Concord to show how it should be done. His *Civil Disobedience* is a purge for the overly co-operative. "My thoughts," said he, "are murder to the state and involuntarily go plotting against her." He believed what he said; and when as a practical protest against government support of slavery he refused to pay a poll tax, he was thrust into jail. Emerson visited him and asked sadly through the bars: "Henry, why are you here?" Thoreau's answer was transcendentally direct. "Waldo, why are you not here?"

Ralph Waldo Emerson, the greatest of the transcendentalists, yet stood aside from its extreme manifestations. Scion of a long line of ministers, he himself had retired from the Unitarian ministry to work out his attitude toward God and his fellow men. The world, as he saw it was throttling law, progress, and individual freedom, and he devoted his life to the battle for individual salvation. "Let men but stand erect," he said, "and they can possess the universe." Serene, high-minded, often accused of pallid thinking, he traveled and lectured untiringly. No settlement was too remote nor its fee too small to divert him from his duty. Concord became the home of a coterie of thinkers who warmed themselves at Emerson's flame but were in no sense subservient disciples. Emerson vigorously championed Jeffersonian democracy but was repelled by the "impudent vulgarity" of the Jacksonians. Nevertheless, he retained his optimism and expressed the faith that some day there would emerge from the racial and social welter of America "a new race, a new religion, a new state, a new literature, which will be as vigorous as the new Europe which came out of the smelting-pot of the Dark Ages."

In 1837 Ralph Waldo Emerson stood before a Harvard audience and issued an intellectual declaration of independence. "We have listened too long to the courtly muses of Europe," he said. "We will walk on our own feet; we will work with our own hands; we will speak our own minds." Conservatives, anxious to preserve their special social and economic privileges, were aghast at this call to break with tradition, and he was in effect outlawed for the next forty years. The struggle that followed his declaration was longer and more bitter than the war which put Jefferson's Declaration into effect; indeed, it still goes on.

The bourgeoning of reformism in the 1830's and 1840's was the most remarkable phenomenon in the social history of that generation. Scarcely a field was left untouched. Emerson, who as a truly self-reliant man, maintained a rather supercilious attitude of aloofness toward programs, attended in Boston in 1840 a convention of the Friends of Universal Reform and recited with some humor the roster of causes represented:

"If the assembly was disorderly, it was picturesque. Madmen, mad-women, men with beards, Dunkers, Muggletonians, Come-outers, Groaners, Agrarians, Seventh-Day Baptists, Quakers, Abolitionists, Calvinists, Unitarians, and Philosophers—all came successively to the top, and seized their moment, if not their hours, wherein to chide, or pray, or preach, or protest."

Abolitionism was to have profound political results but its examination falls more properly under the story of the sectional conflict. Utopianism was nothing new in America, but it now received a new lease of life. Its most startling and successful manifestation was Mormonism. If the Utopian experiments of the time prove anything, they prove that socialism cannot be suddenly put into effect (at least in a complex society) except when those concerned are skillful and industrious workers ready to yield obedience to a wise and practical leader whose ascendance amounts to absolutism. Nor could they live a completely self-sufficient existence; indeed, in most cases they succeeded only when their idealism was sparked and disciplined by deep religious feeling.

Van Wyck Brooks suggests that the prominence of Vermonters in the Utopian movement was, after all, the legitimate offspring of

New England's Calvinist theocracy, of its search for the City of God and its determination to bend mankind to conformity to the divine plan; but at the same time it was the child of revolt against the individualistic transcendentalism of Concord, which was to become the apologist for the philosophy that "the business of the United States is business." They show that the American spirit is not unassailably competitive—even in that most American of all the states, Vermont. It yearns for a peaceful and cooperative order of society and is sometimes optimistic (or foolish) enough to launch into bold experimentation in the search.

The reform which in the long run was to prove most fundamental and most significant was in the field of education. It was promoted by nearly all reformers in the conscious hope of building a more enlightened democracy. As a matter of fact, parsimony had combined with prejudice to hamper the growth of common schools. The revolution in education began in 1823 when Samuel Read Hall established a little normal school in Vermont. Hall developed many of the features now familiar in teacher training, held conventions, wrote textbooks, and devised teaching aids. The movement spread rapidly. Horace Mann in Massachusetts and Henry Barnard in Connecticut became evangelists in the new cause. One of the most serious obstacles to taxation for the spread and betterment of free schools was the objection that it was a violation of the rights of property; another objection came from the churches, which had traditionally considered education their private field, though they had not cultivated it very thoroughly. The issue was bitterly fought everywhere, but particularly in Pennsylvania, where a dour, club-footed ironmaster named Thaddeus Stevens led the battle for free public schools. By the 1850's the opponents of free schools were losing nearly everywhere. Unfortunately the Civil War seriously handicapped the movement in the South.

The American people were too apt to regard democracy as a revealed faith and to sink back in the secure belief that it would bring Utopia without too much effort on their part. Cooper was a critic of democratic excesses and of the idea of progress. Nathaniel Hawthorne, born in the decaying old seaport of Salem, in his novels pointed out the truth that pain and sorrow and struggle are the human lot, and that there is no pleasant and secure railroad to Utopia. Edgar Allan Poe, a gloomy and gifted Virginian, master of the romantic mood, inspired writer of poetry and short stories and inventor of the detective story, was the literary American of his generation to receive highest acclaim in Europe. To the tragedy of Hawthorne and the "blasted hope" of Poe one is tempted to link the pathos of Pittsburgh's Stephen Collins Foster, the composer of enduring folk songs of a downtrodden race. All three were out of step with the heedless optimism of democratic America and each sought refuge in a world of his own, far from the self-assurance of transcendentalism.

The most slashing critic of the democratic dogma, however, was Herman Melville. As a runaway sailor on a Pacific isle he had seen the idyll of native life and also glimpsed the ugly cannibalism beneath. Now in his tremendous allegory, *Moby Dick,* he sounded the warning that there are no automatic guarantees of human progress. Man is fate's lieutenant; good and evil are eternally with us. Captain Ahab must always pursue the white whale. Our purpose on earth is to engage in the strife; this is our delight and the expression of our individualism, even though in the end we go down like Captain Ahab before the fury of evil. Man's alliance with good against evil, the everlasting search for truth even though we may be destined to know it only in part—these were the facts of life as Melville saw them. Ralph H. Gabriel succinctly points up the two wings of democratic thought: "Emerson said: Trust thyself because God is in you. Melville replied: Trust thyself because no god will aid you." Some of Melville's novels attained success, but *Moby Dick* was received with silence or misunderstanding. America was not ready to be jolted from its smug security by such warlike realism.

The democracy of the 1850's was an incongruous and contradictory mixture without philosophy or direction. In the South it was Athenian in nature, based on slavery. In the North it was smug and contented, overgrown and soft, ready to be bent to selfish purposes. Jeffersonian democracy, suitable for a simple agrarian society, was out of date in the developing industrial society, and its doctrine of individualism was to be the support of the very interests Jefferson had sought to overthrow. These were the men of action, the builders and money grubbers who saw democracy as the pillar of their own power. Such men are necessary for material progress, but society in taking the gifts they offer in one hand must be wary lest the other hand lift the watch and fob of eternal values.

Hawthorne and Poe could offer little but resignation, noble or delirious. Melville's trumpet call to battle was sounded for the heroic, but few of us are heroes. Emerson saw the confusions and contradictions and gave self-reliance and dignity to the American spirit—which was all very well but quite useless without integrated dynamism. For a few years the Civil War gave purpose to democracy, but with the apparent passing of the crisis the old smugness returned. It was the mission of Walt Whitman to strike the spark which has kindled the watch fires of democracy in our generation.

Walt Whitman was a New York Quaker, a carpenter, typesetter, and journalist who knocked about from job to job. Fired by Emerson's faith in man, he applied himself to forging the declamatory poems which he set in type and issued in 1855 as the first edition of *Leaves of Grass*. The book was an immediate and undoubted failure, and it was not until praise found its way back from England that the country awoke to his great gift. Meanwhile he added to his poems, served as an army nurse during the Civil War, and clerked in a government office in Washington. It seems to have been Whitman who first used the phrase "democratic faith"; certainly no more joyous nor impassioned affirmation of it has ever been written than appeared in his work. Van Wyck Brooks has said that he "precipitated the American character." Rude, impulsive, and affirmative, he lived among people and loved them. He looked upon himself as a primitive poet whose function it was to focus tribal aspirations and stir the people to action. He spurned the pallid, unimaginative, duty-bound reformism of the transcendentalists and put iron tonic in the veins of their self-reliant man. He gathered together the disparate, warring elements of democracy and gave them organic being and dynamism. There he stuck, for he was not a man of ideas and did not know how to build the democratic future. That has been the task of our century, in so far as it has been done.

The men we have been discussing did not necessarily exert direct effect upon the common people but were read and interpreted by the leaders and teachers. Probably more direct was the power exerted by George Bancroft, the historian. In the florid style then in vogue his *History of the United States* vigorously championed democracy and found many instances in which Providence had intervened to protect and mold it. Bancroft profoundly influenced statesmen, teachers, and editorial writers, though his views were after all but reflections of American popular opinion. No less significant in the growth of democracy were the orations of such statesmen as Webster and Everett which were printed in the newspapers, reprinted in readers, and recited in schoolrooms. Webster, in particular, was regarded as the champion of union, which was in the North regarded as an aspect of democracy, and his "Reply to Hayne" was recruiting men for the Union Army a generation before the Civil War.

VII

The Emergence of American Character

THE term American Revolution is in reality a misnomer, for the war did not change American directions but only accelerated certain trends which were already evident. These trends, it must be obvious by now, were toward democracy and nationalism. At the time they were regarded as inconsistent, and the adherents of each fought for its own program as the only salvation of the nation. In 1787 they accepted the Constitution with crossed fingers, each hoping to interpret or mold it to his ideal. The result was that this became the period in which the battle for the democratic process was fought and won, with the surprising outcome that the two ideals were found to be not inconsistent but complementary.

The half century which followed the drawing-up of the Constitution saw the steady development of American nationalism, nationalism in the sense of co-operative and aggressive patriotism. When the Constitution was completed, thirty-five of the thirty-nine men who signed it lived on or near Atlantic tidewater; sixteen years later that Constitution gave law to the peaks of the Rockies. The American flag had appeared in the Oregon country and the ports of the Orient and was soon to fly over the Barbary castles of North Africa. The rocks of New England and western sectionalism were successfully passed by 1815, but before the end of the period it was evident that the nation might yet founder on the rock of southern sectionalism. Nevertheless, this was the period in which the consciousness of American nationality took hold of so large a part of the people that a generation later they were willing to offer their lives in defense of the ideal.

Modern nations are the creation of historical and political forces among which language, race, religion, geography, economics, and culture may have played parts. As a distinct motivating force nationalism was recognizable in a number of European countries before the end of the Middle Ages, but it received its great impetus from the French Revolution. Nations are not likely to spring suddenly into full maturity; they usually evolve slowly. This gradual process certainly applies to

the United States, for it created the machinery of a national government long before its people were agreed that they constituted a nation.
The American people, indeed, long thought of themselves first as
citizens, say, of Vermont or Virginia and insisted that the Constitution
of 1787 had set up an alliance rather than a nation. This was shown
by the common way of referring to the country as "these" United
States; it was not until after 1865 that "the" United States became
the common form.

Here we find evolving nationalism basing itself upon a common
vision of expanding democracy and expanding national prosperity and
power. But this was the gawky age of America, a time when the
operation of the national glands was uncertain and one never knew
whether to expect heroism or cowardice, wisdom or shortsightedness,
generosity or selfishness in national policy. Tremendous struggles
were shaping between rival economic interests, as the foundations of
industrial and financial empire were laid. The deplorable side of
nationalism—its selfishness and intolerance—was too clearly evident.
The new was being glorified because it was new, and change was
being identified with progress. But the credit side of the ledger was
even more evident. Reform was making headway in social, cultural,
and intellectual lines. Material advances were raising the standard
of living of the common man. Best of all, there had emerged a
systematic understanding of the meaning and method of democracy
and of the fact that if democracy was to live, the nation must be a
unit in its defense.

The generation of the War of 1812 saw the emergence of the American character in the form it was to bear for a century, with only
minor changes. We usually have been materialistic, vaguely idealistic,
rashly optimistic, emotional, sentimental, and easily diverted from the
pursuit of difficult objectives—in other words, immature. These characteristics in an older nation would rightly be called psychopathic; of
course nations, no more than individuals, exhibit all the characteristics
of immaturity. In this immaturity lies the explanation for many of
the vagaries which have marked our social, economic, and political
policies as a people.

American humor of the early nineteenth century showed the national
immaturity in its ostentatious robustness and utter callousness. It
challenged the giant wilderness with gargantuan fantasies, for those
were the days when Davy Crockett carpeted the Mississippi Valley
with bearskins, when Mike Fink roared up and down the rivers, when

black John Henry wrestled cotton bales and drove railroad spikes with one blow, and when Paul Bunyan was born in the north woods. It was the day when personal combat was preceded by a ritual of poetic "brags," and Westerners spoke in words chosen for onomatopoeia and mock pomposity.

The decades before the Civil War saw an undercurrent of change, though scarcely the beginnings of subtlety or understatement. Life had not yet beaten the American down, but he was dimly aware that its complexities would not vanish before sound and fury. Nor was American humor standardized. The crackle of Irish wit rose up against Celtic giantism. Burlesque was sometimes softened to satire. The New England Yankee, masking his thoughts behind his native caution like a fox peering from a burrow, carried his wooden nutmegs and ironic jokes over the country. He became the picaresque hero, the butt, and the instructor of the frontier humorist. Humor came more often to lie in the manner of telling rather than the matter. A gust of the primitive, however, lived on in the practical joke, designed to injure or embarrass; the modern "hot foot" is an example. A more refined sadism lay in the seemingly harmless tale or apparent compliment told in a straightfaced and guileless manner with the brutal barb suddenly disclosed at the end. Lincoln was a master of the barb. Once when he spoke from the same platform as the rotund and bibulous Stephen H. Douglas, he referred to the latter's statement that the elder Douglas had been a cooper. "I am certain that he was a very good one," said Lincoln, bowing to his opponent, "for he has made one of the best whisky casks I have ever seen."

One of the most striking and significant American characteristics has been rootlessness: the lack of attachment to any certain place. The European peasant's chief quality is a love and respect for the soil. Historically this has existed in the United States principally in areas where the European peasant managed to preserve some measure of aloofness, as among the Pennsylvania-Dutch or the German and Scandinavian settlers of the Northwest. Americans have rarely loved the soil, despite the spoutings of sentimental novelists. We have "wrested a living from the soil"; we have been subduers of nature, not children and partners. Because the forest and the tough sod of the plains were seen first as enemies, it was difficult to develop an affection for the acres that had been won with suffering, and they were frequently abandoned for any reason or no reason. Wondering European observers early noted that American affection and loyalty turned toward institutions, specifically our social and political systems. Had Americans had the characteristics of peasants, it would have made more difficult the ruthless exploitation of nature which has made possible the tremendous physical power of the United States.

Another fundamental trait, which we have had occasion to mention before, was dualism. This struggle exists, of course, in all human beings, but its emphasis in the Englishman was exaggerated in America because we were not mature and well-balanced. The democratic process, moreover, prevents the reaching of a permanent social or psychological balance because it will not accept any current condition as perfect but insists on further changes to meet changing situations. Let us examine a number of these conflicts and suggest—rather than assert—how they influenced American character.

The conflict between individualism and community controls went on in the East as well as the West. Now individualism was sometimes lawlessness, but it was also the basis of that courage which is so essential in a democratic society. A man could make his own decisions; if he thought the law was unjust, he defied it or took it into his own hands, though of course he accepted the consequences. That such actions may be necessary if salutary changes are to be made was recognized by Thoreau when he went to jail rather than pay an unjust tax. Joseph Palmer, one of the "universal reformers," wore a beard in a day when beards were practically unknown and spent a year in jail for "inciting" a riot among those who gathered to cut it off. It was such courage that prevented the growth of an American proletariat, that is, workers with the slave mind. Even our Negroes are marshaling their social and political weapons like free men.

On the other hand society countered by laying emphasis upon the humdrum virtues. Proposed social and political changes had to be examined in the light of their morality, and reformers had to insist that they wanted reform in order to promote the reign of morality. Even Bob Ingersoll wanted America to become atheistic in order to promote the homely virtues! The intellectual stimulus to progress too often failed to crash through this rigid social and moral system. Mediocrity was the result. As Mark Twain said: "We have freedom of spirit, freedom of conscience, and the prudence never to practice either of them." This was exhibited in social disapproval of any manifestation of better than average education or refinement of taste— that was "putting on airs." Such manifestations were called "aristocracy," though actually they were no more than the vague and inexpert gropings of the plutocracy for something higher. The will of the majority was accepted, not so much because it was right (there was always vigorous opposition to that idea) as because it would inevitably prevail until a new majority arose to overthrow it.

Social insistence upon conformity and mediocrity meant that men who would otherwise have led truly progressive movements had to devote their lives to strengthening the tribal mores. A few broke away and despite taunts and mobbings sought to smash their prison barriers; they were the great reformers, or the faddists and fakirs. For other individuals with initiative and ability there was still one exit open: the road to the amassing of wealth. Probably this road was left open because the material needs of a new continent were so clearly evident, even though there was risk that the one who gained wealth would break through the crust of mediocrity by his mere economic strength and destroy the careful barriers against individualism. At any rate, that is what happened. Since material gain afforded the one road of exit, it was well traveled; and those who reached the mansion at its end were regarded with admiration, a little suspicion, and in time growing hostility. This materialism should not be confused with realism; the latter is a proper grasp of *all* the factors in a situation—material, psychological, and idealistic.

And yet just as plain was the existence of idealism, so close beside materialism that the two seem joined together. The materialist dreamed of factories, cities, and railroads, and he made them come true. He dreamed of setting the American flag on the Pacific coast, and he did. These accomplishments to him were not solely material, for over them all was spread the mantle of equality of opportunity and free institutions. He knew nothing of art or literature, but he did know something of an idealistic way of life, and he coveted it for his children's generation. His own peccadilloes he saw as temporary and necessary in the rough beginnings of civilization; once the material basis was laid, those who came afterward could go on to higher things. Money was simply a measure of accomplishment and perhaps of power.

Another significant contradiction lay between our inferiority complex and our complacency. It is a well-known psychological fact that one boasts in order to offset a feeling of inferiority. We could not match the art, the traditions, or the elegance of Europe, but we did have size. Therefore we found something incomparably admirable in size, mass, weight, quantity, and numbers. American accomplishments became unique, simply because they were American. Boastfulness easily became complacency. The crude bumpkin, Yankee Doodle, and the slippery Brother Jonathan (both British characterizations) became the shrewd, tolerant, and benevolent Uncle Sam. With peace and prosperity came greater self-confidence. God must be on our side, men thought, or we would not have prospered so mightily. Edward Everett remarked smugly that "our government is in its theory perfect, and in its operation it is perfect also. Thus we have solved the great problem in human affairs."

The average American was too often bored by other cultures and contemptuous of other ways of life; this attitude gave him an air of confidence and relaxation, which was often interpreted as the consciousness of power and has even passed muster as sophistication. Indeed, the American has been a strange mixture of loneliness and gregariousness, of naivete, curiosity, shrewdness, and of contemptuousness of what he cannot understand or cannot have, even though he may have cloaked his feelings in good-humored ridicule. Americans have had a sort of swaggering air, which moved Chesterton to remark that they were born drunk. Sometimes we have been thin-skinned and suspicious; again, we have been bumptiously self-confident or friendly as Newfoundland pups. Kipling, perhaps, was not far wrong when he described an American in these biting lines:

> Enslaved, illogical, elate,
>   He greets the embarrassed Gods, nor fears
> To shake the iron hand of Fate
>   Or match with Destiny for beers.

This brings us to the closely related but equally amazing contradiction between the American desire to dominate and the desire to be loved— or, if you prefer, to be accepted and depended on. Both were natural human traits but were accentuated by our circumstances. Americans had usually themselves or in the persons of their ancestors fled from an unequal contest in Europe. They brought with them a host of resentments, for instance, their fear of aristocracy, of established churches, and of standing armies, and they sought to prove their own worth by winning a position of dominance. Unfortunately Europe persisted for the most part in regarding its lost sons and daughters as barbarians. Naturally we were puzzled, hurt, resentful, and at times unreasonable. Suspicion marked our private and public actions. We laugh at the Japanese classification of foreign nations into friendly

THE EMERGENCE OF AMERICAN CHARACTER 125

enemies, neutral enemies, and hostile enemies; actually we had rather similar feelings through much of our early history.

We were conscious, nevertheless, of our inexperience, and uncomfortable because our great wealth bred jealousy abroad. We tried to purchase goodwill by unparalleled gifts. We poured out our money like water in the support of missionaries and for famine and earthquake relief, and we were naively puzzled that the world loved us so little. Even today we have still to learn that the rich and powerful are seldom loved, no matter how generous or helpful they are; the world calls such manifestations arrogance and shows jealousy and resentment. The best we can expect—and, indeed, far more useful than love—is respect, and then only when we have earned it, not bought it.

This pathetic desire to be loved was shown sometimes by the way in which we rejected our prospective friends before they had a chance to reject us. Perhaps we used it to cover our own fear and hostility. The history of our foreign relations is haunted with illustrations of our fear of being rooked, especially by England. The clearest example, however, occurred in 1782 at the close of the Revolution. We had by the terms of our alliance with France agreed not to make peace without French consent, but John Jay, fearful that France would deny us the trans-Appalachian West, hastened to get in the first double cross by making an arrangement with England to get that West; his argument was dubious, but Congress accepted its benefits.

One of the most striking inconsistencies in American character was the simultaneous existence of tolerance and intolerance. We believed in free institutions and equality of opportunity, and by and large we probably had the highest batting average of any great nation. On the other hand, it is a very human tendency for the pleasantly situated to regard their society as the permanently desirable one. We have never, therefore, been without bases of intolerance both on the part of those who want change and those who resist it. One such controversy rages over whether to accept Orientals and Negroes as first-class citizens, and it breeds the view that they should be accepted at once without regard to their fitness, and on the opposite extreme the view that they should not be permitted to prepare for acceptance. When it is asserted that capitalism is synonymous with democracy, both capitalists and socialists rush to take their place in the battle lines.

Optimism has been exalted in American history, optimism because of past successes and future prospects. The American accepted the idea of progress without serious cavil. The shortcomings of the past did not worry him; this was not the land of his fathers, but of his children. James Wilson, who helped to write the Constitution, regarded it as setting up a nation founded on men's likenesses, not their differences as in other nations. Democracy is an act of faith, and the very boldness of its optimism calls forth a response in the people. They obey the laws because they make them. "It is really an incredible thing," said De Tocqueville, "to see how this people keeps itself in order through the single conviction that its only safeguard against itself lies in itself." At the same time our optimism asserted that all problems have a solution, and this very assertion prevented deep understanding. We had a strong tendency to oversimplify, partly because we were bored by what we could not understand, partly because we thought in terms of black and white. In American novels and movies the hero and the villain have usually been sharply distinguished. When we looked at troubles in a foreign nation we saw only two parties, the one that was right and the one that was wrong—unless we decided that both were wrong—and we took sides with the "oppressed."

Pessimism, save when used for dramatic effect, has been the unforgivable sin, and yet it has never been far from the surface. The Federalists, it will be remembered, fervently distrusted human nature; and in the end they vanished, at least partly because the country got tired of their glooming. The conservatives learned their lesson and since then have concealed their pessimism. They became professional optimists, and their booster clubs have given a rather desperately determined air to American optimism. Nevertheless, both optimism and pessimism are basically expressions of Calvinism's doctrine of predestination. Everything will turn out all right because God is on the side of America; the majority is right, or if it is not it will be succeeded by one that is, because the peoples' hearts are open to truth and justice. Or conversely, everything will turn out wrong because human nature is depraved, and the masses will be too strong for the enlightened few and will bear them down in a vast Ragnarok.

These conflicts and contradictions in American character caused us to vacillate between extremes and rightly laid us open to the charge of being inconsistent and unpredictable. Emotionalism was illustrated in religious excitements, in reformist fads, and foreign relations. Our anger was easily stirred by real or fancied insults to national honor. Our sympathies were easily evoked by the sight of hardship and oppression. We repeatedly put our hands to the plow of responsibility, then proved ourselves unfit for the kingdom by looking back and wandering off to hunt for birds' nests. Such wisdom as there was in foreign policies was of executive creation, often against the will of Congress, and such responsibilities as we shouldered were thrust upon us by sudden crises. We have been unusually susceptible to newspaper propaganda and to slogans such as "Remember the Maine!" and "Fifty-four forty or fight!"

Too often we found relief from emotionalism only by taking refuge in sentimentalism—the refusal or inability to recognize reality and the embracing of a myth. It was illustrated above by Everett's statement that "we have solved the great problem in human affairs," a statement made at the very time when the operation of democracy had never been so seriously threatened. Sentimentalism governed whenever we refused to look at the facts but nevertheless boasted of perfection in civil rights, social equality, and freedom of opportunity. Sentimentalism thus excused our evasions and permitted our sores (foreign and domestic) to strike inward.

The American has been, perhaps more than anyone else, a man of conscience. It is commonly said by cynical critics that the "American way" is one of intolerance, race prejudice, and legal and economic oppression. Nothing could be more wrong. American history is concerned with those problems not because they are more common here than in other nations but because we have refused to become reconciled to them and have never for long given up the fight against them. The tremendous part played in American history by conflicts over land, abolition, race equality, and economic concentration are but outward manifestations of bitter inner tensions, which rise from the refusal to be reconciled to what is regarded as wrong. Conscience, in its social sense, rises from the ability to look in two directions at once— toward the practical program and toward the ideal—and from the realization that the ideal program cannot succeed unless it has yielded enough to the practical to give it a firm foundation. Hence the bitter struggle all through American history over what shall be the terms of the compromise between the practical and the ideal. Hence also the necessity for defenders of slavery to rationalize it as a public, private, and moral good, and hence Ingersoll's rationalization that atheism would promote the homely virtues. The cynic (one who denies the existence of moral standards) was rare in America until the twentieth century.

The American has seen this struggle as part of the universal search for moral values. Hence the American mission. We have pointed out that the contradictions in the American character arise both from national immaturity and from the opportunism of democracy. So long as we are democratic we can never settle down to a completely predictable pattern, nor should we desire to. Nevertheless, we have possessed from the eve of the Revolution to the present day a distinct sense that we have a national mission. Every nation convinces itself that it has something good to offer the world and usually it has, though not always the thing it prizes most highly. Our mission is to spread the gospel that in the democratic process we have found a universally applicable way of life; our youthful optimism and reformism makes us certain that sooner or later the world will accept it.

Older nations have accepted their function to influence and lead others as so natural and inevitable that they seldom think of it as a mission. The "mission civilisatrice" and "the white man's burden" therefore have been presented more as "destinies" than as "missions." Younger nations do not possess the same bland certainty and they search more consciously for something to give them significance. As early as 1650 Edward Johnson was regarding New England as the place "where the Lord would create a new heaven and a new earth, new churches and a new commonwealth together." A few years later William Stoughton noted that "God had sifted a whole nation that he might send choice grain into the wilderness." The Utopian view of America thus began with the Calvinists' belief that they were planting a City of God, and the idea has run all through American history.

The Revolutionary fathers of the United States did not always sense clearly the evolutionary method of democracy but they did believe that America had a mission. They had at first regarded it as their mission to preserve the liberties of both England and America or see them buried in a "common grave." But they grasped a new concept when Tom Paine in his *Common Sense* cried that "Freedom hath been hunted round the globe. . . . Receive the fugitive, and prepare in time an asylum for mankind." From that moment they saw America as destined to be the ark "in which all the liberty and true religion of the world are to be deposited." Washington's First Inaugural proclaimed that "the preservation of the sacred fire of liberty and the destiny of the republican model of government are . . . finally staked on the experiment entrusted to the hands of the American people." Jefferson frequently expressed his opinion that "the last hope of human liberty in this world rests on us." More than this, "we are destined to be a barrier against the return of ignorance and barbarism."

It was obvious to them that God had designed North America, or at least the better part of it which was bound together by the Mississippi River system, to be one nation. There was a smug sense of physical security. As that arch-Federalist, Timothy Dwight, put it in an optimistic moment:

> See this glad world remote from every foe,
> From Europe's mischiefs, and from Europe's woe.

The Calvinist concept of a chosen people flourished vigorously. "We are the peculiar people," said a Charleston editorial writer in 1845, "chosen of the Lord to keep burning the vestal flame of Liberty, as a light unto the feet and a lamp unto the path of the benighted nations, who yet slumber or groan under the bondage of tyranny." This was uttered in blank disregard of the existence in Charleston itself of a class which "slumbered or groaned" under the bondage of slavery! As levelheaded a man as Lincoln shared the sentiment. The Declaration of Independence, said he, gave "hope for the world for all future time. It was that which gave promise that in due time the weights should be lifted from the shoulders of all men, and that all should have an equal chance."

It is obvious that however sincerely Americans have held to their sense of a mission, and however significant and useful a factor that mission may be in world history, it nevertheless rose not solely from our security but from our insecurity. Separated from the main stream of Western Civilization, we sought a means of unifying ourselves around a concept that would give us world significance. Because we were rootless we had to build our own contribution, and we found it in the glorification of our free and equal institutions. One cannot read widely in American history without being struck by the real anxiety in every time of crisis lest democracy be stamped out and the hope of the world vanish with it.

The means of implementing the American mission has been a fruitful source of contention throughout our history, though never more than it is today. It would be too much to ask for consistency, for other factors always entered into the individual's attitudes toward the problem. One school has insisted that it was our business to evolve the democratic way in isolation, to afford an example which the world could follow when it came to its senses. J. Q. Adams expressed this in unequivocal language.

"America goes not abroad in search of monsters to destroy. She is the well-wisher to the freedom and independence of all. She is the champion and vindicator only of her own. She will recommend the general cause by the countenance of her voice and the benignant sympathy of her example. She well knows that by once enlisting under other banners than her own, were they even the banners of foreign independence, she would involve herself beyond the power of extrication in all the wars of interest and intrigue, of individual avarice, envy and ambition, which assume the colours and usurp the standards of freedom. The fundamental maxims of her policy would insensibly change from liberty to force."

This aloofness has at times taken on the character of Pharisaism: one of the defenses of isolationism was that we could not afford to soil our pure democratic robes by intimate contact with the wicked world.

The expansionists of the nineteenth century accepted the isolationist view with the amendment that we must expand in order to build a country strong enough to defend democracy, and that we must be ascendant in this hemisphere in order to insulate democracy from effective attack. Before the Civil War, Southern expansionists argued quite sincerely that since America was democratic the expansion of slave territory meant the expansion of freedom. Toward the end of the century the insulationists were to be challenged by a third school which advocated an active crusade on behalf of democracy and presently came out for international co-operation.

VIII

Engines of Democracy

THE groping so evident among the American intellectuals of the middle of the nineteenth century was also partly due to the early phases of a dilemma which was not to become clear until our own century. Here we can only forecast what we will analyze at length later on. The American *vernacular,* or native workmanship, was finding expression in the artifacts of the American artisan and in the functionalism of the new machines. On the other hand, European art was rooted in the cultivated tradition which had developed with more or less symmetry from classical times to the Industrial Revolution. The two were quite incompatible, and each stubbornly refused to give way; it was in effect a struggle between the aristocratic élite of the cultivated tradition and the democratic vernacular which sought to exploit the machine to defeat the élite and elevate the masses. The first promised static order; the latter threatened change with all its danger of bringing on chaos. We know that status sooner or later brings revolution, but that was not so apparent to men in 1850. Hence, American intellectuals were torn between the supposed security of status and the democratic demand for change.

It is a general misapprehension among Americans that historically we have been the most inventive of nations. This is not quite true. Nor have we been until this century a leading scientific nation: American history before 1900 offers only three notable "pure scientists"— Benjamin Franklin, Joseph Henry, and Willard Gibbs. The word *invention* has several meanings. It may, as is popularly supposed, refer to the sudden production of something new and useful. It may refer to a process to which numerous men each add a little, a process that may take many generations. Again, invention may refer to carefully planned and integrated technical research and experiment by a team or corps of men.

Inventions are of two kinds: basic inventions and improvement inventions. In the beginning it is likely that both were the result of accident or of a technique of trial-and-error made necessary by ignorance of scientific principles. The Greeks, however, made some inventions by consciously applying scientific truths, and in modern times this method has become much more common. Nowadays the creation of useful machines and processes usually comes through three steps: the pure scientist discovers the principles; the inventor combines and applies them; and the engineer-technologist adapts and refines the invention. Indeed, the two last steps may sometimes be identical, for very often the inventor is simply an engineer or chemist with an imaginative and experimental flair. It is in the third step, that of technology, that the United States has historically held primacy, though it also has a proud record in the second. Many of our supposed inventions were really engineering refinements of inventions already made abroad; among these were the steamboat, the cotton gin, the rotary press, and the automobile.

Though many improvement-inventions are made by men who are conscious of the needs, it would be an error to suppose that mere need is enough to bring forth the mechanical solution. The Roman Empire had dire need of efficient and speedy transportation and communication, but the steamship, railroad, and telegraph failed to appear, and the empire broke up. It is a common saying that necessity is the mother of invention; in more cases invention is the mother of necessity, for the invention brings such changes in society and economy that it cannot be dispensed with.

The need for inventions cannot be perceived, nor can the invention be made until the component parts have been invented. This fact is so clear that inventions seem almost to be plucked from the atmosphere of the time. Many inventions are duplicated in two or more places by the work of men or teams who have never heard of each other. The classic example is that of Elisha Gray, whose *caveat* on the method of the telephone reached the patent office only two hours after the application for a patent on the completed invention was filed by Alexander Graham Bell. Modern inventions do not necessarily improve the quality of the work; metallurgical products are superior, but some other articles—such as linens and cut gems—are no better now than they were in ancient Egypt. The principal effects are social and economic in as much as modern methods reduce costs and increase production.

Most of the inventions fundamental to early nineteenth-century industry were a part of our European heritage or were imported soon after they were made. The steam engine, based on principles familiar from the time of the ancient Greeks, was utilized in simple forms in France and England for pumping water from mines. The invention, in fact, was essential to the coal-mining industry, for otherwise mines were invariably flooded and rendered useless. James Watt, a Scottish instrument maker, turned the simple mine engine into a mighty force by adding the condenser, the steam jacket, and the cylinder head, all of them patented in 1769. Textile machinery was the work of a series of brilliant English inventors. Machine tools had made headway on the European continent after 1450 but were vastly improved in England, largely due to the necessity for precision work in the building of steam engines. English industry was built chiefly on steam power; that of the United States chiefly on water power, at least in the early stages. The long dominance of water power made New England a permanent industrial area and has infected the American engineer with a yearning to harness rivers and waterfalls even when they are not the cheapest source of motive power.

Americans have long been justly famed for mechanical ingenuity; most significant have been the contributions of New England, which, because it was not well adapted to agriculture, had taken up wood and metal working, and where machinery of a sort had been in use almost from the time of settlement. Even before the Revolution the British prohibition of the export of iron-working machinery threw Americans in that industry on their own resources. After independence Parliament not only widened the embargo on machinery and plans but forbade the emigration of mechanics. Americans were thus stimulated to make their own developments, and with certain important exceptions technical progress was of native growth up to about 1840.

America was a raw continent, with all the heavy work of building a civilization to be done and but few inhabitants to do it; in these straits it was perhaps natural for an American to see the uses of steam in lifting, moving, hauling, sawing, crushing, and grinding. Oliver Evans, a mill mechanic in the wheat region along the Delaware River, saw that Watt's low-pressure engine did not generate enough power to perform heavy duties, and so in the 1780's he worked out plans for a high-pressure engine. This engine he adapted to many practical uses. One of them was to power a new series of machines which revolutionized the flour-milling industry by making it all but completely automatic. Though investors were in no haste to avail themselves of the fruits of Evan's genius, he persevered. On one occasion in 1804, in order to move a steam dredge, he actually built a steam-driven machine which not only traveled over land but took to the water and paddled to its destination.

One of the earliest and most significant American inventions was the cotton gin, or engine. British improvements in textile machinery had caused an unprecedented demand for cotton; the trouble was that there was no efficient means of separating seeds and fiber. Much cotton was cleaned by hand, though a crude roller gin (*churka*) had been brought from India by way of Brazil or the West Indies and was useful in seeding the long-staple (black seed) sea-island cotton grown on the coastal islands. Unfortunately short-staple (or green seed) cotton, which adhered to the rough seeds, was the only kind that would grow inland, and the roller gin did not clean it efficiently. In 1793 Eli Whitney, a Connecticut Yankee on a visit to South Carolina, invented the spike-toothed cotton gin, which successfully cleaned inland cotton. The machine was so simple that he could not successfully defend his patents, and he eventually returned to New England and took up gun manufacturing.

The effect of Whitney's gin on history has been tremendous. Cotton had never been an important crop in the Thirteen Colonies, and as late as 1794 John Jay agreed not to export cotton—apparently ignorant of the fact that it was grown in the United States! Not only did the production of short-staple cotton now leap, but it became the economic basis of most of the South and put the profits back into slavery, which had apparently been a dying institution. The result was the Cotton Kingdom, a powerful agricultural domain devoted to slavery and to political reaction, which was regarded by its enemies as a dragon blocking the path of progress. The greatest internal crisis in American history was the result.

The first half of the nineteenth century saw the groundwork laid for the later development of American mass production. Most significant features of the new era were the adoption of power to machinery, the amazing growth of the use of machine tools, the invention of the principle of the interchangeable part, and the utilization of semiskilled labor. The last three developments were chiefly the work of a galaxy of New Englanders, most of them gunmakers of Massachusetts and Connecticut. Though the interchangeable part had been used in England in making marine blocks and in France for muskets, it was not carried to perfection. Eli Whitney and Simeon North separately worked out the principle in their gun factories about 1800. Whitney, however, showed more genius as both an inventor and an organizer.

Before he turned out a single weapon he spent two years at his factory near New Haven, building special machines and training green workmen to do specific jobs. Then one day late in 1800 he dumped a box of parts upon the office floor of the Secretary of War and picking them up at random put together ten muskets, which stood the tests.

Other gunsmiths prominent in the machine-tool business were Thomas Blanchard, inventor of the copying lathe for making articles of eccentric shape, such as gun stocks; Samuel Colt, inventor (or at least perfecter) of the revolver; and Elisha King Root, an associate of Colt, who perfected the drop hammer and the die forge and also designed numerous other tools. Equally important in developing the machine tools of the textile industry was David Wilkinson of Pawtucket, brother-in-law of Samuel Slater, the Englishman who set up the first successful power spinning machines in New England.

The names of inventors and improvers could be greatly extended; suffice it to say that long before the Civil War the machines of New England were pouring forth a steady stream of bolts, nails, tacks, screws, wire, small tools, and other objects too numerous to mention. The crowning achievements of Yankee ingenuity were the turret lathe, the grinding machine, and the universal milling machine; with these it was possible to attain automatically a precision hitherto undreamed of. One amusing illustration of the growing significance of American industry will serve to illuminate the whole. Before the 1830's wooden clocks had cost five dollars and metal clocks as much as fifty, but in 1838 Chauncey Jerome of Connecticut utilized the system of interchangeable parts to produce brass clocks which could sell for fifty cents. When a shipment of his cheap clocks reached England the British customs official, thinking that he was trying to beat down the amount of the duty, decided to punish him by buying in the clocks at the invoice price of $1.50 apiece. Jerome was delighted and sent another shipment. It was also seized and prompt payment made. It was not until the third shipment of brass clocks arrived at the same low invoice price that the British discovered that they had been had by the Yankee clockmaker.

The conquest of distance was on the whole the most serious problem that confronted Americans, for the United States was not compact like England or France but even in its infancy sprawled over nearly a million square miles. Roads received little attention in the colonial period and were, according to season, streaks of heavy dust or quagmires, and unbelievably rough and dangerous. Travelers in the East, if they were wise, moved from city to city by packet sloops. Freight, of course, was carried by sea far more quickly and cheaply than by road. Industrial growth in all parts of the country was clearly doomed to be limited until some means was found of carrying on cheaply and efficiently the necessary interchanges of manufactures and agricultural products. The existence of numerous navigable rivers in most parts of the country suggested the development of boats propelled by steam engines. John Fitch, John Stevens, and Robert Fulton were the pioneers in this endeavor. Stevens was also an early experimenter with the steam locomotive. By the 1840's the railroads were creeping toward the Appalachian Mountains and during the next decade they began to divert Western products from their old course down the Ohio and Mississippi and to pour them into the ports of the Northeast. The Erie Canal which had begun that movement in the 1820's and had boomed New York City was now permanently eclipsed.

The childlike eagerness with which technical advances and new products are now received by the general public is in striking contrast to its former attitude. In 1807 Fulton was called a fool for insisting that he could propel a boat by steam; it would be a hardy skeptic now who would deny that men may soon set foot on the moon. Many people, gullible enough in other ways, sought to show their sound sense by guffawing at nearly every attempt at basic technological improvements. The railroad was opposed because trains scared horses and prevented cows from letting down their milk, and sparks set fire to crops and forests. There was, moreover, a perceptible opinion that if the Lord had intended men to travel in this outlandish fashion he would have equipped them with wheels, steam engines, and bells. Not only did people oppose inventions because of inertia, but religious, social, and economic training made many suspicious of any change that threatened vested interests—not merely vested financial interests but vested interests in established prejudices and opinions, and in social position or prestige, actual or hoped for. Even the tolerant and intelligent did not always understand what was going on. In 1838 the chief clerk in the Patent Office resigned. His reason was that steam and electricity were the ultimate secrets of nature; all inventions worth making had been made, and he wished to find a job with a future!

*   *   *

The merchant capitalist was primarily a trader and financier. His traditional interest in speculation and place utility was shown by his investments in turnpikes, canals, river steamboats, and railroads. True, he financed some production, but he did it with little vision. Country people produced surpluses of homespun or barrel staves over what they needed, and such surpluses were collected by the merchant and traded in the city or in foreign parts. Such people were encouraged to produce greater surpluses, and sometimes they became "cottage" workers chiefly engaged in the production of handmade articles such as textiles, shoes, hats, and nails. The next stage brought the mill, which performed by machine one or more of the steps in hand manu- facture. Thus, Slater's spinning mill in Pawtucket was operated by children who spun thread which was used by their parents in cottage weaving. Just as typical was the system of payment in kind, which had been handed down from time immemorial and which was a real service in rural vicinities, but which came to be resented as giving the merchant capitalist two profits. These methods were dominant at least until 1850. The factory with its integration of the manu- facture of the finished product in one continuous, supervised opera- tion was the exception until the Civil War suddenly called into use the technologies which had been developing.

British economic theorists, convinced that their country, because of its resources and its early start, was destined to monopolize world manufactures, heartily agreed with Adam Smith's dictum that in- dustry should be permitted to develop where it had the natural ad- vantages. Southerners approved of this doctrine of laissez faire, since it meant that they should buy their goods in the cheapest markets. The would-be manufacturers of the North and West, however, were aghast, and sought to find some way of thwarting Adam Smith. Hamil- ton came to their rescue in his *Report on Manufactures;* presently a school of economic writers began making the necessary amendments to the English economists chiefly by upholding the protective tariff.

Mathew Carey, a Philadelphia publisher who had been born in Ireland, wrote *Essays on Political Economy* (1822), in which he linked together the protective tariff and internal improvements at Federal expense and gave Clay the cue for the American System. Carey's son, Henry, followed in his footsteps. Friedrich List, a German resi- dent in Philadelphia during the 1820's, absorbed Mathew Carey's argument. When List returned to Germany he took with him the American economic doctrines, and they became a powerful factor in the growth of German industry and nationalism. Late in the century, partially transformed and very much criticized, they were returned to the United States and influenced the modern American science of economics.

Mathew Carey aimed at more than profits for manufactures or even national self-sufficiency. If democracy were to be realized, he held, it must offer wider opportunities. As the country then was, the ambitious young man was limited in choice to a few callings, and these could be increased only by trading simplicity for complexity. Wider opportunities could be created by industrialization, and that could come only when England's throttling hold on the American market was pried loose. Then talent and ingenuity would be rewarded, general prosperity enhanced, and personal life cultivated and enriched. Carey gave battle on multiple fronts. He attacked the smug conservatism of the merchant capitalist, the traditionalism of farmer and planter, and the desire of the industrial capitalist to keep benefits for himself rather than to share them with his employees.

Henry Carey was no less zealous and much more logical. Laws, he insisted, are unitary, so economic law must agree with moral law. Away with the Economic Man of the English school, devoid of altruism and shaped only to pursue wealth! To bring in the Real Man he proposed the "principle of association"—much the same as national planning—by which each nation should shake off the shackles of England and develop its own economy and culture. The mission of the United States was to hasten this day by its own example. Only when by such means the economic problems of humanity had been solved, could there ensue harmony of interests and the universal reign of tolerance, peace, and morals.

A considerable body of economists of our day believe that the United States would have won industrial power regardless of the Hamiltons, Careys, or Clays, simply because it had the resources and conditions.

(1) The American economic climate was capitalistic from the first. The weakness of state churches permitted freedom of education and thought. We had no guilds to monopolize crafts and to limit and control production, wages, and labor; on the other hand, we did have the psychology of Calvinism with its stimulus to industry, thrift, and initiative, its approval of wealth as a proof of righteousness, and its urge to remake society.

(2) American resources were so abundant that equality of opportunity

all but became a reality. Land, timber, and minerals were available almost as gifts, especially to the shrewd; and, since capital was scarce, most enterprisers were on a rock-bottom status of financial equality. It was personal qualifications (often including unscrupulousness) that brought success.

(3) From the time of the Revolution both state and Federal governments were shorn of their power to interfere with individual business. Government planning was abhorrent to all but a few theorists like Henry Carey and John Quincy Adams. The nationalist decisions of Marshall were chiefly aimed at undercutting the states' attempts to interfere with private business and at enhancing the Federal power to promote private business by granting gifts and privileges and setting up a national bank.

Mercantile organization was usually simple. Ventures too extensive for the resources of one merchant were undertaken by two or more in a partnership which might be confined to the one venture or prolonged for years. The joint-stock company was merely an undertaking with many partners, each of whom contributed a share of the capital and received a share of the profits. Merchandising, manufacturing, and private banking could be conducted by these private partnerships.

Presently, joint-stock companies sought state charters, which set them up as legal persons known as corporations. The form was of obvious value in such ventures as insurance companies, which required a longer span of life than it was likely the founders would enjoy. In addition they could sue and be sued as legal persons; management was simplified and placed under the control of the holders of a majority of the stock; and shares could be sold on the market and bonds floated. Scattered capital seeking investments which freed the owners from the cares of management now found entrance into banks, insurance and manufacturing companies, turnpikes, canals, and presently railroad companies.

*   *   *

Workingmen, especially in the cities, regarded themselves as very badly exploited, and perhaps they were in the light of what should have been. Still, their conditions, though far from enviable, were better than those in similar occupations in Europe. Wages which seemed low to Americans were eagerly accepted by immigrants, either because they were desperate or because the pay seemed generous. Foreigners, indeed, swamped the mill towns from the 1840's onward.

Irish laborers did the construction work of the country, even in the South, and in the seaports Irish and Negro dock workers fought for jobs. Organized labor did not get under way effectively until after the Civil War. There were numerous reasons. Public opinion opposed unions on the grounds that they raised prices and interfered with the owner's right to administer his own property; if a workingman was dissatisfied with his wages or conditions of labor, let him get another job or go west. In the beginning relations between employers and employees were close, and this closeness doubtless reduced friction. Nevertheless, labor organizations began to rise in the cities, usually confined to handicrafters such as the carpenters, printers, and cordwainers (shoemakers), but at first they were chiefly devoted to insurance benefits and only cautiously touched the problems of their relations with capital.

Labor organization entered a new phase in 1827, when the Philadelphia crafts set up a central association. The movement spread to other cities, and in several cases the city associations became the core of local political workingmen's parties. These flourished modestly in prosperous times, but scarcity of jobs during times of depression gave employers a weapon against them, and caused heavy mortality in the roster of party workers and voters and cut down the number of unions. Workingmen's political parties pushed many useful and much-needed reforms but were successful chiefly in promoting free public education, the abolition of imprisonment for debt, and the passage of mechanics' lien laws.

Presently there arose a demand for a shorter work day and for the regulation of the labor of women and children—chiefly from a desire to spread the work and to reduce the competition of women and children, though there was also a perceptible desire for more leisure for amusements, education, and home occupations and recreations. Eventually the ten-hour day was adopted in New Hampshire (1847) and Pennsylvania (1848); Massachusetts (1843) and Pennsylvania (1848) regulated the employment of children under twelve. The Federal government had also adopted the ten-hour day for its laborers and mechanics in 1840. Actually much of the credit for these advances must go to the Democratic Party, for its leaders sought to absorb the workingmen's parties by adopting selected parts of their program.

The most significant labor advance, however, was made against the law of conspiracy. The tide began to turn in 1842 when the supreme court of Massachusetts under Chief Justice Lemuel Shaw, in the case of *Commonwealth v. Hunt,* reversed the direction of judicial treatment of labor. The Boston cordwainers had struck to impose a closed shop, and the commonwealth had taken legal action against them. By the decision labor unions were accepted as lawful in so far as their means were "fair or honorable and lawful"; the strike was declared a lawful weapon for gaining a closed shop and better wages and working conditions; and it was held that union members could not be held collectively responsible for the unlawful acts of individual members. It was an epochal decision and gradually won acceptance over the nation.

IX

The Southern Search for a Veto

THE older historians viewed sections primarily as ideological alliances, but Frederick Jackson Turner demonstrated that they were and are at bottom economic and cultural areas. During the two generations before the Civil War the sections of the new nation took various and sometimes shifting stands on the great questions of the tariff, internal improvements at Federal expense, and the sale of the public domain at low prices to encourage rapid settlement of the wilderness. The 1830's saw a gradual coagulation of the sections. New England and the Middle Atlantic states found common interests. The Northwest's interest in general farming, lumbering, and incipient manufactures separated it from the Southwest where cotton culture and slavery were rising. By about 1840 the South and the Southwest had moved to undertake a common defense of cotton, slavery, and free trade. Nevertheless the three emergent sections were so nearly balanced that agricultural interests in South and Northwest were able to ally to rein the ambitions of the industrialists of the Northeast. At the same time a network of canals and railways were slowly diverting Northwestern commerce from New Orleans to the Atlantic ports and promising to weld Northeast and Northwest into the North.

The sectional struggle was the opportunity and the Nemesis of ambitious politicians. Jackson clinched his rule by breaking down the Bank of the United States and minimizing the issue of internal improvements and the protective tariff. When South Carolina rejected the nationalist program, John C. Calhoun, its most brilliant political leader, was forced to choose between changing his principles or leaving politics. It was probably the bitterest choice an American politician ever had to make, but his roots were in his section and held him there. He did the best he could to show that he had wanted and still wanted a *reasonable* tariff, but the northern trend was against him; he saw himself isolated with his section, and his ambition to become President ended in bitter disappointment.

The Census of 1790 showed that population was almost evenly

divided between North and South. The latter, indeed, profited by the Three-Fifths Ratio and expected population growth to place control of the Union in its hands; otherwise, as some candid souls admitted, the South would not have approved the Constitution. By 1840 the inferiority of the South in population and economic power had become plain as a pikestaff, and was resulting in Southern defensiveness and in a search for a means of protecting its interests.

Though aristocrats and "cotton snobs" may have been socially and economically ascendant, the yeoman farmers had been strengthened by the Jacksonian movement and their political power had to be reckoned with. Nevertheless the South was fundamentally united by a common acceptance of belief in white superiority and Negro inferiority, by allegiance to localism—or at the widest, sectionalism—and by faith in the power of "King Cotton." The South held the fantastic belief that only its cotton had made possible the movement toward industrialization and a higher standard of living recently evident in Western Civilization. It even went so far as to hold that it had a natural monopoly on the growth of cotton and could dictate its own terms to the textile manufacturers of Europe and the United States. "Cotton is King" became the watchword of the South, and it was asserted that the fall of textiles would bring down the entire industrial structure and involve the world in ruin.

Of course, this does not tell the whole story. The Southern way of life had a special attraction for all classes, each after its own fashion, but with certain fundamental values in common. It was these values that helped to balance the picture of economic loss in the minds of individuals. They believed that the unique rural civilization of the South had stemmed from England, but that it had been improved and stabilized by the new milieu. To the more obvious joys of politics, hunting, and social gatherings they added the rich texture of days passed in unhurried pursuit of business or in frankly relaxed leisure. "Southrons" saw themselves as individuals first, and only secondarily as members of society, and they took such pride in this attitude that they held an erroneous picture of the Northerner as a wage slave, a mere robot. Only Southerners knew how to "live," and they regarded any change as dangerous to their perfect existence.

The South clearly had a poorly balanced economy, and most of its ills rose from this fact. Since cotton's margin of profit was narrow, it had to exploit the soil and go on to new; when suitable cotton lands were used up, disaster was sure to follow, barring the little-expected

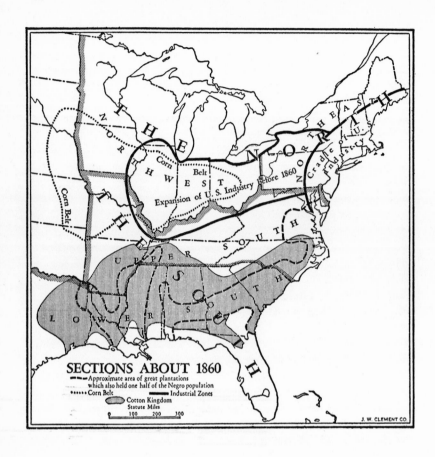

SECTIONS ABOUT 1860

‑ ‑ ‑ Approximate area of great plantations
        which also held one half of the Negro population
•••••• Corn Belt   ———— Industrial Zones
        Cotton Kingdom
        Statute Miles
        0   100   200   300

J. W. CLEMENT CO.

interposition of science. The planter was extravagant, and low prices merely spurred him on to greater production. The cotton planter was over-capitalized, but he could not easily reduce his labor force. Even if he were willing to defy social taboos and go into manufacture or transportation, he would have found it difficult to transfer his capital; and in any case the result would have been to undermine the way of life of which Southerners were so proud. It was begging the question to lay the entire blame for the South's economic subservience upon either slavery or exploitation by Northern industrialists and merchants. It was a Gordian knot which could be done away with only by the sword of a Grant or by the passage of time.

*   *   *

The new significance of slavery forced its first clear entry into politics when the South backed Missouri's demand for admission to the Union as a slave state. The Missouri Compromise (1820) divided the public domain between slavery and freedom on what was at the time regarded as an equitable basis. Proslavery sentiment was now firmly established, and when in 1825 eight Northern state legislatures proposed emancipation at Federal expense, the plan was harshly rejected by the South. From now on the South devoted itself to: (1) the search for some Constitutional means of guarding its special interests; (2) the moral defense of its special interests; and (3) the stabilization of the *status quo*.

The Southern search for a Constitutional means of guarding its special interests passed through four stages; (1) local self-government, or state rights; (2) the concurrent voice; (3) Constitutional guarantees; and (4) independence. The weapon of local self-government was wielded by the states either in single or group opposition to the Federal government. State rights were never invoked in a vacuum, that is, they received little allegiance as mere abstract principles unconnected with practical problems. If any state or section was politically ascendant, it saw its interests as those of the nation and was inclined to be nationalist; if it was out of power, it tended to uphold state rights as a protection against the tyranny of the majority.

The eminent Virginian political writer, John Taylor of Caroline, rejected Jefferson's concept of conflict between balanced social forces and depended upon the states' holding the balance between a selfish financial aristocracy in control of the central government on the one hand and the chaotic tendencies of the people on the other. The

Constitution was a compact between the states, and the latter were the judges of its terms. Taylor authored a stream of books, articles, and pamphlets, but the most significant in his later career was *Construction Construed and Constitutions Vindicated* (1820), which countered implied powers with the compact theory and asserted that the real issue in the Missouri controversy was the balance of power between the sections. This was followed in 1822 by *Tyranny Unmasked,* a prolix argument against the protective tariff and its creation of an industrial and financial monopoly.

Taylor adapted *American Physiocracy* to the plantation system. It opposed tariffs, banks, and "paper wealth" and rapidly approached Athenian democracy—a society of aristocrats (or at least privileged citizens) erected on an economy of slavery. As the common interests of the Southern states drew them together to resist Northern attacks, the localism of Jefferson and the compact theory of John Taylor were united into a dogma which a group of embittered Southerners, led by John Randolph, preached in Congress and spread throughout the South at dinners, barbecues, and private gatherings. The rise of the young nationalists during and after the War of 1812 drew the "Antique Republicans" of the South into a desperate little band of "statriots" determined to sell their lives dearly. Actually the economic and psychological tides of the South were running in their favor. The tobacco and cotton kingdoms were drawn together, and the latter took command. South Carolina leadership supplanted Virginia, but it was not until Calhoun was driven over to the ranks of the localists by the events of Jackson's first administration that the faction was able to develop the discipline of a party and the dynamism of a political program. To be sure, Calhoun was defending a status, but in the process he became probably the only really original political theorist of the so-called middle period of American history. His chief works are the *South Carolina Exposition,* published anonymously in 1828, and the *Disquisition on Government* and the *Discourse on the Constitution,* not published until after his death.

The freedom of the ballot, said Calhoun, was no guarantee of liberty, for it instituted the tyranny of the *numerical majority.* Only when every interest exercised a check on the others and decisions were watered down and compromised until they satisfied all, only then was there a *concurrent majority,* the one effective guarantee against a tyranny. Every public decision must be tailored to the satisfaction of the minority, not of the majority. No majority (meaning the North) could institute a policy such as the protective tariff, which injured the interests—which might merely mean desires—of a considerable minority (meaning the South). To prevent such injury the minority was entitled to "a concurrent voice in making and executing the laws, or a veto on their execution." The veto could be overcome only if the minority upon reflection and investigation withdrew it. The concurrent voice has reappeared in our own day, first in Wilson's idea of the self-determination of peoples, and more strongly in the veto in the United Nations. The concurrent voice is the weapon of a minority not simply to protect its rights but to enforce its will.

The concurrent voice found practical expression in the unwritten law which arose from the Missouri Compromise that there must be a balance between slave and free states so that one might check the other in the Senate. There was still the menace of a Northern President, and this Calhoun proposed to meet by having a dual executive, two Presidents, one from each section, and each entitled to disallow the acts of the other and to veto Congressional legislation. However, the specific mechanism which Calhoun proposed to use in finding the concurrent voice or in interposing the veto he called "nullification"; and while he may not have been its inventor, he certainly ranks as its greatest champion.

Any state which felt that its interests were being injured by Federal acts or legislation should call a special state convention which could declare the obnoxious acts or legislation null and void within its borders. The Federal government could (1) yield and withdraw the offense, or (2) propose a Constitutional amendment giving to itself the disputed power. If the amendment were rejected by the states, the Federal government could not exercise the power. If it were accepted, the objecting state would be overruled; it must submit or consider the course of secession from the Union. Thus, said Calhoun, the creators of the Constitution (the signers of the compact) decided what it meant. Actually the decision was to be made by a minority composed of one fourth of the states plus one, the number necessary to defeat an amendent. The South would have a permanent strangle hold on the Union, which was what Calhoun basically desired, whether or not he saw it in those terms.

When South Carolina in 1832 declared the tariff of that year null and void, and forced upon the Federal government a compromise that was almost humiliating, the protective tariff began a thirty-year retreat which was stopped only by the Civil War. The rise of the abolition movement did much to convert the leaders of the Cotton States which had not supported South Carolina in 1832. In their distress Southern leaders who loved the Union began increasingly to look upon Calhoun as their strategist in command of a campaign to save the Union without sacrificing Southern Rights.

The South was indeed confronted by the necessity of choosing between the horns of a dilemma, with the certainty that either one would fatally pierce its heart. In the North the Hamiltonians and Jacksonians were carrying on the conflict from which modern America was to emerge. Southern leaders, though they favored aristocratic and property privileges, could not bring themselves to support the Northern Whigs with their mercantilism and loose construction of the Constitution. On the other hand, they could not stomach the democracy and reformism of the Democrats though their sympathies as agrarians lay with that party. In the end Calhoun chose the agrarian Democrats, but stipulated that democracy and reformism must be hushed up in the interests of political spoils and Southern security. The Democratic Party became essentially the prisoner and the tool of proslavery interests.

The Mexican War, as Calhoun bitterly foresaw, intensified the sectional struggle. It owed its origin partly to the Southern demand for fresh lands, but Northern abolitionists and free farmers did their best to keep those lands from being dedicated to slavery. The concurrent voice lost its last defense when in 1850 California came into the Union as a free state and thus destroyed the balance in the Senate. The Compromise of 1850, however, gave to the South certain guarantees of the existing status, and in the Dred Scott Decision of 1857 the Supreme Court took the side of the South. Southern leaders put their hope in Constitutional guarantees and fought to maintain national parties as opposed to sectional. With the rise of the Republican Party with its leaning toward industry and its opposition to the extension of slavery to the territories it became evident that a sectional party, devoted to the destruction of these guarantees, was gaining ground. With the Republican capture of the presidency in 1860 the South seized its last and sharpest weapon: secession.

If southern extremists were determined to dominate the Union or leave it, Northern extremists were just as determined to dominate the South and force it to remain in the Union. It is true that a few abolitionists of the Garrison school were willing to break up the Union, but the vast majority of abolitionists favored no such symbolic washing of hands but proposed to eradicate the sin of slavery by fair means or foul. Free-soilers, a little less concerned with sin than with economics, were not so much worried by slavery in the states as by its extension. Abolitionists and free-soilers together formed a mighty army devoted to Union and willing to mix their blood with its cement.

The South's support of slavery was solidified by the rise of cotton, but it was the black abolitionist angel that stirred the economic and social waters into moral motion. It is now less than two centuries since any important segment of mankind began to look upon human slavery with any appreciable degree of abhorrence. Granted that it is morally reprehensible in our modern context, the fact remains that the nations were not willing to part with the institution until it had become unprofitable or interfered with profits in some ways. Even Northern sentimentalists waited until then to make their monumental discovery that slavery in one part of the nation interfered with the proper working of democracy everywhere.

In the great days of antislavery agitation there was a sentimental tendency to see slaves only where slavery existed in *legal* form. Actually slavery can take other forms: social, economic, political, and psychological. The South, in defending legal Negro slavery, was quite correct in pointing out that the North held slaves as truly even if not as obviously in the persons of apprentices, many wage earners, and women who did not control their own lives and property. The fact that the Negro slave had a higher standard of living than many free white men was tossed aside by abolitionists on the ground that a man's economic condition meant nothing unless he had the political and civil rights to defend it. This fact was true, yet again the South was correct in pointing out that the North did not have clean hands, that Northern Negroes were the victims of all types of discrimination only a little less than Southern slaves.

*   *   *

A story is told about a party of Northerners who met in Paris at the close of the War between the States to celebrate their victory with those sentientious toasts characteristic of the day. Presently a Bostonian arose and in cultured accents offered the following:

"Here's to the United States, bounded on the north by British

America, on the south by Mexico, on the east by the Atlantic Ocean, and on the west by the Pacific."

Next came a Chicagoan. "My eastern friend has too limited a view," said he. "We must look to our Manifest Destiny. Here's to the United States, bounded on the north by the North Pole, on the south by the South Pole, on the east by the rising, and on the west by the setting, sun."

Prolonged and boisterous applause followed, but the next gentleman, a Californian, considered the toast too moderate. "With Manifest Destiny in our favor," he cried, "why limit ourselves so narrowly? I give you the United States, bounded on the north by the Aurora Borealis, on the south by the Precession of the Equinoxes, on the east by Primeval Chaos, and on the west by the Day of Judgment!"

The exuberance of the Californian typified the great era of American territorial expansion. The words Manifest Destiny seem to have been used first in July 1845 by John L. O'Sullivan, editor of the *Democratic Review* of New York, in an article on the Texas annexation question which decried the attempts of European powers to "check the fulfillment of our manifest destiny to overspread the continent allotted by Providence for the free development of our yearly multiplying millions." This was not by any means the origin of the *idea* of Manifest Destiny, for it infected the Revolutionary generation and played the major role in bringing on the War of 1812.

The new wave of territorial aggression, which began to rise in the 1830's and reached its crest with the Mexican War, reflected in its origins the growing complexity of the American scene. The movement was still basically agrarian. Of course, there was plenty of second-quality land left and, strictly speaking, Oregon and Texas were not needed yet. The planter wing of the agrarian imperialists feared that unless slave Texas were admitted the slave states would leave the Union and unite with Texas. Exponents of state rights felt that expansion and the admission of new states would weaken Federal power to interfere with local institutions, and they pointed out that the abolitionists, the foremost advocates of Federal aggrandizement, were the bitterest opponents of annexations. The proslave argument, offered without humor or intentional deceit, was that the expansion of slave territory would also expand the territory of freedom.

The second great cause of the resurgence of Manifest Destiny lay in fear: American fear of Europe and European fear of the United States. The chancellories of conservative Europe were fully aware of the sprawling inefficiency of the United States in its gawky democratic youth, but the lesson of the country's inherent power had been driven home by De Tocqueville's half-admiring, half-horrified, but altogether fascinated analysis of the American scene. The rising industry of the Northeast was regarded as a menace to Manchester and the industrial belt of Paris. The cold-eyed Yankee merchants of New York were molding a financial and commercial wall about the United States which Britishers would soon be unable to pass without their permission. The Cotton South was arrogantly boasting that it could at a word bring civilization down in chaos. Worst of all, the success of the American democratic experiment was encouraging restiveness of the European masses under their kings and nobility.

Just as strong was American fear of European interference. Industrialists feared direct competition. New York feared that Europe not only would breach its wall but would carve out private domains on the Pacific coast and in Latin America. The South feared that its rule of cotton would fall before the competition of the vast prospective cotton lands of a British-controlled Texas. Along with these separate fears went one which shook the nation. A threat to the United States or its welfare was a threat to the existence of democracy and to the American democratic mission. The very least to be expected, proslave men and abolitionists agreed, was the weakening of democratic purity. The welfare of democracy came first; this was the "higher law" of Manifest Destiny.

This view was supported by a series of curious rationalizations: democracy's rights were superior because it was democracy; the necessity for new lands gave a natural right to them and, moreover, Americans would make better use of them than their present barbarous owners; these lands were sparsely occupied, were contiguous to our borders, and were within our "natural" boundaries—boundaries which the God of Nature and of nations had marked for our own. The last argument soon developed until its advocates likened the growth of a human political society to the biological growth of plants and animals which ruthlessly overrun or devour weaker competitors. The resemblance to the philosophies of modern dictatorships cannot be escaped. It is a psychology which is common to nations which are building empires, along with the usual protraction that its political and economic and cultural institutions are superior to those of decadent peoples. From this was drawn the curiously inconsistent corollary that therefore it is the "duty" of the strong to "protect" the weak, to bring them the blessings of superior institutions, and to eliminate the international nuisances which exist in the behavior of primitive or decadent nations.

Europeans and Latin-Americans were dismayed by the remorseless progress of the American pioneers, so like the march of faceless and conscienceless soldier ants. Mexicans were particularly alarmed, and early analyzed to their own satisfaction the method of American advance by finding the common factors in the absorption of Louisiana, Natchez, Baton Rouge, Mobile, and finally Florida. Lucas Alamán, a leading conservative historian and statesman of Mexico, thus epitomized it before the movement for Texan independence and long before its greatest application in the "purchase" of 1848 from Mexico:

"They commence by entering the territory they covet, upon pretense of carrying on commerce, or of the establishment of settlements, with or without the consent of the government to which it belongs. The settlers grow, multiply, become the predominant party in the population, and as soon as a foundation is laid in this manner, they begin to set up rights which it is impossible to support in a serious discussion, and to bring forward ridiculous pretensions, founded upon historical facts which are admitted by nobody. . . . These pioneers excite, by degrees, movements which disturb the political state of the country in dispute. When things have come to this pass, the diplomatic management commences; the unrest they have excited in the territory in dispute, the interests of the settlers there, the incursions of adventurers and savages instigated by them, and the persistence with which the opinion is set up as to their right of possession, become the subjects of notes, full of expressions of justice and moderation, until, with the aid of other incidents, which are never wanting in the course of diplomatic relations, the desired end is attained of concluding an arrangement as hard on one party as it is advantageous to the other."

Here, then, were the two sides of Manifest Destiny. It is impossible to assess to each the exact justice of all the arguments. One thing sure is that no party, European, North American, or Latin-American, approached the court with the first requirement of equity, that is, with its own hands clean. Each party had its own "higher law," carefully tailored to its own needs, and insisted upon its priority. Now it so happens that such "higher laws" are in a practical sense enforced only by the judicial administration of the sword, hence one

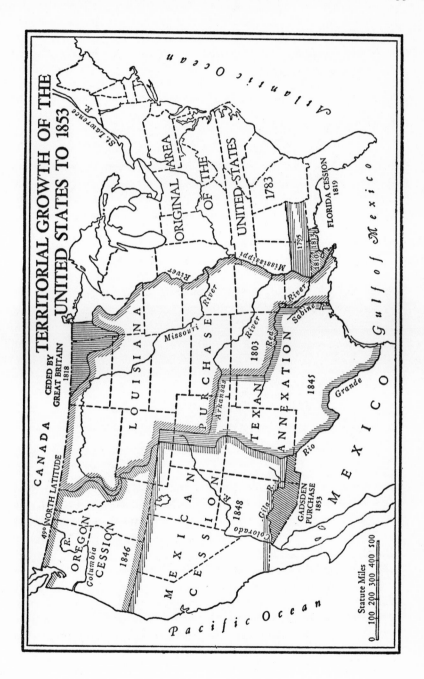

important cause of the Mexican War. It was in this process, however, that there arose within the United States a struggle over how the welfare of democracy was best to be promoted, and this is what turned the expansionist movement into a quarrel over slavery.

*   *   *

It has in considerable part been historians of Southern origin who have clarified the issues and introduced some measure of impartiality into the study of the causes of the Civil War. Their facts have been painfully winnowed and honestly weighed, yet the conclusions they have drawn have sometimes been curiously ambivalent. Southerners have been confronted by one embarrassing fact: the South's support of slavery was patently against developing moral standards. The result sometimes has been a strangely illogical denial that slavery could have been the cause of the Civil War. Slavery, they say, was the *symbol* of sectional conflict; the real subjects of strife were labor, race, and agrarianism.

Actually, however, it may be held that even with Negroes present in the United States, unless they had been slaves there would have been no plantation economy with its effective *American Physiocratic* opposition to industrialization and to the democratic process; no block to European immigration into the South; no alleged question of white supremacy or of a Negro social menace which would have brought war, for the North would not have gone to war to enforce race equality; and finally no crucial question of the extension of slavery to the territories. But since the Negro would not have been here except as a slave, it is almost impossible to imagine his racial influence up to 1865 apart from his status as slave.

Slavery—not simply the Negro, but the Negro as slave—was woven into every aspect of Southern life. Southernism and the Confederacy were based, as Alexander Stephens put it, on the "great truth" that slavery was the Negro's "natural and normal condition." The *primary* basis of sectional division was between slavery and freedom, not between agriculture and industry or white and black labor, nor from any deliberate Republican intention to menace white supremacy. This basis of division was well recognized before 1860. A nonslaveholder in the Kentucky Constitutional Convention of 1849 proclaimed that "Kentucky, sir, will be ready for emancipation when she is ready to cut loose all her feelings for the South."

Slavery, then, lay at the root, but it is not our concern to place the ultimate blame in a moral or causal sense on any section. If slavery was a sin, that sin lay at the door of both North and South. Our objective is to try to understand why the democratic process broke down. At the risk of oversimplification, let us note the basic contradictions between North and South. First, the North believed that slavery was the root of a menace to the democratic way of life, an attempt to override both the rights and the political majority of the free farmer and the growing industrialist. On the other hand, the South distrusted democracy because it ruled by majorities—or rather, the South defined democracy as based upon the concurrent majority, which of course put the whip in the hand of the minority. In a democracy, according to the Northern view, all subjects of dispute can be tossed into the political arena if they are not first settled otherwise. The South not only refused to yield to changing economic and moral standards but sought to prevent the submission of its "peculiar institution" and its results (such as the territorial issue) to the democratic process. The North, whether or not justly, felt that it was forced to organize a sectional political party which should bring the country up-to-date, not only on the slavery issue but in problems of governmental organization and finance, tariff, land, and education.

Second, the North saw a further menace in the South's denial of civil liberties. It is only just to say that most Northerners were but little concerned with the rights of the Negro *per se,* and some Northern state laws discriminated outrageously against the free Negro. The North's complaint, however, was that Southern actions against Negroes directly affected the civil liberties of whites, and cited a long list of cases in which (the North said) the South had in the more purely political sphere got its way or at least satisfactory compromises by threats of nullification and secession. Some observant Northerners were now convinced that the South would never be content until slavery was legalized in all the states. These interpretations were of course prejudiced, but nevertheless they reflected the solidifying Northern view that Calhoun's right of minority veto had developed popularly into a demand for minority rule.

Northern capitalists resembled the South in seeing democracy as based upon property, but they meant industrial property rather than land or slaves. To them democracy must guarantee the freedom of industrial property to multiply itself freely. They now began to see

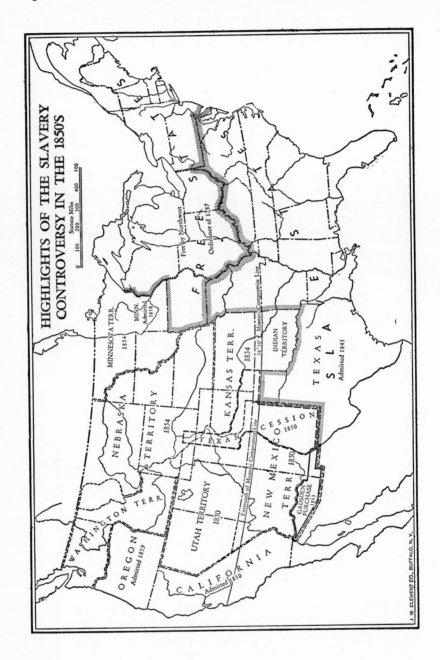

HIGHLIGHTS OF THE SLAVERY
CONTROVERSY IN THE 1850'S

Statute Miles
0   100   200   300   400   500

FREE BY NORTHWEST
Ordinance of 1787

MINNESOTA TERR.
1854

MINN.
Admitted
1858

NEBRASKA

TERRITORY
1854

KANSAS TERR.
1854

Missouri Compromise Line
36°30' Missouri Compromise Line

INDIAN
TERRITORY

TEXAS
SLAVE
Admitted 1845

WASHINGTON TERR.

OREGON
Admitted 1859

UTAH TERRITORY
1850

TEXAN   CESSION
1850

Extension of Missouri Compromise Line

NEW MEXICO
TERR. 1850

GADSDEN
PURCHASE
1853

CALIFORNIA
Admitted 1850

J. W. CLEMENT CO., BUFFALO, N.Y.

that it was not enough to assure Federal subsidies in the form of cheap raw materials, government-financed railroads, and protective tariffs, even where and if these could be obtained. These would be of limited use if the South and its farmer allies could interfere with the right of property to multiply itself freely. In other words, "due process of law" must be transformed from a mere guarantee of a fair trial to a substantive limitation of the power of both the states and the Federal government to interfere with the rights of property. Capital probably did not foresee the steps which it took, nor is it likely that it deliberately sought war. But when the Civil War came it saw how war could play into its hands, and presently it stumbled upon substantive due process of law as the answer to its need for freedom of property.

Third, the North saw in the Southern course a growing threat to the Union. Developing nationalism and democracy had become so intertwined in the North that most people in that section could not envisage the preservation of democracy without national supremacy. Northerners saw the United States as a democratic babe in the woods with the wolves of monarchism and authoritarianism howling for its blood; the view was essentially correct. They felt also that the United States had a mission to furnish an inspiration and an example to the world by fostering and developing democracy. At any rate, many profound and well-balanced American thinkers, while recognizing the shortcomings of our democracy, felt that Southern independence would be a fatal blow to any hope of a democratic future for the world. Successful secession would perhaps be the signal for the breakup of the Union into its component states or sections. At best the remaining Union would be so weakened and so discredited in the eyes of the world that democracy would lose its fighting chance for survival.

These were the bases of sectional controversy, but secession did not need to follow unless politicians and statesmen failed to find solutions. Their failure lay essentially in too great a reliance on the political Federalism of the Constitution of 1787. Americans of 1787 were but vaguely aware of the tremendous currents which were to sweep the world during the next two generations and thought of their problems in relatively simple economic and political terms. Their invention of the Federal system was of tremendous importance, but the framers of the Constitution left unsettled a host of problems because they were ignorant of them, could not agree upon solutions, or did not regard them as the concern of the convention.

One of the most serious questions concerned the nature of sovereignty. Was it divisible, as the Constitution seemed to imply? If not, where was the location of ultimate sovereignty—in the states or the Federal government? Was the Union a permanent national sovereignty or a temporary league of sovereign and independent states? In the answer lay the final decision as to the exact character and the permanent value of the Federal system. Until 1860 the Union managed to rock along by pretending that national and state sovereignty could exist on parallel lines. Einstein was yet to come, and the geometry of Euclid ruled.

In neither section, unfortunately, was there enough *effective* statesmanship to make political federation work by mapping out supplementary federations of economic, cultural, and emotional diversities. It was, unfortunately, the opportunity which extremists had long sought and which they had deliberately helped to create. Secession followed when they were joined by such men as Davis, who hoped to use secession as a weapon to force a re-formation of the Union. The parallelism of national and state sovereignties as apparently envisioned by the framers of the Constitution had broken down. The Euclidean dream was over; Abraham Lincoln, the Einstein of Federalism, announced that parallel lines do merge and that the nation was sovereign.

Effective statesmanship might still have found a way to save the Union without war and have afforded time for the slavery issue to settle itself. It is readily apparent that many of the subjects of sectional conflict were mere wish-fulfillments and at their most tangible were based on prejudiced views. Thus the economic, social, moral, and political factors may have been tinder to the fires of sectional war, but war was not in any practical sense irrepressible or inevitable. None of these problems was unsolvable by reasonable men. Indeed, the world before and since has seen similar bitter differences settled without war. The spark which turned sectional differences and secession into war must then be sought in another direction, the psychological.

American society wore a superficial air of broadclothed solemnity; men strutted behind an amusing variety of beard designs, spouted flowery clichés with hands smugly on hearts, leaned perilously on Latin quotations, and turned every puny public address into an impassioned oration on property, respectibility, constitutionality, and the American eagle and the British lion. And yet this owlish sedateness was easily dissolved into an emotionalism which might bring on a vulgar, belly-rending guffaw or a murderous stabbing affray between men rolling in the mud. The per-capita consumption of liquor was appalling, and even some revered statesmen almost invariably advanced from a genial glow at noon to a full conflagration at midnight. Liquor and custom and a semibarbaric demand for personal dominance led to amazingly sordid personal and political vilification, justified neither by truth nor expediency and hinging upon absurdly petty causes. The mortality among editors and politicians was something to consider before choosing those careers.

Southerners, especially, despite their self-bestowed reputation for good manners, their basic good-heartedness, and their loud-mouthed, backslapping good fellowship, were touchy and unpredictable. Northerners never knew just how to take them, for they were the most astute of political traders, claiming everything in sight, yielding a little to gain a lot, and often flying into a rage and proceeding to direct action when they lost an argument or perceived an obscure insult. They made their bewildered political opponents and finally the entire Northeast skittish at every proposition; the Southern version of the situation, naturally, was that the Yankees were trading and squeezing the South out of everything worth having—and beyond cavil, some of them were doing their best at it.

In those days Americans took their politics seriously, perhaps because there were fewer rival amusements. What with local, state, and Federal elections, there were mass meetings, resolutions, barbecues, banquets, and toasts in almost any month of the year, the more so because elections were not concentrated as they are now but were spread out so as to occur perhaps as often as twice a year. Not only was this the result of the search for the entertainment of speeches and parades, but there was an almost savage faith in annual elections as the safeguard of democracy. Politics was poorly articulated: national parties were little more than state alliances and localities and states were able to make supposed national elections the vehicle for local feuds.

Elections, as 1860 proved, thus hinged so often on local problems and animosities that they were poor indexes of popular attitudes toward national issues. The unfortunate result of all these conditions was the continual exacerbation of party feeling. There was no way in which issues could lie fallow while the electorate considered them calmly. Debates on slavery or its related problems only confirmed prejudices and rubbed salt on unhealed wounds. "Reactions," as Avery O. Craven says repeatedly, "were more important than realities." Each side stubbornly interpreted every action as an assault upon its rights, and with this attitude came unreasoning confusion, prejudice, and finally, fear.

A pointed illustration, which might be multiplied on both sides, was Robert Toombs's speech in Congress in 1850. "We have the right," he taunted the North, "to call on you to give your blood to maintain the slaves of the South in bondage! Deceive not yourselves; you cannot deceive others. This is a proslavery government. Slavery is stamped on its heart!" Of course, he was saying that the North must help to preserve not only Southern property rights but that social order which (he presumed) could be maintained only by slavery. But he was casting the helplessness of the North into its teeth, glorying that the South held the whip hand. Of course, on the other hand, Benton offered his breast to the leveled pistol of Foote; and Thaddeus Stevens spoke iron-faced in the House, lashing the "slavocracy" with the scorpions of his scorn while Southerners surrounded his desk, cursing and snarling but fearing to break through his bodyguard, the gigantic Roscoe Conkling of New York. Such episodes as these helped to convince the self-righteous partisans of each section that their opponents were not so much fearful of losing their rights as bent on domination.

The essential immediate cause of the Civil War lay in fear, deliberately induced fear which promoted in both sides a stubborn self-righteousness which created a political hotbox. Politics became so heated that it lost its ability to function in its true sphere: the compromise and solution of conflicts. It failed to prevent economic and social factors from being transposed into moral principles. For this failure we can blame the extremists of both sides. They knew perfectly well that principles cannot be compromised, so they made it their object to convince the public that they were championing eternal moral standards.

Unfortunately conditions and events played into their hands. Their activities present an instructive warning of the way in which two stubborn extremes can wear away the moderate center and precipitate an entirely unnecessary conflict. Each demanded a complete surrender and refused to let the issue die with anything else. The discontented, whatever the source of their discontent, were convinced by specious but plausible arguments that the other extreme was to blame. Lurid novels, poems, anecdotes, and even nursery rhymes and arithmetic problems were summoned to the aid of editors and evangelical orators as propaganda of self-righteousness and fear and hatred. Worst—and most powerful argument of all—the Deity was summoned through the Bible to give witness for and against slavery, and the followers of the meek and lowly Jesus split into mutually hateful denominations on the issue. Finally as each partisan presentation failed to convince the opposition, the sense of moral outrage and sectional injury mounted and emotions spiraled until a tension was built up which was exploded by the attack on Fort Sumter.

*   *   *

The Civil War has been called the ridgepole and the watershed of American history. Examination of most of the currents of national life shows that they led, whether or not inevitably, to that grand climax. It is no less clear that the great problems and movements of American life in the last three generations have flowed out of the dislocations of that war and its aftermath or taken form because of the decisions made then. On the other hand the drama of war and reconstruction has tended to obscure the fact that the same social, economic, and political reforms might have been made by peaceful methods without bringing desolation and sectional hatreds in their train. That would have been the democratic method. Such thoughts as these must have been in the mind of the poet when he sang his requiem over the grave of the fallen Confederacy.

> Bury the bygone South.
> Bury the minstrel with the honey-mouth,
> Bury the broadsword virtues of the clan,
> Bury the unmachined, the planters' pride,
> The courtesy and the bitter arrogance,
> The pistol-hearted horsemen who could ride
> Like jolly centaurs under the hot stars.
> Bury the whip, bury the branding-bars,
> Bury the unjust thing
> That some tamed into mercy, being wise,
> But could not starve the tiger from its eyes
> Or make it feed where beasts of mercy feed.

Bury the fiddle-music and the dance,
The sick magnolias of the false romance
And all the chivalry that went to seed
Before its ripening.

—Stephen Vincent Benét, *John Brown's Body*

Whatever might have been, the fact remains that there was a Civil War and there was a Reconstruction period, and both were instruments of change. Most obvious result was the amendment by arms of the Constitution to the effect that the Federal government was supreme—that a state could not secede. True, the doctrine of state rights remained an issue and still does, but there is no longer a question of where ultimate sovereignty resides. At the same time the question of allegiance was settled. The old state pride lingers here and there, but in the long run the first allegiance of the American is to the nation, not to the state.

Inalienably linked to the prosecution of the war was the tightening of Federal controls. This was inevitable, for it was the task of the Federal government to organize the nation for war and to suppress treasonable movements within the states; in short, to assume war powers which if they had been strictly enforced would have turned us into a dictatorship after the pattern of the Roman Republic in time of crisis. There was much muttering among those who valued state rights whatever the cost to the nation and feared that the very purchasing power wielded by the Federal government might lead to a control over men's souls. The Radicals failed to break down state rights by reducing the states to super-counties and they failed to consolidate all Federal functions in an all-powerful Congress. Nevertheless, the American nation was never to be the same again. A social, economic, and political revolution had whirled it into the stream of change, and the current was too strong for a return.

The democratic process was inevitably affected by these changes in Constitutional meaning, if not actually forms. Northerners had fought, probably above all else, to vindicate democracy and to open up to evolution the road which the South had blocked. The basic tragedy of Reconstruction lay in the fact that scarcely had one road block been removed than another was substituted. Industry and finance had forged in the fires of sectional strife a control that, while far from absolute, was strong enough to throw the balance of democratic conflict off center again. Thenceforth political and economic protest on the part of farmers and workers was directed toward re-establishing the balance with industry.

This imbalance requires further comment. We have noted that there were in American life contradictory urges to equality and to dominance. The first was expressed in the democratic concept of a balance of social conflict, the second in the intense individualism which resulted in the rise of the industrial capitalist. The North was during the Civil War essentially an alliance of these two principles against the Southern principle of an Athenian democracy based on slavery. A slave régime always discourages practical technologists because labor is socially unacceptable.

Whether the North was consciously fighting the battle for free science may be open to argument, but it certainly was fighting for the free application of technology—and technology flows from science. The Northern victory cleared the way for the study of science and its technological application in ways which made profits for the entrepreneur, raised the American standard of living for the masses, and in time made the United States the economic giant whose world impact has shaken the foundations of civilization. And it will reinforce them against the uncertain future.

The acceleration of technology and industry by the temporary demands of the war itself may not have been so great as is sometimes supposed, for the country was undergoing tremendous economic expansion in the 1850's. Nevertheless, it is probably fair to credit the war with some of the growth in mining, heavy industry, and agriculture. Progress in mechanization was marked during the war years in agriculture, in shoe making, and in the manufacturing of ready-made clothing. The petroleum industry got on its feet during the war years. Tariff protection became a permanent policy, and the income tax and the internal revenue on luxuries were added to the American scene. During Reconstruction Northern industrial capital made its entry into the South and won the battle to force the South to protect it. The economic policies which the Hamiltonians had long been advocating were now triumphant.

There was nothing for the South and the West to do but act as purveyors of food and raw materials and do what they could to raise themselves to industrial equality with the East. This was an ambitious program, but there was a good chance of its fulfillment. Now the bolder members of the planter class and ambitious yeomen and poor whites found tremendous opportunities in commerce and industry and turned their energies to remaking the South. The West had made good progress toward industrialization before the war, and in the ensuing decades it is possible to follow its progress by the swelling wave of political and economic conservatism which moved westward and finally crossed the Mississippi in the 1890's.

The Civil War confirmed the American antipathy toward Europe and reinforced the conviction that European governments were inveterate enemies of democracy. Even the South bore a grudge against the European nations for their failure to render more positive and decisive aid. Europe's vague uneasiness at the growth of the western democratic republic was turned to alarm lest with its overweening power and prestige it upset the uneasy political and economic balances of the world—which, of course, it eventually did. On the other hand, the strength of American Federalism was an encouragement to German federation, and the victory of American nationalism and democracy gave a filip to the parallel movements in Europe. The triumph of the Southern slave states would have spelled disaster for the democratic movement on the European continent and might seriously have retarded it in Great Britain.

Not the least of the psychological results of the Civil War was the creation of the Lincoln Legend, for over much of the country, at least, the kindly, homespun Lincoln receives more worship than the aloof patricians Washington and Lee. It has been said that Lincoln died at exactly the right moment to insure immortality, yet the legend began even during his life; the tragic circumstances of Lincoln's death only caused it to mushroom more amazingly. The revulsion against the rather common portrayal of the ugly gorilla from the prairies of Illinois started the poets and other creators of folk myths upon their task, and even sneering *Punch* regretted its failure to recognize "this rail-splitter, as true-born king of men." In life Lincoln was the most complex of men, and along with his better attributes he was skeptical, brutally realistic, acute to the extent of foxiness, coarse to the extent of vulgarity, and indifferent to cultural nuances.

Now his other side came uppermost. He was the patient, tolerant, innately dignified, melancholy, yet whimsical man of the people, agonizing over the travail of his country like a modern Christ. "New birth of our new soil, the first American," he became the typification of American opportunity, the model boy who was bound to rise. Born in a log cabin, he studied before a flickering fire, learned to write with charcoal on a slab, and walked miles to return a few cents overcharge. He split rails; lifted out hogs when they were stuck in the mire; never drank or swore; told off-color stories only as parables; and spent his years in the White House snatching widows' only sons from the firing squad. He loved and lost Ann Rutledge, and thereafter heard her voice in every sighing wind.

Lincoln has been portrayed as a Westerner, a Southerner, and even as a Yankee. The fact is that he is all things to all Americans. He has concentrated in himself the heroic essence of the war years as Emancipator and savior of the Union, and finally has become the exemplar of the best in democracy, the proof that the democratic process can stand the test. And yet there is truth in Basler's statement that "Lincoln is not so much the type of democracy as he is an abstract embodiment of the ancient and cosmic forces of genius and wisdom." His rise to fame was heralded by nature's portents; he wrestled in prayer; he foresaw the future in dreams; he walked with the spirits of the dead. Nancy Hanks became a wilderness madonna, and the log cabin in Kentucky a Bethlehem. His putative father was a carpenter, but his real father was a Virginia aristocrat! He could save others but could not save himself—and died on Good Friday! And Judas Booth varied the legend only by shooting himself!

Each year we repeat in February the ritualistic observance of the birthday of the folk hero. No visit to Washington is complete without a pilgrimage to the classic marble structure over whose portal we read: "In this temple as in the hearts of the people for whom he saved the Union the memory of Abraham Lincoln is enshrined forever." There are his greatest speeches which the commoner reads with reverent, moving lips while a shaft of light falls upon the white statue of the pitying hero. Nothing can be clearer than that here Americans find the sanctuary and embodiment of their dreams of the sacredness of human dignity and of the American mission to point the way to a better life for the world. When in the hungry winter of 1931 the American people were beaten down by forces which seemed about to shatter the American dream and Lincoln's successor in the White House recommended a diet of faith, a minister lifted his prayer to the folk hero: "Oh, Lincoln. Arise! Stand forth that we may gaze upon thy furrowed face. Look upon us; pity us; speak to us as thou didst at Gettysburg; stretch forth thy hand; point the way of destiny and duty that America may be thy living monument down to the end of time. Oh, Lincoln, come down from thy summit of bronze and march."

*   *   *

The Northern Radical Republicans had disfranchised Southern "rebels" and enfranchised Southern Negroes in order to entrench the power of industrialism and to enjoy the spoils of office. By 1877 it was evident that the Northern masses were weary of the Radical program and were ready to see the South restored to the control of its whites, rebels though they might have been. The hung election of 1876 offered an opportunity for a compromise. The Republicans were given Hayes as president, but they gave to the South a free hand over the Negroes in return for Southern local and Congressional encouragement and protection of their investments. The industrialists were now sure of the South and of the great Middle West and saw no reason for keeping these Radical nemeses of the South in power, especially since their Southern extensions were such bad financial risks. The Radical either faded from public life or turned to other interests, while Southern "brigadier generals" surged through the doors of Congress. Technically the old quarrel was forgotten, but occasionally on provocation the old hatred ran through the Congressional delegations like a chilling wind. Nevertheless, the Southerners kept their bargain in so far as their unreconstructed constituencies would permit and in so doing swung the bulk of Democratic strength to the support of industry.

The Southern leaders, now known as Bourbons, had seen from the first that the North had won because of its overwhelming material might, and they sought to build up similar strength in the South. Honest manual labor was now presented in a different light. It was—they said—the white man of the South more than the Negro who had been freed by the Civil War. It is true that the leading Bourbons reestablished their fortunes with the aid of their Northern contacts and in the 1880's emerged not only as political dictators of the South but as managers or lawyers of Northern enterprise in the South. Still, they may have been right. It is difficult, in looking back, to see how the task of building the New South could have been handled better, for the common Southerner was still averse to being reconstructed and Northern Republican politicos were no help.

Perhaps, after all, the Radical program, however brutal, had not been without its astuteness. The South and the West of 1865 would probably have downed the Northeast in a great neo-Jacksonian crusade. Now the South, worn down by war and Reconstruction and bought off by economic and social sweets, was ready to cooperate. However, the South was more than ever convinced of the rectitude of the aristo-agrarian ideal, and made white supremacy the standard around which all loyal Southerners must rally. The necessary economic surrender of 1877 made its leaders more than ever determined to protect the citadel of white supremacy by imbuing their people with the psychology of a closely disciplined, beleaguered garrison. They made internal politics a means of enforcing that discipline, and external politics a continuation of Calhoun's search for a veto on the nation in any policy that affected Southern interests.

The Peace of 1877 resulted in placing the Negro in a peculiar status of second-class citizenship. Few Negroes were able to compete economically with their white neighbors, so presently they settled into a condition that bore some resemblances to serfdom and some to peonage. Socially they made a few advances, but they were still the bottom layer of society. Civil liberties were drastically curtailed, but more by social than by legal pressures. Curiously enough, the franchise was not technically withdrawn until after 1890, though of course it was limited in its practical use. By about 1900 the old agrarian tradition and the rising industrial interests of the South had worked out a *modus vivendi* which suited them fairly well and which was to survive deep into the new century. Southern Negroes had little choice but to accept their assigned role, whatever secret protests they may have harbored. The rural areas, especially the cotton, rice, and sugar-cane regions, relied largely on Negro labor. The factories, with some exceptions, preferred white labor. Negroes were disfranchised and wherever possible they were confined to menial work by methods not always free from violence. They could hold land, but on the whole it was not wise to show too many marks of expertness, prosperity, or self-respect. In the cities Negroes received less pay for the same jobs than white artisans, but the threat of Negro competition was useful in hampering unionization and hold-ing white wages down. Technically the South still held to state rights, but there was a growing readiness to accept Federal gifts if there were no strings attached and if they were not intended to benefit the Negro.

Rural and city interests had their clashes, but these were fought out in the white primaries, and when the general election came the interests showed a solid front. After all, they had one common meet-ing ground: white supremacy. In a general sense, the ruling class succeeded in its original objective of preventing white and black workers from uniting, and the policy of race division suited Northern investors very well. It was not the first nor the last time that local conditions had lent themselves to the illustration of the motto "Divide and rule."

Nevertheless, the Negro made remarkable progress, both by his own efforts and by the aid of some of his white neighbors. The present-age Negro, naturally views his second-class status with impatience and resentment, yet it is worth pointing out that he is advancing in exactly the same way in which successive classes of whites have risen. The democratic process has never envisioned the award of democratic privileges to any class which has not earned it by showing an earnest and determined intention to measure up to standards of courage and self-restraint perhaps even higher than is required of those who have already arrived.

The Southern battle to enforce internal discipline sentenced it to the one-party system. The white political rebels of the 1870's who cooperated with the Republican Party were punished, and those of the 1890's who went over to the Populist Party were ruthlessly driven from politics. Successful rebels had been shrewd enough to operate within the Democratic Party and thus avoid running counter to the fear that if the whites were divided Negro voters would wield the balance of power. The Southern garrison had won its struggle for the preservation of internal discipline.

Meanwhile the battle for the veto on national actions had been progressing on a wider front. This battle for a veto, to which Calhoun devoted his life and which led to secession and war, continues with unabated vigor a century after his death and plays its part in nearly every political issue. Its motivations are the same as with Calhoun: the protection of white supremacy and of the South's economic interests. The Bourbons accepted the Peace of 1877 because they had to; actually neither they nor their successors intended to submit to permanent economic domination by the North, and they have sought diligently to use their political power to break its hold.

The forms taken by the Southern veto are familiar. Even before the Civil War the Democratic Party had accepted the Two-thirds Rule in its presidential nominating conventions. This practice meant that after the war the presidential candidate would always be a Northerner but must be satisfactory to the South. The abandonment of the rule in 1936 seemed at first to indicate the healing of old wounds, but it has since led to renewed strife.

The Two-thirds Rule was not the South's only weapon. Its solid allegiance to the Democratic Party meant that less reliable states could wield power and furnish candidates in crucial elections, but it also meant that after the election was won the South came into its own. Its Senators and Congressmen were returned with humdrum regularity and so amassed the seniority which made them chairmen of committees and big wheels in the party organization. Each Democratic President learned that to get his program passed, he must win the support of Southern legislators. If he did not, the result was an informal but none the less effective alliance with the Republicans to thwart his program. The tactic could be worked at times even when the Republican Party had a narrow majority in Congress.

With these weapons at its disposal the South has usually been able to enforce its veto. Democratic presidential aspirants (until 1948) have had to be assured of its favor. It has blocked or watered down legislation which it feels attacks its interests, such as election-control bills, antilynching bills, and fair-employment bills. It has been able to fill its basket with Federal plums and to bring in Federally-supported war industries on terms which promote Southern industrialization without seriously violating its concepts of race relations.

The strength of Northern economic imperialism in the South was rooted in the psychological colonialism of Southerners. Basically this was no different from the sentimentalities, the prejudices, the credulities, and the sympathies which laid all Americans open to self-defeat through some form of exploitation. The American paradox is a perpetual puzzle to foreigners; the Southern paradox is a perpetual puzzle to other Americans, and sometimes to Southerners themselves. There was a never-ending clash between Southern individualism and the discipline inculcated by generations of living in a garrison besieged by race and sectional conflicts. Hedonism and puritanism strove for mastery: on the one side the appreciation of leisure and its pursuits, of good manners, good conversation, and good whisky; on the other, prohibition of alcoholic liquor in ten states, social conformity as lip service to the aristo-agrarian ideal, political conformity as a defense of white supremacy, and religious conformity to a fervent fundamentalist creed as a bulwark against the infiltration of modern ideas.

The Bourbons who negotiated the Peace of 1877 had found their strongest opponents among defiantly unreconstructed Southerners, especially in the rural areas, who insisted that the old aristo-agrarian order must be preserved in its pristine purity at any cost. Enthusiastic romantics joined in creating the Southern mythus of "the time that never was." The contented darkey, the plantation hoe-down, the mint julep, the lavish hunt breakfast, the scholar-planter, the code of chivalry, indeed the whole tradition of lavender and old lace was built up by representing the unusual as the universal condition. The whole South joined zealously in the holy game, turned every Cotton Snob into an aristo-agrarian, and refurbished its genealogies and where necessary invented them.

"The South" (says Cash, himself a Southerner) "was, of course, being continually driven more and more on the defensive. The need to justify itself in the eyes of the world and in its own and to assert its pride as against the Yankee was more imperative now than it had ever been before. Moreover, there was naturally a great aversion on the part of the individuals who made up the master class to sur-render the glory which had been theirs under the *ancien régime*. And like many other people come upon evil days, the South in its entirety was filled with an immense regret and nostalgia; yearned backward toward its past with passionate longing. And so it happened that, while the actuality of aristocracy was drawing away toward the limbo of aborted and unrealized things, the claim of its possession as an achieved and essentially indefeasible heritage, so far from being abated, was reasserted with a kind of frenzied intensity. It was in this period that the legend of the Old South finally emerged and fully took on the form in which we know it today. With the ante-bellum world removed to the realm of retrospect, the shackles of reality, as so often happens in such cases, fell away from it altogether. Perpetually suspended in the great haze of memory, it hung, as it were, poised, somewhere between earth and sky, colossal, shining, and incomparably lovely—a Cloud-Cuckoo-Land wherein . . . life would move always in stately and noble measure through scenery out of Watteau."*

---

* Wilbur J. Cash, *The Mind of the South* (1941), 124.

X

The Gospel of Wealth

EUROPEAN adventurers, explorers, businessmen, and noblemen—
object matri-money—who took the boat for the United States
in 1909, carried with them a little red guide book written by an
unsung German humorist named Baedeker. "Throughout almost the
whole country," they read with a sense of happy relief, "traveling is now
as safe as in the most civilized parts of Europe, and the carrying of arms
unnecessary." But their contacts with the *genus Americanus* both in
Europe and in its native lair never failed to fill them with a sense
of bewilderment, which could not always be concealed under an air
of assumed superiority. Europeans, if Henry James wrote truly, looked
upon Americans with much the same fascinated repulsion as one
might look upon his own suddenly withered hand.

America was a wilderness of contradictions—a democracy under
plutocratic controls. Descendants of first settlers indulged in snobbery
toward the descendants of those who came to settle a few years
later. It was a society which looked down on cultured German and
Slav professors and musicians if fortune had ordained that they must
labor for a living, yet was eternally apologizing to British visitors
for the national crudity. The people derided the land of their ancestors
yet imported its music, its art, its literature, and its dancing masters,
and strove to mold taste to the European model and to build up a
new aristocracy which should reign over the masses as European
nobles reigned over their peasants. It seems reasonable that many
of the new entrepreneurs saw what the snobs among the newly-rich
were doing and refused to connive at setting up a new order which
violated their instincts.

The old aristocracy of which Washington was the finest flower had
placed emphasis upon character. It is clear that men like the Adamses,
Jefferson, Robert E. Lee, and Abraham Lincoln (to name only a
few) were men of character, and their sense of duty was shared
by millions of men and women unknown to history. Various factors,
including the reaction from war and the effects of the long battle

against the wilderness, were in danger of making slickness and love for power more prominent as American traits than the sense of ordered responsibility—of devotion to duty—which we call character. The task of subduing this wildness, of making character a part of the American grain, was an absorbing interest of the Gilded Age.

The new entrepreneurs who objected to the snobs' program, which aimed at transplanting the European social order, found the cult of respectability more to their taste. They could become "good providers" for their families, go to church, contribute to charity, commit their sins in privacy or in discreet company, and keep within the letter of the law, even seeing to it that special privileges were granted by kept politicians with all due formality. Gentility was diligently cultivated; men became "gentlemen," and women "ladies"; even the working classes assumed the titles.

Reliability was the watchword of the new order. It was, in effect, the principal aspect of the cult and, as such, tended to confuse respectability with character; the danger in this was that respectability without character is likely to produce a rascal or a stuffed shirt. It was the old mediocrity of the Jacksonian period endowed with dynamic force. Still, it was in the spirit of the English motto, "Manners makyth man." Its attempt to implant a respect for the humdrum virtues was a healthy sign and a necessary step to the building of both culture and social-conscious wealth. It was also necessary in preparing the nation for the responsibilities which were to descend upon it in the twentieth century.

Appearance, manners, and behavior became second only to sound financial standing. The book of etiquette was more diligently read than the family Bible. Bearded patresfamilias comported themselves with a painful dignity, which they flattered themselves was quiet elegance. Women were models of prim decorum and presumably were helpless without proper male escort. The sight of a mouse was the signal for a faint into the arms of the flattered swain or for a graceful ascent to a chair—not forgetting to show a pretty ankle in the process. Little girls were taught to model themselves on their mamas, and little boys in their Fauntleroy suits were reproved for unseemly noise. Gold watches, Malacca sticks, neat clothing of good quality, punctuality, reserve without coldness, and refinement without artiness were the marks of the devotee of the cult of respectability.

Predictability was prized. One moved week after week on the same unvarying round; he sat in the same pew on Sundays, ate

with the same relatives of holidays, went to the same resort of summers, lived in the same house and sat in the same chair during his
entire adult life. Unpleasant social facts were ignored or glossed
over and probably were not mentioned in the presence of women or
children. Genteelism afflicted literary and artistic circles; even the
magazines ignored all but the most respectable subjects unless they
wished to point a moral.

* * *

The period from the Civil War to World War I was marked
by the ascendance of the middle class, and it possessed the virtues
and vices that go with a bourgeois society. The dominant Republican
Party was the party of the middle class. It found its mission in en-
suring Federal complaisance toward rising industry. Enterprisers
were permitted to purchase natural resources at low prices, they were
granted protective tariffs against foreign competitors, and the laws
were tailored to their satisfaction. Republican policy, be it noted,
was in conformity with the effective public will. Since business
prosperity lay at the root of national prosperity it was considered only
right and proper for government to lavish natural resources upon it.
Attempts to hoard resources were regarded as against the public interest. Suggestions that government regulate private enterprise were
considered as obviously socialistic; indeed it might well be that they
would have been morally and materially destructive, for after two
generations of experiment we are still uncertain what form regulation
should take. The genius of America had risen from the energy of
its people and from their insistence that they must be left free from
institutional interference in exploiting the vast natural resources of
their country. Even the Constitution had been deliberately drawn to
prevent governmental interference with the citizen and his enterprises. Employers' guilds and laborers' unions were weak. A vast free
domestic market, constantly being expanded as population grew,
beckoned to the manufacturer, and a superb transportation network
offered access even to remote parts of the country. It seems fair
to say that even without the Civil War the triumph of industry
was inevitable.

The Civil War years saw the rise of the group of industrialists
who have become known as the Great Entrepreneurs, and who for
the most part dealt in the new products which were entering the
industrial world or were opening up new markets and sources of

supply and new methods of transport. Among them may be mentioned Carnegie in steel, Rockefeller in oil, McCormick in agricultural machinery, and Vanderbilt in railroads. While it must be granted that such men took advantage of every loophole in the law in building their empires, yet they did build up a much-needed industrial plant at a social cost which in retrospect seems amazingly low. Their mission was to pave the way for mass production, which was to lay the foundations of national power and of the American standard of living.

Without denying that there were deliberate abuses, it is clear that the basic evils of the period rose from economic ignorance. Classical economics was based on the belief that there would always be a scarcity of goods in relation to demand and that competition for the market must be bitter and at times brutal. As a result a secure place in the market could be held only by the monopolist, who naturally would reduce output and raise prices; our social and mass production ideal of maximum production for the lowest price would have been regarded as absurd, and doubtless would have been in the context. At any rate the effect of this "economy of scarcity" ideal was that competition (the basis of laissez faire doctrine) must logically end when one competitor succeeded in absorbing or ruining the others. Free enterprise meant the right of a man to risk his stake in the competition—and the right of the victor to keep the spoils.

When the risks are great there is a tendency to ensure success by undercutting the rules of fair play. Laissez faire theory insists that the market is automatically regulated by the law of supply and demand and that the function of government is merely to serve as an umpire. This has always been as much theory as practice, for there are always men who are willing to accept and even ask for government intervention when it helps them—though of course they loudly champion laissez faire when government action would hamper them. Indeed it has been held that the campaign against monopoly which we will presently notice was launched not so much because of popular support but because little businessmen feared being swallowed by big business. If this is true we have the curious situation of a long government battle against laissez faire fought with the intention of preserving laissez faire.

The war among competitors frequently resulted in wastefulness and mutual destruction, and this was made worse by the rise of a group of reckless financiers and market manipulators—to say nothing of the erratic nature of the business cycle and of the political struggle over a sound currency. Industries and railroads were so weakened that the Panic of 1893 hit them hard, and many went bankrupt. The return of the Republicans to power under McKinley in 1897 brought —or at least coincided with—a renewal of business activity, but responsible businessmen were now determined to take steps to see that the debacle was not repeated.

Leadership in this movement was exercised by the great financier capitalist John Pierpont Morgan and by the associates of John D. Rockefeller, tremendously successful oil entrepreneur who had gone into banking. Such men, as bankers in a nation with an expanding economy and a serious shortage of credit, were in a position to dictate terms to the chaotic industrialists. The bankers argued that chaos could be forefended only if industrialists and railroaders adopted a live-and-let-live policy which they called "community of interest." To do this it was necessary to form a monopoly in each field of enterprise, or at least a semi-monopoly which could dominate the field and dictate common policies. They hoped also to minimize the rise and fall of prices and to pad the disastrous effects of the business cycle; to make savings in buying and manufacturing; to control prices and raise profits; and to block the rising power of labor which they felt was leading to socialism.

Accusations were not lacking that the bankers (actually *private* rather than commercial bankers) were deliberately forcing the government to retain a gold-based currency in order to limit the amount of available credit and thus advance their program of seizing control of American industry as European bankers had already done with European industry. This was the favorite thesis of the Western and Southern populists and gave rise to their demand for expansion of currency either by printing it or by freely coining silver. Whatever the merits of the rival arguments the masters of capital were able to launch the reign of finance capitalism—that is, the control of enterprise by banks and other financial institutions.

The *holding company* is the institution which facilitated the rise of finance capitalism. Common law had discouraged corporations from holding stock in other corporations, but in 1889 New Jersey made it legal and in time other states followed. The holding company is a corporation that may or may not be engaged in production but whose primary function is to acquire enough stock in other corporations to enable it to control them. Each of these subsidiary corporations may in turn control others, and so on downward. The wide spread in the ownership of stock makes it possible to control a corporation's policies by voting a block of stock as small as five per cent of the whole.

The Great Entrepreneurs could scarcely avoid the knowledge that their actions were violating even the harsh tenets of Calvinism by ignoring its injunction to social responsibility. What was needed was a philosophical justification of their course. It was the mission of Herbert Spencer to furnish it.

*   *   *

By the middle of the nineteenth century organic evolution had been widely accepted, but savants had been pretty much at a loss to explain how one species developed into a more complex species. Then in 1859 Charles Darwin published his *Origin of Species,* which propounded the theory of natural selection as an explanation. This suggestion, worked out in parallel by Darwin and Alfred R. Wallace, has now been amended, but its effect on the nineteenth century was tremendous. Man had not been created but had evolved from the brute and was himself an animal, though the highest one. Man had not fallen, but had risen. As for evolution as the result of design, it was cast overboard in favor of change through adaptations, mutations, and struggles which gave every evidence of chance. Worst of all, it knocked the props from under the *a priori* method of finding truth by reasoning from pleasant basic assumptions and insisted upon reasoning from unpleasant facts—in other words, inductive reasoning knocked out deductive.

The result was that just when the economic world was entering upon a stage of upheaval and men needed a sense of security, Darwinism took from them the age-old comfort of trust in a loving and watchful Providence and confronted them with an impersonal universe which coldly ordained the survival of the fittest. On the other hand, for the first time scholars felt that evolution was demonstrable and could be used as a premise for further thought. The theory has affected virtually every aspect of modern life and is in no small part the impetus for all modern thought. It is worth noting, also, that the emphasis by Karl Marx on the class struggle apparently dovetailed neatly into Darwinism's theory of the struggle for survival.

Darwinism's triumph in the United States was delayed by the Civil War, but soon thereafter it was put to use, under the name of Social Darwinism, to explain and justify the methods of the Great Entrepreneurs and the Finance Capitalists. One might think that Darwinism's emphasis on the struggle for survival would have made pessimists; probably it often did, yet more often it strengthened optimism because it preached progress. The great interpreter of Social Darwinism was the English philosopher-engineer Herbert Spencer, whose influence in America was so enormous that he has been called an Apostle to the Americans. His many volumes covered all cosmic phenomena and were heralded in America by John Fiske, the Harvard historian, and by Edward L. Youmans, the founder of *Popular Science Monthly*.

Though Spencer was regarded by philosophers as superficial and by scientists as half-educated, he was able to apply Darwin's theory and scientific data so glibly to the social scene that it fascinated and delighted American economic conservatives, who knew exactly what they wanted. Spencer, in fact, had published his *Social Statics* in 1850, eight years before Darwin's epochal *Origin of Species,* but the new light only confirmed the old. He preached a cosmic "equilibration of mechanism," which justified laissez faire, and applied to society the biological idea of the survival of the fittest. Of course, he saw this as a struggle among individuals, and so intense was his view that he was in effect a philosophical anarchist. Human relations must be governed by natural law, and the state must confine itself to the function of an occasional umpire. He violently opposed the forcible burdening of the superior (the successful) for the support of the in- ferior (the unsuccessful)—an obvious discouragement of reform.

State regulation of industry was therefore bad and the graduated income tax unjust, decisions which the courts presently rubber-stamped. State support of hospitals, schools, roads, and fire departments was bad; they should either be supported on a basis of private charity or thrown into the pot, where entrepreneurs could struggle to make a profit by administering them. Oppression of labor fulfilled the grand purpose of the cosmos by weeding out the unfit, and the man about to fall into a pauper's grave could comfort himself with the consciousness that he was in tune with natural law. The sugar-coating on the bitter pill was that evolution could "end only in the establishment of the greatest perfection and the most complete happiness." That great day, fortunately, was just around the corner, a great comfort to American optimists. There was even a word of encouragement for the pious in Spencer's assurance that science and religion were recon- cilable and that the veneration of the Unknowable—God—could never be displaced.

Spencer was now in the position of giving the approval of nature and morals to the changes which would have taken place in Western Civilization in any case. Of course, he did not invent racism and imperialism and he was technically a pacifist, but Social Darwinism was a definite encouragement to the men who launched the world imperialist race. Just as definite was Spencer's encouragement to those who sought to arrest American society at the *status quo* in order to free their hands to promote material progress and to amass property. His doctrines seemed to fall into line with American experience and to justify so many things we wished to do. In effect they stripped from the Protestant Ethic many of its inconvenient admonitions and left intact the practical aids to material aggrandizement. William Lawrence, a proper Bostonian and Episcopal bishop, proclaimed that "in the long run, it is only to the man of morality that wealth comes. . . . Godliness is in league with riches." Geneva's Calvin had come to life again.

It must not be thought that Social Darwinism made brutal misanthropists of the Great Entrepreneurs and the Finance Capitalists. They were, by and large, too simple-minded for that; it was only an intellectual like W. G. Sumner who became a misanthropist. "Bet-you-a-million" Gates was one of the boys, joyously betting a thousand dollars that one raindrop would beat another one down a pane of glass. Carnegie was a hail-fellow-well-met who nursed the ambition of becoming the literary spokesman of the gospel of wealth and succeeded with the help of his secretaries. Even "Jupiter" Morgan used to go to his church on slow afternoons and sing hymns to the accompaniment of his favorite organist.

Late in the century an epidemic swept their ranks—an epidemic of art collecting; they seem to have taken up the game not only as a form of ostentation and sound investment but also as the result of vague esthetic gropings. Not many of the wealthy learned much about art, but they collected like mad. Few cities of today are without art museums which contain the good and bad evidences of this craze. Charles Francis Adams II summed up the tycoons of the fin de siècle. "I have known, and known tolerably well, a good many 'successful' men—'big' financially—men famous during the last half century; and a less interesting crowd I do not care to encounter. . . . Not one that I have ever known would I care to meet again, either in this world or the next."

*   *   *

The funneling of most Americans' energies into material channels was natural. The problem of conquering a continent was a material one, and it needed material methods and undivided attention. Action was glorified because action was necessary, and the man who produced the most in goods or bank credit was the acknowledged leader. In the true Puritan tradition prosperity became the proof of righteousness, and education, art, literature, politics, and the church played soft accompaniments to the role of the inspired millionaire, as Van Wyck Brooks named him. The rich man blandly accepted his position as conferred by divine right.

Still, he was a likable rascal! Brooks has pointed out that the English man of wealth, however self-satisfied, still lived in a sort of underworld apart from the aristocracy and the intelligentsia, who constituted the cream of society. But in America the best brains and blood went into business and occupied the center of the stage. The American businessman was "a gay, sprightly, childlike being, moved and movable, the player of a game, a sportsman essentially, though with a frequently dim perception of the rules." He was the inspired millionaire, the envy of all those on the lower rungs of the ladder. If this description does not seem to apply, it is because this generation no longer knows the ways in which the Gateses, Morgans, and Carnegies disported in their leisure moments or the deadly practical jokes which they played on each other in the rivalry of the market place.

The campaign to preserve the economic *status quo* found one of its outlets in an attempt to preserve proper moral attitudes—which, of course, must approve the *status quo*. This campaign, though quite unintegrated, managed to penetrate every nook and cranny of American life. Wealth naturally took an important part in the movement, but it was not the only initiating and controlling factor. True enough, churches, educational institutions, missions, and charities were subtly influenced where necessary, but probably not often. Lecturers, writers, courts, and press staunchly and courageously said what they believed, a matter which was not difficult since the American people and their economic, social, and cultural leaders were enthusiastically Spencerian. The Salvation Army, introduced from England, was accused by radicals of touting to the rich and of fighting discontent with earthly rewards by offering heavenly rewards. The Young Men's Christian Association, also a British importation, devoted itself to ethical teaching, night schools, and physical culture. It would be a mistake to label as conscious hypocrites either the overlords or the ministers of the gospel of wealth. Says Ralph Gabriel:*

"Its basic emphasis was upon the responsibility of the individual, confronting the hard uncertainty of life. The gospel of wealth explained the meaning of life with a metaphor that called life a testing period in which those selected for distinction must unite character with ability, and magnanimity with power. It was the philosophy which lay behind the private charity for which the Americans of the Gilded Age became justly famous. It was an effort to carry the idealism and the moral code of Christianity and the democratic faith into a rapidly developing capitalism. The gospel of wealth sought to harmonize competitive acquisitiveness with the fundamental moral law."

It must be remembered that the depressions and labor troubles of the era did not destroy Americans' optimistic faith in the democratic way or in the future. Capitalists, indeed, began to assert that the brutal economic struggle bred leaders who because of their economic power could and would do more for the masses than corrupt political leaders. To reach this desirable end they demanded that the state give them tariffs and cheap raw materials and that it hedge in property rights with sympathetic courts and favorable currency and banking laws. Beyond these functions the state must leave wealth alone to work out its destiny of making America the paradise on earth that Eden had once been. By and large, Americans deferred to the rich man as leader. He had proved his expertness in making money, the most important of human pursuits; therefore he could speak with authority on all subjects. No one else could hope to be accepted as so expert in problems involving the social, economic, religious, political, and even artistic aspects of life as the man with a million dollars.

The effect of the rising dominance of industrial wealth was the culminating proof of the Calvinist axiom that God prospers the righteous. Poverty was due to vice, laziness, thriftlessness, or occasionally to bad fortune. By far the most of the country's rich men were paragons of piety. Rockefeller was a leading Baptist layman, and Morgan was beyond doubt the leading Episcopal layman. Morgan's will reads in its religious fealty like a document out of

---

* Ralph Henry Gabriel, *The Course of American Democratic Thought*, (1940).

sixteenth-century England. There was nothing of the cynic in Rockefeller when he testified on his method of building up Standard Oil:
"It was right between me and my God." Again he stated: "I believe
the power to make money is a gift of God. . . . It is my duty to
make money and still more money, and to use the money I make
for the good of my fellow man according to the dictates of my conscience." James J. Hill, technically a Protestant, once donated a
million dollars to a Catholic theological seminary and defended the
action as necessary to ensure that immigrants were properly educated
in "their social view, their political action, their moral status."

It would be wrong to accuse the churches of having been bought;
they did not need to be purchased, for they saw eye to eye with
their benefactors. But they did need support. Russell Conwell built
the 3,000-seat Baptist Temple in Philadelphia, the largest Protestant
church in the country, and packed it every Sunday because he believed in and preached the morality current among rich and poor.
Frederick T. Gates, another minister, became Rockefeller's mentor
in distributing 500 million dollars. There is a story that a minister
who asked a tycoon for a donation to a worthy cause was answered,
"I am not of your church." "That does not matter," replied the
minister, "your money is orthodox."

Pious men saw the hand of God working when great gifts poured
in to worthy enterprises. When Rockefeller's initial gift of $600,000
for founding the University of Chicago was announced to the convention of the Baptist Educational Society, a witness recounts that
there was "a perfect bedlam of applause, shouts, and waving of
handkerchiefs. One of the godly men present sprang to his feet,
exclaiming, "God has kept Chicago for us! I wonder at His patience!"
Without direction the audience rose and sang the Doxology. Before
long public opinion, which had been critical of the oil trust, began
to turn, and it was pointed out that it was an enterprise begun and
carried on by Christian men.

Universities were not always controlled by wealthy donors, but
there certainly were instances when professors were dismissed for
preaching doctrines hostile to "property." Administrators could not
have been ignorant of the connection with the spigot that controlled
the cash. The students at Syracuse University sang a touching appeal
to John Archbold, Rockefeller's associate:

We have a Standard Oil pipe running up to John Crouse Hall,
And a gusher in the stadium will be flowing full next fall.

We need the money, Mr. Archbold,

We need it right away.

It was not necessary to inspect school texts to see that they set forth the proper principles, and copybooks to see that they set forth the proper maxims; those who prepared the material were glad to do it free of charge, for the old morality of thrift and integrity which they favored was the very same which business rather flatteringly ascribed to itself. Perhaps even more effective were the "Alger books," stories by Horatio Alger, a warm-hearted Unitarian minister who lived among the street gamins of New York. His numerous books usually dealt with poor boys who made good through hard work, honesty, and thrift; and, though highly sentimental, they were read with avidity by a generation of boys who were not as blasé as are their grandsons. On a more adult level there were the lectures of Robert G. Ingersoll, who actually saw agnosticism as a step toward the realization of traditional morals and the amassing of wealth.

Elbert Hubbard wrote *A Message to Garcia* and saw 40 million copies distributed. The reader of this sermonette will learn that the older generation, which complains of the softness of modern youth, was in its turn denounced as incapable of independent action, However, the 40 million copies were sold to those who saw in the sermon encouragement for hard work, independence, initiative and getting ahead. George Horace Lorimer, long-time editor of *The Saturday Evening Post,* allowed that "there're just as many chances for a fellow as ever, but they're a little gun shy." His *Letters from a Self-Made Merchant to His Son* (1904) is still good for many a chuckle and packs into its shrewd wisdom the mythus of the capitalistic system.

The high priest of the gospel of wealth, however, was the Russell H. Conwell, mentioned above, who was the perennial flower of Chautauqua. He specialized in one lecture, *Acres of Diamonds,* which he delivered 6,000 times and with the proceeds of which he founded Temple University because of his sincere belief that education paved the road to success. He was the real founder of the American success story which still haunts our magazines and which is indubitably true, whether or not he was correct in his claim that out of 4,500 millionaires in the United States 3,900 began as poor boys. His cry "I say, get rich, get rich!" rang into the ears of receptive audiences and became the marching order of the gospel of wealth.

But Conwell had a further word of advice. There was no use

going abroad to look for diamonds; they lay in the opportunities abundantly available at one's own front door. The attainment of wealth was a social duty, and of course wealth should be spent in a Christian way. "We ought to get rich if we can by honorable and Christian methods, and those are the only methods that sweep us quickly toward the goal of riches." Thickening evidence of economic oppression never penetrated Conwell's armor. His philosophy, of course, was blatantly materialistic, but it was in line with public opinion—and won the orator a million dollars.

The worship of success gave rise naturally to a study of the means of attaining success. As psychology had evolved, the swarm of fakirs on its fringes had multiplied. The 1890's saw the introduction of personal magnetism, mental control, and other psychological emanations which were soon to give birth to the high-pressure salesman and the public-relations counsel. Advertising had been growing ever since the war and had been an important element in the inception and success of the yellow press, as well as in furnishing the money for the artistic improvement of highbrow magazines. As early as 1876 Bret Harte could satirize the outdoor advertiser:

> One Sabbath morn, as heavenward
> White Mountain tourists slowly spurred,
> On every rock, to their dismay,
> They read the legend all the way—
> SAPOLIO.

Americans had always been slogan-conscious, and advertisers knew it. The public was now confronted everywhere with arresting statements: "It Floats," "Children Cry for It," "You Press the Button; We Do the Rest," and finally by such commands as "Watch the Fords Go By."

Self-censorship was a natural development in a society which desired no changes save material ones. There remained, however, the Puritan belief that sex was somehow shameful, sinful, and, unless it was strictly controlled, destructive of moral and social order and economic enterprise. The prime mover in the postwar campaign against obscene books and pictures, lotteries, gambling houses, patent medicines, and fake advertisers was Anthony Comstock, a Connecticut Yankee who found his happy hunting ground in New York. As secretary of the Society for the Suppression of Vice he conscientiously prosecuted all kinds of vice, but it is difficult to avoid the impression that he was most active in suppressing sex. He spearheaded the movement which tightened up postal laws and customs regulations against books and pictures which did not meet his rigid standards.

Comstock prosecuted not only actual or claimed obscenity but anyone who expressed ideas which he considered morally corrupting. He inspired the organization of the famous Watch and Ward Society (1876), which still keeps watch and ward over Boston's books, plays, and moral behavior. In this case Boston's native Puritanism is reinforced by the powerful aid of the Catholic Church, which has found a solid foundation among Boston's Irish. Comstock's animus was often clearly personal, as in the case when he prosecuted the producer of one of Shaw's plays apparently because the playwright had coined the word "comstockery."

* * *

It is quite clear that Spencer had nothing to do with the origin of the American stereotype of rugged individualism. Jefferson had drawn it from American life but saw it exemplified in the self-reliance of the farmers more than in cutthroat competition among them. Adam Smith had propounded competition, and the classical economists had given it its soulless sheen in the concept of the Economic Man, moved only by economic considerations. Hamilton and the Careys, still under the influence of the Enlightenment, were not inclined to go as far, though they promoted corporate privileges and government protection. It was Spencer's task to add the approval of natural law, thus changing the Economic Man to the Universal Man and enabling the American stereotype to stand forth in all its perfection. After that, regardless of consistence in details, Americans swore by it. The result has been one of the most amazing rationalizations in history. Observe the transformation.

Spencer's rugged individualism justified the cutthroat tactics of some of the Great Entrepreneurs, but it was not so easily adjusted to the community of interest and monopolism of Finance Capitalism. But it was too neat a justification to discard, so the rationale was carried over even though Spencer himself declined in repute. Monopolies rose naturally out of free competition; therefore they could not be rejected by rugged individualists. The monopoly simply stepped into the place of the individual, and the courts recognized the substitution by declaring the corporation a legal person. Americans accepted natural law but determined to help it along. As Cochran and Miller put it:*

"American economists sympathetic to industrial business simultaneously could be high tariff men and sternly antiunion; they could boost government patents, subsidies, bounties, loans, while contending in the same breath that free competition was the life of trade. They could approve tax remissions to encourage new businesses while opposing as destructive interference with the operation of 'natural economic laws' factory acts regulating conditions of labor. . . . Thus free competition became the keystone of the triumphal arch of American business philosophy, while monopolistic tendencies were ignored; science and mechanization became the grand avenues of progress while patent pools and social regimentation were obscured; thrift remained the first commandment in the decalogue of the new business society though conspicuous consumption was its sign of grace."

When Wilson began to regulate corporate privileges by his New Freedom, Spencer, though knocked into a cocked hat by Pragmatism, was appealed to as the ultimate authority on the evils of government encroachment. Charles W. Eliot, president of Harvard, Senator Henry Cabot Lodge of Massachusetts, and Nicholas Murray ("Miraculous") Butler, president of Columbia—three of the most ponderous intellects in America—called as with one voice on Spencer to save them. Even Spencer's opponents were influenced so subtly that in many cases they found themselves willy-nilly on his side. They were fascinated by natural law. "Adopt all the cunning devices that social science has invented," said one of them, "and you cannot be sure that direct or indirect help of the poor does not undermine their self-respect and weaken their independence." This is still the majority American view in the upper and middle classes and is given at least lip-service by labor. It was the basis upon which the challenge to the New Deal was rallied in the 1930's, and there is no indication that it has yet run its course.

American symbolism, as Ralph Gabriel calls it, had been expressed in the Declaration of Independence, in Fourth-of-July and Memorial Day orations, and in the cult of Washington worship. These were now supplemented by the Lincoln cult and by a new resurgence of

---

* Thomas C. Cochran and William Miller, *The Age of Enterprise,* (1942) 121, 123.

reverence for the Constitution. Today the Constitution has function and value as a brake on hasty and ill-considered action and as a cogent argument for conservatives. The Gilded Age, however, saw it as the arcanum of property and awarded it a divine origin, an expression of absolute eternal values regardless of popular will. "Oh Marvellous Constitution," cried an orator. "Magic Parchment! Transforming Word! Maker, Monitor, Guardian of Mankind! Thou hast gathered to thy impartial bosom the peoples of the earth, Columbia, and called them equal."

This age was the seminal season of the reforms which have come in our own age. It is no less true that it gave us or passed on to us the false standards and neurotic frustrations which we are striving to overcome. The spectacle of the American shifting hesitantly between smugness on one side and, on the other, the uneasy feeling that there was something better if he could only find it, is fraught with the humor and the tender pathos that we see in the efforts of the adolescent to act like an adult. The "plain people"—those without intellectual or social pretensions—were conscious of the flux that was occurring in the nation and yet on the whole regarded the future with confidence and accepted the rhythm of the present as something satisfying akin to a divine order. Henry Seidel Canby, a most perceptive analyst of the society of the 1890's, has this to say:*

"I believe that there were values in that period called the nineties and scandalously misdescribed in current films and novels, which were as worthy (greatness aside) as any cultural period has ever developed, and which are now lost, perhaps irrevocably. . . . But I believe also that no one . . . can fail to see in looking back the seeds of dissolution, the shame, the animated corpses of belief, the diseases of culture, which were also coexistent with this pausing time in our American history, when there was such real content, and such a complacent yet enviable and sometimes splendid trust in the future; when . . . for the last time in living memory everyone knew exactly what it meant to be an American."

---

* From *The Age of Confidence,* (1934).

XI

The Pragmatic Challenge

SOCIAL Darwinism may have dominated the scene after the Civil War but at no time was there a lack of knights errant to tilt against it in defense of the American way. This they did, not only by showing that Spencer had misread the true meaning of Darwin, but more importantly by challenging denial of the old American belief that we were consciously and of our own volition heading toward a moral goal—that is, toward a democratic society in which Christian ethics should rule and the individual should find maximum freedom consistent with social good. Spencerianism, they asserted, was tearing down the progress we had made toward this goal. Its elevation of the successful individual was denying the rights of the mass of individuals and in so doing was destroying the basic federation between the individual and society which was the aim of democracy. Jefferson's individualism meant self reliance with due regard for the social context; it did not mean a cutthroat competition which would result in the triumph of a few at the expense of tearing down the social fabric.

By the 1890's William James, Harvard biologist, psychologist, and philosopher, had emerged as leader of what was coming to be called the pragmatic revolt. His ideas were so repugnant to philosophers that he spent his career in joyous conflict; indeed, unlike his novelist brother, Henry, who had fled to England, William delighted in the turmoil and clamor of America. He saw its "tough-mindedness" as the hope of the future, and sought to find ways to utilize its fighting instincts in building a better society. James, like most Americans, was an optimist, a believer in progress; yet as an intelligent thinker he could not accept progress as inevitable. Society could advance or deteriorate: accident, community decisions, and the acts of individual leaders would all enter into the equation and decide the outcome. He accepted science as a tool—but not as a Spencerian master. Ideas were meant to be put into action. Truth must be tested by experience, and if there was any Absolute—final, perfect, divine Truth— it was unknowable. This was all to the good, for if society was governed by natural laws there was no freedom for humanity to strive to better itself. Said he: "the practical consequence of such a philosophy is the well-known democratic respect for the sacredness of individuality, —is, at any rate, the outward tolerance of whatever is not itself intolerant."

It was Vermont-born John Dewey who made clear the social evolutionary method of pragmatism, and under the name of Instrumentalism placed his mark on educational theories and practices. The key of his method is that ideas are useful only if they aid in solving problems; the greatest hindrances to social good are the prejudices, slogans, and myths which bar our road to control of our moral and social environment and allow natural science to outdistance social science. Dewey emphasized the learner rather than the subject taught; preached the value of learning by doing—hence the blossoming of laboratories and vocational training; and sought to instil the ability to examine, evaluate, and judge ideas and facts. To him life and thought were continual invitations to adventure. "If it is better to travel than to arrive," said he, "it is because traveling is a constant arriving, while arrival that precludes further traveling is most easily attained by going to sleep or dying." In his ninetieth year he stood before an audience and recounted the dangers of the present-day world and called them a challenge to "bold and imaginative venture in thought. " "All it requires" he added, "is some ideas, imagination and, I warn you, guts."

The world's dislike and fear of all that America stands for has found expression in the battle against John Dewey. His championship of a democratic society in which cultural and material assets shall become the property of the masses rejects the intuitive absolutes on which the élite classes have traditionally based their ascendance. If these mystic insignia of class are displaced by science and experiment their preferred position is lost. Even some liberals have felt that Dewey went too fast and too far; especially have they criticized his belief that war may sometimes be a more efficient use of social energy than submission. The democratic method of utilizing pressure groups, they point out, lends itself to the abuse of democracy by selfish interests which are never absent even in the United States. They assert that Dewey's own Instrumentalism has been used by industrialists to oppose high schools and colleges as "Bolshevistic" and to substitute vocational education; Dewey himself vigorously opposed such misuse of his teachings by special interests.

Though he acknowledged the fact of class warfare, radicals resented his insistence that it is an unreasonable weapon because it is based on the acceptance of an absolutist "religion" (as Communism) and rejects the practical method of experiment. No man in the democratic world was hated more cordially by the Soviets than John Dewey. How just these various accusations are may be left to those who care to labor through his thirty turbidly written books. It would seem, as so often happens, that his teachings have been misused to make science master rather than tool, and to cultivate vocational and professional skills rather than "creative intelligence." Be that as it may, there can be no doubt of Dewey's permanent influence. Alfred North Whitehead,* who certainly did not always agree with him, had this to say:

"John Dewey is to be classed among those men who have made philosophic thought relevant to the needs of their own day. In the performance of this function he is to be classed with the ancient stoics, with Augustine, with Aquinas, with Francis Bacon, with Descartes, with Locke, with Auguste Comte. The fame of these men is not primarily based on the special doctrines which are the subsequent delight of scholars. As the result of their activities the social systems of their times received an impulse of enlightenment, enabling them more fully to achieve such high purposes as were then possible. . . . John Dewey has performed analogous services for American civilization. He has disclosed great ideas relevant to the functioning of the social system. The magnitude of his achievement is to be estimated by reference to the future. For many generations the North American Continent will be the living center of human civilization. Thought and action will derive from it, and refer to it. We are living in the midst of the period subject to Dewey's influence. For this reason there is difficulty in defining it. We cannot observe it from the outside in contrast to other periods also viewed in the same way. But knowledge outruns verbal analysis. John Dewey is the typical effective American thinker; and he is the chief intellectual force providing that environment with coherent purpose."

* * *

Transcendentalists had believed that truth could be known, that good and evil were clearly separated, recognizable, and unchangeable.

---

* In Paul L. Schilpp, ed., *The Philosophy of John Dewey* (1939,) 477-478.

Evolution had introduced the belief that everything is in process of change, and suggested that morals and laws are in each generation the product of social consciousness. The American is dualistic—torn between good and evil, or as some would define them, the ideal and the material. Hence to the materialist the material consequence indictates truth; to the idealist the ideal consequence indicates truth. Pragmatism, like the behavior and institutions of the English-speaking peoples, refuses to choose, but straddles; it operates through compromise, which an undergraduate once aptly described as the lowest of the goods and the highest of the evils.

It is not our purpose here to enter into the philosophical concepts of Pragmatism. Our interest is in its social and economic meaning and effect. Much to the merriment of absolutists, Pragmatists have been subject to a very human confusion as they have groped for definitions, but in the end they have pretty well agreed on the social meaning of their doctrine. With its eyes firmly fixed on the facts of any proposed solution to social problems Pragmatism asks three questions: (1) Will it work? (2) Will it have a good effect on society? (3) If the effect is not completely desirable what compromise shall we draw between the two in order to keep as much as possible of practical program and social good?

Now this is hard doctrine for those who demand certainty. Timorous souls want a world that is tightly and compactly organized on well recognized rules of logic, a world whose actions they can predict and accept, in which they are assured that even if they cannot be lords of the castle they will at least have a snug berth in the kitchen. The Pragmatist, on the other hand, has no patience with the ivory tower but sallies into the world of affairs. The Pragmatists battle long and hard over what constitutes good in the context of any given problem; then there is a meeting of minds in what is quite frankly a compromise. Rarely do they solve any problems in a single conclusive gesture. Rather they go about it little by little, making changes as democratic opinion develops. That is, they attack confusion bit by bit, rather than by sweeping generalizations. The method of democracy is their method of change, because it obliges the individual to share in determining the policy and destiny of his group. To the Pragmatist the fun comes in the fishing—and now and then a fish drawn from the ocean of truth.

Pragmatism's rise marked the reassertion of the democratic spirit in American thought, and its critics, many of them, attacked it because down underneath they were too pessimistic or determinist to accept democracy's process of experimentation. They wanted immediate certainty. William James had rudely jostled the academic mortar-boards on the heads of the philosophers and they rallied to the attack. Pragmatism, said they, is a way of doing without a philosophy—which may be true, at least so far as an elaborate metaphysical structure is concerned—and the idealists accused him of judging everything by its cash value. Pragmatism's recognition of facts has frequently been interpreted wrongly by both idealists and materialists as cheerful acquiescence in materialism. Thoughtless materialists who welcomed Pragmatism to their ranks did not have wit to see its social implications. They set a style, for to this day it is a popular delusion that Pragmatism asks only the one question (Will it work?) and accepts the solution regardless of consequences.

Philosophical, literary, and religious intuitionists have deplored Pragmatism as superficial, on the ground that things are really much more complicated. Probably they are, but trace all philosophical and religious structures to their foundations and we find that they are built deductively on certain assumed axioms or dogmas—such as the Marxists' belief in economic determinism, or Descartes' assumption that "I think, therefore I am." Their comfort lies in their certainty that they have the applicable-on-earth part of the Absolute (eternal Truth), and that since they know good from evil there can be no compromise and everyone must meet their standards. A clear case is the Christian's belief in his creed. Faith, in the beautiful words of St. Paul, "is the substance of things hoped for, the evidence of things not seen." It is the impregnable ground for action, and confidence comes when "we walk by faith, not by sight," holding before us the "shield of faith, wherewith ye shall be able to quench all the fiery darts of the wicked." St. Paul was an absolutist, "for by grace are ye saved through faith; and that not of yourselves: it is the gift of God."

St. Paul also pointed out that practical "Israel, which followed after the law of righteousness, hath not attained to the law of righteousness. Wherefore? Because they sought it not by faith, but as it were by the works of the law." Here undoubtedly lies the Achilles' heel of any "practical" program—its tendency to subordinate ethical aims to immediate objects. American democracy is no exception to the human tendency to forget the ideal at times. The Pragmatist, caught between two absolutes—Christianity and godless authoritarianism—takes refuge with the God whom John the Evangelist portrays: "God

is a spirit, and they that worship Him must worship Him in spirit and
in truth."

When Pragmatism's democratic method is traced to its source it
also is found to be based on an axiom—faith in human dignity and
freedom. Now Christianity also believes in the concept of human dignity
and individual responsibility; so in daily life Pragmatism is reconcilable
with Christian ethics. The Pragmatist, however, does not know eternal
Truth, so he cannot try to apply it. Each generation brings up new
crises which the old rules may not fit, and to meet which new policies
must be evolved. His only axiom is a firm faith in human dignity and
freedom, and he examines all crises and programs with that in mind.
He operates inductively, feeling his way by successive compromises
and referring constantly to experience, to the existing social context,
and to the ideal of human welfare toward which he strives. He believes that we must preserve and reconcile the rival sovereignties and
moral values of the individual on one hand and of society on the
other, as positive aids toward a higher moral order.

He insists first of all in preserving flexibility so that he can be
ready to meet any crisis. He regards all sweeping generalizations
(statements of absolute truth) with suspicion—even this one. He
fears absolutes so much that he is sometimes accused of becoming an
absolutist in his determined rejection of absolutes. The pragmatic
democrat thus espouses a process rather than an absolute, but if he
sees the continuance of that process jeopardized he will fight as fiercely
as any convinced believer in the absolute. He believes with Arthur
Koestler, who learned through bitter experience with Sovietism, that
"the end justifies the means only within very narrow limits; that ethics
is not a function of social utility, and charity not a petty bourgeois
sentiment but the gravitational force which keeps civilization in its
orbit."*

One more word about Pragmatism. The above outline undoubtedly
oversimplifies the actual situation, but it has been necessary to avoid
metaphysical subtleties. Of course even the most rigid idealists have
always made compromises in their daily living and the most confirmed
absolutists have always understood perfectly well that they could not
know all that was in the mind of God—which alone has the right to

---

* Richard Crossman, ed., *The God That Failed: A Confession* (1949), 68.

be the Absolute spelled with a capital "A". As Pragmatism evolved during the Progressive Era it simply gave intellectual respectability to an approach which is as old as humanity and which appears wherever formative civilizations have material problems to overcome. Nevertheless its method has been more common among the so-called Anglo-Saxon peoples than among others. They have showed the greatest disinclination to bind themselves in the chains of logic, and the greatest genius in overcoming unexpected obstacles which more logical peoples would insist were insurmountable. Pragmatism was in the American air, and its manifestations did not always wait for William James or John Dewey to give it official utterance. American conquerors of the wilderness had judged programs and actions by their consequences, and it was natural that many teachers, thinkers, and reformers should do likewise. Long before this James Russell Lowell had advised the pragmatic method in meeting an American crisis.

"New occasions teach new duties; time makes ancient good uncouth;
They must upward still and onward, who would keep abreast of
    Truth;
Lo, before us gleam her campfires! We, ourselves must Pilgrims be,
Launch our Mayflower and steer boldly in the desperate winter sea,
Nor attempt the Future's portal with the Past's blood-rusted key."

* * *

European art was rooted in a civilization which had developed with more or less symmetry from classical times to the Industrial Revolution. The American vernacular, on the other hand, to quote one of the ablest students of the subject, is the folk art "of the first people in history who, disinherited of a great cultural tradition, found themselves living under democratic institutions in an expanding machine economy."* This definition does not include such inherited "folk art" as that of the Pennsylvania Dutch, in so far as it sought symbolism or prettiness.

Pragmatism was the expression in politics, society, and intellect of what the vernacular was in art. Hitherto the prestige of the cultivated tradition had drawn American artists to Europe, and many of them had stayed there because there was not enough sand in their souls to

---

* John A. Kouwenhoven, *Made in America* (1948), 15.

face life in the sprawling, formless, noisy country of their birth. As a result, the vernacular had been relegated to the common craftsmen and to a few rebel artists, architects, and engineers. They had the vision of something new in the world, a civilization built upon service to the people and appreciation by the people; and in pursuance of this dream they were trying to grasp the way to utilize the material resources of America and to express its values in new artistic forms.

The political institutions of the United States were based on democracy, but many of its social institutions were based on distrust of the people. The inexorable pressure of democracy was shaping a machine culture to exploit our resources in the service of the masses; the inexorable pressure of the American inferiority complex was calling for the absorption *in toto* of the European cultivated tradition. The conflict which grew out of these clashing pressures not only pained artists but confused the public. Nevertheless, generations of simple American mechanics refused to feel inferior but asserted that function should govern form. They deplored European "art" and "beauty" as mere artificial prettiness but never realized that they themselves had found the nub of art and beauty in their vernacular. This fact is evident to anyone who examines the simple architecture of the ante-bellum period such as the Shaker barn or the Cape Cod cottage, or the common artifacts such as furniture and tools—for example, the ax, a light, utilitarian, and graceful descendant of the European's unwieldy broadax.

The American vernacular influence sprang from the masses and has persisted despite the determined effort of the top crust to bastardize it by putting Corinthian pillars on steam engines and coruscating their framework with pomegranates and arabesques. Europe feared the machine and wished to hide and prettify it. The American vernacular wished to strip away unnecessary bulk, weight, and ornamentation in order to simplify and cheapen the machine, and to increase its efficiency. The difference in approach was fundamental. Europe wished to preserve the old, which itself had once been functional but was now outmoded by new techniques, because the old represented the ascendance of an age-old élite. The American instinctively realized that if the machine was to serve *all* the people it must not be subjected to the old artistic forms.

The American was short-cutting European evolution and entering the era of mass production; the same struggle went on in Europe, but the European was more firmly rooted in the past. Thus, about 1870, Americans used a cast-steel plow which weighed forty pounds, while the British clung to a wrought-iron plow (intended to do the same work) which weighed two hundred fifty pounds. Even though the ornamental lines and coruscations of the European tradition were then sadly afflicting American machines, the most impressive exhibit at the Centennial Exhibition of 1876 was the enormous, starkly functional Corliss steam engine. Even Europeans recognized its artistic quality. The *London Times,* little inclined to praise things American, noted that "the American mechanizes as an old Greek sculptured, as the Venetian painted."

Horatio Greenough, a sculptor, was one of the first to recognize the clash which was beginning even in his day. We, said he, found our institutions on hope; Europeans on the past. "We hoist the sail and are seasick; they anchor and dance." The struggle between native and alien forms afflicted not only art, mechanics, and literature but politics, for the Civil War was in a way an aspect of this conflict. The cultivated tradition refused to adapt itself to the vernacular, and the result was for a long time the sterilization of both on the American scene: drab cities dotted with pompous classical monuments. Even the vernacular builder was too often affected (where his patron could afford it) and broke his vernacular plane surfaces with the horrible jigsaw lacework sometimes called Carpenter-Gothic.

The battle was under way when in 1898 George S. Morison, builder of famous bridges, published *The New Epoch as Developed by the Manufacture of Power.* Power, he said, would mold a new civilization and a new ethics, destroying the old in so far as necessary to the development of the new era. He saw the spread of education to all the world, but there would be danger in the transition epoch when the half-educated masses "do not know enough to recognize their limitations, but know too much to follow loyally the direction of better qualified leaders."

The above is not meant to imply that we must cast the old aside or sneer at the traditions of the race; but if we wish to reach fulfillment we must not allow them to confine us too strictly. Rather, we must select from them building stones to insert at proper places into the new structure. America is building a new phase of Western Civilization which will mold the old traditions to the new machine age and will give a better life to the common man. Perhaps it is only natural that we should be torn between our nostalgia for the old and our faith in our power to create the new.

It is sometimes difficult for the layman to understand that it is the artist who is the vanguard of new phases of civilization. This fact was shown during the Gilded Age, when a group of rebel artists began to work toward impressionism, partly inspired by Paris, partly by Oriental art, and partly self-taught. The dreamily sentimental Hudson River School gave way reluctantly to the deeper insight of George Innes, while marine subjects found advocates in that son of whaling New Bedford, the fiercely questing Albert Ryder, and the spacious Bostonian, Winslow Homer, who found his happier medium in water colors. Even beyond these was Thomas Eakins of Philadelphia, who in painting for himself was painting for a coming generation.

Meanwhile an architectural revolution had been wrought by new materials and a host of new utilities which required a maze of pipes and conduits. Associated in designing the buildings of the World's Columbian Exposition were a number of Chicagoans who were to exercise a vital influence on American architecture; out of their daring and imagination came the skyscraper and the modern style. That the new day of iron construction was not solely American was shown by London's Crystal Palace and Paris's Eiffel Tower. But for the most part it was the proud development of Chicago.

Louis Sullivan, a bitter and cantankerous Bostonian of Irish and Swiss lineage, who was established in Chicago, found in the skyscraper the "emotional synthesis of practical conditions." His guiding rule came to him one day in the quiet of the Vatican's Sistine Chapel when Michelangelo seemed to be audibly saying, "Form follows function." Sullivan looked on architecture as a social manifestation and read in it the social state of mind. His functionalism, cool and intelligent without bleakness, whether in skyscrapers or dwellings, was in striking contrast to the garrulousness of the average American architect which, then and since, seems to betray a confusion in values.

Some of his pupils failed to comprehend his method and produced bleakness, but the greatest of them, Frank Lloyd Wright, a product of rural Wisconsin, may yet be the harbinger of a new day. Building on the simplicity of Jefferson and rooting his creations in the earth, the rocks, and the trees, Wright proposed an architecture worthy of self-reliant democracy, which could learn principles from the past but not forms. Taking from the Orient or from any other source, Wright read, wrote, and spoke as he designed, and by 1910 he had marshaled his ideas for unity, sincerity, simplicity, and repose. "As for the future," said he, "the work shall grow more truly simple . . . more fluent . . . more organic . . . for only so can architecture be worthy of its high rank as a fine art." Sullivan, ignored by important clients, found solace in a series of small banks, "jewels on the shoddy main streets of the prairie towns." Wright, however, was never without clients, and before long his ideas inspired a new school of the modern in Europe—a school whose hangers-on he soon repudiated.

*   *   *

There was a saying at the turn of the century that the United States imported art and exported artists. It was tragically true that in their zeal to copy European good form in art, Americans were unable to recognize the artistic pioneers in their midst; such artists took what commissions they could get at home or moved to Europe where there were more rebels to make them welcome. Young artists, of course, could expect recognition only after a term of study in Paris, Munich, or Rome (and here the word "artist" applies not only to painters, but to sculptors, architects, writers, and musicians). The popularity of the European flavor in American art, fiction, poetry, and historical writing must have betokened a desire to escape from the present and the real.

Such absorption bred in them a nostalgia which gilded even the lamp posts of Paris and made it impossible for them to distinguish between the good and the mediocre—let alone to appreciate the promise of their own country. Tradition was poorly understood but none the less revered; there is the instance of a dean of women in an American university who quite naively "started new traditions." Like Henry James, who gathered "a golden-ripe crop of English impressions" as soon as he crossed the threshold of his inn, the American exile found stimulus in an environment which the natives regarded as depressing or accepted as routine. He wistfully endowed its trifling mannerisms with an aura of leisure, charm, and grace, without sensing that underneath ran a current of brutality as cynical—more so—than that in the United States, and without the American promise. If only America could have these mannered traditions! It was William Dean Howells who answered with gentle irony that perhaps it was as well that we had no sovereign, no court, no aristocracy, no clergy, no church, no country gentlemen, palaces, nor manor houses—we had simply the whole of human life left!

The age rang with the clash and din of the change from agriculture to industry, from the culture of the few to the culture of the many.

There was in the potential intelligentsia little faith in the future, little determination to put their shoulders to the wheel of national destiny. Their superficial optimism evaporated in the uproar. With the exceptions of the hardy souls whom we shall take up later, they fled in distaste or alarm, some into a sullen silence; some into the arms of the brute they feared; some to Europe, hoping thereby to turn charm into power, to nurse the flicker of aspiration into the flame of genius. They hated competition, probably because they felt they could not win, and they suspected democracy because (in the current milieu) it called for competition.

Even the sincerest artist was prompted to flight by the feeling that he could never set down in writing or in paint or carve in stone that sprawling giant, America, with all its turmoil, confusion, and contraditions. He failed to see the age-old connection between conquest of physical problems and intellectual and esthetic growth. "We're the disinherited of art," cried Henry James of the American expatriates, and failed to see that Europe also was striving, even more bitterly, to disinherit its pioneers. Expatriates mistook for freedom the European weariness which merely shrugged at their experiments.

The presiding genius of American expatriate artists and writers must always be Henry James. The talented James family, one of the most inexhaustible studies in American history, is notable for the two brothers: Henry, who fled, and William, who stayed to do his bit. When Henry decided to become an expatriate, his brother pled with him. "Europe," he said, "has been made what it is by men staying in their homes and fighting stubbornly generation after generation for all the beauty, comfort, order that they have got—we must abide and do the same. . . . A man always pays in one way or another for expatriation, for detachment from his plain, primary heritage." Perhaps Henry would have been smothered had he stayed; at any rate, he settled into the literary life of London to write the "mandarin" novels which bear his name.

Presently he became almost morbidly fascinated by Americans as social phenomena, particularly in contact with the old civilization of Europe: their "absolute and incredible lack of culture." Most notable is his portrait of the direct and self-confident Christopher Newman in *The American* (1877), who falls in love with a Parisian noble lady. Though she returns his love, the relationship can only end in driving her to a nunnery. James's Americans knew defeat in their contacts with the older civilization, but somehow they always emerged the victors—greater in spiritual stature but no less American.

Could he have been portraying his own history as he would have wished it to happen? He became the dean of literary London and, in his dissection of the inner mind, the inspiration of a whole school of British and French novelists; yet when the romance palled and he sought renewal of strength in America after an absence of almost thirty years, the new America seemed more horrible than the old one, and he fled back to England. He had been defeated in every respect in America, where it was well known that Americans won material victories and suffered spiritual disaster; yet when his American characters suffered defeat in Europe, they seemed to have an inner strength and resilience which he lacked.

It was in 1899 that Hamlin Garland visited James at Rye, and in the course of their conversation the expatriate fixed a somber eye on his guest and made this remarkable confession:

"If I were to live my life over again I would be an American. I would steep myself in America, I would know no other land. I would study its beautiful side. The mixture of Europe and America which you see in me has proved disastrous. It has made of me a man who is neither American nor European. I have lost touch with my own people and I live here alone. . . . I shall never return to the United States, but I wish I could."*

It was the architect Louis Sullivan who laid his finger on the malaise of the expatriate when he issued his war cry: "Form follows function." Forms *had* followed functions in the past, and those forms had become fixed in modern minds as the sine-qua-non of the good life. Without disparaging traditions, for it is clear that new cultural forms must build on old ones, it must be observed that esthetes of the Gilded Age failed to realize that the New World (the New World of time rather than of geography) demanded new forms to accompany new functions. The Machine Age was upon us with its inexorable demand for new forms in art and life. The esthetes hated the machine less for what it did to the masses than for what it did to the old forms of art which they had imbedded in their subconscious as unalterable.

The Great Refusal of the United States to take its place in the world during the first half of the twentieth century may be laid at

---

* Hamlin Garland, *Roadside Meetings*, (1930).

the door of its once-potential intelligentsia. The American public distrusted them and their ideas and confused them with the "corrupt"
world from which the pioneer ancestors had fled. Under the paint
of the Gilded Age, Americans could not help feeling that the man
with an idea worth-while did not give up until his last breath was
gone. The expatriates had been false to their stubborn Puritan heritage,
which demanded that a man go through fire and rack for what he
believed.

XII

The Pragmatic Corporation

THE United States made relatively few contributions to pure science before World War I, but it was in the front rank in the development of practical applications of science and in making engineering refinements. Even in these fields, while it may have had primacy, it was by no means dominant; nor for that matter was any single nation. Advancement was the product of international interchange of information; the so-called "inventions" were mostly the culmination of successive evolutionary changes made by a series of contributors. Indeed, the developments in mathematics, physics, chemistry, and metallurgy were so essential to each other that in their applications they could only move abreast. True, the United States did make unique contributions to industry, but these, as we shall see, were overwhelmingly in the fields of management, marketing, and sometimes engineering.

American industry (given the human and scientific requisites) was certain to prosper because water power, coal, petroleum, wood, ores, and the silicates proper for glass and ceramics were present in such abundance. Of these petroleum was for a time all but an American monopoly. The significance of petroleum derivatives in lubrication and heating is obvious. They drive internal-combustion engines, and as such power automobiles, airplanes, locomotives, motorships, and stationary engines. Coal and water power built a tremendous electrical industry which revolutionized lighting, the power basis of industry, urban transport, communication both by wire and wireless, refrigeration, air compression, and the extractive industries.

The chemical industries, based partially on coal-tar and petroleum derivatives but drawing heavily on mineral and agricultural resources, revolutionized medicine and food preservation, introduced plastics, developed soil science, found new uses for rubber, founded a new entertainment industry, and seared the face of Mother Earth with explosives. In so far as the technological aspects of living are concerned, George

Washington would have been more at home in ancient Egypt than in an American city of 1920.

Effective mass production developed first in the United States because it was promoted by a combination of fundamental and peculiar characteristics which around 1900 existed there and nowhere else. First was American receptivity to new methods, promoted by liberal patent laws, the early application of laboratory tests and research, and by the fact that no restriction on new processes had been laid down by guilds, labor unions, or hereditary social or economic castes. Second was the intelligence and know-how of American workmen who had been familiar with tools from boyhood—often power-driven tools, at that. Third was the scarcity of labor which promoted the invention of labor-saving devices. This meant that power was applied to manufacturing processes wherever possible, that machinery and parts were standardized, that American products were pre-eminently machine-made, and that the bulk of our manufactures made small changes—as in meat packing, flour milling, lumbering, dairying, and oil refining. Fourth was the vast store of natural resources easily and cheaply available to entrepreneurs. Fifth, and as vital as any of the above, was the vast expanding domestic market, unvexed by internal inspection or customs barriers. Lastly was a unique contribution possible (at the moment) only in America: this lay in the American genius for teamwork, on the part of both management and labor, for out of these rose the triumph of mass production.

We have seen how the evolution toward mass production had gotten well under way before the Civil War. The gunmakers of the Connecticut Valley had introduced the interchangeable part, designed elaborate machine tools, and applied power to machinery. These applications had spread throughout the country, and the demands of the Civil War had accelerated their application. As soon as machine tools began to pour out nuts, bolts, nails, wire, and gadgets, the early stages of mass production were really under way. Efficient methods and laboratory tests were introduced. Bill Jones, manager of the Carnegie steel mills, never hesitated to discard even a good machine for a better one, and Carnegie used to open his board meetings with the query, "Well, what machines shall we throw away this time?"

Oliver Evans had long since developed his process of automatic flour milling, but apparently it was not the first example of continuous automatic production, for as early as 1617 an English traveler saw the principle at work in a Spanish mint. Probably as early as 1835

Cincinnati meat packers introduced an overhead conveyor which carried carcasses along a "disassembly" line. In the 1890's freight-car trucks were hauled along a track while workmen on scaffolds alongside completed the superstructures. Actually the assembly line was not new. As early as the fifteenth century Venetian shipbuilders had floated their hulks down narrow canals while workmen stationed in windows en route completed the ship.

These preliminaries, though doubtless each of them was carefully thought out, were basically no more than common sense. There remained the fourth step: scientific management. The leader in this advance was Frederick Winslow Taylor, a Philadelphia engineer who in 1893 set himself up as an engineering consultant with "Systematizing Shop Management and Manufacturing Costs a Specialty." Taylor believed that by planning and routing work through the factory and by job and time studies he could set up reasonable and efficient production standards. The slide rule, the stop watch, photograph, and Taylor's own development of high-speed tool steel were essential parts of the research of the new school. He was well aware that workmen "soldiered" on the job, and he laid it to the existing antagonism between worker and manager. He hoped to allay this growing antagonism and at the same time increase production by advocating a wage system based on the "differentiated piece rate," which would stimulate and reward the efficient workers and would introduce a new spirit of co-operation—essentially the extension of democracy to industry.

Taylor and the enthusiastic associates who quickly gathered about him saw the industrial problem not only in terms of machines and efficiency but also in terms of human relations. High wages, high standards of safety, and good working conditions entered into their calculations, and they were even aware of the effect of the social conditions in the community upon the job. At first business, rolling luxuriously in profits, hesitated to adopt Taylor's ideas, and they actually found a warmer reception in Europe. By the time his book, *Principles of Scientific Management,* was published in 1911, profits had come down and entrepreneurs were ready to try anything which would reduce costs. Possibly this came about at least in part through the closing of the frontier and the growing realization that easily adaptable materials were no longer to be had for the taking; probably other factors such as overcapitalization and the demands of labor were also responsible. Unfortunately management refused at first to adopt Taylor's well-rounded plans but accepted only the aspects which immediately cut costs and raised production. The adoption of the remainder has come about partly by enlightened management, partly by legislative and labor-union pressure.

*　　*　　*

The logical outcome of "Taylorization" was the assembly line, and it was only natural that it should first reach perfection in the automobile industry, then the least enslaved by tradition. The man who inspired this revolutionary change was Henry Ford, a Michigan farm-boy machinist who had become an Edison power-company engineer. As early as 1893 Ford began to construct a car out of odds and ends, and when it actually worked he resolved to make cars for the market. After two heart-breaking false starts, in 1903 the Ford Motor Company finally got under way. The company had been financed only with difficulty, and competition was brisk, but business was excellent, at least partly because Barney Oldfield, recently a bicycle racer, began a long automobile racing career by driving a Ford to a walk-away victory over Winton.

During the first summer the new venture, financed with $28,000 in cash and notes, cleared $36,000; in the depression year of 1907 it made a million. Much of this was due to Ford's own courage. At this time motor-car makers were forced to pay royalties to the Electric Vehicle Company of Connecticut, a concern which had acquired George Selden's basic automotive patent and which was owned by W. C. Whitney, the Wall Street plunger. Ford refused point-blank to pay and after eight years of litigation broke the motor monopoly (1911). However, fifteen years of association had laid the groundwork of the cross-licensing system which has kept the automobile industry relatively free from patent conflicts.

During the early years automobiles were largely luxuries which could be afforded only by the well-to-do, and manufacturers accepted the fact of a limited market and added to the price as much as they dared under the highly competitive conditions. Mass-production methods were used in the production of American cars from the first, and in 1906 Cadillac mechanics in London amazed British manufacturers by assembling three cars from piles of parts and then putting them through track tests with perfect scores. Henry M. Leland was the genius behind this demonstration, but it was only the beginning of what was to come.

Ford now resolved to mass-produce a good light car which would be cheap enough to tap the rural and middle-class market. Economies were made in design and fuel consumption, vanadium steel was utilized, and production was limited to one type of engine and chassis. Even the bodies were strictly utilitarian, and no aberrations were permitted; a current joke had it that the customer could have any color he wanted so long as it was black. This was the famous Model T, which was first produced in 1909 and with slight changes remained in production until 1927. Altogether about 15 million copies of Model T were sold, half the cars on American roads, while the price descended from $850 at the beginning to $290 in 1924.

In 1914 Ford wrought two revolutions: the introduction of the conveyor-belt assembly line and the institution of the five-dollar-a-day wage. More than this, he resolved to pour practically all of the profits into expansion, and when the minority stockholders objected he won independence by buying them out. Meanwhile he bought ore and coal mines, ore boats and a railroad, put up blast furnaces and steel mills, and acquired parts factories. By 1927 he had set up a new center for his vast empire at River Rouge, where endless conveyor belts carried the slowly growing cars before lines of automatons, each devoted to his minute task and nothing else. Ford's crisis came in the primary postwar depression of 1920-21, when he was financially overextended and General Motors, backed by Wall Street capital, was fighting for the market. Ford could have obtained relief by surrendering to the bankers, but he refused. Gathering up all available parts, he put together 125,000 cars and shipped them to his dealers, in effect forcing them to furnish emergency finances. The Ford Empire was saved.

Ford was tall and thin, with the eyes of a zealot and the persistence of a leech. His leaping imagination was that of an empire builder, but—and this is the secret of empire building—it was strictly limited by the practical and by the ideals of the people who were to compose the empire. All his life Ford sought to strengthen in the American people the Calvinist virtues of caution, self-assurance, thrift, and deference to success. Provincial in speech and manner, ignorant of everything save mechanics ("I don't like to read books; they muss up my mind"), utterly unable to compose or deliver a speech, Ford was a man of action rather than thought. He seldom pondered abstract matters for long and apparently reached his decisions by intuitive jumps. A self-made man and in the beginning something of a populist, he despised the *rentier* who lived on unearned profits, and he never learned from the past ("History is bunk") beyond catching a nostalgia for old pewter and square dancing. To him beauty lay solely in utility.

He domineered over his executives, sweated his employees, all but ruined his distributors and parts contractors, sowed racial bigotry and unrealistic pacifism with equal conviction and naivete, was a faddist on food, tobacco, and alcohol, and quite innocently disavowed any inclination to do-goodism which did not also bring a profit in dollars and cents. Hard-souled, stubborn, efficient, wrapped up in his work, suspicious of amusements, reverencing accomplishment and power, indifferent to the fate of individuals, determined to have social and economic progress but to make it pay its own way, Ford was simply the typical American raised to the *nth* power. And the American people awarded him a faith in his capacity for industrial statesmanship and in his dictum that "machinery is the new messiah" that was not shaken until the Great Depression. Such were the characteristics of the people whom he found, the characteristics which despite himself he was to alter so profoundly.

Henry Ford's engineers in their search for means of speeding up production and lowering costs had adopted some of Taylor's principles and had laid out their departments and machines in such a way as to feed parts efficiently to the central assembling area; in the latter area specialization was already under way, as certain workmen were assigned to gangs which performed certain functions in the assembling. This led to a greater demand for parts, and experiments were begun in specializing parts production and assembly. Gravity slides between benches helped to hasten the work, but presently the engineers began to apply the overhead-conveyor principle already in use by the Chicago meat packers. The result was that sub-assembled parts were fed to the assembly area so fast that chaos threatened.

The desperate engineers then devised an endless-chain or belt conveyor which carried the chassis past lines of workmen, each of whom performed a carefully planned and limited function in assembling the car. The introduction of the automatic conveyor (January 1914) was the final step in the evolution of assembly-line mass production. Within three months Ford workmen were assembling a Model T in ninety-three minutes; on 31 October 1925 they turned out a car for each ten seconds of the working day.

*   *   *

Ford thus expressed his method: (1) Centralized management; (2) Control of raw materials by the manufacturer, (3) Specialized tools and machinery without regard to initial cost; (4) Subdivision and specialization of labor; (5) Motion study and efficient shop management; (6) High wages and short hours, but no tolerance of shop rules or trade-union demands that might curtail production; (7) Abolition of red tape and ritual.

This is the technique properly called mass production. Anything less falls short by so much of true mass production until at some undetermined point it becomes merely large-scale production, which, as in most European industries, makes up in weight of hours and manpower and individual skill for its lack of the mass-production technique.

In practice mass production means that the shaping of every part must be reduced to its simplest terms—so simple that it can be performed by an automatic machine or by a machine operated (in most cases) by a worker who at best is semiskilled. Ford estimated in 1922 that of his jobs eighty-five per cent required less than a month of training, while forty-five per cent took only one day. Drucker describes the preparations for mass production of planes in World War II.*

"First came the design—not of machines but of the plane as an assembly of identical and interchangeable parts. Then came the analysis of each part as a problem in mass production, as something that is being produced in a sequence of elementary and basic operations, performable fast and accurately by an unskilled or semiskilled worker. Next came the task of merging the production of each part into a plant producing the whole—a task involving three distinct problems of organization; one of people working as members of a team to a common end, one of technical processes, one of materials-flow. Finally came the job of training thousands of new workers and hundreds of new supervisors many of whom had never seen the inside of a plant before. On those four pillars, design of the final product as a composite of interchangeable parts, design of the production of each part as a series of simple, repetitive operations, design of a plant to integrate human labor, machines and materials into one whole, and training in skills and in team-work, rested every achievement of our war production. Whenever, because of ignorance or urgency, the attempt was made to slight one of these four tasks of organization—and the

---

* Peter Drucker, *Big Business* (1947), 24-25; also issued as *Concept of the Corporation* (1946).

temptation to do so was great as each of them is time-consuming and can be speeded only with difficulty—the result was failure to produce."

Thus it is not enough to put the principles of centralization into operation. Once established they must be kept up to date. Successful mass production calls for continual alertness and study by management; a willingness to change methods and machinery frequently; a large and, if possible, growing marketing area; and the cooperation of labor. European industries which have tried to adopt mass-production techniques have almost invariably failed at one of these points; they are unwilling to replace a new machine by a better one, they sweat their labor, or they do not possess a large enough market to absorb their product.

Henry Ford violated some of his own canons and paid a severe penalty. His relations with labor were bad (after the first few years), and his boasted high wages turned out to be shams inasmuch as they either were not paid as claimed or were earned by an unmerciful speed-up of the production line. Even more serious, perhaps, the Model T was practically frozen for nineteen years, and the Ford organization did not develop the knack of retooling for a new model without seriously interrupting production. The result was that by 1927 Chevrolet had passed Ford in sales. The Model T was so outdated that it had to be dropped, and the vast thousands of Ford workers were thrown on public charity for more than a year while the factory retooled.

The mass-production technique had passed beyond the ken of its greatest genius and had become devoted to flexibility of method and product, more organizational than technical. It was this fact which made possible the production miracles of World War II. There was a limit beyond which even the mass-production process could not be profitably subdivided. For example, Ford stubbornly handicapped himself by insisting upon too many special-purpose machine tools; General Motors found it better to use more general-purpose tools, which would not have to be scrapped with every change of model.

The mass producer brings his materials in either raw or finished form from all over the country at calculated intervals; to build up too great a stock would tie up capital and perhaps wipe out the thin margin of profit. In effect he makes lumber camps, mines, glass, paint, fabric, and tire factories, and railroads and steamship lines a part of his assembly line. Just as revolutionary are the marketing concepts of mass production. Basically it is not brought on by demand but creates its own market. Said Ford: "Mass production begins, then, in the conception of a public need *of which the public may not as yet be conscious* and proceeds on the principle that use-convenience must be matched by price-convenience. . . . Mass production precedes mass consumption and makes it possible, by reducing costs and thus producing greater use-convenience and price-convenience."

Thus, with every reduction in cost a new market is tapped among people in the next lower income stratum. Mass-production industries are easily affected by changes in economic conditions, for it is possible to make a snug profit at ninety per cent of full production but to lose heavily at sixty per cent. The result is that there is a limit to which mass production can be applied with social profit. One way in which industries sought to overcome this situation was to open new markets by wooing new buyers with advertising. The serious overproduction of the 1920's led to an astounding development of this "art."

Mass production is popularly identified with the assembly line. Actually that is the final stage of only one type. Behind it lies the production line in which each part, for example a crankshaft, is machined by a succession of workers, each performing a separate operation. Then comes the sub-assembly line in which the parts are fitted together to form, for example, an engine. The sub-assembly lines then feed their products at proper intervals to the assembly line on which the automobile, the reaper, or the refrigerator gradually take final form. But the assembly line is *not* an essential feature of all mass production, as will be recognized by anyone familiar with those automatic "ribbon" production-line industries such as paper making and strip steel milling, and with incandescent lamp manufacture, which are automatic in a way that automobile manufacture can never be. Oliver Evans's automatic flour mill of 1783 was as authentic a form of mass production as Ford's assembly line. Then, of course, there are mass-production industries in which hand work still necessarily plays a large part—as the garment-making industry. It may be technically possible to invent machines which by certain alterations with wrench and screw driver can be used to make automatically a variety of articles, but it is difficult to conceive of machines that can make garments without human intervention.

Since World War II we have seen the dawn of a movement which undoubtedly will bring in a second industrial revolution. It is *automation,* the use of machines to run machines and thus to minimize direct human intervention in the actual processes of manufacture even of articles as complicated as automobile engines. Tape controls and electronic gadgets can direct the handling of materials and the setting of machines, and can process data and exercise routine judgments. Norbert Wiener, one of the foremost founders of automation, speaks of it as preparing the way for the "human use of human beings." There will be few workers visible on a factory floor, but behind the scenes as production increases under the new scheme there will be even more workers engaged in doing the things which machines cannot do—thinking, analyzing, synthesizing, deciding, and acting purposefully.

It is apparent that under such a regime the "trained barbarian"— the technician—will be of minimum value. There will be an overwhelming demand for men and women who are disciplined thinkers. Already the prospect is beginning to revolutionize industrialists' attitudes toward the aims of education and is beginning to restore the old respect for training in "academic" subjects and to point up the old truth that the proper study of mankind is man. The transition should not be difficult, for American engineers have never quite lost sight of the social and humanistic objectives of mass production.

Automation, no more than the older mass production, can provide a straight and easy path to the gates of paradise. There will be, as always in human affairs, forks which can lead to destruction. There is danger that automation may cut out competition and thus reduce the consumer's protection. Its demand that the *whole* business be automated (else it will go bankrupt) may bring about a captive market and a captive consumer. Its demand for highly intelligent workers may pose the problem of what to do with those who are not as highly endowed but who are entitled to an outlet for their creative energies and who have a right to feel that they are *needed*. These are problems which can and will be solved in ways that are consistent with human freedom and dignity.

It might be well to interject a word of caution here. The mass-production technique has *not* taken over all of American industry—nor can it. We have seen how the Model T created a market which it could not hold against the Chevrolet and Plymouth with their greater power and luxury and more graceful lines. In the same way mass production has called forth tastes and needs that we never knew we had, while rising income enables us to gratify them. The demand for specialty, luxury, and custom-made goods is rising. In 1939 by far the most of our industrial establishments—about one tenth of one per cent of the total—employed more than 2,500 workers; 40 per cent employed five or less. Out of 8 million industrial fabricators 30 per cent worked in factories which employed 100 or less, and only 25 per cent worked in factories which employed 100 or more.

Nevertheless, the American standard of living depends basically on cheap raw materials and on the mass-production technique. Ford's egomania led him to disclaim "any dependence on scientific management." His engineers knew better. Ford might claim the credit for the development of mass production, but actually he was merely the latest and greatest of a long line of contributors which included such names as Evans, Whitney, North, Blanchard, Colt, Edison, Sprague, and Taylor—not to mention Ford's own men: Couzens, Flanders, Knudsen, Emde, Klann, Avery, and above all the blustering, brilliant "Great Dane," Charles E. Sorensen. Ford's publicity machine was geared to give him all honor, so it was natural that before long public and industrialists alike were acclaiming him as the father of mass production. The world listened with respect when he proclaimed that "Machinery is the new Messiah" and had faith in his glowing picture of a new and better material world. In Europe mass production became known both as "rationalization" (from its reasoned, scientific orderliness) and "Fordism."

Nevertheless, it was the genius of Ford as an engineer and manager which lay behind the triumph of the mass-production technique. The effect upon the United States can best be illustrated by brief reference to the automobile. Its first effect was industrial, for competitors were forced to ape Ford's methods, and the technique presently leaped to other fields. The entire emphasis of the economy was shifted, and the American standard of living shot upward. The automobile industry gives direct and indirect employment to six million workers and is an enormous consumer of steel, nickel, lead, alloys, plate glass, fabrics, and plastics. It put Texas and Oklahoma on the map of prosperity with its booming demand for gasoline and oil. Its rubber purchases raised Malaysia to enviable prosperity—until Japanese conquerors and synthetic rubber came along.

The automobile industry speeded up the marketing of farm products, accelerated the turnover of goods, and hastened business procedures. It lifted the country out of the mud by a stupendous roadbuilding program—in 1950 there were over three million miles of improved roads and streets for the use of forty-two million vehicles. It has remade the political, social, and psychological outlook of the country by telescoping rural distances, spreading out the cities, affording a cheap and easy means for shifting population, has changed leisure habits, popularized the "touring" vacation, and integrated the nation as never before.

On the other hand the country's railroad system, already ailing from financial abuse, was reduced almost to bankruptcy by the competition of trucks, buses, and passenger automobiles. The automobile has encouraged foot-looseness and irresponsibility, inculcated the bad habit of installment buying, has weakened family ties, and has taken a million lives and maimed many more. The taste it gave of luxurious living whetted the American appetite for more and gave an impetus to the propaganda for the welfare state. When the coo of the political turtle dove was heard over the radio, the citizen was ready to listen. In the nineteenth century it was Daniel Webster who had taught the sovereignty of the nation over the state; in the twentieth century it was Henry Ford, the cantankerous and individualistic populist of Dearborn.

*   *   *

Nineteenth-century men lived in an economy of scarcity, in which it was believed that supply could not overtake demand. The interests of the producer and of society seemed irreconcilable; an industry was sure it must seek monopoly in order to keep from being wrecked by competitors, but society felt it must prevent monopoly in order to keep from being milked. Now we live in an economy made by mass production, in which the supply is prospectively unlimited, but demand is limited only by effective purchasing power. For the first time maximum profit can be obtained by maximum production at minimum cost—exactly what society has always wanted. We have not worked out all the details, but the broad outline of the future is clear. Mass production can introduce an economy of plenty, a state which up to our own time only utopian dreamers dared to contemplate.

A thoughtful view of mass production will show that there is far more to it than careful technical blueprinting and management. It is even more basically a social effort. Now the success of a social effort depends upon the co-operation of the participating individuals. It is perhaps true that machines and many aspects of scientific management could have been developed without the inspiration of democracy. Nevertheless, the ultimate secret of the American know-how lies not in machines nor in scientific management nor even in financial and corporation organization. Basically it depends upon the fostering of the spirit of freedom, cooperation, and *esprit de corps* on the part of the workers, engineers, management, and capital. This condition may bring an upstanding demand for high wages and miscellaneous benefits (often enforced by strikes), but this demand is only a realization of Taylor's original concept that mass production could be successful only if the workers shared in pride and effort.

Progressivism's transformation of democracy aided in achieving the desired result not only by forcing the corporations into line but by creating a new atmosphere, in which labor could strive for its rights with more hope of success. Only in so far as this democratization has been achieved can American mass production be said to have succeeded. This idea is something which foreigners usually can not or will not understand, and it must be admitted that many Americans have fallen short in realization, even Henry Ford himself. On the other hand, it must be recognized that industrial democracy exercised without a proper sense of responsibility and self-restraint on the part of the workers will lead to what we now call "featherbedding" and eventually to break-down. The purpose of mass production is to raise production; only then can it raise wages. In the production process it relies chiefly on semiskilled workers, but this is possible only because its preparatory stage utilizes an ever-growing number of skilled men— tool, die, and pattern makers, engineers, chemists, and psychologists.

Experience has shown that the corporation is the most practical agent in working this modern miracle of technical, financial, and social co-operation; and the corporation is useful whether the economy is capitalistic, socialistic, or totalitarian. The more vigorously theorists and politicians have denounced the corporation, the more it has flourished. Today we deserve no special credit for realizing what the Progressives of 1900 often denied: the big corporation is here to stay. Internally the corporation is like a planned society. It brings together the factors of production—land, labor, and capital—and adds a fourth, the manager, who makes the whole greater than the sum of its parts.

Before World War I the corporation had taken on pretty much the color which is familiar to us today. As in an army, no one man is indispensable. Frederick Taylor recognized the new nature of business when in 1911 he stated that "no great man can (with the old system of personal management) hope to compete with a number of ordinary men who have been properly organized so as efficiently to co-operate." Specialization within the organization was already well under way: specialization in the various phases of manufacture, sales, maintenance, construction, research, purchasing, finance, and labor relations. Industrial and personnel engineers were trying to learn the art of co-ordinating all these activities.

"The great corporations had their own politics, their own internal diplomacy, their own bureaucracies and hierarchies of power. They had their own court conflicts and court scandals, their own hereditary offices and strategic marriages, their own ministerial cabinets composed of men brought up occasionally from the ranks and their own pensioners who played polo or sailed yachts, held balls and horse shows while great corporate machines ground out profits or consumed capital."*

Mass production has given the corporation a significance which it could not otherwise have enjoyed. This fact was just as true in those businesses which could not or did not adopt mass-production methods in full. Those countries which put their industries under state control have found that the corporation meets their need for an operational instrument. This has proved to be so satisfactory—for instance, in the Scandinavian countries—that the theory of socialism has begun to shift away from government ownership of the means of production to government *control* of private producers. Expropriation of production is to be limited to basic industries, and not all socialists agree even to that, for it imposes a burden of debt on the state.

The present trend of socialism, then, is to retain the private profit system under government controls. In the light of this redefinition the New Deal can certainly be accused of promoting socialism. The problem in our country is whether private corporations can manage Big Business to society's welfare, or at least to its satisfaction. Thus far the issue remains undecided, and private control remains on probation. In spite of certain inconsistencies in the situation, even the New Deal was willing to preserve private control—but in producing units rather than in holding units.

If private control of the corporation is to survive, it must meet on three levels the test which any institution must undergo.† It must (1) be functionally integrated, that is, have the organization to pro-

---

* Thomas C. Cochran and William Miller, *The Age of Enterprise,* (1942) 308.

† Much of what follows is based upon Peter F. Drucker, *Big Business: A Study of the Political Problems of American Capitalism* (1947).

duce, the leadership to advance, the flexibility to meet new conditions, and the ability to assess realistically how well it is performing its functions; (2) be able to mold its internal policies and relations so as to fulfill society's beliefs and promises; (3) square its own purpose for existence, the making of profits, with society's view of its purpose for existence, the supplying of cheap goods or services. These three problems must be solved interdependently, for they are equal in importance to survival; failure in any one means death.

Corporations have on the whole successfully met the first test. They have learned that efficiency is best promoted if the organization is neither too big nor too small; hence the halt in the movement toward the unification of steel and of automobile manufacture. This limit still enables them to afford research and pioneering, to take long-term interests into account, and, by amassing adequate reserves and shifting orders among plants, to avoid undue retrenchments and promote company and social stability. Intelligent decentralization within the corporation has promoted flexibility, brought out new leadership, and made more positions for able men.

Corporations have not failed on the second test as dismally as is often claimed. Management has earnestly sought "within the framework imposed by external financial control" to ease the social and psychological problems raised by mass production. Modern economy probably offers a poorer chance to become independent than there was a hundred years ago, but the chances of rising to foreman or into the managerial class would seem to be greater than ever—in spite of a common public belief in the contrary. Nevertheless, the belief, however ill-founded, is having clear political effects, chief of which may be mentioned the long tenure of the Democratic Party.

There is a common complaint that assembly-line work is monotonous, and so it is, though perhaps not so monotonous as the weeding of onions or the ululations of vocal training. The assembly line, however, employs only part of the men in a factory, nor is it an essential feature of all mass production. Anyhow, there is a tendency among fickle moderns to resent continuous and arduous effort; we forget that monotony is the price not only of security but of knowledge.

Compared with those in other countries American labor-management relations are remarkably successful—even cordial. Nevertheless many problems remain. Workmen complain that advancement is capricious, or that it is based on formal academic and technical training and there is little chance to develop latent abilities. It is demonstrable that the managers often fail to give the worker an understanding of the significance of his part in the production process. Instances are told of how morale problems in wartime airplane factories were cured by bringing in finished bombers with crews to show the worker exactly what he had accomplished.

The corporation, moreover, has failed to raise the workingman's social dignity and status. The result of corporation policies has been that labor unions have copied capital's old tactics and have found their mission in purely negative opposition to any force in business, society, or government which threatens their "rights" and have made the situation worse by their featherbedding, jurisdictional strife, and the initiation fee and other rackets. Under the circumstances it is no wonder that labor unions have also not won dignity and status for their members. There is good reason to believe that responsible managers and labor leaders would more frequently find common ground for agreement if it were not for the pressure of capital on one side and radical agitators on the other.

The third test brings up the problem of balancing the corporation's need for profits against society's need for cheap goods. The human desire for achievement, prestige, and power finds many outlets, of which the profit motive is only one. It is used in our society, which demands material results, as the best way to "co-ordinate individual drives into social purposes and action." Even the USSR uses economic incentives and rewards more widely than does capitalism; true enough, it rejects private profit, but it brazenly pumps out of its official monopoly trusts greater profits than capitalistic corporations would dare to demand.

It is begging the question to blame corporate shortcomings solely on greed, for underneath all the evidences of these lies the inability of both the public and the corporation itself to recognize the true nature of the problem and its solution. The original type of monopoly lay in control of production and the market—as in the case of Carnegie's threatened throttle hold on the steel market. Actually such a monopoly will in the end be self-defeating, for there is endless interchangeability of materials, processes, and finished goods. Even in the automobile market no one corporation would get tight control, for second-hand cars compete with new ones.

*   *   *

We cannot leave the subject of capital without noting the progress which has been occurring in its relations toward labor. Frederick

W. Taylor had warned that his scientific management depended upon a willing and cooperative labor force—that the basis of mass production would be destroyed if labor was suppressed to the point where its cooperation became mechanical and sullen. It took a long time for management to learn the lesson, but there are numerous signs that it is finally learning. Among those responsible was Elton Mayo, an Australian sociologist transplanted to Harvard. His experiments showed that labor discontent rose not so much from inadequate wages as from nervous strain and the feeling of being no more than an animated cog in a machine. Wage incentives were of little help, nor was the specious camaraderie of shop picnics where the boss joked with the floor sweeper and called him by his first name. What did matter was attention to such things as illumination, rest periods when the solitary worker could enjoy the companionship of his fellows, and a recognition by management that there is a line at which efficiency becomes self-defeating.

In other words, workers are people. They wish to know *why* they are doing a certain thing; they need a sense of pride in workmanship; a consciousness of getting somewhere; and the knowledge that what they do is in its way as important as what the boss does. Fear cramps their output, but appreciation boosts it. The boasted efficiency of scientific management was put to shame when in a Pittsburgh steel plant the union showed what could be done by raising the output of the most productive department 210 per cent in a single month. General Motors has sought to approach the problem of human relations by negotiating a wage contract which boosts wages with the cost of living, and provides for an additional increase based upon rising productivity. Unions are now agitating for a guaranteed annual wage, which they may well get.

The significance of the so-called fringe benefits is being finally grasped: that the worker prefers continuous employment, good treatment, and recognition of his humanity, over mere high wages. These facts are working a quiet revolution in industry. Plants are being broken up and the departments placed in suburban or rural areas where the workers find life more pleasant. Air conditioned, noise-proofed shops and offices are excluding the old distractions of drafts, heat, and clatter. The honor system is replacing that old devil, the time clock. Workers are told what the part on which they are working will go to make. Open house days are held during which the families of the workers and the community are invited in to watch the factory in operation. Sports and leisure-time activities and amusements have become a well recognized activity of personnel departments.

This does not mean that the millenium has come to American industry, nor is it just over the horizon. Hard-bitten, old time managers still sneer at human relations and insist that the worker is activated only by greed and fear. Nevertheless the Supreme Court's validation of the Wagner Act in 1937 made farsighted businessmen realize that they had to learn to live with unions. The changes have not always come about without union prodding, but this has only made intelligent entrepreneurs realize that intelligent union leaders who are really seeking to serve the welfare of the members are as important to production as plant and department managers. Even the hard-headed National Association of Manufacturers has been hearkening to the portents of the new day. Clarence Francis, chairman of General Foods, strikingly expressed the new concept of human relations before a NAM convention:

"You can buy a man's time, you can buy a man's physical presence at a given place; you can even buy a measured number of skilled muscular motions per hour or day. But you cannot buy enthusiasm; you cannot buy initiative; you cannot buy loyalty; you cannot buy the devotion of hearts, minds and souls. You have to earn these things. . . . It is ironic that Americans—the most advanced people technically, mechanically, and industrially—should have waited until a comparatively recent period to inquire into the most promising single source of productivity: namely, the human will to work. It is hopeful, on the other hand, that the search is now under way."*

---

* *Time,* 14 April 1952, 97.

XIII

Pragmatism and Progressivism

PRAGMATISM always present, even during the heyday of transcendentalism, after the Civil War became the instrument of a
new age of experimental search for answers to American problems.
That it exercised such a vital influence at this juncture was probably
due less to its newness than to the formalization of its method in a
way which could win the acceptance of the new generation and could
direct and inspire it in its battle for betterment. We shall now see how,
despite many human failures, this new realization remolded every aspect
of American society.

The problems that confronted the sprawling, inchoate country were
enormous. They rose not only from conditions bred by its internal
development but from the millions of foreigners who were crowding
through the gates. In every generation since 1830 the United States
has been confronted by the task of educating and indoctrinating in
democracy a new horde of strangers. It is also true that we have had
a difficult task of adapting ourselves to the rush of material and cultural
change—some of it brought by the immigrant—and of learning to
live with the problems we could not solve. Post-Civil War America
was a melting pot of nationalities, cultures, and prejudices, into which
went not only the newly-arrived immigrants but the native American
as well. The American as a rule objected fervently to the melting
process and built up a most interesting insulation of rationalizations
and prejudices, but in the end there emerged a new and perhaps in
some ways a better nation.

The half-century after the Civil War saw the most tremendous folk
movement in history, excepting perhaps the present Russian movement
into Siberia. During that time a total of nearly 25 million immigrants
came to the United States, by far the most of them to stay; during
six separate years after 1900 over a million a year entered the country.
In 1870 one person in seven was foreign-born, in 1920 one person in
nine; though the number of foreign-born residents had more than
doubled, the population of the country had jumped about 280 per

cent—from 38 million to 106 million. In 1890 the foreign-born in New York-Brooklyn were two fifths of the population; in Philadelphia one fourth; in Boston one third. At one time New York City boasted (whether or not correctly) that it had more Italians than any city except Rome; more Irish than any city except Dublin; more Germans than any city except Berlin; more Greeks than any city except Athens; and more Jews than any other city in the world. At the base of the Statue of Liberty, Bartholdi's heroic bronze of "Liberty Enlightening the World," contributed by the people of France and placed on Bedloe's Island in New York Harbor in 1886, were placed these lines by Emma Lazarus:

> . . . Give me your tired, your poor,
> Your huddled masses yearning to breathe free,
> The wretched refuse of your teeming shore.
> Send these, the homeless, tempest-tost to me;
> I lift my lamp beside the golden door.

The first mass immigration had occurred during the 1840's partly as a result of the Irish famine and German political troubles. The movement continued during the next decade and was reinforced by Hollanders and Scandinavians. It is said that a million Swedes, a quarter of Sweden's population, came to America. All of the new comers made cultural contributions to the American scene. The English and Scots because of their similarity to Americans left the least trace; the Irish had little to offer that was unique intellectually, though their share in song and drama is evident; the Scandinavians and Hollanders were for the most part solid people of the lower classes, religiously conservative and quietly interested in education and culture. The Germans made the greatest impressions. Many of them were educated men, leaders of liberalism in German thought, politics, and professions. They looked upon American puritanism and its peculiar reformism with distaste and fought the temperance movement, blue Sundays, fossilized theologies, the lack of dignity and depth in politics, and the bleakness and mediocrity of American life. There was a great deal of misunderstanding and underestimation of American ways, with much resultant bitterness, but in the end the German critics did more good than harm by their precepts and examples.

German teachers, theologians, engineers, architects, scientists, foresters, horticulturists, and brewers left broad streams of influence in their lines of activity. They were long prominent in the trade-

union movement, and socialism as a political manifestation was regarded as a German importation. German societies, such as the
Turnvereine, were not only active in adult education but helped to
turn the American mind toward scientific physical training and organized sports. Most impressive contribution, however, was in music.
In the American West the best fiddler was the one who finished the
tune first. When little German bands and orchestras appeared, the
puzzled Americans found each member playing a different "tune."
Orchestras and choral societies spread from German communities,
and presently musical conservatories began to appear. Germans were
indispensable teachers, impresarios, conductors, composers, and, not
least of all, musical instrument makers.

European ignorance of America was abysmal in the earlier years, and
such information as existed was often drawn from Cooper's novels,
which were translated into many languages. Misconceptions were
increased by the way in which some British travelers set forth their
experiences; these books usually were translated into German. Around
1830, however, strictly factual guidebooks for immigrants began to
appear, and these did much to correct romantic or hostile views. Most
important of all were the letters—"American letters"—written home
by immigrants. The appearance of a single letter in a community
might spread the "American fever" for emigration and strip it of
able-bodied citizens.

In spite of undoubted drawbacks, the romantic view of America
remained deep-seated. Laziness, bad management, or bad luck might
tell against the immigrant, but usually industry and reasonable shrewdness were rewarded. Letters are evidence of the awe-struck amazement
of the immigrants at the opportunities offered by America. The Irishman, lately starving on his blighted potato patch, found that he could
have meat three times a day. A German farmer could sell his land,
buy tickets to America, and still have enough left to buy a cleared
farm with buildings for himself and each of his three sons. True,
the farms were sometimes in poor condition, but Germans knew how
to restore their fertility and were not afraid of work. Those who
had no resources found that wages were so high that after two or
three years of careful saving they could buy the coveted farm.

Faith in Europe was gone, and even those who could have lived
comfortably at home often left because they felt they could do better
abroad. "America," wrote Goethe, "thou hast it better." In America
there was no enforced service in the army, taxes were negligible, and

so great was the government surplus that Congress was actually troubled by what to do with it. Peasants who had lived under extortionate taxes, rents, and tithes, and had been harassed by government spies were amazed to find that government cost so little and interfered so little with the citizen. One observer who asked German emigrants why they were going to America received from them all the same answer: "There is no king there." No white man in America, the immigrants found, acknowledged a master. Farm hands and house-maids sat at table with their employers, and American women were not accustomed to field drudgery. "There are no large estates," wrote a Swedish newcomer, "whose owners can take the last sheaf from their dependents and then turn them out to beg." Another Scandinavian recounted his blessings, then added the simple truth so telling to the people at home: "Neither is my cap worn out from lifting it in the presence of gentlemen."

One of the most striking things about the immigration of the twentieth century was the change in its sources. In the decade of the 1860's almost nine tenths came from Northern and Western Europe; in the decade of World War I about six tenths were coming from Southern and Eastern Europe. That is, immigrants were no longer the easily assimilable elements whose culture and political institutions were much like those of the United States, but the quite different Latins and Slavs. Hard times in Europe may have stimulated the movement, but it is quite evident that the reasons lay more in the American invitation and in the immigrant's hope of betterment. There were, however, the additional incentives of escape from military service and from political or religious persecution. Political refugees, especially from the Slavic lands, were sifting into America all the time. The principal religious refugees were Jews, also from the Slavic lands.

The greater tendency of the "new immigration" to be clannish rose naturally from its relative difficulty in learning American ways and from the hostility of English-speaking natives and immigrants. The "old immigration" persisted in the pattern set before the Civil War: the Irish settled in the cities, Germans in the cities and the rural areas of the upper Mississippi, Scandinavians in the woods and wheat-lands of the North, and English and Scots quietly sank into American life wherever it suited them without leaving much trace. The Jews invariably preferred the cities, particularly New York. Italians settled largely in mining and industrial centers as laborers, barbers, shoe cobblers, stone masons, and building contractors; many of them, as soon as they won a stake, bought up run-down farms in the surrounding areas and became truck farmers and dairymen. Slavs in general became miners and laborers, then rose to mechanics or went on the farm. Portuguese went into the fisheries in New England and on the Pacific Coast. Levantines operated restaurants and fruit stores, were pack peddlers or rug merchants.

Chinese, after a long and discouraging effort against native opposition to get a foothold in lumbering, mining, fisheries, and agriculture, gave up and went into hand-laundry work, merchandising, or small manufactures, usually in urban areas called Chinatowns. The Japanese at first refused to be segregated and sought to compete with natives on all fronts, but were gradually pushed into the occupations of gardeners, truck farmers, and merchants. Three immigration movements that were little noted amid the clash of incoming Europeans were the passing of numerous French-Canadians to the mill towns of New England, of English-speaking Canadians into American professions and industries, and of Mexicans finding a precarious living in the border states as herdsmen or seasonal workers in fields, orchards, and canneries.

American natives, especially laborers, have never been disposed to welcome newcomers without reservation. The opposition to Germans and Scotch-Irish was sometimes violent during the colonial period, and later on the flood of Irish and Germans which began after 1830 was regarded as a menace to political institutions and the standard of living. Opposition increased as the "new immigration" swelled. It was asserted that Latins, Slavs, and Jews were weak stocks, given to disease and crime. Instances in which European judges gave criminals the choice of "prison or a ticket to America" were cited as evidence that the United States was becoming the cesspool of Europe. The "new immigration" was declared to be politically unassimilable and therefore not wanted.

There is no denying that the "new immigration" has greatly affected American history since 1865. There can be no doubt that it slowed down cultural unification and development and encouraged political corruption in urban centers, though political corruption certainly existed in rural communities in which few foreigners lived. Probably the labor-union movement was retarded by the antipathy between natives and foreign-born. It would be unfair to blame all urban shortcomings on foreigners, yet it is true that it took three generations for most of the "new immigration" to become acclimated to American life, and in the meanwhile there were serious maladjustments which encouraged delinquency and crime.

On the other hand, immigrants contributed in labor more than they received in wages. Individuals contributed largely to every field of professional and political life. Even in the early years the "new immigration" was prominent in the professions. It is evident now that Latins, Slavs, and French-Canadians make as good Americans as the older elements, while Jews and Italians have so frequently beaten Americans at the game of competition that they have been accused of not playing fair—often a rationalization for losers.

The inundation of immigrants served to multiply the number of political pressure groups, of which the Germans and the Irish were before World War I the most powerful. The Irish, indeed, showed a genius for the small change of politics which goes to make up the bank accounts of the national parties, and Irish political bosses became familiar phenomena. The Irish were by tradition Democrats, and when they took over the political direction of New England (under the suzerainty of the "spendthrift trusts") the antipathetic French-Canadians of the mill towns flocked into Republican ranks. Unfortunately there was a tendency to make Irishness a profession and to measure all things in foreign policy by how much they would damage Britain. There is evidence that it was the professional Irish of Boston who dictated Henry Cabot Lodge's opposition to the League of Nations and so may possibly have changed world history.

Germans, whether or not they or their fathers were refugees, were notably loyal to German culture, and during the World Wars this loyalty was too often translated into support of the German cause and so became a ticklish problem for politicians. An alliance of Germans and Scandinavians actually forced Illinois and Wisconsin to permit public schools to teach in the language of the immigrant settlement in which they were located. The use of the immigrant pressure group to force American policy to favor their interests or those of the nation from which they had come had been well systematized by World War I and was sometimes invoked by home governments. Its real power was shown later on when the Irish-Americans practically forced the British to permit the setting up of Eire; when Germans plumped for the cancellation of World War I reparations; and when the Latin and Slavic nations fought the imposition of the quota system on immigration unsuccessfully, but accepted loans instead. The crowning example came when American Jews were able to force the Executive to adopt an anti-British and anti-Arab policy during the Palestine crisis of 1948.

Americans expect each man to look out for himself; immigrants, especially the "new immigrants," found this obligation difficult because the new milieu was so strange and the language so different. They had built up a dream portrait of America which could not possibly be true, and those who found themselves trapped in a city sweatshop or pounding the pavements in search of jobs blamed America rather than their own gullibility. Such people were loath to admit that what they had found was at least an improvement over rule by lords and cossacks.

On the other hand, America was by no means blameless. Immigrants needed to be patient, industrious, and thrifty, for their right to work at reasonable wages and under reasonable conditions was so frequently violated by selfish employers that they sometimes became cynical about American tolerance and goodwill. Even the law frequently lifted a prejudiced hand against them at the behest of the employers. To make matters worse, there developed in every immigrant element human bloodsuckers who preyed upon their more ignorant fellows, using every wile to deceive and exploit them. The Federal government made a few regulations to govern immigration and imposed a few health and literacy tests, but there was no attempt at selection on the other side of the Atlantic, and Ellis Island, the principal receiving station, was slackly run by political appointees.

Worst of all, there was no official Federal attempt to help the immigrant to become adjusted, once he was in. Settlement houses and schools undertook special programs to teach American customs and institutions and the English language; but "Americanization" was, as observers have pointed out, merely benevolent nativism. The aim was to get the immigrant to slough off his old character in a hurry and take on the American character. Naturally this was resented by the foreign-born, who, like as not, regarded their own culture as superior to American. More tragic was the situation of the second generation, which often despised its parents and their culture without yet understanding American culture and institutions. The result was the deliberate destruction of much in immigrant culture which would have enriched the pattern of American life.

* * *

For twenty years after the Civil War leading politicians united in hushing any attempts to expose the social and economic ills of the

country and it was left for a spate of more or less obscure third parties
to bring them to public attention and to suggest remedies. On the
whole the public agreed with businessmen's claim that they were administering the political and economic affairs of the country in a
fairminded and even benevolent manner. Farmers and laborers, however, took exception and tartly pointed out that business had set up
a double standard of morality, one for itself and one for them. A
candid examination of the scene must uphold the farmers' and laborers'
contention, yet they themselves were partly responsible for the situation.

Farmers were rushing into the new territories and glutting the
markets with surpluses. Farm boys were pouring into the cities and—
added to millions of immigrants—threatened to glut the labor market.
The farmer irascibly insisted that his interests should dominate the
nation since all wealth came from the soil; the laborer asserted that
his interests should come first since value should depend upon the cost
of the labor spent in producing an article. The laborer regarded the
farmer as a capitalist, and the farmer regarded the laborer as only
less a parasite than the capitalistic monopolist. Not only did the two
clash, but each of them failed to unite effectively to support their
interests; they went on their headlong individualistic way and blamed
the bitter results on capital. The businessman might justly have accused
them of wanting a double standard of morality to benefit themselves.

Labor and farm protest, reinforced by the liberal ferment which
is never absent in American life, forced Congress to make a start at
regulating big business. The Interstate Commerce Act (1887) and
the Sherman Antitrust Act (1890) were the entering wedges, though
both were for a number of years blunted by court decisions. The
Sherman Act was even interpreted to hamper labor unions' activities
on the ground that they were conspiring to restrain trade. The Fourteenth Amendment's protection of *persons* was interpreted to include
protection of corporations, which were *legal persons,* and was used to
limit the states' exercise of police power whenever it interfered with
property rights. The courts also developed the injunction as a weapon
to limit or forbid actions by labor unions or individuals. The Federal
courts, led by the Supreme Court itself, were clearly engaged in preventing the erection of obstacles to industrial centralization. The
significance to the growth of American power is manifest. In its early
stages the campaign was directed against the states but when Congress
presumed to set up obstacles these also were washed out. Critics felt
that there was an increasing tendency on the part of the court to

judge expedience as well as constitutionality. This was seized upon by injured parties to carry practically every important act of Congress to the courts for adjudication. By the beginning of the new century this had become so confirmed a custom that the Supreme Court had in effect become a third legislative chamber. This situation was to continue for a generation.

It would not be fair to portray the period as thoroughly reactionary; actually the Supreme Court showed in several cases that it was willing to make liberal rulings when issues permitted. It may be that it was changing as public opinion changed, and public opinion may have been changing because the factory and mining population was rising. There is no doubt but what labor's standard of living was improving, yet labor's outlook remained determinedly pessimistic. Basically the laborer compared his condition with what he thought it *ought* to be rather than with comparable European trades; the result was that he was glumly convinced that he was not receiving his fair share of the stream of goods which he was fabricating from our enormous natural resources. Nevertheless, even though he lost most of his strikes, union pressure was slowly forcing employers to make concessions, and in the sum these made considerable difference. This was all the more possible because corporations were not burdened by the cost of a heavy military establishment and they could afford to give way. The growing efficiency of industry, already verging on mass production, was cheapening goods and increasing the number of semiskilled workers who traditionally were better paid than the unskilled. No less influential was the political and social progressive movement in both states and nation which made the rights of labor one of the chief items upon its agenda.

American farmers had traditionally been stronger and more vocal than labor, and their protests gained urgency from the way in which farm prices were declining while those of manufactured goods were rising. Crux of the so-called Battle of the Standards was in the Plains states where during the 1890's the Populist Party threatened to gain complete control. At this time the miners of the West were pouring forth silver so plentifully that the market price had dropped disastrously in terms of gold, which was at that time the monetary standard. The Populists were reformers, but they soon found that the people were more attracted by the specious promise to cure all economic ailments by inflating the currency, coining silver at the artificially high ratio of sixteen ounces of silver to one of gold. The movement swept into the Democratic Party, and in 1896 the Democrats annexed the Populists and ran for the presidency one William Jennings Bryan, who as the "Boy Orator of the Platte" had been a spokesman for silver inflation.

The "gold bugs" rallied against "free silver" and in a campaign engineered by Republican strategist Mark Hanna elected William McKinley to the White House. The outcome may have been affected by the recovery in agricultural prices which was evident even before the election, and perhaps also by labor's suspicion of any alliance with agriculture. As it was the Republican victory was so close that a change of 14,000 votes in half a dozen states would have swung it to the other side. One may in retrospect cast doubts upon the thesis that the election of Bryan would have been disastrous, but it seems clear that the middle class believed that it would. At any rate the outcome was a defeat for agrarian protesters and such labor elements as had joined them. It was moreover a victory for big property, and it set in motion the great day of industrial concentration which we have already noted. The agrarian revolt may in one way be regarded as the last gasp of simon-pure Jeffersonianism. Thereafter the middle class (aided somewhat by the masses) was to become the standard bearer of protest and it added certain aims of its own to those it had inherited from the Populists. The scene was now set for the Progressive Era which, as we shall see, differed markedly from the Populist Era.

*   *   *

By a progressive we mean one who, as Allan Nevins puts it, favors the gradual introduction of wholly new processes of government intended to achieve novel aims. As such he is distinct from the mere reformer of the Cleveland type, who seeks—again in Nevins's words—to purify the existing processes of government in order to effect more completely its traditional aims.

The problems that confronted the Era were all the greater because the industrial beneficiaries of the Civil War had advanced slowly in their political and economic ideas while American social and material conditions had entered on an epoch of unprecedented change. There was the problem of the city with its teeming masses and noisome physical conditions, the first in dire need of social engineering, and the latter of sanitary and civil engineering. There was the too-frequent breakdown of personal and political honesty which arose from the transition from one epoch to another, from the old life of comparative leisure to the new one of haste and ruthless competition, and to the confusions incident upon shifts from country to city and from the farm to the factory. There was the problem of the concentration of economic power with its potential ability to tyrannize over the bodies and the minds of men. There was the influx of European mechanics and peasants bewildered by a strange language and no less by strange customs and institutions; the task of acclimating them to the American way was one which too frequently could not be done in less than three generations.

Lastly there was the task of overcoming cultural crudity and the crass materialism which feared or distrusted good manners, good taste, and clear thinking on public problems, lest they weaken the pillars which supported the old structure of popular prejudices and plutocratic privileges. Progressivism's attitude toward the cult of respectability was ambivalent. It approved the cult's steadying and refining influence but distrusted its glorification of mediocrity and its acceptance of imposed standards. The result, unfortunately, was to breed a certain amount of confusion and to cause a decline in allegiance to standards. Progressivism, as we shall see, had its customs and institutions.

The so-called classical economists of the early nineteenth century had systematized a philosophy of competition which was a reasonable portrayal of the economy of their times. By the turn of the twentieth century, however, the American economy had begun to grow away from the competitive model toward a system in which one corporation, or at best a few friendly rivals, would control each field. Either situation was regarded with alarm, and this alarm was not lessened by the way in which big business, perhaps quite sincerely, regarded itself as abiding by the classical injunctions such as the law of supply and demand.

The Battle of the Standards had been an early phase of the protest against the passing of competition and it was to be continued during the next two decades by the progressives. European liberals have opposed government interference in the economy; American liberals, somewhat to their own surprise, found themselves advocating it. American reformers had traditionally sought to return to a purer age of competition by pruning away the monopolistic practices which they regarded as evil and artificial; such men wished to break up the "monopolies" (in practice they meant any large corporation) and force the pieces to compete—hence they are called Atomists. The influence of evolution had fostered a school of reformers who regarded large corporations as a legitimate product of evolution; they merely wished to regulate them so far as seemed necessary to protect the public welfare, hence their name of Regulationists.

As early as the 1880's Lester Frank Ward's fight against Spencerian determinism had laid the foundations of sociology. The economist, Simon N. Patten, criticized the economy of scarcity and he was reinforced by a galaxy of professional economists, including the embittered Thorstein Veblen. The Protestant churches were affected by a program known as the Social Gospel, which preached their duty to ameliorate the appalling social and moral conditions which were plainly the outcome of industrialism. One result was to widen the already existing split between Fundamentalists and Modernists. While the Roman Catholic Church rejected Pragmatism, it did seek a social system which it regarded as suited to the masses; its program was based upon the Encyclical *Rerum Novarum* (*On the Conditions of the Working Classes*) promulgated in 1891. The rising tide of pragmatic democracy resulted also in the birth of professional social work which went beyond charity in an effort to help the unfortunate to help themselves.

The state of American society was forcefully called to public attention in the early 1900's by a group of writers whom Theodore Roosevelt impatiently dubbed muckrakers. True, there had been voices raised before this, notably that of Henry D. Lloyd, whose intemperate *Wealth Against Commonwealth* (1894) had been directed against the Standard Oil. The great day of the movement, however, came when it was taken up by certain popular magazines, notably *McClure's, Collier's,* and *Cosmopolitan.* Of course their principal target was corporation practices, but they also exposed the white-slave trade, child labor, the adulteration of food and drugs, and numerous other abuses.

The most significant effect of the muckrakers, however, sprang from their demonstration that social and economic abuses and political corruption were almost invariably connected. The public was appalled by the evidence that it was respected community leaders who bought and paid for special privileges: either franchises and contracts which were under the control of politicians, or protection by the politicians from competitors and racketeers. The fact that many otherwise high-minded businessmen were convinced that such tactics were the only alternative to ruin did little to excuse them in the public mind. Some of the muckrakers were convinced that if businessmen had not originally sought special privileges and protection, neither political corruption nor the prospect of ruin would have ensued. At any rate the exposure of the situation furnished Progressives with issues which they felt could be solved by concrete political action.

Lincoln Steffens, the most perceptive of the muckrakers, found that reform movements which threw out politicians to put in a "businessman's government" often put in men who were worse because they were confused, cynical, or self-seeking. The fact was that "some of our laws run counter to the forces of nature, to the economic pressure of business." Monopolies might or might not be wrong, but they were inevitable because they were economic necessities. The businessmen who were corrupting politics were not intentionally corruptors but might even be high-minded. Steffen's cure for hypocrisy was— more hypocrisy. Since businessmen could not operate without controlling government, "make it impossible for them to be crooks and not know it. We have, we Americans, quite enough honesty now. What we need is integrity, intellectual honesty."

Social comment was not limited to editorials, books, and magazine articles which would be read only by the relative few. Cartoonists had traditionally traded in abuse, as may be seen by reference to the cartoons directed against Jackson and Lincoln. They now discovered that a fly swatter is sometimes a more efficient instrument than a meat ax, and they began to utilize a brand of humor and understatement which was often more persuasive than abuse. Not that moral indignation was lacking, for such left-wing cartoons as those of Art Young carried unmistakable messages.

The rise of the pragmatic spirit led to increased public censure of the origins and disposal of the fortunes of the Great Entrepreneurs. These men believed that their tremendous development of national wealth was sufficient justification for their own wealth. Nevertheless, they grew restive as they became increasingly aware of public antipathy, and they began to counter with gifts to worthy objects. One millionaire after another warned his fellows—and took his own advice—that the amassing of "wealth without purpose must be stopped, or the public will stop it." Carnegie besought his fellow Pittsburgh millionaires not to die "without leaving behind them some evidence of love and gratitude for the city in which they made their fortunes." Here and there misanthropists denied the sincerity of the new reformism and harked back to Roman aristocrats who imported shiploads of Egyptian wheat to feed the mob and stave off revolution while they sought out and destroyed the leaders.

Regardless of the motives, these gifts wrought enormous public benefit in a day when custom did not permit government to take much interest in scientific and social advancement. They have even, perhaps, enriched the lives of all Americans in ways which government gifts could never have done. By 1910 the outpouring of money into public-spirited enterprises had reached an amazing magnitude. Foundations, institutes, universities, and medical centers multiplied across the nation. Rockefeller disposed of about 500 millions, chiefly for education, research, and medical service, and Carnegie put 350 millions into his libraries, research institutions, and other benevolences. The once antipathetic names of Sage, Guggenheim, Duke, Huntington, Mellon, Frick, and Kresge took on a new sheen in the public mind, and this even served to cover those millionaires who took no interest in such activities.

The management of these enormous gifts has opened up a new field of administration and has, incidentally, changed the ownership of the stock (though not always the control) of some of America's greatest corporations. It would not be unfair to say that many of these bequests were made in the hope that they would make more secure the owners' hold on the remaining millions. It is certainly conceivable that the hope was realized on a short-term basis; yet these gifts sowed the seeds of the millionaires' downfall. Research has raised the standard of life and health, and education has bred shrewd and intelligent leaders of the masses who have given direction to the movement for expropriation by taxation or wage raises. Lastly, and perhaps most significant of all, the millionaire himself has changed—or at least his grandson has. There is a new spirit of responsibility and sympathy among many men of wealth which gives them the attitude and standards of the steward of a trust fund.

The growth of cities made it possible to increase the number of years during which the child was exposed to public-school education, and toward the close of the period the school bus began to lead to the consolidation and betterment of country schools. Unfortunately the poverty-stricken South lagged far behind the rest of the nation, though it found this fact a happy reason for failure to educate Negroes properly. Teachers everywhere were underpaid and the turnover was immense, but progress was made. New buildings sprang up all over the land, improved methods were introduced, the curriculum was enriched, and free texts were provided.

Though there was some criticism of "frills" and "crazes" in education, the schools on the whole did a good job in reducing illiteracy and acclimating immigrant children. Public high schools began to replace local private academies, and businessmen began to prefer to hire high school graduates as clerks. At the same time business "colleges" multiplied until no small city was without one. If it is possible to hold that culture must be broad before it can be deep, then American education was on the right track. Already, as James Bryce noted in 1888, "the average of knowledge is higher, the habit of reading and thinking more generally diffused, than in any other country."

There was a certain promise in the remodeling of American universities which followed upon the foundation in 1876 of the Johns Hopkins University as a graduate school under the guidance of Daniel Coit Gilman. American universities, particularly the graduate schools, were in many respects frank copies of the German university. The basis of their courses was found in lectures and research seminars. Libraries and laboratories were for the first time put into general use. Faculty members were drawn from men who had proved themselves able and willing to advance the frontiers of knowledge and to stimulate student interest. As a result the graduate schools and the analogous professional schools have become intensive intellectual training grounds. Harvard pioneered by allowing the student a wide selection of electives in place of the prescribed classical course. The summer school came out of Chautauqua and met the needs of ambitious teachers.

The nation was in the happy situation of being able to spare young people from production and service in order to give them a chance to broaden their education. There was also the advantage that education of all classes in the public schools (that is, tax-supported schools) weakened class-consciousness. John Dewey's instrumentalism was profoundly altering methods of instruction by its tenet of "learning by doing" and its deliberate emphasis upon the teaching of democracy.

On the other hand, critics justly pointed out that American education from bottom to top shared certain defects. Education was the democratic right of the individual and was intended for his own satisfaction and advancement less than for the promotion of social aims, though not exclusive of the latter. Since everyone was entitled—and up to a certain age forced—to go to school, the public schools and presently the colleges invented mass education on the lines of mass production. There was increasing confusion between training, in the case of learning a trade, and education in the sense of indoctrination in the traditional arts and social values. The curriculum was "a rope of sand" formed with the intention of informing rather than teaching to think. A rigidly standardized and regimented credit system ruled with its bells, books, examinations, and courses cut and dried so as to offer the least obstruction to the attainment of a diploma or a degree. The aims were to teach social and professional skills (laudable in themselves), while the intellectual aim was touted but rarely honored in practice—there wasn't time!

We had occasion in a previous chapter to show how law had come to be regarded as the expression of natural moral law; law was not *made,* it was found. It was the task of Justice Holmes to overturn this attitude in his treatise *The Common Law* (1881) and show how law had been molded to the changing needs of an evolving society, in other words was an "organic" growth. The Constitution was not the ultimate and absolute truth; it had resulted from centuries of growth, and the growth had continued since 1787. Its nature was determined by facts; the United States, originally a congeries of states, had now by one means or another evolved into a nation in which the Federal government was supreme.

Oliver Wendell Holmes, son of the poet of the same name, was a maverick Boston Brahmin who was salted by native wit, toughened by war, tutored by profound study and long contact with the pragmatic questioners at Harvard, and trained by years on the Massachusetts bench. He went to the Supreme Court in 1902, and his tall figure, drooping cavalry mustaches, and pungent witticisms remained familiar parts of the Washington scene until his death, though he retired from the Court at the age of ninety-one. During his long service Holmes championed the evolutionary view of law against a conservative majority and became a figure revered alike by friend and foe. An early friend of William James and the Pragmatists, he had a speculative turn of mind which made him delight in "twisting the tail of the cosmos," and perhaps out of such experiences came his sense "of the limited validity of legal principles"—that the "law has not been logic; it has been experience."

He has with some accuracy been described as a conservative with sensible ideas, not primarily interested in social reform, but with a keen appreciation of what was possible. No American has more clearly or wisely expressed the pragmatic conscience. "Life is action, the use of one's powers," said he. "As to use them to their height is our joy and duty, so it is the one end that justifies itself. Life is a roar of bargain and battle; but in the very heart of it there rises a mystic spiritual tone that gives meaning to the whole, and transmutes the dull details into romance. Man is born a predestined idealist, for he is born to act. To act is to affirm the worth of an end, and to persist in affirming the worth of an end is to make an ideal."

Holmes's demand that the Federal government take up Jefferson's battle for the rights of the little man and adapt his principles to an industrial society rallied around him a group of brilliant younger men. Best-known of these were Roscoe Pound, Dean of the Harvard Law School; Louis Brandeis, a notable champion of social legislation; and Benjamin Cardozo. The last two eventually rose to the Supreme bench. The new school of legal realism was willing to keep capitalism but insisted that it be regulated for the protection of the people. Yet, having been reared under Anglo-Saxon institutions, the reformers had to find excuses in the old Constitution—else they would be promoting revolution, not evolution. They found their reasons, as Anglo-Saxons always do. They took over for their own purposes the conservatives' own instruments—the interstate-commerce clause, the elastic clause, and the Fourteenth Amendment—and gaily proceeded to demand that conservative decisions be reversed. These decisions were reversed, but that is a later story.

The pragmatic breeze which swept through the temples of law and learning led to a search for cause and effect which overturned many a musty belief. James Harvey Robinson of Columbia not only applied evolution to all historical development; he went further and called historical writing "a pragmatic weapon for explaining the present and controlling the future of man," a view which he called the New History. With Charles Austin Beard he set a new fashion of looking for causes and of bringing into historical study the social, economic, scientific, and cultural strands hitherto omitted by the chroniclers of dynastic fortunes. Historians probed into the causes of the American Revolution, the effect of economic status on political attitudes, and the roles of the frontier and of the sections. The fact remains that even some of the more important American historians were so bemused by the drama of American history that they had a tendency to draw universals from their national experience. Their spade work had significance, but the keys which they offered were sometimes of glass which broke in the hand.

In a very real sense the political struggles of the Progressive Era missed the point actually at issue. The Progressive was one who applied liberal reformist ideas to the American scene but with the additional faith that he was helping out progress through evolution. Jefferson and Jackson had believed in progress but hardly in evolutionary terms; they had more of a feeling that they were peeling away unhealthy excrescences and *returning* to the conditions of a purer age. The atavistic survival of this concept split the Progressive movement into two wings, and the Atomists and Regulationists began to walk warily in each other's presence. The Atomists, who wished to break up the "monopolies" and force the pieces to compete, were (the Regulationists insisted) trying to thwart the economic law which dictated the continual cheapening of goods through the savings of concentration and mass production; continued tampering with the course of nature would bring economic breakdown and chaos. On the other had, the Regulationists (the Atomists insisted) were building a new Leviathan which must be either the superstate controlling business or superbusiness controlling the state.

As perceptive Progressives became fully conscious of their apparent dilemma, the realization angered and embittered some of them. Instead of a glorious sweep straight on to the gates of Paradise, they saw the road fork before them and disaster waiting on both forks. History, instead of being progressive, seemed to be cyclical. Atomism led to economic trouble and brought breakdown or revolution; Regulationism led to what we now call fascism. Apparently we were headed for destruction, either on the horn of dictatorship or on the horn of economic breakdown. It was not given to that generation to know that the interests of producer and of society could be reconciled, that mass production could make maximum profit obtainable by maximum production at minimum cost to society. It is to the eternal credit of Henry Ford that he saw this condition, even though as through a glass darkly.

*   *   *

The Populist reform movement, as Henry Demarest Lloyd said, had been pushed from the nest by the cowbird of free silver and lay smashed upon the ground. But neither the forces which had given it life nor the leaders who had fostered it were dead. For something less than a decade the struggle was carried on primarily in the states and cities, and it gradually became apparent that the movement was developing a labor and middle-class as well as an agrarian basis. The traditional Jeffersonian agrarian was perforce learning to get along with the urban masses as they sought for ways to adapt democracy—designed for an agrarian economy—to an industrial civilization.

The Progressives adopted, perfected, and in large part put into effect the Populist program, and in addition, as might have been expected, they laid more stress on labor legislation and industrial controls. In the political sphere they worked for the direct primary, initiative, referendum, recall, the Australian (secret) ballot, the short ballot, woman suffrage, popular election of Senators, corrupt-practices acts, and publicity for campaign expenses. Not only did they seek to overthrow local and state machines (sometimes substituting their own), but they vigorously renovated the legislative machinery in city councils and state legislatures. They promoted the rise of the city manager, the city commission, and the use of technical experts in government.

In the economic sphere they sought to break up monopolies and force the pieces to compete. They set up commissions to regulate the practices and rates of railroads and public utilities. They worked for fish, game, and timber conservation and promoted practical programs for the better use of farmlands. They legislated minimum wages and hours, workmen's compensation, factory safety and sanitation codes, and protection for female and child workers. They agitated for and confidently looked forward to a Federal income-tax amendment, postal savings, parcel post, currency reform, and tariff reform.

Though they were predominantly Atomist in their philosophy, they made certain other steps toward the service or welfare state by their agitation for reform of old-age assistance and other aspects of social care; laws for the inspection of foods, drugs, and dairies; laws to foster public health and sanitation and to control diseases; and a mushrooming interest not only in improving the quality of education but of expanding its coverage in the high school, college, and technical fields.

No city or state was without its would-be reformers—sometimes practical idealists, sometimes disgruntled politicians or business elements seeking to overthrow the old régime, sometimes aspiring young men ready to seize any entree to power and pelf. The idealists might sweep an election and then blow the chance because of their ignorance, gullibility, or hardheadedness. Even the more realistic reformers had their troubles, and no city or state was permanently reformed, though many were permanently improved. The Progressive movement bore certain resemblances to the Jacksonian movement. Most of its leaders thought in the traditional terms of restoring Atomism, that is, enforcing business competition. Just as evident was the willingness of its leaders to use every political weapon, even the most ruthless. They traded, they logrolled, they bribed with money and patronage, they allied with rebel elements of the bossism they sought to overthrow, they built inexorable machines, vindictively punished their foes, and sold out their friends for a percentage of reform.

Lincoln Steffens, the demon muckraker, confronted the ruthless reformer U'ren of Oregon with the accusation that he had made bargains with the devil to get his support. Like Moses he had broken the covenants of the Lord, and though he might see the Promised Land he would not be permitted to enter it.

"You may have saved the people of Oregon," urged Steffens, "but haven't you lost your own soul? Won't you go to hell?"

U'ren considered for a moment, then raised his clear gaze. "Well," he answered, "I would *go* to hell for the people of Oregon!" Sometimes it is the duty of the democratic leader to suffer damnation that the people may live.

Among the prominent state leaders of progressivism were William E. Borah of Idaho, Hiram Johnson of California, George W. Norris of Nebraska, and William Allen White of Kansas. But Robert ("Battling Bob") Marion LaFollette of Wisconsin stands head and shoulders above the rest. The triumph of the "Wisconsin Idea" in 1905 brought into power a machine which was to dominate that state for forty years under the leadership of LaFollette and his sons. When LaFollette moved on to the Senate to introduce the "Wisconsin Idea" to the nation he found another progressive, Theodore Roosevelt, entrenched in the White House. Gifted with youth, energy, and a flair for the dramatic, TR had risen from New York state politics to the vice presidency; then the assassination of McKinley precipitated him into the presidency and the leadership of Republican progressives. It was Roosevelt and LaFollette who were to represent best the opposing wings of progressivism and were to move from uneasy friendship to bitter enmity.

LaFollette was an Atomist, that is he wished to break up the monopolies—in practice he meant any large business—and force the pieces to compete. It is also worth noting here that like many other Middle Western progressives he saw the United States as a nation apart from world currents and was later to become a violent isolationist. LaFollette was deadly earnest in his trustbusting program, too earnest to see certain pitfalls which were evident to the more sophisticated Roosevelt. The latter accused "Battling Bob" of advocating "a form of sincere rural toryism" which was attempting to turn back the clock. He pointed out that if the corporations obeyed the law and competed sincerely they would either kill each other off or one would be left to monopolize the field—which was against the law. When TR asserted that the great corporation was here to stay and the only way to deal with it was to regulate it, LaFollette accused him of favoring big business.

Truth to tell, TR was himself in a dilemma. The middle class, long the backbone of the Republican Party, was angered by the current evidences of corruption in politics and business and alarmed by the rising cost of living—but not enough to relinquish its faith in the mythus of laissez faire and run the risks of root-and-branch reform. Probably it feared that serious reform would mean the end of its pleasant reign and its replacement by the common man. Roosevelt doubtless recognized all this, and after the manner of politicians from time immemorial took refuge in sound and fury, and in moral rationalizations. He was thus able to work up among his followers a fine crusading glow without seriously endangering the fairly satisfactory status quo. Before criticizing him it is well to recognize his belief that the country was not ready for drastic action but that he must find substitutes for action lest LaFollette be able to implement his disastrous atomistic program.

TR's significance lay in two things: his popularization and redirection of progressive issues, and the start that he gave to the conservation of natural resources. That he actually accomplished little may be attributed in part to his own doubt and hesitancy, but perhaps even more to the political situation: he had to keep East and West together, and he would have been helpless without the aid of some of the more tolerant members of the Old Guard (the ultra-conservative wing of the Republican Party) and even some of the more susceptible Democrats. "A lot iv us," confessed Mr. Dooley, "liked Tiddy Rosenfelt that wudden't iver be suspected iv votin' f'r him."

TR was clearly alarmed by the lawless ways of some members of the plutocracy and the growing desire of resentful labor to get something for nothing—two ends of the same game. The Republican Party had built its strength on the rising power of Big Business in days when the people approved of that growth. Roosevelt saw that the people were changing their attitude, and he warned the party and Wall Street that if they expected to remain in power they must yield to the rising popular demand. So keenly did Roosevelt blame Wall Street for the situation that it is said that at the Gridiron Dinner in 1907 at which Morgan was present, TR during an exposition of his policies shook his fist in the Magnifico's face and shouted, "If you don't let us do this, those who come after us will rise and bring you to ruin." He and his advice were rejected, and conservatism enjoyed a few more years of untrammeled power. But in the end the Democrats under TR's great kinsman mounted the wave of protest and rode to victory.

Progressives like LaFollette were able to make reforms in many states, but they lacked the dramatic appeal and the political skill to charm the new generation of urban sophisticates, whose support was necessary to win national attention. Roosevelt knew how to charm. The left-wing Progressives, moreover, failed to see that the great corporation was necessary to American power and to the American standard of living. They were not hampered by idealistic scruples in their political maneuvers, but their ideals beclouded their view of their objective; essentially their Atomism was an attempt to return to the golden age of the past which, like most golden ages, had never existed. Roosevelt was not the first to recognize this fact, but it is to his credit that he actively tried to do something about the matter by offering something which he firmly believed was better: Regulation. Atomism, he asserted, would inevitably have been destructive; Regulation at least offered a chance of healthfully controlling evolution. How well it has been used is, of course, another matter. At any rate, what we now know as the First New Deal was built upon the bequest that he left to the American people.

When Roosevelt split the Republican Party in 1912 he ensured that the presidency would fall to the Democrats. The beneficiary was Woodrow Wilson, governor of New Jersey and recently president of Princeton. Though he was accused of being coldly aloof and intellectual, Wilson was in every sense of the word an extraordinary man. A master of English, he possessed the knack of presenting ideas in a way which convinced by the very clarity and sincerity of their expression. Though he believed in the power of intellect to move the world, moral principles were nevertheless everything and he lived in doubt, uncertainty, and torture of soul until the principle was found in any problem. His approach, whether or not he recognized it, was pragmatic, but once he had found the moral basis—or rationalization, if you wish—he was possessed of a most unpragmatic certainty. Nothing, literally nothing, could change his mind because, forsooth, he had the Absolute by the tail. This is why Boss Smith called him a "Presbyterian priest," why he could with no sense of either naivete or hypocrisy call upon "the conscience of the world."

His zeal made him regard political opponents as personal enemies and made him cast off friends who doubted his infallibility. It led, of course, to belief in leadership by an élite—the Calvinist "elect." It led him to turn opinions into principles quite unnecessarily and, since principles cannot be compromised, to block the road to political accommodations. It had the advantage of carrying conviction because his "call to duty" was obviously clear, calm, and sincere; on the other hand, though the stress upon the moral was a decisive urge to action, his slighting of selfish and material motives left out the sound bases so necessary to sustained exertion. As Steffens said, he had not sinned enough to understand sinners. The tragic consequences were seen in the moral crusade of World War I and the quick popular revulsion from idealism. Worst of all, he never learned that in real life there are times when a democratic leader must violate his conscience and compromise even on the most cherished principle; when he must accept damnation for the good of the people.

In his Princeton days Wilson had sought a cure for the evils of finance capitalism not by trust busting but by espousing moral regeneration of its leaders by "pitiless publicity" and legal action. It was the individual who would be punished, not the corporation— the driver, not the machine. Herein probably lay Wilson's first appeal to the Wall Street crowd, for they believed that his ideas would thwart radicalism but prove ineffective in action; after all, the courts were on their side.

With Wilson's awakening, however, he recalled his lessons in British economic liberalism with its faith in competition. Moreover, the sap began to stir in his Jeffersonian roots, and he cast about for ways to defend the middle class—the modern version of Jefferson's small property. These as well as political expediency forbade the aping of Roosevelt's Regulationism, and he modified his past preachments about Atomism trying to force a return to the eighteenth century. After all, by now Hamiltonian centralization had triumphed to the extent that the issue of whether or not government should interfere in business had dropped from the political scene; even the Old Guard's President Taft had interfered.

Wilson sought to hold a position between TR's Regulationism and Brandeis's extreme view that mere bigness was bad. He took a firm stand in favor of enforced competition—"a body of laws which will look after the men who are on the make"—and he opposed the corporations "growing big by methods which unrighteously crushed those who were smaller." He denied that the death of competition would increase efficiency, but he was ready to admit that bigness might have been gained by intelligence and efficiency. "We mean," said he, "to make little business big, and all business honest, instead of striving to make Big Business little, and yet letting it remain dishonest." He agreed that the corporation was the inevitable form of business enterprise and that it was impossible to return to the old order of individual competition. Whether or not Wilson foresaw and favored the growth of rival giants in each industrial field may be open to argument, but it is probably fair to say that he implied this growth. Government action has helped it along, but perhaps it was in the cards anyway.

Wilson had defined his New Freedom as a movement to "purify and humanize every process of our common life." Government now had a positive function "to cheer and inspirit our people with the sure prospects of social justice and due reward, with the vision of the open gates of opportunity for all." His inaugural address was a clear, calm call to duty that came with soothing coolness after the fevers of the Roosevelt era. It also outlined a program of reform legislation, the principal items of which were a lower tariff, renovation of the banking system, a strong antimonopoly act, and agricultural aid.

Wilson's competitive philosophy was extended to his conduct of foreign affairs. The nation, after all, was but a larger competitive unit; and, while it should live and let live, it should never lose its competitive identity in an international political and economic monopoly. In terms of British economic liberalism, Wilson believed that if free trade, freedom of the seas, and equal access to raw materials could be guaranteed, the result would be the end of wars. He saw international relations as a "handsome rivalry," a "rivalry in which there is no dislike, this rivalry in which there is nothing but the hope of a common elevation in great enterprises which we can undertake in common." This belief led him to refuse to clap an embargo on shipments to the warring powers of Europe and to deny the right of the powers to interfere with American trade. It led both to his espousal of the self-determination of nations and to his refusal to recognize governments which seized power by force.

It was this belief in reasoned and limited co-operation among competitors which led him to enter war against predatory Germany. Even the League of Nations, while reflecting in its formation many conflicting pressures, accepted his concept of national competition. It was in effect a sort of super-Federal Trade Commission, which should express the "organized moral force of the world." Wilson had apparently failed to see that the very success of capitalism was preparing for its transformation into another economic form. His antitrust policy was defending the passing small competitor from being crushed less by the big competitor than by historical forces, which gave a chance (if properly handled) of bringing a higher material and intellectual standard to all mankind. In the same way the League of Nations approved and imposed a passing economic and political order which was probably not in keeping with the spirit of evolution.

XIV

The New Deal and the Welfare State

WILSON saw World War I as a crusade whose idealism was being sold out by the overly practical Allies. His purpose was to point up the idealistic reasons for conflict and make the war a great step in the moral development of humanity. That is why, as we can read in his speeches, he sold the war to the people of the United States as a war for democratic and national honor, imbued the Allied peoples with the same spirit, and even sought to convince the people of the Central Powers. The over-all result was that Wilson succeeded in putting new life into the Allies; now their people were fighting not for lost territories or colonial or trade grabs but for the democratic, economic, and cultural rights of nations and individuals. The surge of enthusiasm that followed was a powerful factor in ending the four-year stalemate, in stopping the last despairing German thrust, and winning the war in a triumphant four-months counterthrust.

On both the domestic and the world scenes the weakness of Wilson's method eventually counterbalanced its strength. People can and do act heroically under the stimulus of an ideal, but for the long pull they need the even more powerful belief that there are practical issues at stake—perhaps even survival. Let the struggle drag out and they become weary of doing good for its own sake; let the struggle end before the emotions have been purged and there is likely to follow an anticlimax of hatred, fear, and selfishness. When Wilson preached hatred of the governmental and social systems of the Central Powers, he unwittingly laid the basis for hatred of the *people* of the Central Powers. It was a human tendency to adopt the simple belief that all good was on one side and all evil on the other. When Wilson underplayed (more frequently ignored) the practical reasons for American entry, he contributed to bringing on the postwar debacle.

The Republican Old Guard was well aware that the American entry into World War I was an extension of the progressive crusade. It was also aware that after a quarter-century of moral tension the progressive cycle had been run and the American people were tired of crusades, domestic and foreign. Harding had expressed this belief when from a Boston platform he proclaimed that "America's present need is not heroics but healing; not nostrums but normalcy; not revolution but restoration . . . not surgery but serenity." Harding was presently swept into the presidency by a wave of revulsion against progressivism and war.

What did President Harding mean by a return to normalcy? It was not long before the pattern became clear: (1) a return to isolation from international affairs, and (2) the return to an economic structure as nearly as possible like that which had existed in the time of McKinley. The first intention bears so directly upon the role that the United States has played in world affairs that we shall return to it later for examination. We may note in passing, however, that the refusal to share in world responsibility was in itself an acceptance of whatever programs and consequences the world might work out without us; in its division of the forces of democracy it encouraged the effort of would-be tyrants to plunge the world into a new age of barbarism. The second intention found expression in the deliberate administrative and judicial destruction of Wilson's reforms. The determination to return to the good old times was unmistakable. As a perceptive observer commented at the time: "You cannot teach an Old Guard new tricks."

Republican economic policies were, by and large, the ones that might have been expected from conservatives who believed in the "shower-of-economic-grace" theory that only if business was aided (and not until then) would the wage earner be helped. The mission of aiding business became the fundamental concern of all Republican policy. Whether or not because of Republican policy, the American economy began a period of expansion in production and investment which continued until 1929. There was a growing problem of how to dispose of surplus capital and goods. Capital accumulations were mounting from war profits, tax rebates and reductions, and from the dividends and bonuses made possible by increased efficiency and by the squeezing of labor's wages. Excess production rose from overinvestment in plants and from the wartime stepping-up of the rhythm of production. Both capital and labor feared to slow down lest they bring on a disastrous panic. Improved technology was grinding out goods faster than America's effective purchasing power could absorb.

Americans had long possessed a petty business psychology, which had risen from the necessity of pinching every penny to obtain needed capital; suddenly they were confronted by a surplus both of capital and of goods. The proper ways to get rid of the surplus—if they were determined not to slow down production—were to raise wages so laborers could buy more goods and to invest abroad so foreigners could buy more goods. The theory that high wages would expand the market was approved by more businessmen than put it into effect. Indeed, one may question whether an industrialist can afford to act on the principle unless his competitors do likewise; Henry Ford saw this point, and while he claimed to raise wages and got credit with the public for doing it, he actually got around it by a series of maneuvers.

Foreign investment was also incompatible with the traditional temper of petty business and so was never promoted very heartily. The United States was all but self-sufficient and could not grasp the necessity of becoming less so. In consequence, interest rates came down and speculation in stocks, building, and real estate ensued. Business concentrated on an effort to expand domestic and foreign markets, but without greatly expanding purchasing power.

Changes both in technology and in business techniques were largely responsible for the mounting surpluses. The manager began to displace the owner, partly because ownership was now distributed among thousands of stockholders. The managerial system was distinguished from the old free-enterprise system by (among other things) its interest in stability rather than in risk-taking and its hierarchical organization which laid a new emphasis on planning, policies, and concern for the future. The movement toward business concentration was resumed at a pace which dumbfounded and dismayed progressives. However size raised problems of efficient management, so many corporations consciously put an end to their growth and sought ways of promoting stability and flexibility. As a result the middle-sized corporations became large and presently a few friendly competitors were holding each field— a situation soon to be called oligopoly. Here at last was an alternative to the old choice between competition and monopoly. Most of these large industries quietly dropped competition in prices and took up competition in advertising, packaging, and in technical features. The last was important because they could afford research and (unlike the majority of small competitors in the old days) were in a position to enjoy its fruits at least for a few years.

Unfortunately there were drawbacks from the social point of view, especially in the oligopolists' threat of collusion. Deny their power as they might, the oligopolists were in a position to set prices, and since they were anxious to prevent ruinous competition they were likely to do what was best for the whole industry. The effect on the consumer could scarcely be different from that of outright monopoly. Instead of continually increasing efficiency and reducing prices there was a tendency to "follow the leader." That is, they accepted a price agreeable to all and stayed with it—though such prices did show a tendency to come down. Not only did the great corporations rather generally cease to compete in prices, but price competition was called an unfair trade practice and presently a prohibition (at least in retailing) was written into law. There was in the 1930's to be no lack of accusations that this collusion had brought stagnation and depression.

* * *

The decade of the 1920's was a period of moral confusion, caused by the reaction to the war and by the new social techniques and the new industrial technologies which were being translated into explosive social forces. Americans had looked into the abyss of world affairs and drawn back in alarm. Now they devoted themselves to building a wall warranted to isolate them from world responsibilities, interferences, and ideas. In their anxiety to shut out foreign ideas they restricted immigration, persecuted liberal and radical doctrines, and washed out the economic reforms of the Progressive Era. They sought to strengthen Americanism by tightening social, and where possible legal, restrictions. Even Prohibition owed its triumph largely to the war and to the American resolve to turn the land into an Eden of peace and prosperity, into which the serpent of foreign radicalism and irreligion could find no entry.

Never before this time had the people made their interpretations in such clearly materialistic terms. The effective majority was convinced (whether rightly or not) that material welfare was most important. The *status quo* gave material prosperity or the chance to acquire it; hence any person or -ism which questioned the *status quo* was automatically an enemy. Now democracy by its very definition questions things as they are and welcomes discussion of better ways of doing things; hence it also came to be regarded with suspicion and sometimes with hostility. We no longer trusted democracy to the full extent as the method to solve our problems, and lacking this faith we became hysterical whenever the *status quo* was questioned. The repressive spirit of the 1920's found dramatic illustration in a great surge of fear and intolerance, which took the form of unreasoned persecution of men who held radical and even liberal opinions; of attempts to censor and direct personal morals; and of a new wave of nativism which sometimes took Catholics, Jews, and Negroes as its victims.

The collapse of Normalcy in 1929 and the coming of the depression toppled idols on every side. The psychological effects were tremendous. It was a period of economic desperation and personal humiliation. Some men suffered from a new disease known as "unemployment shock" which robbed them of initiative and pride and made them let the wife and children scrabble for a living. Especially noticeable was the blow to American optimism. Hitherto depressions had been limited in duration and usually they had been softened by the half-rural conditions under which millions of the workers lived. Moreover, the economic mythus assured people that depressions brought their own cure. Now some of the economists followed the famed British economist John Maynard Keynes in asserting that depression was as normal as prosperity and its cure lay in a radical departure from cherished concepts of the relation of government to business.

Even businessmen were impressed by the fact that the great financiers to whom they had always looked for leadership were now as baffled as they were. The blow to the morale of the common man was stunning, and he developed a deep-seated distrust of the boasted automatic controls of capitalism. The shame that proud and hitherto self-reliant persons suffered at being on relief made so indelible an impression that it cannot pass until the death of the last man who carried his sack of free flour through the back alleys in order not to be seen by the neighbors. The result was seen in the universal pessimism which followed World War II as men of all classes confidently expected another devastating depression. This was reflected in the way in which labor and agriculture were more concerned with security in the enjoyment of what they had than in the traditional search for higher wages or prices.

Radicalism increased, but it usually took the American pattern of populism. Though there was serious talk of revolution as early as 1931 and more than a tang of it in the atmosphere, the interesting thing is that there was never danger of the American workingman going communist even though Reds were active leaders and stimulants to protest and violence. There was, however, a strong resurgence of the populism and Utopianism which has so frequently appeared in American history. This offered the opportunity sought by a horde of ambitious leaders in the preparatory stage of fascism which we can call proto-fascism. Their aim was to place all the economic power in the hands of the government, even at the cost of destroying democratic controls.

The new radicalism never took on any country-wide features either of organization or ideology—nor did more than a few abandon at least a lip service to democracy, though, of course, some weird meanings were given to the word. The Northern middle class showed the usual fear of Reds, labor unions, inflation, and even of fascism, while it lingered lovingly over proposals to disfranchise anyone who was receiving charity. Workers and farmers feared Reds and fascists, believed the worst about unions, and proposed to clip the power of Wall Street by government action and inflation. The South was particularly prone to proto-fascism, though it was too localistic and distrustful of authority ever to allow its proto-fascism to become more than a limited and intra-state phenomenon.

Under the pressure of the depression crisis President Hoover had begun the evolution toward government direction of the economy. He did it reluctantly, but toward the end he was recommending measures which no doubt would have scandalized Secretary of Commerce Hoover. Strangely enough, it was the Democrats who blocked his program, the same men who were soon to tie government so irretrievably to the economy that it probably can never be detached. Whether Hoover's program would have cured the depression can never be known, but certainly it was worth trying. If successful it would perhaps have forefended many measures of government interference which even moderates have come to regard as alarming. But that was not the way it happened.

*   *   *

The man who under the guise of public necessity was to carry to an undreamed of extent the evolution Hoover had begun was a Hudson River country gentleman, a sufferer from infantile paralysis who could only with great difficulty move from his wheelchair, a man who bore the magic name of Roosevelt. No man in American history, not even Jefferson, Jackson, or Lincoln, was to become the center of such a storm of controversy. No man except Washington played for so long a time the dominant role in public life. No man (except perhaps Lincoln) possessed such a broad grasp of affairs along with the subtlety and imaginativeness which enabled him to use it. No other

man had ever in the public estimation come so close to being the indispensable man, or been elected to the presidency four times. Like
it or not, Franklin D. Roosevelt must be recognized as one of the
half dozen towering figures of American history, and his role was
cast in such a time of crisis that his stature as a world figure was
scarcely less.

The fact that the Rooseveltian policies of the 1930's were called
the New Deal should not conceal the fact that they stemmed from
and were in a sense the long-delayed culmination of Progressivism.
We have seen that the period between the Civil War and World War
I was the heyday of the middle class in America. Its values, as in
any bourgeois society, were moralistic, and for a while it managed to
conceal its own evils behind the facade of the Gilded Age. But presently
Pragmatism began to tear down this facade and demand that changes
be made—though of course it demanded amendments rather than complete rebuilding. Moreover, the high cost of living was destroying
the preferred position which the middle class had occupied since the
Civil War. The middle class was in a quandary. Duty demanded
reform, but self-interest was unwilling to alter the existing very pleasant
mode of living. The stage was now set for the entry of Progressivism.

TR by his Regulationism showed the middle class how to enjoy the
glow of a moral crusade by striking at business abuses, which were
now undermining its standard of living, and at the same time permit
the continued growth of the mass-production economy which had made
life so comfortable and convenient. The City of God was to be a
place of brotherhood and co-operation where only occasionally would
the angelic cop find it necessary to thump his jeweled nightstick on
the golden pavement. This, said TR, was evolution, the predestined
course of the American Way. This was all very well, but—curious
omission for the apostle of the strenuous life—it did not satisfy the
Calvinistic urge for growth through struggle.

The ascetic Wilson sought to supply this lack. The City of God
would be given over to a "handsome rivalry" conducted with Prince-
tonian gentility which (the angelic cop would see to this) would result
in every man winning a prize, graduated according to ability and effort,
of course, but nevertheless a prize. And yet, and here the transcendentalist side of this modern Calvin appeared, the prize itself was not the
goal; rather was the goal the spiritual strength gained in the struggle
and the joy of seeing the City of God erected on this earth.

We have seen how Wilson sought to force his "handsome rivalry" upon the domestic and international scenes, and how the moral strain was too great for the American people. The result was the reaction of Normalcy, with its favored materialism and its ten-year struggle to suppress the twinges of the conscience which Pragmatism had revived and which Wilson had given a sense of urgency and responsibility. And yet, in a curious sense, Normalcy did not lose sight of the pragmatic goal. With a strangely warped sense of fact it interpreted Progressivism as the revolt of the common man rather than a bourgeois effort to reconcile conscience and comfort. The common man has failed to bring the City of God, said Normalcy: now let the businessman and the engineer take over. The approach was proto-fascist, as was the custom of the time—in itself not out of keeping with Calvinist belief in the social and political responsibility of the "elect."

The significance of the collapse of Normalcy is open to various interpretations. Was it brought on by a mere cyclic depression? Was it the death throe of capitalism brought on either by its suicidal dissipations or by a natural evolution toward another economic system? Or was it merely the crash of a structure which was made top-heavy by concentration and which should have covered more ground instead of having ambitiously grown so tall? And what was the remedy— patient waiting enforced by machine guns on the house-tops, traditional Atomistic reform, TRooseveltian Regulation, or root-and-branch socialism? Could the democratic process still be made to run, or had its pistons rusted in their cylinders during the winter of Normalcy?

The New Deal has come and gone, but we do not yet know all the answers, nor are we likely to know them in this generation. There has been bitter controversy over whether the New Deal was revolution or evolution. Perhaps it was neither—or both. The New Freedom had ended in 1916, and Normalcy had sought to destroy or to prevent the effective use of its reforms. The result was that time built up a flood of changes which in the end were bound to break down the dam of Normalcy. The refusal of Normalcy to let evolution work resulted in their coming at last with a rush, whose very speed made it seem like a revolution.

Even before his nomination Roosevelt had promised "bold, persistent experimentation. If it fails, admit it frankly and try another. But above all, try something. The millions who are in want will not stand by silently forever while the things to satisfy their needs are within easy reach." The result was that the New Deal was consistent neither in philosophy nor in policy. Actually it falls into three more or less distinct stages which we shall call First, Second, and Third New Deals.

The first one accepted the idea that the American economy was mature, that agriculture and industry were overexpanded; as a cure it sought a national self-sufficiency which carried with it a strong effort (now almost forgotten) to restore business to its old primacy and to refurbish its reputation by asking it to give the other fellow a break. When business refused to play along, the New Deal sharply reversed itself by forcing reforms and seeking international co-operation. But even this did not bring the desired recovery, and in the stage which we shall call the Third New Deal the administration settled down to a permanent policy of pump-priming of which World War II was the most tremendous phase. And there, apparently, we still are.

The basic trouble with the country (it was thought) was the maldistribution of wealth which made it impossible for the actual producers of goods and services to purchase the wares which they produced in the service of an overexpanded industry. The problem that confronted the incoming administration was two-pronged. It had to save the financial structure and prevent general bankruptcy by raising prices so that debtors in business and agriculture could earn the dollars to pay off the debts incurred when prices were high; essentially this action meant reinflation. In the second place it had to prevent a further decline of business and to start the wheels of industry to rolling by getting business to raise wages faster than prices.

It is evident that the blame for the depression was thus laid at the door of business, and business was asked to assume the major responsibility for correcting its mistakes. Many thoughtful businessmen were ready to have the government impose a control of competitive practices which would save business from itself, but others never agreed that the basic trouble was maldistribution, or if they did they blamed antitrust legislation. The latter group preferred letting nature take its course—that is, at least with their rivals. Labor was badly split, as always. One wing would have been satisfied with wage raises; the other demanded not only that wages be raised but that profits be lowered. Farmers were for the most part shortsightedly content to get higher prices for their products and could not realize that at the same time the prices of their purchases would rise.

Another serious split was within the ranks of New Deal experts, particularly the lawyers and economists. A strong element favored the theory of the British economist, John Maynard Keynes, that "compensatory spending" of borrowed money by a government in time of depression was necessary to take up the slack in private spending. Taxes and expenditures should benefit the poor most and the rich least, on the ground that the former spent what they received and in this way stimulated production.

Then there were the Atomists and the Regulationists. The Atomists asserted that the re-establishment of competition by breaking up the great corporations would automatically restore good order in business and with it prosperity. On the other hand, the Regulationists insisted that Adam Smith's automatic market controls could not be revived and the only reasonable alternative was bold government regulation. Roosevelt never made up his mind between the two wings, but stubbornly insisted that he had blended them. The result was growing vacillation, bafflement of supporters, alienation of well-wishers, and ridicule by critics.

The "Hundred Days" session (March-June 1933) of the newly-elected Seventy-third Congress was one of the most dramatic periods of American history. Conflict of interests by no means disappeared, yet it was minimized by the decisive leadership of Roosevelt, a new soberness in the attitude of Congress, and a readiness of all elements of the population to substitute action for debate in an attempt to do anything which would give some promise of hauling the economic ox out of the pit into which it had fallen—or had been pushed. This changed, however, even before the session was over and the various interests began the gyrations which make the New Deal era one of inexhaustible interest.

Jefferson had held that government is the natural enemy of the citizen, and it is not yet certain that he was wrong. The New Deal faced once more the old, old dilemma. Either direction that it took around the circle might wind up at totalitarianism. Should political democracy enlarge economic democracy, or should economic centralization restrict political democracy by refusing to feed the unfortunate? Should we switch from legal protection of the fortunate individual at the expense of society to the protection of the unfortunate individual as a member of society at the expense of the fortunate individual? The New Deal stalled and vacillated. It borrowed capital's surplus and gave it to the consumer by means of made work, placating capital's bankers by allowing them to create part of the credit which the government borrowed. It forced up wages in order to increase purchasing power, and prices in order to preserve the life of the capitalist structure by making it possible to pay debts and interest.

The First New Deal made a heroic attempt to save capitalism by imposing Regulationism with the consent of enlightened businessmen. It had proposed to business that it save itself by granting to labor and agriculture a degree of equality which should result in an effective social and economic balance among them. But the operation performed by the First New Deal surgeon resulted in an excruciating pain, which convinced business that the surgeon was determined to kill rather than cure. Nevertheless, its power to move had been restored, so it hopped off the operating table, threw its crutch at the surgeon (as FDR said), and presently managed to bring down its presumed benefactor in ruin.

A glance back over the demands made on business by the First New Deal will bring understanding of the businessman's point of view, even if it does not stir sympathy. After all, he had merely tried to bring the City of God after Progressivism had failed; was he now to be blotted out of existence for a failure which at worst was only temporary and which a few more years could easily see reversed? Business never agreed that the First New Deal was in the authentic stream of American evolution and that it was made inevitable by the excesses of Normalcy.

Business had refused to propitiate labor and agriculture in order to provide a political substitute for the middle class. Labor and agriculture rebelled when they found that they were being rooked out of their recompense for agreeing to set up the pro-business National Recovery Administration. The Second New Deal, deprived of business support, was driven to rely on a farmer-labor alliance and to revert to the farmer-labor favorite policy of Atomism. The actions of business (and of its ally, the Supreme Court) convinced the Second New Deal that fundamental reforms were necessary to adjust the nation to the new day. Some of these it managed to force through, but in the end it was checkmated chiefly by the South, always an element in the collapse of American reform. The puerile aggressiveness of the Third New Deal and of the Fair Deal may or may not have been the dying lunges of a great historic movement.

The New Deal was to the end torn by the conflict between Atomism and Regulation. Roosevelt insisted that he had harmonized the two views, but in doing so he only exposed his ignorance of economics and business confidence. He admired Pragmatism, which judges a policy by its results, but as time went on he became increasingly unwilling to judge by results; many policies begun as experiments were plainly failures, but he convinced himself that they were well thought-out and irrevocable. Those around him who protested were dropped, and the narrowing circle of the faithful was more and more composed of those who responded satisfactorily to their master's voice.

Business objected to the Regulationism of the First New Deal on the ground that it was creeping socialism. Certainly the 1930's saw the government put into effect or seek to put into effect most of the planks of the Socialist Platform of 1932 with the significant exception of government ownership of the means of production. Even this, said critics, was implied in the vast expansion of government corporations such as TVA. It was not as evident then as it is now that socialist doctrine is being redefined to permit the retention of the private profit system under government control. The problem of whether such a system is socialism or capitalism cannot be settled here. At any rate, when business washed out the First New Deal, it laid up trouble for itself. It should have considered while it was crowing over the *Hoosac Mills Decision* that laborers and tenant farmers have a weak sense of the sanctity of property. If the anchors of the middle class and the owner-farmer are dragged, the next wave of reform may well bring socialism. There is some logic to the judgment that FDR was the greatest conservative since Hamilton.

Both FDR and Truman were well aware that capitalism was committing suicide, and their attempts to redistribute economic power were intended to reinforce the decreasing middle class with new blood—to endow workers and tenant farmers with enough property to ensure that property would become at least a little more sacred to them. Thus the Second New Deal's return to Atomism was a desperate attempt to revive the middle class, or at least supplement it, as an element in the balance of social forces. Not even yet do more than a handful of businessmen seem to grasp the probable fact that it was the New Deal that saved private enterprise. It sought to pacify public resentment and yet preserve the bigness necessary to mass production by fostering the growth of rival giants in industrial fields where they did not already exist. This was in a way the putting into effect of Wilson's amendments to La Follette's original Atomism, which would have been disruptive. At any rate, it suggested a way to avoid the dilemma posed by Atomism and Regulationism.

The surrender of the Supreme Court to the New Deal was the vital step in the eclipse of laissez faire by governmental responsibility for the public welfare. It was at long last a recognition of the fact that political democracy was in danger in a world where the individual no longer could stand alone against economic power. The court's change over also clarified certain governmental trends which had been evident for some time. It removed the twilight zone between sovereign state and sovereign nation from which predatory economic power had been able to dictate to both. It amended the old doctrine of separation of powers by removing the obstructions which it had erected to prevent Congress and President from solving the complexities of the new day. Lastly the court tacitly abandoned at least the more extreme of its claims to judicial supremacy; that is, it admitted by inference that its actions had been based upon captious prejudices, limited views of what was or was not reasonable, and nostalgic allegiance to custom. The court has not lost its traditional functions, but has consented to use them moderately and to speak with assurance only when the plain meaning of the Constitution is at stake.

In a way, the New Deal's own mistakes and confusion helped to conceal what it was trying to do. It violated traditional morals and gave too much room to political opportunism and to a too-human stubbornness or resentment. But the fact remains that in demanding government aid, business lost part of its independence. It became necessary for the Federal government to assume control of credit, to tinker with the gold standard, to finance exports and imports, and to enter even the fields of private, state, and local finance. The government has thus become responsible for and responsive to economic ups-and-downs as never before.

In looking back upon the leaders of the New Deal, it is apparent that as individuals they were usually incorruptible and were filled with high ideals and with a sense of responsibility for the public welfare. Unfortunately this is not the whole story. They were overly slick in political maneuvers. They purchased loyalty, misrepresented facts, and made easy promises which were soon broken. As a class they lacked political integrity. This judgment, however, requires to be set in the background of the times and of American history. There is no evidence that the opposition to the New Deal could boast of any greater integrity, and apparently the voting public distrusted its ideals. The New Deal was accused of being faithless and ruthless, and perhaps it was. Yet this was the traditional pattern of American political reform movements, as we saw in the time of Jefferson, Jackson, and the Progressives.

In this sense, at least, the New Deal was in the authentic stream of American History.

Regardless of the theoretical and actual dangers involved in change, the complexities of the twentieth century made it necessary to explore the possibility of using government as the protector of the citizen. This entailed a number of new departures. One of them was the enlargement of the old definition of democracy as a political process by the acceptance of the belief that the citizen also has economic rights. Up to 1932 economics had in general wagged politics; now it was necessary for politics to wag economics—merely the American phase of what was going on all over the world.

To implement this it was necessary to oil the creaking wheels of democracy by resuscitating the party system, restoring the atrophied powers of the President, and altering and extending the administrative bureaucracy so that it could cope with its problems. The purpose of all this was to undertake at least a moderate degree of planning, both social and economic. The government acknowledged and carried out its duty to promote the welfare of the individual citizen. It made and carried out plans for the restoration and conservation of natural resources. It accepted the responsibility to rebuild blighted areas all the way from city slums to the rural slums of the Tennessee Valley. This has been called welfare statism, and probably it is; what is often forgotten is that it came because business and Progressivism between them had undermined laissez faire, and with decreasing opportunity the average man saw no other way to assure himself of reasonable security.

The New Deal has been accused of a long list of crimes. One of them was indifference to the piling-up of the public debt; if that was a crime, the responsibility should probably be laid at the door of the advertisers' campaign to destroy the ancient virtue of thrift. It has been accused of turning the people into a supine herd whose votes could be purchased by relief and made-work handouts. Actually the voters attitude toward government has always been based upon an opinion of whether or not it promotes his welfare. Even the Republican Party received its long tenure for no other reason than the belief of the middle class that Republican policies promoted its welfare. If the New Deal used bribery, it was merely a change in the form rather than the fact. In any case, it is true that the New Deal partook of the popular tendency to resort to trick phraseology and juggling of statistics to prove a case. Such antics confirmed the country's growing skepticism, which was well illustrated in the saying that there are lies, damn lies, and statistics.

The New Deal has been accused of destroying state sovereignty and with it the motivation of state pride by winning an ascendancy over state policies by its grants and its dollar-matching with or without strings. The charge has merit, but the policy may well have grown because the states had lost their dynamism and were no longer properly fulfilling their functions. It seldom occurs to such critics to look behind the fact to see what can be done to restore local dynamism. Paradoxical as it may seem, the states are busier than ever, for they have received new powers to experiment and to tax. They have become partners with the Federal government in administering a vast complex of legislation. They can and do attack their problems by interstate compacts. All in all, the state still touches the daily life of the citizen far more than he is touched by the Federal government.

The significance of the New Deal is not found simply in its attraction to the voter or in its verging upon the service state as an alternative to social and economic chaos. Even more important was its search for an alternative to the break-down of democracy. It is easy enough to say that the answers it found were incomplete and socially expensive— but when have answers been both cheap and satisfactory? If it departed from the stream of American evolution, which is as yet not at all certain, the departure was forced by the hardheadedness of its enemies. Two things are sure. By one means or another it maintained and strengthened democracy in a world from which the process was rapidly disappearing. No less important, it shored up American economic power so that when the crisis came the country was ready to be the arsenal of democracy.

*   *   *

The last generation has witnessed a startling reversal in the attitude of the American people toward political and military cooperation with the world. No less startling and doubtless arising from the same roots has been the change in the attitude of capital toward its role in society. The pity is that the world at large (including the American public) has lagged in its comprehension of what has occurred. The public still thinks too often in terms of an Opper cartoon or of Upton Sinclair's *Jungle* which portrayed capital as purely exploitive. Many foreigners also think of the United States as a huge predatory capitalistic beast, thereby more or less unconsciously seeing what both Red and fascist propagandists wish them to see. There may have been some excuse a generation ago for painting capital as an exploiter, but that is no longer true. It is even sometimes argued that agriculture and labor are now the exploiters. Capitalism has been too successful for its own good; there is a tendency for the public to forget that its high standard of living was won in great part by the thrift, the initiative, and the calculated risks of businessmen.

The depression and the teachings of Keynes had made pessimists of American businessmen and of the public, and after World War II the National Association of Manufacturers' prophecies of gloom rose in something of the same ratio as the stock market. Men who thought in terms of the classical economists were sorely puzzled to explain why an economy which violated all the rules continued to operate. The competitive model of the classical economists survived in such enterprises as coal mining, cotton textiles, clothing manufacture, and farming, save as they were influenced by actions of trade unions, cooperatives, and government. Without these "artificial" supports they would still have been depressed industries as they had been in the 1920's.

The typical producing units, however, were in the hands of corporate giants which Adam Smith would certainly not have recognized as competitors. Theoretically, at least, they controlled production, prices, and employment, and so—in the opinion of liberals—must exercise an evil influence over the public welfare. Another violation of old standards was the way in which government was interfering in the economy by regulating corporate and financial practices, loaning money to private business, fostering the growth of new producers, and even itself engaging in production; this condition—in the opinion of conservatives—must have led to ruin long since. And yet liberals and conservatives both had to admit that prosperity and the public welfare had never been higher.

To explain this puzzle Harvard economist John K. Galbraith offered in his book *American Capitalism: The Concept of Countervailing Power* (1952) a synthesis which deserves attention. After pointing out the illusions which rose from continued obeisance to Adam Smith, he offered the key to the changing economic picture in what he called "countervailing power." This means (much oversimplified) that the power of the great producing corporations over prices is countervailed by a number of forces. One of these is the corporations themselves, which as buyers of crude materials try to force down prices; an example would be the way in which the auto industry long forced the steel industry to make an exception in its favor in its general imposition of the basing point system. Another force is composed of the great retailers, the department stores, chain stores, and mail order houses, whose business is so important to producers that they can usually make savings which presumably are passed on to the consumer. Then there are labor unions' pressure for high wages and farm cooperatives' pressure for high prices for farm produce; both have used political means to attain their ends.

This leads into the role of the government in creating and sustaining countervailing power. Not only does it interfere in favor of labor and agriculture but it keeps a watchful eye upon big corporations, not simply the producers but also the countervailers, as proved by its prosecutions of the Atlantic and Pacific Tea Company. Probably no less important has been the way in which it has used its lending and contract-awarding powers to build up rivals in those fields in which it felt that competition was needed. It backed Henry Kaiser's efforts to break the monopoly of the Aluminum Company of America, to set up a steel industry on the West Coast, and to get into the business of auto manufacture. Government has thus sought to create oligopolies in place of monopolies.

Galbraith's comfort is cold enough under ordinary circumstances and in peace time, but even that vanishes when for any reason such as the Korean War the demand for goods presses upon productive capacities with the result of bringing inflation and a "seller's market." Countervailing power then loses much of its effect. Rising prices enable management to give raises to labor with the result that prices are raised farther and presently another wage raise is demanded; they may not see it that way but labor and management are effectively in coalition. Not until the pressure on productive capacity is removed—perhaps cut to a level considerably below it—can prices recede. The Korean War convinced many that inflation was permanent and raised the demand for goods; this, added to the government deficit and to the huge private savings available for expenditure, made it unlikely that there would be an early drop in prices. Indeed, though no one would admit it for himself, many were benefiting from inflation and opposed measures which would effectively stop its spiral; Congress and administration were afraid to act and each salved its conscience by laying the blame on the other. In the end Congress evaded the issue of inflation by forcing the Truman administration to assume a series of controls over industry, prices, and wages, which even the New Deal had never sought.

*　　*　　*

By the 1940's the character of the new capitalism was clear. It was no longer based on Adam Smith's "supply and demand"—if it ever had been—but had become reconciled to a system of controls which would have scandalized Smith, though Henry Carey would probably have approved. Competition had largely changed base and was now most evident in packaging and advertising. Prices tended to "follow the leader" and retailers were limited by law in their right to attract custom by cutting prices. Manufacture and even some branches of retailing required so much capital that the little man frequently found himself unable to launch out into new enterprises. The freedom of business to do as it pleased was now balanced by a reduction in risks due to the government's efforts to minimize the effects of the business cycle. Whether the economic system was still based on "free enterprise" was hotly debated; as a matter of fact the term itself did not come into use until the depression era at the very time when traditionalists felt that its practice was passing away.

Though the American mythus still upheld Atomism, actual practice more nearly resembled Regulation. The Federal government supported farm prices, protected labor by complicated legislation, and permitted bankers to create the credit which it borrowed and pumped into the economy. In one way or another it subsidized air lines, truckers, inland and ocean waterborne commerce, scientific research, education, and publishing. Federal services burgeoned: weather reports, trade analyses, air navigation facilities, river and harbor improvements. Industrial expansion was encouraged by tax write-offs or by charging it to national defense. Even the cheap power furnished by the New Deal's hydro-electric enterprises became a form of subsidy to the manufacturer. It is claimed that in 1946 the Federal government granted $2.25 billions in subsidies to business and agriculture, turned over another billion to the states as grants-in-aid, and made Federal payments to around 16 million people. During the years immediately after the war the government pumped about $40 billion a year into the credit structure.

Enough has been said to show that American capitalism is not as self-reliant or self-sufficient as "free enterprise" propagandists still sometimes claim. No doubt the government has intended its activities to promote the public welfare and individual security. Thus far they probably have, but only the future can show whether the price is too high. It is certainly true that socialist theory is turning away from government *ownership* of the means of production to advocacy of government *control* of privately owned (and in details privately operated) productive machinery. Sometimes this is called "soft socialism." One point of view is that government interference, whether to regulate or pamper, will presently put an end to private initiative and economic expansion. Another view is that this mixed system will prove to be a practical way of avoiding the pitfalls of socialism on one side and of a too rugged individualism on the other. One thing is thus far certain: compared to the regimentations of fascism and communism the American mixed system preserves an amazing degree of freedom.

The decline of Wall Street as a source of new capital has been one of the little-recognized accompaniments of the transition of capitalism. Industrialists have avoided Wall Street control by using their profits to expand their facilities. The change was further hastened by the Federal controls set up by the Securities and Exchange Commission, by the splitting apart of commercial and investment banking, and not least by the way in which the government furnished capital through such agencies as the Reconstruction Finance Corporation. Brokers are supervised, margins prescribed, and offers of new stock have to be accompanied by disclosures of all pertinent facts. Bulls, bears, wolves, and lambs are gone, and with them has departed the dramatic glamor of the Street. The once flourishing business of lending capital abroad has hesitated with the foreign tendency toward expropriation, regimentation, and socialization; in consequence the Federal government has had to step in with such lending agencies as the Export-Import Bank. There still linger a few leaks and crevices by which abuse may enter, but a vigilant Uncle Sam is stuffing them up with reams of regulations.

Another aspect of the financial scene is the way in which commercial banks have been abandoning their old function of encouraging community enterprise. In such old areas as Boston this has frequently forced industry to turn to Federal financing or to move to more progressive areas. Of course this is due in part to the multiplication of legal regulations which make it unwise for a bank to risk a loan on any but the most gilt-edged of security. Moreover government agencies like the Reconstruction Finance Corporation have proved willing to make loans on the more risky enterprise—but it should be noted that RFC gets back 99 per cent of its loans. The new attitude of the banks may be partly due to the conservatism of age and to resentment against government's new role as financier. Another reason may arise out of the very situation they deplore: they are able to create credit (on the basis of their deposits) for the purchase of government bonds which remain at a guaranteed level, draw trouble-free interest, and will be readily cashed by Federal Reserve Banks; recent Federal Reserve modifications of these guarantees have not as yet removed their attractiveness.

* * *

Social subsidies are almost certain to be affected in case of a depression, but just what will happen to other subsidies opens up an enchanting vista. Big Agriculture, Big Labor, and Big Business may be able to force the government to support parity prices, provide made work, and guarantee profits and investments. It requires no gift of prophecy to describe the shape of the future for it is being molded before our eyes under the guidance of Congressional blocs, both Democrat and Republican. The picture may be clarified by the victory in 1952 of the Young Republicans over the Old Guard—essentially a struggle between two wings of big business conservatives in which Atomistic little business may more frequently than not be found on the side of the Old Guard. The latter, steeped in traditional concepts of isolation and self sufficiency, prefers to let nature take its course with the Eastern Hemisphere and to wait out any foreign or domestic peril—military or economic—which may come from that direction.

The other wing is made up of men who are intelligent and imaginative, and who are no doubt actuated by the best intentions. At least superficially they believe in democracy—but a democracy which follows qualified leaders. They have seen how in a century the United States has lifted itself by its economic bootstraps to world leadership, and the example of the New Deal intrigued them where it horrified their more unimaginative brethren. True, they still express horror of the New Deal, but it is a well known psychological fact that people go on with the old verbalizations long after they change their minds. Probably they envision a partnership between Big Business and Big Government—the cooperation of the First New Deal brought up to date, complete with bureaucratic experts and proto-fascist pump priming service to special interests. Big Labor and Big Agriculture would doubtless sit in on policy discussions and would be able to moderate and delay decisions, but would wield no veto except on close decisions. The object of the new regime would be to do for the world what the New Deal did for the United States. World rearmament against Russia and Point Four aid to underdeveloped countries offer logical and readily defensible gambits for their policy. Indeed they may be essential if Western Civilization is to be saved. Moreover they have the virtue of warding off depression, for though the American taxpayer will have to provide much of the money, it will be spent in the United States and so will act as a subsidy to American business.

What we have described is the cooperative-plutocratic state. It is a union of pressure blocs, each retaining its identity but with Big Business really ascendant. It is clear that such a regime *could* be more proto-fascist than democratic, more like the Italian fascist *theory* of the corporate state than like traditional capitalism. Actually it might be as satisfactory to the little man as socialism, for there is always the gnawing doubt that socialism can preserve democracy. Certainly he would benefit by the rise in production, for the first interest of the state would be to foster production. However there is still no indication that Americans are disposed to regard business control as "moral" any more than government control. Federal and state governments and the economic pressure groups can still be played off against each other and if history is any guide they will be.

This would be no world for either the old-fashioned Atomistic Progressive or the old fashioned Economic Liberal. Just how much individual liberty would survive under the cooperative-plutocratic state is a matter for struggle. Trade unions and agrarian senators might well exercise enough power to prevent the growth of a monolithic state, and the habit of civil liberties would remain strong upon the land. Certainly in such a regime democracy could not expect to shape every decision of government—for that matter it never has. Only the general trends could be subjected to political action; the details would be worked out by experts, and inevitably their decisions would alter—perhaps even thwart—those of the electorate and perhaps in the end even subordinate big business also.

The genius of the English-speaking peoples for organizing community and special interest pressure groups might here become more important than ever before. Chambers of Commerce, "service" clubs, women's clubs, junior mechanics, Arbor Day societies, block organizations, granges—such organizations now number something like 200,000—all would make it their business to remind the experts that every question is octagonal. It is even possible that the syndicalist dream of shop management by workmen's committees would be obtained. The strength of democracy has always lain in non-political organizations which are able to get out the vote on specific issues and thus exert pressure on the political parties. Obviously they can operate only in a society where the citizen is free to investigate, decide, and recommend—and in the last extremity veto the experts. The danger, of course, is that the experts may constitute themselves as a closed oligarchy which ignores and eventually suppresses community opinion. This means that the democratic virtues of courage and restraint will have to be inculcated more carefully than ever before in order to assure respect for the democratic will. It means that the courts will have to be more vigilant than ever before in their protection of civil liberties against both government and private pressures.

It is clear that there can be no automatic solutions, no abandonment of total responsibility to the experts. The democratic method of advance by experiment and evolution will be confronted by new and ever more baffling complications and dangers. It has always been thus. Democracy is not intended for the lazy, the timid, and the irresponsible. It is the way of life for those who live courageously.

XV

Mass Production and the Mass Mind

WHEN Henry Ford proclaimed that machinery was the new Messiah he was upholding a social program which even he understood only dimly. The great day of mass production was dawning, with all its potentialities for good and evil. It could become the savior of the masses or it could become their master. True, the effect of the machine on society had been obvious a century before, but its great impact may be said to have begun after World War I. No one standing before a Cleveland Automatic and watching it pouring out bolts made without the intervention of human hands could remain unaware that an uncanny power had entered the world—the creation of man, yet perhaps like the monster of Frankenstein fated to be his master and destroyer. Already Rube Goldberg was satirizing in cartoons the futility of modern mechanization. But he was not the first to look behind the curtain. William Blake had portrayed the peculiar terror of the machine in his "dark Satanic mills," finding something soul-destructive in their inexorable monotony just as Charlie Chaplin did later in his portrayal, *Modern Times* (1936). Actually the concept of the machine as master is not altogether implausible; perhaps it was inevitable from the time that accurate timepieces began to put humanity into a straitjacket laced with inexorable cross stitches of hours, each of sixty unvarying minutes.

The mastery of the machine—long recognized by the thoughtful—is not exhibited always by a demand for mystical veneration, as among the ancients, who portrayed the machine as the peculiar creation of the gods or among medieval men, who regarded machines as magical creations of the devil. The genius of its mastery lies in another direction. It intrigues us by its ruthlessness, its efficiency, its speed, its inevitability—its rewards for patient service and its punishments which are dealt out for no apparent reason. Labor's inferiority is indicated by the way in which the fixed capital expense of the machine means that in case of conflict of interest labor must yield. It promises us leisure and income for a full life, but its tempo hurries us along with no intervals for reflection. It fills young and old with the craving for the sensation of mastery over power and speed. It shrinks the once-vast expanses of the world into a day's journey. It feeds with new instruments the age-old desire for imperial domain. It is obviously complicated, but it demands simplification, systematization, a neat cataloging of functions which discourages deep understanding. It demands worship of the new; not only must we cast aside old machines but sometimes old ideas, old wisdom, history itself. Nor can we reject it by refusing to pay its price; to do that would destroy social equilibrium and presently bring chaos. We must learn to control it or else be ourselves controlled.

Aldous Huxley has put the satirical and yet alarming accolade on the machine in his *Brave New World*. This is a novel of the future in which society is strictly regimented and held in subjection by drugs and spies, babies are gestated on production lines, time is reckoned from the incarnation of the Model-T, and men make the sign of the T and swear by "Great Ford." Even more terrifying are the portrayals of a machine civilization in science fiction—in the novels of H. G. Wells, in George Orwell's *Nineteen Eighty-Four* and Karel Capek's play, *R. U. R.*

Now of course the above arraignment is only one side of the page. For every evil count we can marshal one for good. The machine can take the place of the slave and of the underpaid servitor, a fact which traditionalists can not or will not grasp. It has enabled us to raise the standards of living, of general education, of public and private health, even perhaps of public and private morality. It gives to at least a few the means of deep understanding, opens new vistas of control over nature, even gives a fighting chance of penetrating the secret of the universe—how something came out of nothing. For the first time in history man glimpses the possibility of analyzing and controlling the forces which we once regarded as mere blind instruments of fate or of the gods.

The common people of the world know all this and resent the reluctance of their masters to act upon it. Call it worship of the material if you wish, but recognize that it is on such resentments that communism builds its plot for world dominion. It is all very well for the élite to praise their mellow traditions and boast of their gracious way of life; the commoner has not shared these save at second hand and is weary of being told to be content with little. It is useless to tell him that Americans pay too much for their standard of living. There is a story told that after long deliberation the Kremlin decided to import the moving picture, *Grapes of Wrath,* in order to prove to the Russian people that Americans lived in bitter poverty. The step was a great success and theaters where it was shown were filled with enthusiastic crowds. Finally a suspicious functionary began to investigate. He discovered that the picture's drawing power lay in its portrayal of a society where even the underprivileged wore shoes and drove an auto truck.

Are Americans happy? No, if by that you mean placid contentment. Yes, if you mean joy or excitement in being part of a great creative process. It is not given to all generations to be content—least of all those who live in a time of flux. The *Toronto Globe and Mail* in observing its neighbor to the south noted that the consumption of medicines had been going up in the United States along with the standard of living, then wrote:

"This confirms the commonest European criticism of the New World. The Americans are rich, yes; but they do not know how to live. Their wealth only gives them headaches, their success only brings them insomnia. What the European critics fail to understand is that the Americans themselves clearly recognize, and cheerfully accept, this state of affairs. They would rather toss and turn on silk than sleep soundly on flannelette; they would rather have migraine in a custom-built convertible than be at ease in a streetcar. As between the curse of wealth and the blessings of poverty, the Americans unanimously and enthusiastically choose the former. (So, it might be noted, do the large number of Europeans who have migrated, or would dearly love to migrate, to the Land of Freedom, Plenty and Duodenal Ulcers).

"Whether the Americans or the Europeans are right, is something for sages to argue. We merely note that the great American headache has made a substantial contribution to freedom's cause in the last generation or so; and that if Western Europe is eating regularly, much of the credit belongs with men in Minneapolis and Mobile who haven't slept a wink for three nights handrunning. The Americans are not a happy people, to be sure; but as one of their own philosophers has remarked, what use is happiness? You can't buy money with it."

*   *   *

While the machine and its utilization of natural resources promises ultimate solutions of many human problems it also reinforces the age-old demand for social conformity. The changes which it has fostered have led to conflicts between the old and the new, and consequently to frustrations which at times seem to threaten the breaking down of society. In a community which has regular, consistent, and easily recognized standards the individual is able to adjust himself to social demands without much difficulty, and he lives in a state of relative psychological tranquility. On the other hand, when a community is undergoing change, when new ideas and new ways of doing things are making their entry, community mores are torn between the new and the old standards of behavior. Social clash and disorganization is reflected in the individual, and he acts without much comprehension of the reasons, or goes to the extreme of obeying the new or the old directives. Not only are his choices of means to an end affected, but his personal needs and desires are drastically altered and perhaps corrupted by the conflict. The end result is anxiety, what the French sociologist Emile Durckheim called *anomie*. Its symptoms are a loss of orientation and a sense of confusion, frustration, and futility. The American has always lived under conditions of transition, but never before have these reproduced such marked results.

Anomie is not solely an American disease, but we are here concerned with its American manifestations. In ancient times aristocrats and priesthood found handy mass media for social control in religious festivals, dramatic presentations, and implanting the fear of gods and demons. One of the most poignant episodes in the human story was the struggle of the Epicureans to free the human mind, and their defeat by the Roman Senate. In present-day America we find a mythus which serves the same purpose as the ancients' fear of the gods. Its core is the democratic mythus of human freedom and dignity, but it has added an amazing encrustation of contradictions between theory and practice and between clashing ideas. It is impossible to live by them all, but they are defined as the essence of Americanism to which one must conform if he wishes to be accepted. The result is a clash between the nostalgic individual and his collectivized society.

Students of American history are aware that conformity has always been one aspect of the American scene, just as it has been an aspect of the human scene everywhere. Doubtless it arose from the same sort of pressures which exist in any society, but it was aggravated here by the wildness incident to the pioneering stage which society tried to moderate by demanding conformity to its preferred mores. Democracy also has a tendency to demand conformity to its pattern of equality, and too often this means mediocrity. To be acceptable the citizen cannot rise above his fellows; hence the folksiness of politicians, public speakers, and advertisers. Conformity has its appeal, for it not only relieves the individual from the necessity of making moral choices, but it gives him the sanitary feeling of being at one with his fellows; it has its resemblance to the "glorious irresponsibility" of life in the army. The danger in all this is that it threatens democracy itself. It has in the past, and it is not likely that we shall ever be free of the threat.

Advertising men—"merchants of unhappiness"—have dinned into our ears clichés which are supposed to evoke a desired response. The menace long evident in such mass media as magazines, moving pictures, and radio, has been suddenly pointed up by television's welding of all their techniques. For some reason they treat the American public as a uniform audience with exactly similar tastes, needs, and mental development. The aim is to cram everyone into an "outer-directed" mold which will make him amenable to the advertisers' campaign to undermine thrift and breed discontent.

These objectives, if accomplished, will open the way to the political demagogue and the preacher of social and economic hatreds. The "inner-directed" man who refuses to conform will be represented as the enemy of society; already this is beginning. Humanity in the mass has never been "inner-directed" and it is asking for the millenium to expect it. Nevertheless the demand for conformity is dangerous if only because the standards presented are false and cannot be reached even by all those who try—and widespread failure among the common people paves the way for revolution and either chaos or tyranny. Anyone who saw Arthur Miller's *Death of a Salesman* can never forget the picture of personal disintegration when Willie Loman failed to meet successfully this demand for conformity, nor could the implication be missed that American society was in similar danger of collapse.

The confusion and frustrations of our time have bred a longing for security which, because our age expresses itself most frequently in economic terms, has been interpreted as meaning economic security. This has been seized upon by advertisers and presented as something actually attainable in this life if only we will follow their advice. Politicos follow with specious promises on which the electorate may or may not expect them to deliver. At any rate economic security as a social objective has been blown up beyond all reasonable size. Actually what people want more than economic security is a secure place in the esteem of their associates; even this will on occasion take second place to such personal values as self-respect or love of power.

The assumption that people are all alike has resulted in a curious inability of the masters of mass media to realize that they are not as influential as they imagine. This is strikingly illustrated by the way in which the press has all but unanimously moved to the right while at least until 1952 the voters stubbornly moved left. The natural human desire for social approval has played into the hands of advertisers, and they appeal to it as well as to economic security. Even more frightening than advertisers are the so-called "social engineers." Their object is to develop "scientific" techniques of measurement and direction in adjusting the individual to the group. The group comes first; it is always right or at least it can be set right by proper social engineering. Tensions and frustrations will be done away with, because one can know and trust the desires of the group. Social engineers analyze the individual as though he were a molecule and the community as though it were a chemical formula, and devote themselves to the "engineering of consent" in promoting the "integration of the employee so that he will be spiritually at one with the organization"—in other words to the protection and perpetuation of mediocrity.

Philosophical idealists chortle over this ultimate step in the so-called pragmatic method of forming morals relative to a situation. Of course it is not pragmatism at all, but totalitarianism. Pragmatism envisions a long, slow process of social give and take; it never loses sight of the continuing values of human freedom and dignity, but seeks to preserve them by federating the individual with the group—not forcing him to submit. The social engineer seeks centralization by a subtle process of engineering consent. The silken glove cannot conceal the same objectives which have animated all the authoritarians from the Pharaohs to Josef Vissarionovich Djhugashvili Stalin.

Frederick W. Taylor, the father of scientific management, once remarked that "no great man can (with the old system of personal management) hope to compete with a number of ordinary men who have been properly organized so as efficiently to co-operate." His hope, however was to make it worth labor's while to be willingly cooperative, and Elton Mayo's "human relations" has done much to attain this goal. Lest anyone think that social engineering is the logical and inevitable result of mass production let the denial be here registered that neither Taylor nor Mayo nor their associates would have consented to such manipulation of human beings.

The danger of our age, as Clark Kerr points out, "is not that loyalties are divided today, but they may become undivided tomorrow." Social tensions and frustrations have their uses; God forbid that we should ever lose all of them. The natural-born leader, the constructive fault finder, the inspired rebel, and the man who pokes at social snakes out of mere curiosity have been the creators of civilization; the first thing a totalitarian regime does is to get rid of them, as the slave labor camps in the Soviet Union can prove. Our task is to find a reasoned medium between destructive rivalry and subservience to the system or the group.

Of course there is another side to the use of mass media. Businessmen have a Calvinist responsibility to lead and improve the masses and this can be done only if they attract and hold people through their use of mass media. The ideal of service to the masses lies at the bottom of American business, however much it may appear turgid and pompous when it comes to the surface. Moreover advertisers and the producers of mass entertainment do some commendable things. Hollywood does occasionally make adult films, and it may be held that the rigid demands of such agencies as boards of censorship and the Legion of Decency prevent the production of more. The radio does bring us good music, drama, and commentary, though there is complaint that they are falling off. Television gives little promise of elevating taste; that may or may not come when its techniques are fully developed. The axiom of the existence of a uniform audience has been most successfully challenged in the magazine field, where there has been an effort to satisfy diverse tastes and even to raise tastes by pitching editorials and some articles considerably above the average of comprehension.

*   *   *

Specialization has become the watchword of this generation and it is rare to find a man who is really expert in two unrelated fields. Faced with the choice between narrowness and superficiality the expert has chosen narrowness. Specialists now specialize within specialties, and as a result threaten the approach of the time when there will be no one competent to tie the numerous specialties together, with the result that each will go off on its own tangent and presently part company from all social reality. There is another danger—that each specialist, naturally thinking his own field is the most important, and without the knowledge to judge among them, will expect his interests to rule. He knows only one thing, but he speaks with authority on all. When medicos unite to teach economic lessons, when engineers lay down plans for the good society and scientists try to influence politics, they are really no more expert than the mill hand or the high school teacher.

But even in his own field there is no conclusive reason why society should accept the word of the expert. The human tendency to resist new light affects the expert as well as the layman; recall with what difficulty men like Pasteur put over their revolutionary ideas. The drawbacks of specialization may be countered eventually by the organization of teams of experts who can check and counteract each other; indeed some studies have already drawn upon experts from all the major disciplines, not merely from related fields.

Some failures have resulted from the American attempt to reach the democratic ideal of mass education. Despite good intentions quantity has too often taken precedence over quality. The pressure of material values has forced training in vocational skills to subordinate thorough indoctrination in the cultural heritage. The result is that democratic mass values—that is, prospective personal happiness and advancement, have taken priority over social welfare.

One of the more amazing popular misconceptions about education is that the public schools are teaching radical doctrines; actually they are for the most part devoted to teaching conformity and to bolstering it by the inculcation of the mythus—even to some of its inconsistencies. There are a number of reasons for the rather widespread failures in education aside from the social pressure for conformity. The schools are poorly supported, with the result that they are overcrowded and the teachers overworked. This generation is balking at the age-old truth that monotony is the price of knowledge and of social survival. The family, the church, and other agencies are sometimes reluctant to share in the responsibility for training the child.

Another reason is that education no longer has a formal social and moral basis. Its purpose is to lead to economic success, with the inevitable result that subsequent failure to reach the top brings frustration. Actually the competition among college graduates for white collar jobs is more bitter than the competition among laborers. Many people who do not go beyond high school are capable of taking a college education but there is no point in their doing it until white collar opportunities increase or until we strengthen the ideal of education for living —as well as working—in society. All through the school years there is a great deal of time wasted because efficient learning is not required; indeed if students are required to learn more they will learn, especially university students who fear being forced to leave school or being refused admission to study for a profession.

There has been a long struggle between those who would base education on science and those who would base it on morals. The former have been led by James B. Conant, former president of Harvard, and they acknowledge John Dewey as patron saint; it is doubtful if Dewey would consider it an honor. The moralists have been led by former President Robert M. Hutchins of the University of Chicago, and advocate the study of "the great books"—a worthy pursuit, but even great books contain a certain amount of twaddle; more to the point they seek a moral system which the world can follow with confidence that it has found an absolute. Hutchins may not agree with his followers who distrust democracy because, they say—quite wrongly—it has no moral code. Conant may not agree with his followers who distrust democracy because it does not approve of a ruling intellectual élite. Nevertheless it is futile to expect science to define the ethical aims of education, while leaving it to the philosopher places undue reliance on a sort of self hypnosis which is taken for inspiration. It is here that the pragmatic process of democracy with its practical search for a moral end should serve as a guide. The central problem of democracy (aside from immediate survival) is whether the mass search for happiness can be tempered by a greater sense of moral responsibility. The answer has to be social and political as well as educational, for the child absorbs more from the atmosphere outside the school than he learns in the school.

It is apparent that education has many failings, yet it is too early to despair either of the educational process or of the next generation. Truly educated men and women have always been rare and there is no reason to suppose that they are fewer today. There is room for optimism, especially when one compares the American educational system with that of other countries. Young Americans *do* learn the Three R's; whether or not in the schools they *do* learn the cultural heritage of the race; and an encouraging proportion of them persist in thinking. The coming of automation gives promise of elevating educational standards not merely along technological lines but by making cultural subjects an integral and necessary part of the citizen's preparation for living and earning a living.

Actually no country has yet solved the problem of education. There is a tendency abroad to educate only the best—or rather most brilliant—minds. Great Britain, for example, even under a Labour Government calmly accepted nature's division of humanity into mental orders of ability. It divides the sheep from the goats at the age of eleven. The goats go into industry and the sheep are eventually educated in narrow disciplines well suited to sheep; of course there is a fond belief that the technique of learning and the discipline acquired can be applied to any field. The result is a degree of specialization even more alarming than that in America, and a bland ability among educated Britishers to make sweeping generalizations which would be forbidden by a broader background of knowledge. Such mental and disciplinary compartmentation might well endanger society's future far more than could be countered by the gain in efficiency. Quite the opposite trend is visible in America; indeed there seems to be growing a faith that improved environment may banish many of the mental inequalities which have hitherto been regarded as natural and inevitable.

American education is broader than foreign, and say critics, more superficial. Actually the best students acquire both intellectual discipline and a broad background of knowledge, and one may express the belief that such students in America outnumber the selected specimens who enter foreign universities. At any rate American education does teach that life and learning are interconnected, and the result is seen in the realistic American approach to social problems. It is certainly significant that engineers are active in solving human problems, a situation not likely to develop in Europe. To sum it up, Americans believe that democracy depends upon an educated citizenry, not merely an educated top crust. We may never reach the ideal, but certainly it is worth reaching for at least once in history.

The proof that American education is not all lost motion is seen in the interaction of management and labor. Without claiming anything like a millenium it is still possible to show that this interaction shows more intelligence on both sides than in any European country. Management is not only concerned with efficiency, but also with reducing worker fatigue and improving worker morale. It creates more grades in its hierarchy in order to afford more opportunity to rise and to give more stimulus to responsibility. More than this, it has a feeling of responsibility for the community as a whole and no small part of its personnel and financial resources are devoted to community purposes which would be scorned by management in other countries.

Workers are interested in the welfare of the firm and of the community, and they are cost conscious because savings give them an argument for higher wages. The quality of education and dress is such that off the job one frequently can not tell which man is the worker and which the manager. Industrial and social hierarchies are to a certain extent posited upon income, but one must not carry this too far. Neither a worker nor his wife necessarily regard his status as inferior to that of the relative who goes into management. Certainly he rarely regards his status as a life sentence and if it so happens that he does he is well aware that his children can escape. Throughout the American industrial complex there is a rather clear comprehension that the only alternative to mass production's reconciliation of producer and consumer is a harsh competitive order which must end in monopoly or the sterility of socialism.

* * *

Democratic living is always a conflict of yea and nay, and nowhere is this more evident than in the triumph of science and the backwardness of the social sciences. Science seeks truth, and its discoveries can be translated into new technologies. Its readily apparent utilitarian basis thus makes it adored by the masses, readily supported by industry and even government, and, most significant of all, attractive to the most brilliant minds. Even the fact that pure science is essential to technological progress is now generally recognized, and it receives more support than ever before. Historically there has been a fairly free international interchange of scientific information, and this situation was so true before World War II that there was amazing progress in its application to medicine, plastics, alloys, agriculture, and indeed to all fields of human material endeavor.

Even more significant, though less known to the public, was the growing scientific realization of the meaning of the discoveries of the Curies (radium), Röntgen (x-rays), Becquerel (radioactivity), Planck (the quantum theory), and Einstein (relativity). None of these, it will be noticed, was American, and indeed Americans made relatively few contributions to pure science until after World War I. Out of this progression, however, scientists began to recognize two things. First, the alchemists' dream of the transmutation of elements was within their grasp and with it vast power over the forces of nature and perhaps even the ability to loose an explosion which would destroy the world. The second fact was that order disappears as one enters the realm of the submicroscopic and that in the final analysis there is no such thing as cause and effect, no certainty or reason.

This discovery was a stunning blow to philosophers, at least to materialistic philosophers, and it was not long until political theorists were saying that if nature had no order then it was time that an élite impose order on the masses. Such was in large part the justification offered by fascists for their seizure of power. On the other hand comes the cheering realization that now that reality is rid of its lumpishness, the way is cleared for freedom of the will.

Fascists and totalitarians of all kinds were indeed stealing a march on democracy. Freedom and democracy depended upon restrained and intelligent social interaction, but it was becoming alarmingly clear that the social sciences were lagging in the effort to educate the citizen to control the vast mechanical power which scientists were heedlessly placing in his hands. There were many reasons, but we can name only a few.

One was the failure of the social sciences to develop a method, and in fact the growing realization that human interactions are so fraught with endless possibilities that (notwithstanding social engineers to the contrary) they can never be organized into a predictable, fool-proof pattern. Not only is the human being unpredictable, but he is influenced by endless natural factors which may or may not come under scientific control. Human views of any subject are thus liable to differences of interpretation which may rise out of timidity, selfishness, incomplete data, or honest inability to agree. The one important attempt to develop a method in the social sciences is the case study, as with the Lynds' *Middletown,* a case study of the social conditions of Muncie, Indiana. The method clearly has value, but even more clearly it has limitations.

A second reason for the lagging of the social sciences is public suspicion. Social sciences translate scientific findings into social terms and ask embarrassing questions, such as why must we have slums, or poverty, or race discrimination. People who ask such questions cannot expect to be popular with vested interests, by which we mean not merely capitalists but our vested interest in a white skin, superior prestige, wealth, education, social position, or the hope of acquiring them if the *status quo* remains unchanged. Vested interests also exist among radicals who work for change because they think they or humanity will profit—and they are fully as suspicious of anyone who insists on consulting social or scientific facts.

The truth is that science itself stands in danger because the social sciences are not educating the masses rapidly enough. There was a time when science was regarded as black magic; let the vested interests once more become aware of the fact that science is more interested in truth than in their selfish welfare, and it will again be denounced and persecuted as black magic. It is happening today in the Soviet Union and it can happen in the West.

The creation of atomic weapons has laid the axe to the roots of the popular beliefs in the inevitability of progress and that science necessarily gives personal wisdom and social adaptability. Now that scientists are confronted by the prospect of losing their freedom to search for "truth" regardless of the consequences they are frightened. Are they frightened by the prospect of the loss or do they really grasp what they have done to society? At any rate they are bewildered and the remedies that they propose are likely to be dictatorial or unrealistic—even naive.

Scientists have rubbed the gloss off their glamor and stirred resentment among the frightened masses, but no one in his right mind would propose stopping their research. Of course they need to re-learn the old truth that the proper study of mankind is man. They need to learn the difference between the freedom to invent and espouse brilliant scientific heresies and the business of engaging in conspiracies against that freedom. The fact is that they are in a position to make or break freedom if the outcome is to depend on force. The eventual happiness of humanity may rest upon the work of social scientists and cultural leaders, but in the present crisis the scientist holds the key.

*   *   *

All down through human history the man or the group with a program unlikely to meet with popular approval has found it useful to create an atmosphere of crisis in which the program can be slipped through. The method that they have commonly used is the smear technique, a method that is equally valuable in case of actual crisis to induce the masses to act as desired. The object is to get rid of the independent man—trample him to death by geese. As Aristotle noted: "History shows that almost all tyrants have been demagogues who gained favor with the people by their accusations of the notables."

The cleaning out of the spoils system in the United States government and the substitution of civil service has reduced appointive jobs to about 12,000 policy-making positions out of a total of around 2,600,000. Since political acceptability is no longer necessary for appointment to government service, crypto-communists are able to get into the civil service and to boost each other up the bureaucratic ladder to positions where they exercise considerable influence on policy makers. The situation was "made to order" for Senator Joseph R. McCarthy. McCarthy, a Republican Old Guardsman of Wisconsin, was a big blue-jowled, likable chap without great gifts who hit upon the trade mark of anti-communism; this was an excellent thing for the country, but in his campaign he had a tendency to rate as a communist anyone who did not conform to his extreme reactionism. Indeed he seemed to be less the leader of a moral crusade than a zestful boxer who took pride in being a rough man in the clinches.

Foreign observers have had considerable difficulty in understanding why Americans have had such palpable fear of communism and by and large have tended to attribute it to innate conservatism, capitalist propaganda, and a hysteria which rises from emotional instability. Without denying the iota of truth in each accusation it is possible to present far more convincing reasons. McCarthyism is certainly in itself an indication of intolerance, but it can also be argued that the fact that opponents of McCarthyism have not invoked the extreme weapons (which are available) to stop it, is proof of basic American tolerance. And in all fairness it should be pointed out that in foreign countries those who attack American McCarthyism most bitterly are the first to cover communist intolerance with the charitable mantle of tolerance—a mantle which somehow is never stretched to cover American policies or events.

The American has been dedicated to the defense of his institutions; they, indeed, have historically taken the place of the European peasant's love of the soil. These institutions have not only the aura of tradition behind them, but their suitability and flexibility have been tested, and they have (together with our natural resources) helped to give to Americans an unprecedented degree of civil freedom and of economic opportunity. Inasmuch as these results are identified with capitalism they make communism's opposition to capitalism seem a greater menace than fascism—for fascism at least in *theory* accepts capitalism.

American radicalism has historically been aimed at the purification and adaptation—not the overthrow—of our institutions, and has championed their basic insistence upon the preservation of civil liberties. This definitely includes freedom of religion—for this is a Christian nation however much some of its people may neglect church duties. It has never accepted Nietzsche's announcement that "God is dead," and to that extent has differed from the atheistic culture of present-day Europe.

The American public has learned by bitter experience that fascism and communism are only the two sides of the totalitarian coin. Communism violates the American tradition of peaceful change by its use of intrigue to pave the way for seizure of power by force. When it comes into power it subverts civil liberties and governs by force. It relies for its support in this country chiefly upon European immigrants and their children; relatively little support comes from men and women who have been steeped in the American tradition. Moreover communists in the United States have boldly subordinated American interests to those of Russia. It is apparent that in two world wars the aggressors made the mistake of failing to knock out the United States first. Russia is not likely to repeat this mistake. At any rate it has concentrated its military, propaganda, and espionage weapons in the full consciousness that the United States is the effective reason why it cannot at once assume ascendance over the world.

The sum of the matter is that the American sees in communism an attempt to subvert all that he holds dear. To those who assert that the communist domestic political peril is trifling he answers that it is supported by a powerful outside imperialism and carried on by a sizable group of native-born but unassimilated and pathologically discontented citizens who give their allegiance to that power. Communism has proved its shrewdness and resourcefulness by dividing the labor movement, fooling a number of political and intellectual leaders, filching defense secrets, placing its minions in key government positions, and by forming a program and an apparatus to promote revolution, to seize advantage of governmental mistakes, and to take control in the event of success.

It is possible, of course, to hold that these are minor matters and that undue concern over them shows distrust of the solidity of our institutions. On the other hand the American feels that he is showing a realistic awareness of the way in which evil grows and spreads in this world. Indeed America has been no stranger to the method, for the United States was launched on a wave of revulsion against ideas which it regarded as both insidious and dangerous. Ever since that, despite a certain reverence for European culture, it has lived in fear of some of Europe's ideas. This has been confirmed in every generation by European immigrants who have stubbornly sought to defend those ideas and have frequently sought to block the education of their children in the practice of American institutions. To the American, communist infiltration and propaganda is the most recent phase, and perhaps the most dangerous, of a struggle which began when dissident elements sought to undermine the "Utopias" envisioned by the first colonists.

Many Western Europeans tend to play down communism as a menace. For one thing their moral sensibilities have been blunted by the illness which rose out of two world wars. Along with this has gone the psychology of "eat, drink and be merry, for tomorrow we die"—a psychology often found among those who rather expect to be displaced. Again, nationalism is firmly implanted—too firmly—and there is the constant hope that communists will turn out to be patriots instead of Russian pawns. There is always hope that communists can still be "saved" or convinced by tolerating them; there is little recognition that communists will have to die off like any other generation of re-actionaries and that the best that can be done is to undertake a vigorous campaign to save innocents from their clutches. Certainly in Britain the public feels that it can afford to regard communists as "queer" rather than dangerous.

The European masses also have less to lose than the masses in America, for they have been held down by the tradition that a con-siderable part of the people must be underprivileged and they have been aware of a strong current of opposition to civil and religious liberties and to economic opportunities for the masses. Another curious fact is that so many Europeans (especially Jews) are still so heartsick over Nazi brutalities that they are quite unable to see the same brutal character in the ideology which insists that it is the enemy of fascism.

Perhaps no less important is the fact that (at least in Germany and the Latin countries) there has never been a complete conversion to the democratic method. These peoples have become hardened to revolu-tion and accustomed to ideological divisions, and there is always room for one more sword in the fray. This may or may not arise from their firm grasp of logic or from a superior devotion to principle, but it means that the people have never been in fundamental agreement in supporting democracy; more than that, they cannot believe that Ameri-cans are united in its support and they show a pathetic eagerness to wrest facts to prove that they are not. This leads into a situation which is further explanatory of Europeans' attitudes toward communism. They cannot easily counter it so there is some tendency to deny that it should be countered. In any case, if communism is the menace the United States seems to think, let that country combat it. Even those Europeans who are worried about communism have convinced them-selves that the United States *must* protect them in order to protect itself; the illusion has been fostered by American internationalists.

* * *

Anti-intellectualism allows a certain flexibility in meeting crises, but it also encourages an oversimplified view of problems and a tendency to pluck answers out of the air or out of emotional or political bias. We are accused of a tendency to hysteria which forebodes failure on the long haul because of a lack of the steadiness and predictability (the "character") necessary to world leadership. Polls have shown that Americans are woefully uninformed or misinformed and Gabriel Almond has accused them of looking for "cues for mood responses" rather than for sound information. He is willing to entertain the idea that the old emotionalism is passing, but is it not possible to go farther? Is it not possible that we have glamorized the democracy of the past by exaggerating the amount of intelligent and informed interest taken in public affairs? These things cannot be measured, but it may be that intelligent and informed interest is on the increase, and that there lies the reason for the subsidence of the old waves of national emotion.

We are likely to confuse comfort with civilization, and to exhibit a corollary faith in the efficacy of gadgets, possibly because we hope that they can reduce the personal and national sacrifices necessary to meet our international obligations. These traits expose a vein of insensitiveness which results in mass slaughter in an attempt to get quick results. But this insensitiveness is more the effect of singlemindedness than of sadism, and it is notable that in Korea the United States official policy sought patiently and persistently to avoid widening the sphere of destruction. In any case there is a quite opposite desire to alleviate the sufferings of defeated nations and their citizens.

We still show a certain lack of taste; lawlessness is still rampant, at least in small violations and in a disregard of the spirit of the laws; "slickness" survives, not merely in the craving to "make a fast buck" but in the almost psychopathic need for winning which vitiates the spirit of sportsmanship. It should at least be a warning to prospective enemies that they are baiting a nation which plays for keeps. We make exceptions to our principles of equality and tolerance, even though no one tries to deny the validity of the principles. There is however always a loud protest against such violations, in any given case a majority protest.

Certainly there is a tendency on the part of too many of our leaders to seek personal advantage by shortsighted or demagogic tactics—a penchant to regard the mission of the political opposition as being to frustrate the party in power rather than to offer constructive criticism. They show too great a tendency to kowtow to public pressures rather than to undertake the true function of leadership which is to educate and lead, not follow. Woodrow Wilson vitiated his work by stubbornly mistaken decisions, but he clearly demonstrated that the people of a democracy will react favorably to reason.

* * *

American liberalism has traditionally been concerned not with the introduction of socialism but with removing abuses and equalizing opportunity. And yet—as one might expect in this land of paradoxes—the only modern long-term instance of successful socialism is found in the barely concealed Mormon control of Utah's economy. Liberalism preaches—even if it does not always practice—the Golden Rule. It stresses fair play toward minorities, for it believes that the social and political diversities represented by minorities are the stuff of progress. It even fosters many of the peculiarities of regionalism, for it dreads the growth of a monolithic national opinion which may be used by demagogues to create a national mob spirit. It teaches that ideas are ideals on the way to becoming realities. The liberal, as Clement Eaton says, is a person who is willing to experiment for the improvement of society.

"To establish a free trade in ideas, it is not sufficient that government shall practice restraint in interfering with private opinions—a purely negative role; nor that a society shall be willing to listen to conflicting views. There must be ideas to interchange; there must be vigorous minorities; there must be a crop of critics, skeptics, and rebels; there must be a changing, dynamic civilization, fermenting and full of creative energy."*

If anything is evident in American history it is the continuous existence of a creative ferment, always present to do battle with democracy's tendency to glorify mediocrity. It is frequently overlooked that perceptive conservatives have been essential to the ferment. Their vision of social and political responsibility and their view of America's place in the world have frequently been broader than the liberals' more narrow interpretation of the solution to domestic and foreign problems. One of the finest harbingers of a new day is the fact that there is a returning sense of responsibility (political and cultural, not merely financial) among the younger generation of the wealthy.

---

* Clement Eaton, *Freedom of Thought in the Old South* (1940) viii-ix.

The decade of the 1930's was a time of crisis, when choices were made and men fought for what they believed. The turmoil, the hunger marchers, the chain gangs, the apple sellers, race brutality, fear and intolerance, the rising indignation of a people who saw their cherished democracy rusted tight—all these are too huge to grasp in one book or one mind. There was a new spirit in the air, or rather a renascence of the old spirit of America. Even those who had homes and jobs took to the road to see what America was really like. All America was learning—and what it decided was carried to the White House as though by osmosis and there found expression in demands for action. It is absurd to speak of Roosevelt as a dictator. He was a democratic leader who heard and obeyed—sometimes too quickly and without sufficient protest.

Here was a time made for the creative artist to exercise his function of elucidation and choice, but in the 1930's he lacked the simple, direct view of fundamentals which was shown by the masses. Still torn between form and function—between the cultivated tradition and the rising vernacular—he oscillated between a pallid version of democracy and a pinkish version of communism which he naively took for the sunrise of a new day. Western Civilization's claim to distinction lies in its faith that the long-term triumph of spiritual values can best be assured by laying a material basis for spiritual advance. The creative artist must reconcile mass production and the art of living. He must tame mass production to social usefulness and to do this he must teach that our aim is not always to find the most efficient method, but rather to find the most feasible degree of individual freedom and development consistent with social survival. Where he cannot find solutions he must show us how to equilibrate uncertainties; society after all is like a man with heart trouble who has to learn to get along with what he cannot cure.

No one should quarrel with those who cultivate belle lettres for their own sake, without reference to philology or social significance. Such writing, however, is not usual in America; aside from the "pulps" and the "slicks" (and even they to a certain extent) American fiction writers have been concerned with the traditional quest for moral values. They have had a freshness and vigor which seems to have had some effect on European writers. The latter have largely been given to sterile self praise or self pity, and to the reiteration of clichés about duty, responsibility, dignity, fortitude, and patriotism—all good in their place but uttered without much dynamism. Americans at least introduced their European confreres to self examination and protest, to a new realization of the human ferment with its wildness, heroism, tragedy, and even perhaps a little to its creativeness.

On the other hand American writers despite their vitality and their trenchant self criticism have been journalists in search of the sensational exception to use in illustrating their bitter protests, a failing in which they resembled Hollywood. The result has been that they have too frequently overlooked the strong and consistent currents in American life. Certainly Hollywood and the novelists between them have given the world an erroneous impression of America and this remains despite all that others can do to portray the truth.

Indeed it has been suggested that this impression of an America that could not or would not act had much to do with fostering the delusion of the dictators that they could embark on their aggressions without danger of American opposition. Social and economic progress has moved at a rapid pace in America, yet it is a peculiar fact that the world still sees us in terms of the fiction and the movies of the dizzy 1920's and of the savage depression years. Germany twice and Japan and Russia each once, made ghastly misjudgments of American psychology; as a result the German and Japanese empires ceased to exist and along with them the empires of Austria-Hungary, Turkey, and Italy.

It is evident that most important American fiction writers have ended in futility. Perhaps their trouble lay in their expectation that by searching they would find the golden thread of truth that runs through human existence, when in fact it is their duty to utter the faith that it exists and in so doing to make it real. Reviews have during the last few decades hailed many masterpieces now fortunately and mercifully forgotten.

For a moment in the 1930's it seemed that writers might rise to leadership, and indeed there was a reaction against the sterile and maudlin self-pity of the Lost Generation. In retrospect it would seem that they were only stirring the ashes of the American Dream and asking when the phoenix would arise. It is curious how the larger figures of American fiction are imbued with a pessimistic determination to stand aloof from the society in which they lived. Hence the frustrations of Hemingway, the braggart, uncertain boy; the anguish and fear of Faulkner and Wolfe; the irony of Ellen Glasgow; the clumsy protests of Dreiser; and the snarls of Ring Lardner and Sinclair Lewis. It is little wonder that most Americans turn increasingly to history, biography, travel, and the escape fiction.

The artistic ferment remains in America, but except in literature it is the work of figures who are little more than names to the average reader. There has on the whole been a shift in the attitude of American intellectuals toward their country. They no longer go abroad to seek a spiritual home, perhaps because they have at last recognized that communism and neutralism are destructive, perhaps because they have begun to understand the American mission. This new affirmativeness toward America does not mean complete acceptance, for they still protest against the evils and the crassness in our culture, but it does mean that they are at last doing their share toward making this a better country. The effect is already noticeable. It may not be correct to say that the United States is undergoing a cultural renascence, but one looms on the horizon and barring world catastrophe it should be with us in another generation.

*　　*　　*

Pointing the finger of scorn at youth is a favorite diversion of the generation which is about to become passé. A 6,000-year-old tablet dug from a Near Eastern ruin was found on translation to bewail the degeneracy of the young and to prophecy the end of the world as the result. One hears accusations that youth is conformist, lacks convictions for fear of being called subversive, and is intellectually incurious. They raise hell—but discreetly. They drink less. They work fairly hard. They are not rude or rebellious toward the older generation—partly because no one tries to boss them. The girls are aggressive, coarse, dominant—but want to get married. The men's ambitions have shrunk; they aim at a good job with a corporation, preferably outside of a city, where they can have a house, a car, a pretty wife, babies—a suburban idyll. Above all they are silent; they issue no manifestoes, make no speeches, and carry no posters. One such assessment ends with the words: "The best you can say for this younger generation is, 'Youth Will Serve.'" As if anything better could be said! The curious thing about such analyses is that they, apparently unconsciously, describe a generation which is mature, responsible, ready to do its duty, and more concerned with personal, family, and community satisfactions than with "getting to the top."

It may be that we are seeing the dawn of maturity, and that our long experience in democratic self government has borne fruit. Counters to the deadening effects of mass conformity are all around us. Some of them even rise out of the very conformity which mass production promoted. Ford's Model-T actually led to a demand for cars with improved lines and better performance, and the demand could be satisfied because mass production had provided the purchasing power. The automobile has built up suburbia and made life more worth living for millions. With more leisure and elbow room, Americans are now interested in gardening and in cultural pursuits. The demand is growing for goods and services that are different, and this has led to study of the principles of art and to improved tastes. Fun for its own sake is no lost art; one evidence is the SPEBSQSA—the Society for the Preservation and Encouragement of Barber Shop Quartet Singing in America. There is a legion of similar organizations, equally useless and equally full of fun. Hobbies have multiplied until today they form the basis not only for personal satisfactions but supplying tools, materials, and instruction for them has become big business. Amateur musicians, players, and painters swarm in every community and show intense interest in classic techniques and in modern experimentalism.

There is a great deal of misunderstanding in the world about the role of standardization, and it is criticized on the ground that it will inevitably impose conformity; quite evident is the desire of the critics to keep cultural and material blessings to themselves. Actually standardization need not necessarily be conformity. The mass production of books, periodicals, and recordings does not necessarily pander to mediocrity. As a matter of fact there is no doubt that public taste has risen—though there is still room at the top. The demand for conformity has thus far failed to undermine America's precious diversities. The nation is knitted together not only by laws and politics, but by the strands of veterans, fraternal, business, and labor organizations and women's clubs. These are basically state and regional alliances which survive by a perpetual application of compromise and logrolling. Our federalism means that we have realized that the efficient way is not always the socially desirable way. Our regional compromises and search for individual participation have avoided the disastrous nationalism and individualism of Europe which threaten to give that continent a hard choice between tyranny and destruction. We have persevered in our attempts to utilize private pressure groups and private collective enterprises as social guides.

We still have a healthful resentment of government controls and taxation as intrusions—even when we agree to their necessity. There is little indication that Americans will come to regard government as dependably "moral," that invariable accompaniment of socialism and totalitarianism. An American is amused by British socialists' accusation that the United States is hopelessly conformist while they are free and individualist. Actually there can be no more certain indication of conformity than devotion to the "moral" government.

There is a certain independence along with a certain understanding of the necessity of inter-reliance, and also a certain cool skepticism. The radio exhortation frequently goes in one ear and out the other, Hollywood's confections are accepted as escape not gospel, public opinion polls are taken with salt—at least since 1948—and the old political clichés have been losing their charm since the collapse of 1929. There are so many Americans that even a small proportion of them can give the impression that a fad or a hysteria is sweeping the country. Actually the main body will still be interested primarily in kids and crops, in home and school and business. They have long been following Lewis Mumford's advice to "resist every type of automatism: buy nothing merely because it is advertised, use no invention merely because it has been put on the market, follow no practice merely because it is fashionable." There is a basic acceptance of facts and an ability to roll with the punches. Americans have "always carried a great deal of moral baggage around with them." Franz Boas insists that where sentiments and values are concerned the judgment of the masses is sounder than that of the classes.

America has become the most significant single factor in the modern world, an object which was not sought but for which we have nevertheless paid a high price. The American has been a pragmatic dreamer who made his dreams come true, a rootless wanderer in his own land and in all the world. He has been self-confident because of his conquests of nature, optimistic because of his opportunities, and pessimistic because of the volatility of youth. The democratic method of taking calculated risks has entered into his blood and reappears as a social and military method.

The United States has had a longer experience in democratic self government than any other nation. Moreover it shows a greater political maturity in domestic affairs despite the superficialty and demagoguery of many politicians and Congress' unfortunate lack of dignity. Even at that the notable thing is that Congress does have a core of responsible men who are able to moderate even where they cannot squelch the demagogues. It is moreover fair to say that we have the most effective government of modern times—not necessarily, thank God, the most efficient, though its efficiency is not to be underrated. The American knows that democratic government can function only where people agree on fundamental principles. Our parties are therefore instruments of government rather than crusaders for new departures in fundamental principles. Hence there is before every election a frantic search for "issues" which will sway the voter, but the attempt to present them as "principles" is more likely to excite derision than belief.

We are less hysterical than we used to be when the raft tilts and we get our feet wet. We are calmer and grimmer in meeting crises. We are less confident that the world moves in perceptible grooves. Our aristocracy (or plutocracy, if you prefer) is showing a new sense of responsibility as the rich man seeks a sense of participation in social affairs. Tolerance is making long-term headway despite the efforts of demagogues to thwart it. We are more curious about universal values. We laugh at ourselves oftener. We do our duty without regard to outside distractions. We no longer—most of us—expect the world to love us for our gifts. We face facts—reluctantly, it is true—but we face them.

Americans still have a minimum of reverence for the man on top. Envy is tempered by pleasure in others' success and by innate friendliness and neighborliness; in the international sphere this is shown by proofs of good will unprecedented in human history. Americans still have an instinctive sympathy for the underdog—unfortunately with some unreasoning exceptions. Human relations are improving in industry; despite our efficiency we have grasped the fundamental of human living, that the most efficient solution is not always socially the most desirable. We still work hard—harder than most other nations. We still believe in human dignity and freedom and we are seeking for ways of spreading their observance at home and abroad. We still have plenty of kickers and experimenters, the advantages of mingled bloods and cultures, enormous remaining resources, and best of all the democratic process for meeting changed conditions and sudden crises.

The way is open to reconcile the paradox of competition and co-operation, but not all problems will be solved. We can never fully understand natural phenomena because we can never see them as they are but must apprehend them through mechanical instruments and through humanity's sensory perceptions. Niels Bohr assures us that there will always be uncertainty in physics because we can never know whether light consists of waves or particles. Similarly we can never know whether life is a mechanical phenomenon or a vital principle, or whether the mind is a camera or the agent of free will. Bohr insists that both are true—that the two views are complementary. If this is right there will always be room for human judgment but there will always be things we do not understand—uncertainties which must be equilibrated. There will be no smug permanent answers. There will always be a danger of taking the wrong track. Living will never need to become boredom.

XVI

How Fares the American Mission?

THE forces which were molding the American way of life were so explosive that there was no possibility of confining them to the United States. The American impact had begun to be felt in the outer world long before the twentieth century. Europe's élite saw the United States as the chief source of the new currents which were eddying through the modern world and which jeopardized their traditional ascendance. Its example of democracy was envied by the masses everywhere and its Constitution had served as a pattern wherever peoples were resurgent. American reformers, both balanced and unbalanced, had for a hundred years been planting their standards on European soil and rallying the do-gooders, the discontented, and the oppressed. Emerson, Whitman, Cooper, and Poe had exercised an influence on European literature and liberal thought, and of late days John Dewey had sowed doubts of its traditional educational system. Louis Sullivan and Frank Lloyd Wright, evangelists of the new architecture, found students and imitators even where beaux arts professed to dominate.

Americans could not before World War I have justly claimed many great contributions to pure science, but their technology was rapidly overtaking that of Great Britain and was soon to pass it. The latter, in fact, showed definite signs of slowing down. American marketing methods were already acknowledged as superior, and they were partly responsible for the stream of American manufactured goods which by 1900 had begun to alarm Europeans. The alarm, it would seem, was more for the future than the present; actually the chief part of American exports were still grain, meat, and raw materials.

Before the present generation came upon the scene there was a rather smug tendency to echo George Harvey's famous witticism that the foreign policy of the United States was "to have no foreign policy." Few generalizations have been less accurate, for the United States did have a fairly well defined foreign policy based upon enlightened self interest and the national concept of the American mission. Allan Nevins points out that these found expression in four objectives that were followed as consistently as most other nations have followed their objectives.

One of these guides had been the avoidance of alliances with foreign powers—popularly supposed to be in pursuance of Washington's advice but actually in obedience to Jefferson's sweeping demand for rejection of "entangling alliances" in toto.

The second objective was freedom of trade, which led to the historic policies of defense of freedom of the seas and championship of the Open Door in trade in China and elsewhere.

The third objective was to prevent (for security reasons) the further extension of European power in the Western Hemisphere; this found expression in the Monroe Doctrine (1823), which proved to be so conveniently vague that it covered any desired policy without preventing us from expanding our own territory and economic power at the expense of our neighbors or acquiring the bases necessary for strategic security. Lastly was the American predilection to support democratic aspirations wherever they appeared, usually by popular opinion, sometimes by financial aid and diplomatic pressure, and finally by war; these actions were regarded quite simply as inseparable from the carrying out of the American mission.

Americans in 1900 might convince themselves that they could hold aloof from world affairs, but perceptive Europeans knew better. The growing economic power of the United States and its dynamic social and political ideas would willy-nilly thrust it upon the world stage sooner or later. This was all the more evident in the light of the fact that the Pax Britannica, which since Napoleon had enforced a relative degree of world peace, had from the 1870's begun to show signs of decay, and this had encouraged a resurgence of nationalism and of imperialism in Europe. Imperialism, after all, is merely the extension of national interests abroad. From this it was only a step to the rationalization that the nations wanted empire for the good of the ruled. The white nations, they preached, had a mission—"the White Man's Burden"—to civilize and Christianize the benighted peoples of the world. It was the use of "brutal force to impose on unwilling peoples the blessing" of one's own civilization; the willingness to fight other civilized nations on behalf of the imposition of one's own superior civilization.

European imperialism sought to claim as an excuse that it needed colonial raw materials, manpower, and markets. The United States needed none of these. American advocates of empire sought their excuses in the *eventual* need of markets, but even more in the desire for national prestige, in strategic necessity, and of course in the claim of responsibility for inferior races. The last sprang from the democratic doctrine of equality, but it came with ill grace from a nation which had at times been very callous in its treatment of Indians and Negroes. The native concept of a master race was reinforced by Social Darwinism, and by the racism of Gobineau and Houston Stewart Chamberlain brought back from Germany by graduate students. From these roots came the mythus of the superiority of the "Anglo-Saxons" and of their "destiny" to rule the world. Fear of the "Yellow Peril"—Japan and China—was a corollary of Anglo-Saxonism and in time there was added a fear that Germany might also become an obstacle to the fulfillment of Anglo-Saxon destiny.

Alfred Thayer Mahan's preachments on the significance of sea power in the rise of empires caught the attention of imperialists and big navy advocates everywhere. Among these was a galaxy of American editors and politicians who stood ready to champion the "inevitable destiny" of the United States to expand. One of the latter, not yet risen to greatness, was Theodore Roosevelt. Spain's clumsy handling of Cuban revolt proved to be a convenient excuse for the expansionists, and they were joined by those who were seeking to assure American strategic security in the Caribbean, and by those who believed in America's mission to promote democracy at least at its doorstep. The result was the brief Spanish-American War (1898) and the acquisition within a single year of Puerto Rico, Hawaii, and the Philippines. In time these were followed by the Panama Canal Zone and the Virgin Islands.

It was the Spanish-American War which saddled the country with the two specific responsibilities which were to mold future American foreign policy. First, the expansion of American strategic and economic interests to the Philippines brought us into vital contact with imperial Europe and Japan; the effect in the long run was to place our western frontier on the China coast. Second, the expansion of our strategic and economic interests into the Caribbean made another vital contact with imperial Europe, especially Germany, which was edging toward a strong position in Latin America; the effect in the long run was to place our eastern frontier on the Rhine. These assumptions of responsibility, unfortunately were not understood by the people at large nor even by Congress, and the executive was left to handle them as best he could without their comprehension or support. Therein lies much of the reason for the ridiculous inconsistencies and the repeated and resounding failures of American foreign policy between that time and this.

A retrospect of American imperialism in the Caribbean brings to light certain facts which were not clear to contemporaries. True enough, Cuba, Panama, Haiti, the Dominican Republic, and Nicaragua had treaties of protection forced upon them, and all the Central American republics had been subjected to the pressure of Dollar Diplomacy or had unwillingly entertained marines. But these protectorates were nothing like the pattern set up by European empires. They were limited in duration, their citizens could not be drafted to fight the protector's wars, and they conducted their own foreign affairs even though certain rules were laid down by Washington. Even in domestic affairs American control was usually confined to the fiscal administration and to supervision of elections. The era of political and fiscal protectorates was ephemeral and passed away as the Caribbean states became more orderly and as the overwhelming power of the United States made it useless for Europe to threaten its strategic security. Such control as survives is based upon economic treaties and common strategic interests.

*   *   *

Many historians seek the origins of World War I in European rivalries and absolve the United States of guilt. The matter should not be thus easily shrugged off. The American illusion of isolation caused us to ignore the signs of coming world conflict and to do nothing about it during the twenty years that the world hung on the edge of the abyss. But this was not all, for we may be justly accused of having made positive contributions toward bringing on the age of conflict. The American democratic ideology played a share in creating unrest among the European masses. Its food and raw materials sometimes undercut those of Europe and bred economic dislocations. The threat of mass production techniques, which demanded great resources and marketing areas and called for the integration of nations, imperilled Europe's existing political structure and helped to convince its statesmen and financiers that they must insulate their countries by conquests of territory, raw materials, and strategic bases. True, American mass production was not yet mature and we cannot assess the precise share it played in European actions, but it is clear that then as now Europe regarded American technology as destructive of traditional economic and cultural patterns. Rather than adapting itself to the new technology Europe sought a means of warding it off and so bred conflicts and hastened decline.

Of course our moral judgment on much of what transpired after the war began should depend upon whether human rights were really at stake. Actually the problems of Europe in 1914 were probably not unsolvable, provided its statesmen had realized the terrible alternative which faced them. Germany's kaiser and its ruling junker class were undoubtedly authoritarian, but there was amazing vigor in its proto-democrats and they might conceivably have won the struggle for Germany's soul had there been no war or had it been brief. Britain's responsibility also was primary, for it failed to envision the era of international cooperation which was the logical successor to the Pax Britannica. As for France and Russia, they might or might not have moved without the assurance of Britain.

Even after the war began destruction might have been forefended by a negotiated peace. It seems true that as late as 1916 Germany was ready to negotiate, and it seems equally clear that the Allies refused because the actions of the State Department gave assurance of effective aid or even hope of American entry into the war on their side. No one can say now what steps the American people would have permitted, but there were a number of courses open to Wilson if he had been determined to halt the war. He could have laid an embargo on munitions. He could have threatened to use, and if necessary used, naval force to prevent Allied breach of the old laws of neutrality; the British foreign minister later admitted that the Allies would have had to yield. He could have joined the Allies at the time of the *Lusitania* crisis but firmly and intelligently used his power to bring about a negotiated peace.

The mistakes of Versailles are now readily apparent. Germany, over Wilson's protest, was saddled with a huge indemnity. The Allies thereby subjected themselves to a dilemma: the only way it could be paid was to make Germany strong, but then it would be strong enough to refuse to pay. Germany was forced to disarm on the reciprocal Allied agreement to do likewise—which the Allies did not do. Germany was forced to sign an admission that it was guilty of having caused the war; in the end this was to be a powerful propaganda weapon in impelling the Germans to seek revenge. Wilson envisioned his self-determination of nations as operating in an atmosphere of calm imposed by the League of Nations. Actually it did not work out this way. The Austro-Hungarian Empire at least had the virtue of forming a vast economic entity and its place should at least have been taken by a Danubian Confederacy of the succession states. As it was these states fell to quarreling over boundaries and economic rights, and these quarrels were to do their share toward promoting World War II. And yet it is a mistake to insist that Versailles led inevitably to World War II. True, it was harsh, but it was enforceable, and that without undue hardship. The great mistake lay not in the treaty itself, but in the postwar failure of the Allies (including the United States) to recognize their common interests and act together. Instead of that they fell to bickering among themselves and soon were playing off the succession states against their late allies and even bidding for the favor of Germany.

The American rejection of the League of Nations and of the Treaty of Versailles finds its explanation in national psychology, in the opposition of Irish-Americans and other "hyphenates," and in the parliamentary maneuvers of the Old Guardsmen in the Senate. By 1920 the people had been under a quarter-century of moral tension, a tension too great for their immaturity to support. They looked about them and saw the promises of the progressive leaders failing to materialize, but on the contrary saw prices shooting up with inflation, and war profiteers riding in limousines and living in mansions. They listened to the sly tales told by returning soldiers of the European civilization to which Americans had long looked for cultural guidance. Worst of all, Europe had turned Versailles into a struggle, not for peace or democracy but for spoils, and had tried to shame the United States into underwriting their booty. It was too much for the unstable American psyche. There was a growing conviction that our moral ideals had been betrayed by a cynical Europe, and we in turn became cynical about any hope of international justice or co-operation. With the Old Guard's return to power it promptly sought and found excuses for withdrawing from Europe and avoided responsibilities in East Asia by spreading them among the signatories of the Treaties of Washington (1922).

It is customary to credit the European democracies with a greater sense of reality than the United States; if that was true they were not blessed with enough of it during the interwar years. There is a common accusation that the United States was basically responsible for the lack of democratic unity because it did not join the League of Nations. This is a severe judgment which may or may not be correct. If the United States had joined the League and acted like the other great powers, mere membership would certainly have been ineffectual. Let it be readily admitted that since the dictators rose basically from economic stress the cure had to be at least in part economic—and this is where the United States could have contributed but did not. American interests were inseparably intermeshed with world conditions and events; like it or not we were now in the world and the stubborn determination to remain apart only meant that we must accept "events shaped by the wills of others." Nevertheless the European democracies had the power to crush dictatorship in the cradle, but they lacked decisiveness; they even lacked a sense of urgency. Above all they lacked the will to preach to their people the old truth that in union there is strength.

* * *

The Europeans of 1900 had portrayed the gaudy American, cocktail in hand, bestriding the narrow world, but as a matter of fact the American invasion began seriously only after World War I. There were several reasons. The war weakened Europe and at the same time gave the United States a surplus of capital for investment. In the second place American technology (again partly because of the war) had stepped up the rhythm of production to the point where a surplus of goods existed and had to be disposed of.

Thirdly, the United States was apparently approaching the end of some of its own raw materials, especially petroleum, copper, nickel, and aluminum, and the wealthy and aggressive industries which had been built upon these now naturally sought to gain control of foreign supplies. In addition, Americans felt obliged to combat the efforts of foreigners to manipulate a number of raw materials so as to create an artificial scarcity and raise the prices; among these may be named rubber, tin, tungsten, vanadium, and jute. Last among our factors but probably the key to all the others was the mere dynamism of a young and vigorous nation which delighted in business enterprise and strife just as a young man delights to pit his strength against his fellows.

World War I had poured a quarter of Europe's wealth down the drain, destroyed or worn out much of its productive equipment, killed and crippled millions of its producers, and disrupted old trade ties. All these had to be replaced or mended before Europe could recover the competitive position of 1914. Meanwhile it would be falling far behind the United States. With this in mind, one can see the feeling of desperation which drove British and French statesmen to undertake shady competitive practices. But this was not all. Recovery was retarded by revolutions, by fluctuating currencies, by trade wars, by lack of raw materials, by bad transportation, and by lost or dislocated overseas markets.

If ever the world needed a planned economic effort, this was the time. But the genius of laissez faire still hovered over the nations in both Europe and America and prohibited anything as radical as mutual aid. The inevitable result was that the Allies and the succession states reverted to internal and external cutthroat competition. Neo-mercantilism had been rising with the imperial surge, and now it came in with a swoop. Actually Wilson's own favorite policy of self-determination of nations encouraged the emerging pattern of economic conflict. Tariffs, subsidies, quotas, trade blocks, and barter agreements prevented the free flow of goods and led to internal hardships and international rivalries. Europe was so fractionated that it was impossible to introduce the savings of mass production; so the standard of living suffered. Individual nations and businessmen made the best deals they could with that great fount of credit and capital goods, the United States.

The war had with dramatic suddenness changed the United States from a debtor to a creditor nation. As a matter of fact, American loans should have been several times as large, for the United States had now reached the stage of economic maturity where it should have loaned generously and collected interest in the form of an excess of imports over exports. However, on the whole, it showed itself willing to dispose of its production on credit rather than risk the importation of great quantities of foreign goods. The reasons are readily apparent: continued fear of slowing down the rhythm of production; we were relatively self-sufficient in agriculture, raw materials, and industry; the opposition of business and labor to the introduction of competitive goods whether or not they were cheaper; and the survival of the old mercantile psychology that even a rich nation must sell more than it buys. The result was that we stubbornly subsidized foreign purchases instead of taking goods in exchange. Another evidence of America's economic ascendancy was the way in which it was taking over world markets; even after it went to war its mass production methods had enabled it to go on shipping considerable quantities of goods to neutrals.

The strange thing is that despite the current worship of material values we were quite unable to judge them soundly and realistically. What the United States really needed was an orderly world in which to trade its enormous production for the many foreign products it needed or could use. And yet the nation with one third the world's developed economic wealth deliberately walled itself off from the goods of the world. *Economic* imperialism was growing; yet at the very time that American investments were invading the world, the nation refused to safeguard them either by treaty or by military preparedness and was actually scuttling its navy, dismissing its army, and plumping for pacifism.

Nevertheless it was evident that the dawning age belonged to America. The American was as ubiquitous in all parts of the globe as the Roman had once been in the Mediterranean. Tourists, salesmen, engineers, bank representatives, exporters and importers, and Herbert Hoover's Department of Commerce boys swarmed everywhere. But it was the machine that was the true invader, either actually or by its products and methods. It refused to be impressed by international boundaries but regarded the world as an integral market. American corporations crept under national barriers by buying or building factories in the desired marketing area, and their backlog of expensive research, designing, and business and production techniques made them almost unbeatable.

The superiority of American goods in quality, attractiveness, or cheapness forced European competitors to adopt American methods or face ruin. But Europe did not have the capital, resources, or market to build up native mass-production industries; and, even more to the point, it could not adjust itself psychologically. Its social ideals clashed with the acceptance of higher labor costs, which alone could build a market. There was the typical petty official's affinity for red tape and ritual, and the thrift which made it impossible to throw away a fairly new but still obsolete machine and replace it by a better one. Most important of all was the failure to put into effect the spirit of freedom on the part of workers and engineers which is the core of the American know-how.

Germany sought to impose Fordism as a national sacrifice to augment its power, and the government devoted a quarter of the national income to the change-over. All it did was to create labor dislocations, lose foreign trade, and hasten the coming of Hitler. The result was that German industry (with a few exceptions) remained based on the skilled worker. German engineers consequently sank into pessimism and warned that in case of a second conflict with America, Germany was doomed to defeat.

Russia was the closest approach to an exception to the rule of European inability to adopt American methods. Lately the USSR has sought to claim credit for all the great inventions. In 1930 even Stalin was

properly humble. "We have never concealed," said he, "and we do
not intend to conceal the fact that in the sphere of technique we are
the pupils of the Germans, the English, the French, the Italians, and
first and foremost, the Americans." Throughout the 1920's American
engineers, either hired singly or representing engineering or manufacturing firms, swarmed into Russia, and some of them remained through the
1930's.

Fordism was carried to Russia by Ford engineers, and the word
entered the language to denote the ruthless speed-up and stretch-out
more usually called Stakhanovism. Curiously enough, this phenomenon
was on the increase in the boasted "workers' state" while it was decreasing in capitalist America. This fact is one key to the Russian
failure to profit fully by American teaching. In the United States
the worker and the engineer retained the spirit of freedom; it brought
discontent and strikes, but it also brought a cure to abuses and a certain
pride in sharing in production. In Russia all decisions had to be made
in conformity with rigid ideological principles which destroyed the spirit
of freedom.

During the seventeenth and eighteenth centuries Europe had flattered
the French by imitating their ways, and in the nineteenth century
Britain had become the model. Now the prestige of the United States
was evidenced by a superficial imitation of things America. Bars, cock-
tails, jazz, dances, food, clothes, and card games imported from America
became the mode. Before the war the plump Viennese woman had
been the ideal of Paris fashions, now the slim American woman became
the standard of fashion—if not exactly of beauty. Bobbed hair made
its way across the Atlantic. American slang, "permeated society from
below," and found a reception among would-be smarties all over the
world. The typical British sports, except football, were not as adaptable to the common people as some of the American competitive sports
such as baseball and basketball, and these found considerable vogue
over the world.

The effect of the American moving picture is hard to estimate with
accuracy, yet the bitterness with which many Europeans resented it gives
evidences of its significance. Hollywood put out a superior product
(or at least a smoother and more highly polished one), and, moreover,
it had the cachet of showing American scenes, fashions, dances, and
living conditions. It was not intended as propaganda, but European
politicians and businessmen rightly regarded it as that, for it spread
dissatisfaction with living and working conditions. Presently the re-

action came, as European leaders sought to build up their own cinema industries and launched a campaign of defamation against the American product.

The significant thing is that though native films have largely displaced the Hollywood products, the world's masses have not changed their minds. They flock to see practically any film from Hollywood but stay away in droves from their own. Of course, the American influence is often even more direct through the returned immigrant. There is scarcely an Italian village which does not hold a former resident of Brooklyn. Many of them have "American" quarters in which returned immigrants have built new houses equipped with plumbing, electricity, and a phonograph.

The European élite may be right in its claim that its culture is superior to that of America and its way of life more gracious. Yet it must be remembered that the élite can speak only for its own condition; the peasant or workingman has enjoyed few of these superior attainments and is unimpressed by aristocratic warnings of American materialism and standardization. He often sees the United States as a land of hope, the traditional refuge from economic, religious, social, and political ills. He knows that some of his friends have failed to succeed there, but so many more have succeeded that he has come to look on America as a Great Rock Candy Mountain.

From the viewpoint of Europe's old élite it must be admitted that there was an American menace. America's overwhelming economic power (aided by the war) had displaced Europe's world economic supremacy, had saddled it with debt, and threatened its very daily bread. It contributed to the ruin of European prestige in colonial areas, by the infiltration both of American economic controls and of economic and institutional ideas. The American example of a high standard of living was spreading discontent among Europe's workers, all the more so since emigration to the United States had been limited after World War I. Even more serious, the American example of democracy was contributing powerfully to the clearly approaching political and social crisis. Beyond all of these was an uneasy feeling that if economic leadership was lost, the leadership in the arts and sciences would soon pass to America.

The European movement to restore its position of world pre-eminence or at least to stave off further American encroachment took on two principal forms, one propagandistic and the other financial. Even before 1900, Europeans had frequently pointed with alarm at the increasing power of *Amerikanismus,* as the Germans called it. Americans admitted the fact of the Americanization of the world, but they saw it as the spread of the creative urge, a willingness to experiment with the new and to trust the people with political power and with a high economic standard.

The European view was not as complimentary. They saw Americanization, as Eric Fischer says, as the "conversion of the world into a purely materialistic state, where economic interests and power would prevail." Crass materialism, standardized mediocrity, and mass rather than quality were its earmarks. Wall Street and Washington, said this propaganda, were co-operating in a carefully laid plan to seize and exploit the world.

This propaganda was created primarily to influence the masses of the world. The European masses have been able to enjoy few of the advantages of culture and are therefore inclined to regard such arguments with skepticism. They may or may not be capable of enjoying the fine and the beautiful, but they none the less resent the implication that they can not or should not. On the other hand, these arguments when used in imperial possessions had considerable success. The masses could accept American economic imperialism as an explanation of the way in which wages were squeezed and prices inflated, while the accusation of materialism appealed to the native élite of nobility and education. These lines had such success that they probably delayed the great colonial crisis; and now that the native élite has taken over, it still pacifies the submerged classes with horrendous tales of American imperialism. Here again, however, it may be that the masses are not as gullible as their leaders suppose.

Propagandists in noncolonial areas found tinder lying about loose, ready for lighting. France and Italy each sought to capitalize on their Latin affinity with Latin America. Spain tried to build up a Pan-Hispanism in America aimed at the Colossus of the North. Britain moved to draw the Commonwealth nations together into an economic alliance. None of these efforts had much success, but whispering campaigns against American goods and American motives stirred a natural human resentment against the overly powerful.

Dominant as the United States was in the economic field, there was only nonsense in the accusation that it had reached that place and was maintaining it by a carefully prepared plan. If, as Coolidge averred, the people had awakened to the drumbeats of a new destiny, their march was strangely out of cadence. For one thing, if the United

States wanted economic power, it refused to assume the accompanying political responsibility. It kept the psychological attitudes of a debtor nation and of a petty merchant. It refused to regard World War I as an organic part of American evolution but insisted that it was merely an unsuccessful moral crusade, a temporary aberration. It reacted sharply against government controls. It was determined that its new production plant must be used for private profit. It rejected credit or production planning and made no surveys of world conditions save such as Herbert Hoover offered. Even capitalistic combinations conducting the invasion of other countries were neither consistent nor co-operative in policies and aims.

There can be little doubt that this fact was well known to the men who inspired the propaganda, but they had a purpose to fulfill. At the outset it was Europe's intention to capture American economic power and use it as her own, but any chance of success which this program might have had was killed by American disillusionment. Europe then passed to a propaganda of villification. This also failed, and was promptly followed by economic warfare with all the weapons of commerce. This is not the place to examine the details of the economic battles of the interwar decades, but the greatest struggles were waged over the control of raw materials, especially metals, rubber, and petroleum. Despite American advantages Europe was on the whole able to hold its own. Private citizens of the United States had no more invested abroad during the interwar years than had Britain, nor did they have as much invested in Europe (outside of the war debts) as did Europe in the United States. American technology and know-how made great strides in Europe, but they did not remake European industry in the American image. American cultural and institutional standards also made headway, but it is even more clear that they did not remake Europe even though their prestige excited much superficial imitation.

* * *

So far as imperialism pure and simple is concerned, a rowboat would hold all the Americans who desire to rule the world. But that is not the ˙ssue. Our problem is how best to carry out the American mission—how best to preserve democracy for ourselves and for the world. Actually World War II did not answer the question, for it still confronts us and may remain for a long time to come. Roosevelt's internationalism asserted that the world was now too small to be able to ignore aggression. A menace to freedom anywhere was a menace to American democracy and to the American mission. The Truman Doctrine made it clear—at least for the present—that the United States reserved the right to intervene forcibly anywhere in the world to fight aggression and protect freedom. As Sam Rayburn put it: "The United States cannot wrap two oceans around itself and stay safe and free."

Isolationists joined zealously in the prosecution of World War II after Pearl Harbor, but Roosevelt's leadership and the logic of events had resulted in a new climate of public opinion. Isolationists were not only aware of this but as true patriots they had to consider the arguments. Some of them remained unconvinced that any reorientation of policy was necessary; some went over to internationalism; others modified their stand sufficiently to accept the method of crusade, but only on condition that the United States "go it alone" and confine its interventions to cases where American national interests—which included its democratic interests but not necessarily all foreign democratic interests—were involved. Isolationists, neo-isolationists, and internationalists all sought the larger welfare of mankind, though by different means. All of them regarded themselves as instruments of morality and all in large part rejected the realistic standard of judging foreign affairs held by the founders of the republic. Only history can determine which is right, but meanwhile we must decide among the courses as best we can. That there is an intelligent basis for each of them scarcely permits of denial.

The isolationists rather generally shelved their arguments during the war but took them down immediately afterward. They asserted that totalitarianism abroad did not necessarily menace the United States. Neither was it likely that we would be shut off to ourselves, for even a totalitarian world would still wish to trade. At any rate we were almost self-sufficient and the few things that we lacked could be provided for by stock piles or by natural or chemical substitutes. History had shown that great powers have been great rivals, and there was even more reason to believe that this would be true of a totalitarian world. An intelligent American foreign policy which took advantage of the opportunities always lying around loose could help these imperialisms to cancel each other. Even in the unlikely event that they did unite to attack the United States their task would be impossible in the face of a nation vigilant, united, and prepared. That the internationalists were wrong, because the United States was not powerful enough to impose its will upon the whole world was the clincher in the argument of isolationists both before and after World War II.

Neo-isolationists, as noted above, were willing to accept certain world responsibilities, but only as American interests dictated; other nations were welcome to join in, but they would have to accept American terms. They would probably have been pleased to have a United Nations in which only the United States held the veto; but this would mean a unilateral *Pax Americana,* imitating the "splendid isolation" of the *Pax Britannica*—a concept which the internationalists and simon-pure isolationists vigorously rejected. The neo-isolationists realistically showed that American economic health was all that stood between the world and Russian domination; therefore we should avoid commitments which would drain off our capital, the life blood of our economy. The army should be small but efficient; the navy and the air force should be our instruments of policy and first line of defense; and every effort should be made to utilize scientific advances. The bloody and expensive attempt to stop aggression in Korea showed that no more such ventures should be undertaken: either pull back on all such danger spots or go for the jugular.

At this point the neo-isolationists quarreled: was the jugular in China or in Western Europe?

There were, of course, valid arguments for both views; curiously enough there was minimum stress on the rather obvious fact that both were important. The issue was warped, moreover, by the fact that the Republican Party had been twenty years out of power and by the natural tendency of a party long in opposition to seek power by frustrating its opponent rather than by proposing a constructive program. It would seem that most Old Guardsmen were nostalgic isolationists—as what American is not?—and it is difficult to say how much their neo-isolationism arose from conviction and how much from political opportunism.

At any rate the Old Guard's leaders fought internationalism by laying stress on China rather than Western Europe. This did not originate with the Korean War but appeared even before World War II when Roosevelt accepted the internationalist thesis with its corollary that the preservation of freedom depended first on holding Western Europe. The logic of this was clear enough to win over many of his domestic opponents who did not rabidly hate him, and of course it had the support of those who felt drawn to Europe by ties of blood, culture, or sentiment. On the other hand it became an article of neo-isolationist faith (and to a certain extent of individuals in both other groups) that China must be saved at all costs.

This opinion was not formed out of deference to Stalin's dictum that the road to the West lies through the East. Nor is it enough to call it an opposite and equal reaction to Roosevelt's belief that it was more important to preserve democracy in Europe. It arose from the historic facts that the United States had always been more ready to cooperate with the great powers in the Far East than in Europe, and that the Republican Party had been instrumental in acquiring the Philippines and still acknowledged a responsibility for their defense. Missionaries had long since drawn American attention favorably to China and had done much to implant the erroneous popular opinion that it was enormously wealthy; it is significant that Henry Luce, publisher of *Life, Time,* and *Fortune,* and the chief internationalist exponent of action in China, was the son of missionaries to China. All of these factors led to a rather general feeling after Pearl Harbor that the first enemy was Japan. This was promoted also by distrust of Red Russia among businessmen and the masses, and in some quarters by a tolerance of fascism. Since World War II isolationists and neo-isolationists have tended to hold that we should have pulled in and let Hitler hold the Continent. They are inclined to believe that Hitler genuinely desired to stay out of Britain and France, and that he even regarded the British Empire as a beneficent institution which he wished to preserve. If only Britain and France—and later the United States—had left him free to move East he would have scotched the Red menace; certainly a victorious Hitler would be no worse than the victorious Soviets are. Sometimes this attitude has imbedded in it a touch of fascism and anti-Semitism. There was at the least an apparent belief that a monolithic and fascist Eurasia would be no menace to freedom in the United States, but a monolithic and communist Eurasia would be. At any rate, after Russia entered the war Senator Taft quite frankly gave it as his opinion that victorious sovietism would be more dangerous to the United States than victorious fascism; he may have been right. In defense of this point of view it must be acknowledged that Hitler's army was organized for eastward expansion and that at no time prior to 1939 did he expect either a long war, a war on two fronts, or a war against a coalition of major powers. So far as is known he had no plans to invade either the United States or Latin America. Nor, for that matter, did Japan before the war plan an invasion of the United States—not even of Hawaii.

Neo-islationists were torn between modern necessities and nostalgia for the old days. This was well illustrated by Senator Taft. At times he seemed to desire the American mission to revert to the method of example and occasional foray. He admitted the existence of a power struggle in the world, but tried to argue away both the fact and American responsibilities. Sometimes there were curious results. For example he argued that we should not take the lead in defending and supporting the integration of the European nations, for if they did not do it themselves it could not and should not be done; on the other hand we should take the lead in defending and supporting Chiang's integration of China, for if we did not do it, it could not be done even though it should and must be done.

The internationalists contradicted the isolationists and neo-isolationists at almost every point. They denied that we could become industrially self-sufficient. They believed that totalitarian philosophies (whether fascist or communist) were so dynamic that they must spread into every corner of the world or perish. Hitherto empires and ideologies had operated in limited geographical areas, and so it was possible for them to exist on the same globe without affecting each other. Now that we had finally reached the limit of geographical perspective we were faced by a showdown. A totalitarian state could not afford to allow the "bad" example of a free state to continue to exist; it could not rest until freedom was extinguished. Moreover the very existence of a free state as powerful as the United States exerted a pressure which forced totalitarians to resist it by creating a monolithic structure. But in this case, if no war followed immediately the free economy was so strained that it must be subjected to controls which would increase to the point where the free state ran the danger of becoming as totalitarian and monolithic as its rival.

As for the possibility of successful defense, they pointed out that offensive weapons are always ahead of defense, and never more so than in this age of the H-bomb and bacteriological warfare. As for the United States imposing its will upon the whole world they agreed that it was impossible, but denied that it was either necessary or desirable. Their hope was to find a basis of common action with other nations; in any case they believed that democracy must be preserved in the vital area of Western Europe by war if absolutely necessary. If that were done the remainder of the world would gradually trend toward freedom.

Here we find the reasons for the actions of Roosevelt and Hull during their approach to war. They had no faith that Germany or Japan could be trusted to settle into the accepted pattern; rather they believed that both would shake up the world and either attack the United States or force it into a position where freedom would have to be sacrificed to national survival. Whether or not Germany and Japan planned attacks on the United States was—said the internationalists—beside the point. They were proved aggressors, and the world was now too small to permit aggression to go unpunished. They believed that the West was confronting a breakdown of international morality which would make order and peace impossible.

Economics—it is still the internationalists speaking—had very little to do with the situation, and certainly economic interests would not alone have excused the stupendous cost of the war; indeed a German-dominated Europe and a Japanese-dominated Asia might conceivably have offered greater markets to the United States. Nevertheless it was clear that both Germany and Japan had overturned business morality. The problem boiled down to whether to risk a Russian Eurasia later, or to let Germany crush Russia and then risk the menace of a monolithic Nazi Eurasia. In a very real sense the decision was up to Roosevelt, for he was in an excellent position to force Britain to make a negotiated peace. The usual objection to his choice is that at Yalta he only ensured a monolithic Soviet Eurasia in place of a Nazi one. Indeed it is true that at one period Roosevelt believed that Stalin might be converted to democracy.

Before leaving this subject a further word of explanation should be offered on the American mission. The word *mission* often bears a connotation of aggressive preaching to the unreceptive, of carrying the light to those who sit in darkness. That is not what is meant here; indeed there is no word which exactly fits the meaning, or rather meanings, intended. The American mission was not originally regarded as evangelical but as exemplary—as an attempt to preserve and protect democracy in the United States until a weary world was ready to accept it. To this day few Americans believe that democracy can be spread by missionary activity but they have come to believe that its champions abroad can be aided in their work. Thus the crusaders for democracy are seeking less to convert than to shore up the defenders of the holy places and prevent them from being overrun by totalitarian infidels. There has never been any American opinion that the United States was destined to rule the world; even the exponents of "Anglo-

Saxonism" who flourished at the turn of the century spoke in terms of the destiny of the English-speaking nations. There has never been and is not now any intention to impose the "American way of life" on the world; those who profess to fear this should examine the receptiveness in the minds and hearts of their countrymen rather than denounce an American aggressiveness which does not exist. In other words if the "American way of life" is being adopted anywhere it is because someone is importing it rather than because there is any deliberate attempt to export it.

The American mission does not even *necessarily* imply the leadership which Britain and France have regarded as so important a part of their mission; America's leadership has been assumed reluctantly and only as the corollary of its power. Finally, if the social and economic techniques developed by the United States carry any hope for mankind, that hope depends upon their acceptance by others. That foreigners may regard acceptance as an alternative only slightly less bitter than totalitarian conquest has nothing to do with the case; the choice is theirs. Any American attempt to make the medicine less bitter would only destroy its curative qualities. It is not uncommon for people who have ruined their health by their own excesses to wish to be restored only on their own terms. Europe is sick because it has refused to enter the twentieth century, and in effect is demanding that American power be placed at its disposal to enable it to remain in its tradition-hallowed doldrums.

*   *   *

Devotion to morals is all very fine, but in international affairs it sentences the moralist to continual interferences in the business of other nations, as Wilson found to his sorrow. Sometimes it confronts a country with a showdown which more "realistic" diplomacy could have avoided. The democratic process forces us to make compromises of questionable morality on the domestic scene, but our ignorance of the world leads us to believe that we can make up for this by championing the moral order in foreign affairs. Here are concentrated the historic American diplomatic flaws. Our sense of mission tends to make us divide nations into good and bad, and to regard as immoral those who disagree with our viewpoint. We confuse good order with good morals; so as long as things are accomplished legally we are inclined to overlook conditions which are preludes to the disruption of order. One example was the "good order" which prevailed in Cuba under the

Machado regime and which led inevitably to a renewal of violence. This disinclination to look beneath the surface means that we have been little inclined to practice the first essential of effective statesmanship—a cold assessment of our own capabilities and those of our opponent, and a decision on how far we are willing to go to get what we want. We have believed that we are omnipotent; "We never started a war and never lost one." When we found ourselves unable to huff and puff and blow the Reds down, belief in omnipotence received a rude shock. The public had to find a scapegoat and it accepted with an indignation comically mixed with relief the explanation that we failed because the State Department was full of communists.

The Senate and the State Department have been feuding during most of our history. The reason is simple: the State Department was confronted by conditions which had to be faced with at least a reasonable degree of realism; the Senate was bound by the moral pressures and the necessary compromises of the democratic process. The Constitution rightly protects the individual against government, but has done it by balancing the parts of government against each other so nicely that the executive has always found it difficult to carry out a realistic and consistent foreign policy. The Senate, conscious of its own weight and responsive to a sentimental and frequently short-sighted public, has sometimes blocked the executive's foreign policy and forced him to placate the strongest pressures. When a real crisis arises he must convince public and legislature by shock tactics. In the long run this leads only to doubt, confusion, and further distrust of executive leadership. Even when one balances these by our economic power, our domestic political stability, and our strong belief in the democratic principles which appeal to peoples everywhere, it is no wonder that the world has doubted American ability to lead. It is curious how a nation that respects specialization has been suspicious of expertness at the government level; nowhere more than in the State Department.

Americans have historically failed to realize that statesmanship is not the art of doing the best or most just thing, but of picking the best and most just cause among unsatisfactory choices. We have wanted to know exactly what is going on, and so we have been continually demanding that the State Department play poker with all its cards lying face up on the table. We have failed to distinguish between short and long term policies; consequently, we have sometimes urged a short term policy which was ruinous to the long term. Two examples out of scores were our rejection of the League of Nations and our tearing down of the armed forces in 1945. The fact that global union may be desirable, necessary, or the only way to prevent blowing up the world is no proof that it is the next logical or inevitable step. May it not be that the next step is the organization of regional associations of nations?

Now of course we have pursued our national interest (usually security) but we have also had a peculiar idea that morals are incompatible with national interest. The tendency, therefore, has been to pose as champions of morals and to try to force others to solve problems by legal and moral rules—that is, by our domestic process of formalized conflict with its successive compromises. George Kennan has shown that in our foreign relations we preached moral solutions however inapplicable to the case in issue, tried to shame others into adopting them, but once they had been adopted we considered ourselves free from responsibility. Kennan proceeds to point out several corollaries drawn from this American approach. One result is to accept nations as instruments of international action and thus arrest the process of organic change which is essential to adapt the world to changing times; in a day when great producing and marketing areas are essential to well being it is dangerous to permit the multiplication of nationalities that we see in Asia and the Arabic world. We have assumed that a nation's internal problems are its own business, when as a matter of fact they frequently burst across national borders to plague the world; the overthrow of monarchy in eighteenth century France, the slavery question in the United States, Leinin's overthrow of Kerensky, and Hitler's anti-Semitism are a few examples. We have had a touching faith in the efficiency of collective action, when as a matter of fact a group of nations never has and never will act together without friction and consequent loss of energy and effectiveness.

A characteristic of democracy is its formalization of the social conflict by laws and customs, with the result that so long as these are observed we tend to be blind to what may be going on behind the scenes. The blunders make it possible for subversives, using accepted customs, to burrow into government and work for its overthrow; the communist coup d'etat in Czechoslovakia broke none of the rules, but it was none the less effective—and we had no ground for protest. We take pride in the fact that this formalization of conflict makes force unnecessary, and so we fail to see when a little force exerted at the right time and place—as against the nascent dictatorships during the long armistice— may prevent a world war later on. The curious result is that when the war does begin we are less angered by the cause of the aggression than by the provocation that made us break our rule and use force. Thus anger over Japan's sneak attack on Pearl Harbor was far greater than over the long course of aggression which finally culminated in the attack. As a result our wars become moral conflicts, and since morals cannot be compromised they cannot end until the immoral enemy is completely crushed.

* * *

The above is a formidable arraignment of American diplomatic defects, and yet upon examination it will be found to be essentially descriptive of any democracy, not merely of the United States. It is not intended to intimate that morality should have no place in the conduct for foreign affairs; on the contrary we can never afford to lose sight of it. The power of the United States has lain not merely in its material strength and in its demonstration that it is possible to have a high standard of living for the common man. Even more significant, it has managed to preserve a relative degree of human dignity and freedom within its borders, and in its dealings with the world it has interfered less with the self-determination of small nations than has any other great power. It has preserved a relatively great amount of social and political equality and of freedom of opportunity. It has championed democracy, the way of life which is so attractive to the common people everywhere that its enemies have been forced to appropriate the name as a cover for their plots against liberty. These are the true sources of American power and these are the factors which can remold the world in a new image.

Preserving and spreading these values has not been easy, and the United States has been forced to use power to do it. Any other course would have been suicidal. Nevertheless it has continually been confronted by dilemmas which, whether it acts or not, bring distrust and hatred. If it does not intervene to support democratic elements it is injuring the democratic fight for security and supporting fascism or communism; if it does intervene it lays itself open to bitter recriminations by all those who feel themselves injured. The history of the United States in the postwar world has been its attempt to escape from the dilemma of power by finding a truly multilateral means of assuring the triumph of its ideals. The American purpose, of course, has been to use the most effective means to save itself and the democratic way of life. Few Americans believe that the world will suddenly go democratic, but they do hope to block totalitarianism so that the nations can go on toward democracy. Totalitarianism can be tolerated only if it is decadent.

The United States was pushed into a position of ascendance by a multiplicity of forces, not the least of which was the Kremlin. This has happened before: Athens was forced into leadership by the Persian menace, Rome by Carthage, and Britain by France. Each of these, however, in greater or less degree retained all arms and controls for itself. In other words it adopted the policy of "go it alone." Thus far, at least, the United States has sincerely sought cooperation among freedom-loving nations. Common problems have been submitted to common examination and to common decision. America's weight has sometimes forced more decisive action than her associates desired, but Toynbee's "No annihilation without representation" was unfair—not to mention its disclosure of a pallid view of the crisis. It must at least be admitted that the United States is showing an increasing desire to accommodate herself to the desires of its friends. That, indeed, is the favorite complaint of the neo-isolationists. At any rate the freedom with which the Western Allies bait the United States is proof to the world that they are not subservient.

The United States has agreed with Latin America in making the Monroe Doctrine multilateral. It has fought aggression by means of the Truman Doctrine, the Marshall Plan, the Atlantic Pact, and by the defense of South Korea. It demanded and obtained equality for the small nations in the UN Assembly and has resisted Soviet pressure to settle world problems without regard to the wishes or interests of those nations. This may or may not have been wise (even the small nations disagree on that point) but it at least shows a desire to use power with due regard to the interests and aspirations of others. Those who deny this should inquire whether their demand for a greater degree of co-operation flows from a desire to prevent action of any kind.

* * *

During the great days of imperialism, capital and the profits it earned flowed without undue restraint between Europe and the outer world. All this is changed now as governments regulate trade, discriminate against foreign firms doing business within their borders, restrict the export of profits, and even on occasion seize foreign investments. It was these conditions which gave rise to the Point Four program. Its intention was, by numerous small projects, based on the expenditure of minimum capital, to help "underdeveloped" areas begin the long march toward a high standard of living; meanwhile the speciousness of communist promises would be exposed and the doctrine would lose its attractiveness. It so happens that there are numerous ways, especially in agriculture, by which a much greater production can be gained quickly and at negligible cost.

The project evolved from Nelson Rockefeller's World War II program to organize and utilize Latin American resources, which was followed by investments in enterprise aimed at showing how the Latin American standard of living could be raised. The United Nations began a study of the problem and undertook a few small projects. The U. S. Export-Import Bank had been making loans for many years for development and reconstruction. Aspirations for world improvement found expression in Point Four of President Truman's inaugural address, 20 January 1949. "We must," said he, "embark on a bold new program for making the benefits of our scientific advances and industrial progress available for the improvement and growth of underdeveloped areas." Technical assistance was to be given to development projects and private investment encouraged. A few months later he asked Congress for an initial appropriation of $35,000,000; this was granted, and further appropriations have followed.

Unfortunately, some of the Point Four programs which have been advocated have proved to be based upon the expectation of a continuous flow of American dollars, occasionally of billions. Since 1916 the United States has sought to maintain its rhythm of production and to help the world out of various awkward situations by exporting something like $110 billions; much of this, plus hundreds of additional billions at home, has gone for the necessary but uneconomic purpose of warfare. If this is kept up beyond a limit (at present undetermined) it will kill the goose that laid the golden egg; this is the hope of the Kremlin and may have been one reason why Earl Browder was an original advocate of the Point Four idea. If the United States is to continue to be a bulwark of power and security it must retain the means of multiplying its own capital—that is capital and profit.

The Point Four idea was evolved because the governments of underdeveloped countries have made it risky for private capital to enter their borders. Their hope, of course, is that the U. S. government can be blackmailed by threats of going communist into furnishing capital without hope of profit—and probably eventually without hope of getting it back. Governments may occasionally have good reason for giving away money and goods for political or social ends, but they must never forget that such capital is thereby removed from the essential business of earning profits, and thereby weakens the donor. An economy (even a socialist economy) cannot long exist without profits. Probably the Point Four program should be handled by the United Nations; the US might not get so much credit, but the UN could draw skills and capital more acceptable in other countries which have an outmoded concept of Western imperialism. There is, of course, the risk that economically backward countries will seek to avoid obligations to foreign private enterprise simply by voting themselves funds out of the U. S. Treasury. In January 1952 they united to cram through the UN Assembly a resolution looking toward the establishment of an International Development Authority. This was unmistakably a move to prevent the one who pays the piper from calling the tune.

Point Four, if abused or if carried too far, is bound to encourage further blackmail and further seizure of American private capital. Actually the U. S. government cannot possibly furnish the funds to make over the world. The only solution is to clear the way for private investments to be reasonably safe and to earn a profit. This must be unequivocal; the U. S. government can extend tax-exemption inducements to investors (as Truman has suggested) but to guarantee such investments only continues the evil. Unfortunately this has already begun. Private investments are the life blood of the world's economy, and if they cannot circulate, the economy will sicken and die. Here is a task for the United Nations. If it can induce some countries to grant reasonable conditions to private investors with UN right to adjudicate disputes, the result may be the renewal of economic vitality all over the world. This does not forbid the expenditure of some capital in attempts to help the peoples of underdeveloped countries to help themselves. But this must be done in terms that they can understand and by methods that they can use. It must begin with simple processes and simple tools— not with vast projects and complicated machinery unless the foreign governments themselves will furnish the capital or encourage investors. The world's standard of living can and will be raised, but it will take time—generations, perhaps centuries. It will take boldness, imagination, and perseverance—and not only on our part. Our share will be useless unless those we help wish to help themselves.

*   *   *

In the light of the easily demonstrable fact that many of the faults of the United States rise from its diligent search for the moral ideal, it seems at first glance strange that Europe complains that we are a nation without morals. Only in part has this arisen from the American disinclination to theorize or to build metaphysical structures. The real reason lies in the democratic revolution which threatens to overturn the ascendance of the élite and make culture and material comfort the property of the masses. The American intellectual has rather too largely failed to see what is happening, and so he is distrusted in his own country; he takes his revenge by blackguarding American civilization and thus furnishes welcome ammunition to the "hate America" campaign in which Europe's élite and its communists have joined. The élite gibe at us for being no different from the communists in our materialism, and the communists (who boast of their dialectical materialism) hate us for having beaten them to their material objective. The intellectual wing of Europe's élite is, despite its sterility, much more influential in Europe than our intellectuals are here, and (among other reasons) it hates America because we do not put the intelligentsia on a pedestal.

It was admitted above that we have failed to build a metaphysical structure, which is apparently the only thing that the European intellectual can understand or respect. We have compounded this fault in our propaganda by laying emphasis on material goods, taking it for granted that the hearer will know what ideals and aspirations lay behind their manufacture. The truth is that the world simply cannot (in some cases selfishly will not) understand our words; indeed, we have gone so far in political methods, human relations, and technology that we have no common vocabulary in which to communicate. Europe fears that in taking the machine it will lose all personal values; certainly we have failed to show how these are actually enhanced by the machine. Indeed Europe has failed so signally to grasp the real meaning of what we offer that there is no more frustrating experience for an American than to talk to a European about this. W. H. Whyte has written that it is "startling to listen to an American businessman just returned from Europe; almost invariably he will so revile its low-wage, high-markup, monopoly economics that he sounds much more the howling revolutionist than the European socialists who so mistrust him."

There have been a number of agencies set up since the war to explain America abroad. The Smith-Mundt Information and Educational Exchange Act (27 January 1948) set up the U. S. Information Service (USIS) as a permanent agency in the Department of State. The object was to pull together, expand, and add to the attempts being

made to explain the United States and its policies to the world. Among
the numerous activities of this agency or among those in which it has
a hand are the distribution of news releases, educational and industrial
films, exchange of students and professors, and supervison of cultural
attachés at American legations. There is an astonishing lack of printed
material (especially reference material) about America even in as
advanced a country as Great Britain, and USIS has sought to remedy
this in part by maintaining reference and lending libraries in foreign
capitals. It has operated radio programs called the Voice of America
(VOA), which are beamed to many parts of the world, especially
behind the Iron Curtain, in a conscious attempt to utilize the strategy
of truth in the Cold War. After the war the U. S. sold surplus property
in many countries and took payment in local currency; the Fulbright
Act of 1946 appropriated part of this money for the support of students
and professors who were selected to be sent abroad to study or teach.
The Smith-Mundt Act appropriated dollar funds which were to be
used to enable foreigners to study and teach in the United States either
on an exchange basis or by direct subsidies. In addition to the public
and semi-public agencies there are private agencies engaged in interpret-
ing America abroad. Most notable of these is the National Committee
for a Free Europe, which operates Radio Free Europe and a further
propaganda effort called Crusade for Freedom. The latter has taken
advantage of the fact that Europe's winds blow from west to east to
send toy balloons laden with gifts and printed propaganda behind the
Iron Curtain.

There has been a great deal of well justified criticism of American
official propaganda efforts on the grounds of its spinelessness and of
its errors in approach. One mistake that has been made is the same one
advertisers make here: considering their audience as composed of in-
numerable duplicates. Actually the variety of the audience is limited
only by the number of people in it and by the moods they can undergo.
It is this realization which has led to U. S. government agencies' bringing over foreigners—teachers, students, industrial specialists—either
with or without exchanges of American opposite numbers. Private
organizations have joined the movement with a will, and in 1951
brought over 40,000—triple the number brought by the government.
Among the Americans who go abroad the labor teams seem to be the
most successful, and that among a class deeply impregnated with suspicion. When a member of one team was asked why they succeeded

his answer was simple: "You talk to the brothers. You go around and you talk to the brothers."

At any rate there is little doubt of the value of bringing to this country so-called "productivity teams" from European industries; 2,750 of them had come over by the end of 1951. The results were not only to give technological stimulus but to give Europeans a new insight into what makes America tick. Here are some quotations from a number of the team reports.

"A visit to the U. S. gives one greater confidence in the ability of democracy to solve its problems . . . The country is still . . . moving *forward* both culturally, socially, and economically." [Norwegian trade-unionists]

"American unions' attitude to company profits is typical of their acceptance of a capitalist economy. However high, profits, at least in competitive industry, are not regarded as immoral or a social evil; indeed they give proof of solvency and assured employment . . . the main concern of unions is to obtain a fair share of them." [British trade-union officials]

"Sometimes we had to ask ourselves whether it was manufacturer or union member speaking to us." [Danish ready-made-clothing team]

"The big surprise to me was the importance American bosses give to human-relations problems. The American employer seems to be a psychologist aware that his prosperity is tied directly with that of the workers." [French unionist]

"If members of the team had learned nothing else from their travels in America and Britain, they would have learned one valuable thing, namely, the remarkable amount of good will which exists between people in the Western Hemisphere." [British gray iron-founding team]*

* * *

The American insistence that to save itself Europe needs to organize into a large producing and marketing area is in line with the historical process and with American thinking about the necessity of backing moral ideals by economic power. The approach is being bitterly criticized in Europe on the ground that it is too sudden and simple a remedy for an incredibly complex problem. Actually it is neither sudden nor simple. It has been under discussion and examination for a generation.

---

* William H. Whyte, *Is Anybody Listening?* (1952), 103-104.

If constitutional unification comes it will be only the first step, though a decisive one. Generations of evolution must follow before real integration is achieved.

As for Asia, it would be absurd for the United States or any part of the West to try to teach it morals. We may, however, offer some technological and psychological processes which can lay a firmer basis for Eastern morals. It is curious that the East, where absolutes were born, should advise sweeping compromise between totalitarian Russia which demands absolute subjection of the individual and democratic America which upholds the absolute of the equality of men under God.

The world's salvation may not lie in economics, but salvation cannot come without the help of economic sanity any more than the spirit can thrive on this earth without the aid of the mind and the body. We cannot know God's ultimate secrets, but we can move toward them if we build the future step by step upon the eternal values of the past. The future will not be a copy of what America offers, but an amalgam of the offerings of many peoples and cultures. If what we have done serves only as a useful ladder for the builders of the future, we shall be content.

BIBLIOGRAPHY

The titles that follow are among those that bear more or less closely upon the development of the central thesis of this book.

James T. Adams. *The Adams Family.* 1930

Frederick L. Allen. *The Big Change: America Transforms Itself, 1900-1950.* 1953

Jack Anderson and R. W. May. *McCarthy: The Man, the Senator, the "Ism."* 1952

Leland D. Baldwin. *Best Hope of Earth: A Grammar of Democracy.* 1948
"   "   "   *God's Englishman: The Evolution of the Anglo-Saxon Spirit.* 1943, 1944
"   "   "   *Recent American History.* 1953
"   "   "   *The Stream of American History.* 2v., 1952

Richard G. Baumhoff. *The Damned Missouri Valley.* 1951

John I. H. Baur. *Revolution and Tradition in Modern American Art.* 1951

Charles A. Beard. *Economic Interpretation of the Constitution.* 1913
"   "   "   *Economic Origins of Jeffersonian Democracy.* 1915

Jonathan B. Bingham. *Shirt-Sleeve Diplomacy: Point 4 in Action.* 1953

David E. Bowers, ed. *Foreign Influences in American Life.* 1944

Roger Burlingame. *Backgrounds of Power: The Human Story of Mass Production.* 1949
"   "   *Engines of Democracy: Inventions and Society in Mature America.* 1940

Oscar Cargill. *Intellectual America: Ideas on the March.* 1941

Jesse T. Carpenter. *The South as a Conscious Minority, 1789-1861.* 1930

Wilbur J. Cash. *The Mind of the South.* 1946

Thomas C. Cochran and William Miller. *The Age of Enterprise: A Social History of Industrial America.* 1949

Edward S. Corwin. *Constitutional Revolution, Ltd.* 1941. The New Deal and the Supreme Court

Henry S. Commager. *The American Mind.* 1950

Merle Curti. *Growth of American Thought.* 1943

Russell W. Davenport. *U. S. A. The Permanent Revolution.* 1951

J. Frank Dobie. *The Flavor of Texas.* 1936

Peter F. Drucker. *The Concept of the Corporation* (1946). Also issued as *Big Business* (1947)

Clement Eaton. *Freedom of Thought in the Old South.* 1940

E. M. Erikson. *The Supreme Court and the New Deal.* 1941

Max Farrand. *The Framing of the Constitution of the U. S.* 1913

Eric Fisher. *The Passing of the European Age.* 1948

Ladd Haystead. *If the Prospect Pleases.* 1946. The West

Bert F. Hoselitz, ed. *The Progress of Underdeveloped Areas.* 1952

Ralph H. Gabriel. *The Course of American Democratic Thought.* 1940

John K. Galbraith. *American Capitalism: The Concept of Countervailing Power.* 1952

Siegfried Giedion. *Space, Time, and Architecture.* 1941
"   "   *Mechanization Takes Command.* 1948
Marcus L. Hansen. *The Immigrant in American History.* 1940
"   "   "   *The Atlantic Migration, 1607-1860.* 1945
Richard Hofstadter. *The American Political Tradition and the Men Who Made It.* 1948
"   "   *Social Darwinism in American Thought, 1860-1914.* 1944
Sidney Hook. *John Dewey: an Intellectual Portrait.* 1939
Alfred H. Kelly and W. A. Harbison. *The American Constitution.* 1948
George Kennan. *American Diplomacy, 1900-1950.* 1951
Halvdan Koht. *The American Spirit in Europe.* 1949
John A. Kouwenhoven. *Made in America: The Arts in Modern Civilization.* 1949
Michael Kraus. *Intercolonial Aspects of American Culture.* 1928
"   "   *The Atlantic Civilization.* 1949
Oliver W. Larkin. *Art and Life in America.* 1949
Max Lerner. *The Mind and Faith of Justice Holmes.* 1943
Joseph R. McCarthy. *McCarthyism: The Fight for America.* 1952
Carey McWilliams. *California: The Great Exception.* 1949
"   "   *Southern California Country.* 1946
John C. Miller. *Origins of the American Revolution.* 1943
Richard Neuberger. *Our Promised Land.* 1938. The Columbia River Country
Reinhold Niebuhr. *The Irony of American History.* 1952
Howard W. Odum. *Southern Regions of the U. S.* 1936
"   "   "   *The Way of the South.* 1947
"   "   "   and H. E. Moore. *American Regionalism: A Cultural-Historical Approach to National Integration.* 1938
George S. Perry. *Texas: A World in Itself.* 1942
Ralph B. Perry. *Puritanism and Democracy.* 1944
"   "   "   *Thought and Character of William James.* 2 v., 1935
Basil Rauch. *History of the New Deal.* 1944
David Riesman. *The Lonely Crowd.* 1950
Max Savelle. *Seeds of Liberty: The Genesis of the American Mind.* 1948
Gilbert Seldes. *The Great Audience.* 1950
George Soule. *Prosperity Decade.* 1947
Lincoln Steffens. *Autobiography.* 1931
George M. Stephenson. *History of American Immigration, 1820-1924.* 1926
Charles S. Sydnor. *The Development of Southern Sectionalism, 1819-1848.* 1948
Robert A. Taft. *A Foreign Policy for Americans.* 1951
Rufus Terral. *The Missouri Valley: Land of Drouth, Flood and Promise.* 1947
Alice Felt Tyler. *Freedoms Ferment: Phases of American Social History to 1860.* 1944
Charles Warren. *The Supreme Court in U. S. History.* 2 v., 1926
Dixon Wecter. *The Age of the Great Depression, 1929-1941.* 1948
Nathaniel Weyl. *The Battle Against Disloyalty.* 1951
William H. Whyte, Jr. *Is Anybody Listening?* 1952. An important treatment of "mass communications."
Charles M. Wiltse. *The Jeffersonian Tradition in American Democracy.* 1935
Carl Wittke. *We Who Built America.* 1939
Harvey Wish. *Social and Intellectual America.* 2 v., 1950, 1952

PERMISSIONS TO QUOTE HAVE BEEN GRANTED

From *The Mind of the South,* by Wilbur J. Cash. Copyright 1941. Alfred A. Knopf, Inc. IX.

From "John Brown's Body," in *Selected Works of Stephen Vincent Benet.* Copyright 1927, 1928, by Stephen Vincent Benet. Rinehart & Company, Inc. Permission granted by Brandt & Brandt. IX.

From *The Age of Confidence,* by Henry Seidel Canby. Copyright 1934. Rinehart & Company, Inc. X.

From *The Course of American Democratic Thought,* by Ralph H. Gabriel. Copyright 1940. The Ronald Press Company. X.

From *The Age of Enterprise,* by Thomas C. Cochran and William Miller. Copyright 1942. The Macmillan Company. X and XII.

From *Made in America,* by John A. Kouwenhoven. Copyright 1948, by John A. Kouwenhoven. Doubleday & Company, Inc. XI.

From *The God That Failed,* edited by Richard Crossman. Copyright 1949. Harper & Brothers. XI.

From *Roadside Meetings,* by Hamlin Garland. Copyright 1930. The Macmillan Company. XI.

From an essay, "John Dewey and His Influence," by Alfred North Whitehead. The essay appears in *The Philosophy of John Dewey,* edited by Paul A. Schilpp. Copyright 1939 and 1951. Tudor Publishing Company. Permission granted by The Library of Living Philosophers, Inc. XI.

From *Concept of the Corporation,* by Peter Drucker. Copyright 1946. The John Day Company. XII.

From "Human Relations," an article in *Time,* April 14, 1952. In the article *Time* quoted Clarence Francis which is the material quoted in this book. Permission granted by *Time* and Mr. Francis. XII.

From *Is Anybody Listening?* by William H. Whyte. Copyright 1952. Simon and Schuster, Inc. Permission granted by author. XVI.

From "Chicago," in *Chicago Poems,* by Carl Sandburg. Copyright 1916. Permission granted by Henry Holt & Company, Inc. I.

Printed in U.S.A. by Waverly Press, Inc., Baltimore, Maryland